June 4–5, 2011
San Jose, California, USA

Association for Computing Machinery

Advancing Computing as a Science & Profession

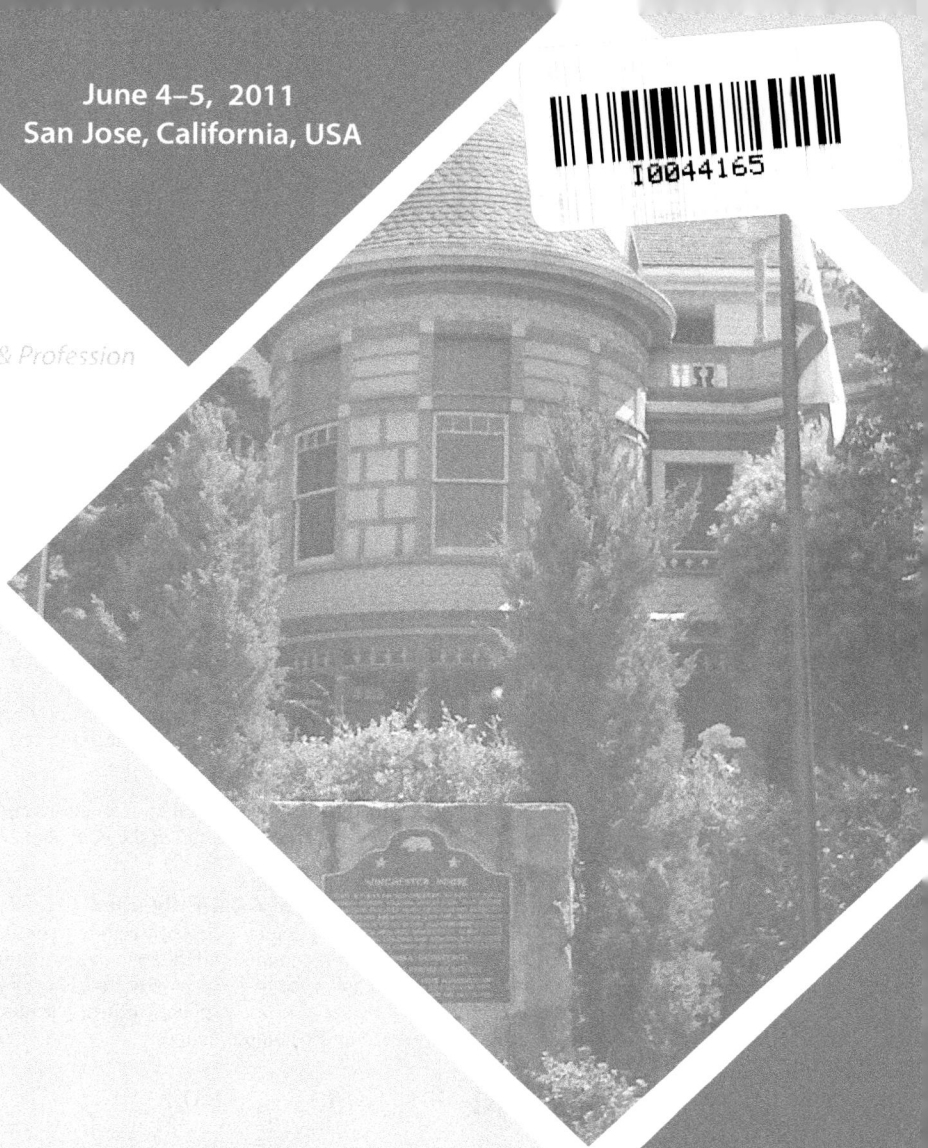

ISMM'11

Proceedings of the 2011 ACM SIGPLAN

International Symposium on Memory Management

In cooperation with:
ACM SIGPLAN

Sponsored by:
Oracle Labs, Hewlett-Packard, and Microsoft Research

Association for Computing Machinery

Advancing Computing as a Science & Profession

The Association for Computing Machinery
2 Penn Plaza, Suite 701
New York, New York 10121-0701

Notice to Past Authors of ACM-Published Articles

ISBN: 978-1-4503-0263-0

Additional copies may be ordered prepaid from:

ACM Order Department
PO Box 30777
New York, NY 10087-0777, USA

Phone: 1-800-342-6626 (USA and Canada)
+1-212-626-0500 (Global)
Fax: +1-212-944-1318
E-mail: acmhelp@acm.org
Hours of Operation: 8:30 am – 4:30 pm ET

Printed in the USA

Welcome

It is with great pleasure that we welcome you to the ACM SIGPLAN 2011 International Symposium on Memory Management. This is the first time that the conference is held as part of FCRC, the Federated Computing Research Conference, allowing attendees to sample a variety of other related conferences and workshops, including PLDI, ISCA, SIGMETRICS, MSPC, and others, during the same week.

This year ISMM received 36 abstracts and 24 full paper submissions, of which 13 were accepted. A single-blind reviewing system was used, and the full Program Committee met in person to facilitate thorough discussion of the papers. In addition to three reviews by Program Committee members, each paper received one review by a member of the External Review Committee, which increased the range and depth of reviewer expertise. Authors were provided an opportunity to submit rebuttal responses to initial reviews, which helped ensure that decisions were not based on faulty interpretations. Program and Review Committee members were allowed to be authors of submitted papers, but Papers co-authored by members of the Program Committee were held to a higher standard to receive consideration; one such paper was accepted.

Putting together ISMM'11 was a community effort. First of all, we thank all of the authors who submitted papers to ISMM. The Program and Review Committees did an extraordinary job in a very short amount of time, and the Steering Committee provided valuable insight and guidance. We thank the FCRC organizers for handling all local arrangements issues, and making the General Chair's job much easier. We thank Oracle Labs, HP Labs, and Microsoft Research for generously providing financial support for ISMM, and allowing us to continue to subsidize student registration.

We hope that you enjoy and learn from the ISMM program, exchange ideas with colleagues from around the world, take advantage of the flexibility offered by FCRC to stop in on other conferences, and reconnect with old friends.

Hans-J. Boehm
ISMM '11 General Chair
HP Labs

David F. Bacon
ISMM '11 Program Chair
IBM T.J. Watson Research

Table of Contents

ISMM 2011 Conference Organization..vii

ISMM 2011 Sponsor and Supporters...viii

Session 1: Parallelizing
Session Chair: Doug Lea *(SUNY Oswego)*

- **Iterative Data-parallel Mark&Sweep on a GPU** 1
  Ronald Veldema, Michael Philippsen *(University of Erlangen-Nuremberg)*

- **Memory Management in NUMA Multicore Systems:**
  Trapped Between Cache Contention and Interconnect Overhead...................................11
  Zoltan Majo, Thomas R. Gross *(ETH Zurich)*

- **Multicore Garbage Collection with Local Heaps**..21
  Simon Marlow, Simon Peyton Jones *(Microsoft Research Ltd.)*

Session 2: Optimizing
Session Chair: Taiichi Yuasa *(Kyoto University)*

- **A Comprehensive Evaluation of Object Scanning Techniques**......................................33
  Robin Garner, Stephen M. Blackburn, Daniel Frampton *(Australian National University)*

- **On the Theory and Potential of LRU-MRU Collaborative Cache Management** 43
  Xiaoming Gu, Chen Ding *(University of Rochester)*

- **Cache Index-Aware Memory Allocation** 55
  Yehuda Afek *(Tel Aviv University)*, Dave Dice *(Sun Labs at Oracle)*,
  Adam Morrison *(Tel Aviv University)*

- **Waste Not, Want Not: Resource-based Garbage Collection**
  in a Shared Environment..65
  Matthew Hertz, Stephen Kane, Elizabeth Keudel *(Canisius College)*, |
  Tongxin Bai, Chen Ding, Xiaoming Gu *(University of Rochester)*,
  Jonathan E. Bard *(SUNY-Buffalo)*

Invited Talk (Joint with MSPC)
Session Chair: Hans Boehm *(HP Labs)*

- **Memory Systems in the Many-Core Era:**
  Challenges, Opportunities, and Solution Directions..77
  Onur Mutlu *(Carnegie Mellon University)*

Session 3: Real-time
Session Chair: Perry Cheng *(IBM Research)*

- **C4: The Continuously Concurrent Compacting Collector**...79
  Gil Tene, Balaji Iyengar, Michael Wolf *(Azul Systems Inc.)*

- **Handles Revisited: Optimising Performance and Memory Costs**
  in a Real-Time Collector 89
  Tomas Kalibera, Richard Jones *(University of Kent)*

- **Short-Term Memory for Self-Collecting Mutators** 99
  Martin Aigner, Andreas Haas, Christoph M. Kirsch, Michael Lippautz, Ana Sokolova,
  Stephanie Stroka, Andreas Unterweger *(University of Salzburg)*

Session 4: Potpourri
Session Chair: Ben Titzer *(Google)*

- **Garbage Collection Auto-Tuning for Java MapReduce on Multi-Cores** 109
  Jeremy Singer *(University of Glasgow)*,
  George Kovoor, Gavin Brown, Mikel Lujan *(University of Manchester)*

- **Compartmental Memory Management in a Modern Web Browser**... 119
  Gregor Wagner *(University of California, Irvine & Mozilla Corporation)*,
  Andreas Gal *(Mozilla Corporation)*, Christian Wimmer *(University of California, Irvine)*,
  Brendan Eich *(Mozilla Corporation)*, Michael Franz *(University of California, Irvine)*

- **Integrated Symbol Table, Engine and Heap Memory Management in Multi-Engine Prolog** 129
  Paul Tarau *(University of North Texas)*

Author Index 139

ISMM 2011 Conference Organization

General Chair: Hans-J. Boehm *(HP Labs)*

Program Chair: David Bacon *(IBM T.J. Watson Research)*

Steering Committee: Steve Blackburn *(Australian National University)*
Richard Jones *(University of Kent)*
Hillel Kolodner *(IBM Haifa Research)*
Doug Lea *(SUNY Oswego)*
Kathryn McKinley *(University of Texas, Austin)*
Guy Steele *(Oracle Labs)*
Martin Vechev *(IBM T.J. Watson Research)*
Jan Vitek *(Purdue University)* (Chair)

Program Committee: Mike Bond *(Ohio State)*
Angela Demke Brown *(University of Toronto)*
Perry Cheng *(IBM Research)*
Daniel Frampton *(Australian National University)*
Rajiv Gupta *(University of California, Riverside)*
Doug Lea *(SUNY Oswego)*
Matthias Meyer *(University of Stuttgart)*
Erez Petrank *(Technion)*
Kostis Sagonas *(Uppsala University)*
Jennifer Sartor *(École Polytechnique Fédérale de Lausanne)*
Guy Steele *(Oracle Labs)*
Ben L. Titzer *(Google)*
Taiichi Yuasa *(Kyoto University)*

External Review Committee: Elvira Albert *(Complutense University of Madrid)*
Dan Grossman *(University of Washington)*
Pramod Joisha *(HP Labs)*
Tomáš Kalibera *(University of Kent)*
Chandra Krintz *(University of California, Santa Barbara)*
Ondřej Lhoták *(University of Waterloo)*
Simon Marlow *(Microsoft Research, Cambridge)*
Tomas Petricek *(University of Cambridge)*
John Regehr *(University of Utah)*
Fridtjof Siebert *(Aicas)*
David Ungar *(IBM Research)*

ISMM 2011 Sponsor & Supporters

Sponsor:  SIGPLAN   **ACM SIGPLAN**

Supporters: Oracle Labs   **Oracle Labs**

hp   **HP Labs**

Microsoft **Research**   **Microsoft Research**

Iterative Data-parallel Mark&Sweep on a GPU

Ronald Veldema   Michael Philippsen

University of Erlangen-Nuremberg, Computer Science Department 2,
Martensstr. 3 • 91058 Erlangen • Germany
{veldema, philippsen}@cs.fau.de

Abstract

Automatic memory management makes programming easier. This is also true for general purpose GPU computing where currently no garbage collectors exist. In this paper we present a parallel mark-and-sweep collector to collect GPU memory on the GPU and tune its performance. Performance is increased by: (1) data-parallel marking and sweeping of regions of memory, (2) marking all elements of large arrays in parallel, (3) trading recursion over parallelism to match deeply linked data structures.

(1) is achieved by coarsely processing all potential objects in a region of memory in parallel. When during (1) a large array is detected, it is put aside and a parallel-for is later issued on the GPU to mark its elements. For a data-structure that is a large linked list, we dynamically switch to a marking version with less overhead by performing a few recursive steps sequentially (and multiple lists in parallel).

The collector achieves a speedup of a factor of up-to 11 over a sequential collector on the same GPU.

Categories and Subject Descriptors   D.3.3 [*Language Constructs and Features*]: Dynamic storage management

General Terms   Algorithms, Design, Measurement, Performance

Keywords   Parallel, GPU, garbage collection, mark and sweep

1. Introduction

As GPUs and their parallel programming model become more popular for general programming tasks, there will be a demand for other features known from traditional programming styles to increase gpGPU programmer productivity. One of those requirements is automatic garbage collection (GC). For GPUs, however, to our knowledge no garbage collection implementation has thus far been attempted where the GPU's memory is collected on the GPU itself. Note that the collector will also work fine on the CPU, but we use the GPU's higher parallelism to show its benefits.

There are a few challenges to overcome on a GPU as a GPU is very different from a normal multi-core CPU. First, a GPU is massively parallel and it is essential to exploit all that parallelism to get good performance out of a GPU, especially as the individual cores are not that fast.

One typically starts a large number of threads (called 'kernels') in parallel on a GPU using a form of `parallel_for`. A GPU typically manages all these threads using a hierarchical scheme. On a GPU one can start a number of fully independent work groups where each work group can run a number of tasks in single-instruction, multiple-thread (SIMT) fashion. Each task in a work group then executes the same instruction at the same time. Therefore a collector needs to be structured such that most of the time all threads on a GPU do the exact same operation. This can be hard to accomplish.

Second, a GPU's memory is more restricted than that of the main CPU. Typically, a GPU has a quarter to a sixteenth of main CPU memory although some GPUs allow main memory to be used as well. Giving the GPU its own dedicated memory will, however, always be faster than sharing that memory with the CPU so it is likely that local GPU memory continues to be used in the future.

Third, although atomic instructions (atomic compare-and-set, exchange, add, etc.) are available, their use is expensive and should be avoided if possible. Also, since current GPUs do not offer instructions to wait for a condition to become true, a busy wait on the GPU is our only option. Hence, mutexes on a GPU are terribly inefficient.

Furthermore, GPUs typically have very little cache (less than 64 KByte L1 and a megabyte of L2 cache). Besides the L1/L2 cache on modern GPUs there exists a high-bandwidth small scratch pad memory per work group that is just as fast as the L1 cache. However, this scratch pad needs to be explicitly programmed for. Given that GPUs are optimized for high-bandwidth operation where data-reuse happens only occasionally, we can expect the trend for small cache sizes to continue.

Finally, today's GPUs offer limited (or no) support for deep recursion. The main reason is that GPUs are mostly used for small data-parallel kernels that are roughly the body of a parallel-loop spliced to a separate function. Since such kernels have low stack requirements (often registers suffice) no need for large per-thread stacks exists. The memory requirements for storing a few local variables and parameters are low so that the software does not drive change. Also, on a GPU potentially 1000+ threads can be started in one step and if each is assigned a few megabytes of stack space, memory consumption would be very high where in most cases the memory would simply lie unused.

Based on the abilities and restrictions of today's GPUs we have the following requirements for allocator and collector. First, memory allocation should be cheap and therefore each kernel should be able to operate independently of the others most of the time. A per-kernel pre-allocated set of blocks partially goes into this direction.

Copying collectors usually add a level of indirection (forwarding pointers) to object access which can be expensive on a GPU. Remember that a mark-and-sweep collector is simple. It traverses the graph of reachable objects from a root set (the set of global vari-

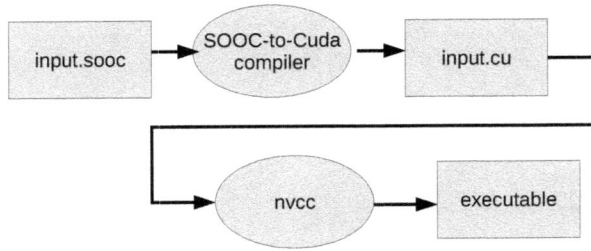

Figure 1. Compilation Pipeline.

ables that hold references). Any object not marked as reachable is garbage and is freed in the subsequent sweep phase.

Parallel mark-and-sweep is traditionally based on threads that pick objects to be marked from a number of shared queues. Work stealing is used to balance the load. This traditional design operates as follows. The mark phase traverses a graph (to find live objects) which is not well parallelizable itself as objects must first be discovered before they can be marked recursively. Once a live object has been discovered, its reference fields must be scanned to find further live objects. Scanning all newly found objects can be done in parallel. This calls for some kind of queue to store a to-do list. To reduce communication, each thread receives its own private queue. Work-stealing achieves load-balancing when threads become idle.

Unfortunately, on a GPU work stealing does not work efficiently because when hundreds of threads start marking there will be hundreds of concurrent accesses to the shared queues. This will cause all threads to diverge execution. Divergence in a GPU's SIMD processor means that upon an 'if-then-else' statement, if some kernels choose the 'if' part and others the 'else' part, the SIMD processor will sequentialize the code by first executing the 'if' kernels while suspending the 'else' kernels. Once the 'if' kernels have finished, the 'else' kernels run to completion. Because only one thread/kernel can access a queue's critical region at a time, all kernels will be sequentialized in a work stealing approach. Parallel mark-and-sweep with work-stealing is therefore slow on current GPUs.

Our solution is to partition memory into fixed size segments. Once a segment has been found to hold *some* live object(s), it is marked as 'should scan it later' in a boolean array. Later all (potential) objects in a segment are scanned in parallel, even those that are unallocated or not known to be live yet. This transforms the marking problem from a graph traversal problem into a data-parallel problem which a GPU is good at.

The contributions of this paper are then as follows:

- iterative data parallel mark and sweep on a GPU;
- reference counted segments to reduce sweeping work;
- delayed scanning of large reference arrays for more parallelism;
- evaluation of garbage collection efficiency on a GPU.

2. Interface to the collector

To test the GPU-based collector we use a simple C/Java dialect which we call Simple OO Cuda (SOOC). It sports objects, a 'new' operator, and a parallel-call statement. The compilation pipeline is shown in Fig. 1. A simple SOOC program is shown in Fig. 2.

By marking the Tree class with 'accelerator' it is marked for compilation and instantiation on the GPU. Its methods only exist on the GPU side, not on the CPU side. From the bottom upwards, the main function starts 1000 parallel threads on the GPU. All of them (in parallel) allocate a few Tree objects.

```
accelerator class Tree {
    int value;
    Tree left;
    Tree right;

    static Tree root;

    Tree(int val) {
        value = val;
        left = null;
        right = null;
    }

    kernel static void go() {
        Tree t = new Tree(1);
        if (t == null) return;

        t.left = new Tree(2);
        if (t.left == null) return;

        t.right = new Tree(3);
        if (t.right == null) return;
    }
};

void main() {
    parallel[1000] Tree.go();
    garbage_collect();
}
```

Figure 2. Example program in the SOOC language.

As these are unreachable after go() finishes, they can all be collected by invoking garbage_collect() back on the host CPU, which in turn starts the parallel mark and sweep routines back on the GPU. Note that the collector we present here only manages the heap allocated on the GPU, not on the CPU which could use some other collector.

To avoid slowing down normal code execution on the GPU, the collector cannot execute in parallel to the user's code (which would add write barriers at the least). This means that the 'new' operator can return 'null' and it is the programmer's task to then return to CPU code to start a garbage collection pass. This is why in the example code all statements that can perform a 'new' test its return value to check if a collection pass is needed.

We chose this design so that whenever the code returns to the CPU, we know that all code on the GPU has finished. Hence, there are **no** live local variables of still running kernels that potentially must be marked. This simplifies the collector immensely. The collector's root set therefore only consists of the global reference-type variables on the GPU and any references that were exported to the CPU. It is conceivable that a compiler can generate code to automatically restart failing kernels after failed 'new' expressions, but this is outside the scope of this paper.

The parallel call statement maps 1:1 to Cuda's kernel invocation with slightly different syntactic sugar. The call to the intrinsic 'garbage_collect()' remains as it invokes the collector.

3. Data structures

The GPU's collectable heap is managed in chunks of K bytes (K is currently set to 128 bytes). If an object is allocated smaller than K bytes, it is rounded up to that size. For each chunk of K bytes an instance of ObjectInfo is statically pre-allocated (Fig. 3). MAX_OBJECTS is pre-computed given the size of the GPU's collectable heap divided by K. If at address P an object is allocated, ObjectInfo P/K is located and its is_allocated bit is set to true.

```
/** each object has one of these
 */
struct ObjectInfo {
  bool is_allocated; // object in use?

  unsigned char mark_phase; // seen in mark phase?

  unsigned char scan_phase; // fields scanned?

  bool is_ref_array; // an array of references?

  // number of entries in ptr_fields
  unsigned num_ptrs;

  // offsets to pointers in object
  unsigned *ptr_fields;
};

// All objects have an entry here:
__device__ ObjectInfo all_objects[MAX_OBJECTS];
```

Figure 3. Object info data structure.

```
class Foo {
    Object A;
    int B;
    int C;
    Object D;
    int E;
    int F;
};

// causes:
struct ObjectInfo {
    ...
    num_ptrs = 2,
    ptr_fields = {8, 24}
}
```

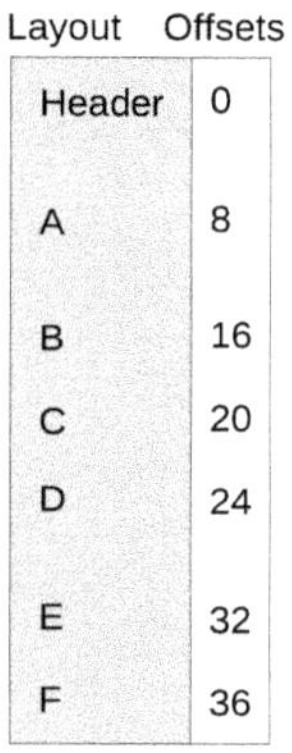

Layout	Offsets
Header	0
A	8
B	16
C	20
D	24
E	32
F	36

Figure 4. Example offset table use

While this adds significant space overheads, it is still better than, for example, a copying collector which wastes at least half of the available memory (a 128 byte chunk with a 32 byte `ObjectInfo` gives a 25% memory overhead). Additionally, there is still room for improvement by grouping similarly typed objects together so that most fields of an `ObjectInfo` instance become superfluous. Likewise could a number of smaller objects be packed into a 128 byte chunk.

The `ptr_fields` field is a pointer to a table of integers that tells at which offsets into an object there are references to other objects. The `num_ptrs` field tells the size of the table. For example, see Fig. 4. Given that pointers on a GPU are 64 bit and given an 8 byte object header, the pointers in the object are at offsets 8 and 24. The compiler therefore statically generates a table on the GPU with those two entries. When allocating an object of that type, a pointer to the offset table is passed to the runtime and set in the `ObjectInfo` instance. When allocating a reference array, the offset tables are of course not used and only the `is_ref_array` field is set to true.

4. Implementation of ' `new` '

The allocator works in two phases, a cold and a warm phase. The allocator starts in the cold phase which trains the allocator to learn how often what object sizes are needed. During the cold phase all memory is partitioned into P chunks (P is currently 16) and allocation is via a bump-allocator (atomically increments a pointer). Kernel K allocates from partition K % P. Once all memory is consumed, ' `new` ' returns null and the user has to initiate a garbage collection pass. After the first collection the allocator permanently switches to the 'warm' phase. Periodically switching back to a 'cold' phase is future work.

In the warm phase the allocator maintains N free-lists for allocating small objects ($<= 128$ bytes) and M buckets for larger objects. A free-list is implemented as a singly linked-list. Retrieving an element from the list is via a single atomic compare-and-exchange instruction. A bucket is an array of free-lists, one per $2^8, 2^9...2^{28}$ request sizes. This increases performance as no search is needed to find a fitting memory block. Kernel K allocates from free-list K % N for small objects and accesses bucket K % M for large objects. If a free-list or bucket is empty, a kernel steals from other free-lists/buckets until success. Only if no free-list holds available memory, ' `new` ' returns null. Typically, N is 1024 and M is 32 as it is more common to allocate a small than a large object. In the measurements later, we will refer to 'N' as 'SFL' (**S**mall **F**ree **L**ist) and 'M' as 'BB' (**B**ig array **B**uckets). The global free-lists and buckets are a centrally shared data structure which can lead to a lot of contention, especially when 1000+ threads on a GPU perform simultaneous allocations (and diverge their SIMT execution paths). Using a large number of buckets allows each kernel to operate independently.

Note that to simplify the prototype, neither allocators nor collector immediately merge two adjacent blocks of memory into a single bigger block. If the program almost exclusively allocates small objects, the free-lists contain almost all the memory after the cold phase. If an allocation of a big array fails in the warm phase, the collector is informed and a separate coalescing pass fits at least the number of bytes requested.

Splitting the allocator into a cold and a warm phase allows the collector to learn typical object sizes. SOOC allows both allocations of objects (which tend to be small) and arrays (which tend to be large). Unfortunately, it is not known a priori what the ratio between small objects and large arrays will be. We can therefore not hand a large amount of memory to the per-kernel buckets at program start-up to reduce the probability of global free-list contention.

Another detail is that the user can invoke the collector early (when memory has not been completely exhausted). In this case, the first collection pass moves left over memory from the P cold memory chunks to the free-lists and buckets in the ratio of small and large allocations performed thus far. For example, if the user allocated 1,000,000 small objects and 5,000 big arrays, the remaining cold memory will be divided between free-lists and buckets in a factor of 1000:5.

The requirements of both allocator and collector for a GPU are minimal. We require some way to atomically add elements to a linked-list to implement our free-lists and an atomic add instruction to implement our bump-allocator for when the allocator is still 'cold'. Beyond these requirements, nothing else is required of a GPU.

5. Implementation of the parallel collector

Like any mark-and-sweep collector, we operate in three phases:

- mark the root set,
- mark everything reachable from the root set, and

3

- a sweep phase that removes any unmarked objects.

Our key idea is to partition memory into fixed size segments. If inside a segment a live object is marked, we scan the entire segment in parallel. To do so, the CPU initiates a parallel-call to the GPU for each potential small-object in the segment. If most of the objects inside a segment are found to be 'live', we have a win as all live objects are analyzed for further live objects in parallel. If most of the objects are 'dead' or not yet known to be 'live', some processors will perform needless work. However, because the work is done in parallel no time is lost (except for the memory bandwidth wasted to touch the object headers). Also, if more parallel processors are available than required, they would have been idle anyway.

To sweep memory in parallel, we again partition the memory into segments. If a segment holds allocated objects, a parallel-call on the CPU to the GPU sweeps out the dead ones.

Before a collection starts, a global mark-phase-counter is incremented. Each object has a mark-phase in its `ObjectInfo` structure. To mark an object, its `mark_phase` is set to the current mark-phase-counter's value. To simplify the collector's data-structures we separate marking an object from scanning it. Marking an object refers to setting the `mark_phase` field in an object's `ObjectInfo` structure. Scanning an object refers to iterating over the `ObjectInfo`'s `ptr_fields` array and setting the `ObjectInfo`'s `scan_phase` to the current phase. An object is garbage if its `mark-phase` still holds the old `mark-phase` value after marking.

Below we will cover each phase of the collector in turn.

5.1 Marking the root set

Because the collector only runs after all kernels on the GPU have finished (by design), the collector does not have to scan the activation records of running kernels. The root set therefore only consists of the (reference type) global variables on the GPU. As a side-effect of this, the collector is precise, i.e., it never has to deal with integers that might be pointers in the root set.

Because there might be many global references, we mark all of them in parallel. Hence, the compiler generates a table of pointers to global reference variables and declares a constant on the host that tells how large the table is. When scanning the root set the collector starts a parallel-call to mark all globals concurrently. See the upper part of Fig. 5. Note that marking the root set only marks the objects, it does not yet scan them. This is performed in the next subsection.

5.2 Marking the reachable set

After all objects that are reachable from the root set variables are marked on the GPU, the parallel-call finishes and control returns to the CPU. Since the CPU does not know which GPU objects are marked (either by the root set marking or by the last recursive marking pass) an extra GPU array called `marked_array` keeps track of segments of memory that hold some object(s) that were marked but not yet scanned. Note that such a segment can also hold objects that are dead or that are marked and already scanned. These can be ignored when marking a segment. For each boolean set in the marked array, the CPU issues a parallel-call to the GPU for marking all objects in the corresponding segment concurrently. See the for loop in Fig. 5. The kernel that marks an element of a segment is shown in Fig. 6.

It first examines `all_objects[id]` to see if the address in the segment is allocated to an object. If true, the object's `mark_phase` field is inspected. If it is set to the mark-phase-counter's value but its `scan_phase` is not yet set, then the object is scanned by invoking the code from Fig. 7 for each of its refer-

```
__device__
Object **global_vars[NUM_REF_GLOBALS] = {..};

__global__
void mark_roots() {
    int i = get_kernel_id();
    Object *p = *(global_vars[i]);
    int id = p->ref_object_id;
    mark_reachable_object(id, gc_phase);
}

void mark() {
    parallel_call[NUM_REF_GLOBALS]
            mark_roots();
    while (true) {
        bool host_marked_array[NUM_SEGMENTS];
        copy_device_to_host(host_marked_array,
                marked_array,
                sizeof(host_marked_array));
        clear_device_data(marked_array,
                sizeof(host_marked_array));

        bool found_something = false;
        for (int i=0; i<NUM_SEGMENTS; i++) {
            if (host_marked_array[i]) {
                parallel_call[SEGMENT_SIZE]
                        mark_segment(i * SEGMENT_SIZE,
                                gc_phase);
                found_something = true;
        } }
        if (!found_something) break;
} }
```

Figure 5. Host side of the marking pass.

ence fields. Scanning an `ObjectInfo` involves iterating over its `ptr_fields` array (see Figs. 3 and 4).[1]

Note that `mark_reachable_object` is concurrently safe. There are two cases to examine. First, if two marking kernels find exactly the same object-identifier live, both kernels concurrently write the same value to `info->mark_phase`. On modern hardware the concurrent write is not a problem. Second, if two marking kernels find object IDs i and i+k to be live and i and i+k map to the same segment, both kernels write the same value to the same element in the `marked_array`. This is not a problem as long as boolean memory writes are atomic. Otherwise, the `marked_array` can be replaced by an integer array without too much overhead as there is only one entry in the array for a whole segment of objects.

Scanning might switch on more bits in the `marked_array` so that more segments need to be processed in the while loop of Fig. 5. If there are no segments that contain any objects marked since the last pass, then the marking phase stops. We detect this by means of the `found_something` flag in the code.

Note that before every iteration the `marked_array` is cleared to avoid needless re-scanning of segments. That way a segment is only marked live if some object in the current iteration makes the segment live.

As can be seen in the code, control flips from the CPU finding segments to mark, to parallel marking code on the GPU, and back.

---

[1] Note that the `mark_reachable_object` is marked with `__device__` to tell Cuda that it is located on the GPU instead of on the CPU. Functions marked with `__global__` can be started in parallel from the CPU using Cuda's parallel-call statement. In the code we simplify this for now with the `parallel_call[N]` pseudo-code.

```
__device__
void scan_object(ObjectInfo *info,
                 int gc_phase) {
  void *obj = INFO_TO_ADDRESS(info);

  for (int i=0;i<info->num_ptrs;i++) {
    int off = info->ptr_fields[i];
    void *field = GET_FIELD_VALUE(obj, off);
    if (field) {
      int ref = GET_OBJECT_ID(field);
      ObjectInfo *P = &obj_info[ref];
      if (P->mark_phase != gc_phase) {
        mark_reachable_object(ref, gc_phase);
} } } }

__global__
void mark_segment(int start_obj_id,
                  int gc_phase) {
  int ix = start_obj_id + get_kernel_id();

  ObjectInfo *info = &all_objects[id];
  if (info->is_allocated &&
      info->mark_phase == gc_phase &&
      info->scan_phase != gc_phase) {
    // object is marked, not yet scanned

    info->scan_phase = gc_phase;

    scan_object(info);
} }
```

Figure 6. Marking a segment, scanning an object.

```
__device__
void mark_reachable_object(int id,
                           int gc_phase) {
  ObjectInfo *info = &all_objects[id];

  info->mark_phase = gc_phase;

  unsigned segment_id = id / SEGMENT_SIZE;
  marked_array[segment_id] = true;
}
```

Figure 7. Marking a reference.

5.3 Sweeping the heap

The sweep phase frees objects that are still marked with the old value of the mark-phase-counter (objects that have not been marked in that collection). To simplify the code slightly, newly allocated objects belong to the current collection phase.

Like for the mark phase, we maintain a boolean array called allocated_array with one boolean element per segment of memory. The invariant is that if allocated_array[P] is true, then there is some allocated object in that segment P. Note that the size of the sweep-segments can be different from the size of the mark-segments so that either size can be changed and optimized independently.

Whenever a kernel on the GPU allocates a new object Y, the allocator also sets the corresponding bit of the allocated_array. Similar to the marker, the sweeper sweeps whole segments that contain at least one allocated object. During a sweep of a segment, non-allocated ObjectInfo structures are examined in vain. But as this happens in parallel, not much time is wasted. If most objects are garbage, all of them are found in one step.

```
__global__
void sweep_segment(int old_phase,
                   int seg) {
  int seg_start = seg * GC_SEGMENT_SIZE;

  ObjectInfo *info = obj_info[seg_start +
                     get_kernel_id()];
  if (info->is_allocated) {
    // object was allocated
    if (info->mark_phase == old_phase) {
      // object was not marked, remove!
      recycle_memory_to_warm_chains(info);
    } else {
      // this segment still has some
      // allocated data.
      allocated_array[seg] = true;
} } }

void sweep() {
  bool has_allocs[NUM_GC_SEGMENTS];

  copy_device_to_host(has_allocs,
                      allocated_array,
                      sizeof(has_allocs));
  clear_device_data(allocated_array,
                    sizeof(has_allocs));

  for (int seg=0;seg<NUM_GC_SEGMENTS;seg++) {
    if (has_allocs[seg]) {
      parallel_call[GC_SEGMENT_SIZE]
          sweep_segment(old_phase, seg));
} }
```

Figure 8. Pseudo-code of the sweeper.

See Fig. 8 for the pseudo-code of the sweeper. The sweep() method copies the allocated_array to the host and clears the array on the GPU afterwards. Only if there is at least one allocated object in the segment, it must be swept for dead objects.

For each segment in parallel we start a sweep_segment kernel. It computes its index into the ObjectInfo array and compares its contents. If an object became garbage, its heap memory is recycled and its ObjectInfo entry is marked deleted. If the allocated object is still live, the sweep-segment still holds allocated objects and is marked accordingly for the next collection pass.

Note that the sweeper could run in parallel to user code. But since not all available GPUs allow multiple different kernels to be started, we stay away from that for portability reasons.

5.4 Optimizations

There are a number of optimizations that we have done to increase collector performance. We go over them now.

5.4.1 Marking or sweeping of Adjacent Segments (AS)

During marking, if we see Z consecutive segments with live objects that still require scanning, we can start Z times $MARK\_SEG-MENT\_SIZE$ kernels in parallel on the GPU to scan any objects on them. This saves us Z times the cost of starting kernels on the GPU. The same we can do in the sweep phase by starting kernels for all Z consecutive sweep segments that were marked as allocated. The larger number of concurrent kernels on the GPU also gives the GPU more flexibility in its scheduling.

5.4.2 Reference Counting marked segments and allocated segments (RC)

One might think that sweeping all segments containing some allocated objects without first determining if the segment is fully

5

marked will negatively affect performance. After all, if all objects in a segment are marked, the sweeper will have nothing to do. However, measurements do not show a significant performance increase. Nevertheless, we have implemented this idea to show that the simpler version that sweeps a segment regardless of whether it is fully marked already performs just as well.

To implement this alternative idea, we replace the boolean array (that tells if a sweep-segment contains some allocation) by an array of integers that states how many objects are allocated on that sweep-segment. Additionally, we introduce another integer array (one element per sweep-segment) in which we record how many objects are marked on that sweep-segment during marking. The CPU-side of the sweeper only needs to issue a parallel-call to sweep a segment if its number of allocations is different from its number of objects marked in the last pass.

This is not for free, since object allocation becomes slightly more expensive as we require an atomic instruction to increment the number of allocated objects on a segment. Similarly, during marking we need to atomically count the number of objects that are marked on a segment.

5.4.3 Delayed Marking (DM) of large arrays in parallel

If the above marker code finds a large array of references, one Cuda-kernel would scan its elements sequentially. This causes an extreme load imbalance and almost sequentializes execution. To counter this, instead of sequentially marking all elements, the marker pushes a reference to the large array (of references) to a queue as a tuple that holds the number of elements and the array-reference itself. Scanning of the array is delayed; once a segment has been fully marked, control returns to the CPU as usual. There the CPU copies the queue's content from the GPU. For each array in the queue, a parallel call is issued to mark all the array's elements concurrently. Each large array is processed sequentially as otherwise we would require multiple different parallel kernel calls which is not portable across GPUs.

5.4.4 RECursive marking (REC)

There is a potential performance problem in applications that use deeply nested data-structures, e.g., long linked lists. The fact that marking deep data structures inhibits parallelism is a known problem, see [6, 7]. Up to now, for such a list our collector marks one node of the list before returning to the host. The host then fetches the marked_array from the GPU, finds that there is one segment to scan (containing the single live next node in the list), and restarts the marking kernels that again find a single live object to scan next. This causes a severe load-imbalance over our kernels and many costly control transfers between CPU and GPU.

Our solution is to sequentialize execution slightly once we know that any further data structures are 'deep'. After (for example) 10 times returning to the host after marking, the collector has scanned the reachable object graph up-to pointer depth 10. At that point the collector will start to recursively mark from inside the scan method using a small fixed size to-do queue to keep the recursive state and to avoid actual recursion. Because the stack space is limited inside a kernel, the size of the queue must be kept small. This avoids the overhead of context-switching as control remains on the GPU for a longer time.

There are therefore two constants used by this optimization. The number of CPU-GPU context switches before enabling the use of the to-do queue and the size of the to-do queue itself. We fix the number of required context-switches to 10 for the rest of the paper and only vary the size of the to-do queue. This size we will call REC from here on.

To implement this optimization the marker calls a slightly different mark_segment function after 10 parallel mark-segment calls inside the mark function. The then called recursive-mark-segment function effectively inlines the mark-object to scan-object chain a number of times and does not immediately return to the host after marking only a single object.

This of course reduces the context-switching overhead at the cost of a potential reduction in parallelism. For example, consider a data-structure that is very deep and has a low enough branching factor such that delayed marking (DM) will not be triggered. In this case, it would be better to mark for a while until enough objects are discovered that the system should return to the default marker by disabling recursive marking for a while. The current prototype does not yet recognize this case and continues to use the recursive-mark-segment function.

5.4.5 Larger Mark Segment (MS) or Sweep Segment (SS) sizes

Increasing the size of a mark- or a sweep segment increases the available parallelism. However, if the larger segments contain only a few live references to mark (or sweep) many parallel kernels are started in vain. Another issue is that the kernel's execution paths easily diverge with large segments when live and dead objects are interleaved. A separate memory compaction phase would solve this. However, parallel memory compaction is outside of the scope of this paper and does not seem crucial for the benchmarks tested.

Varying the sweep segment size will have less effect as during sweeping a segment is examined only once whereas during marking a segment can be examined multiple times. Any accumulative effect of varying MS will therefore be larger. The effect of varying segment sizes will, however, be negated somewhat by the AS optimization (Sec. 5.4.1) by issuing a single parallel call of adjacent sweep (or mark) segments that need to be swept (or marked).

Finally, a larger segment size causes fewer segments to be needed to cover the GPU's collectable heap. This in turn reduces the size of the administrative data that needs to be copied from the GPU to the CPU. On each parallel mark iteration (the size of the host_marked_array array in Fig. 5). As this array traverses the PCI bus, the savings can be significant.

5.5 Implementation of the sequential collector

To demonstrate the effectiveness of the parallel collector (described above), we also implemented a sequential collector. Both collectors use the same allocation routines, only the collector differs.

The sequential collector uses two arrays. One to store object references found but not yet scanned and another to hold references to allocated objects. The sizes of both arrays are computed from the maximal heap size and the minimal object size. Whenever an object is allocated, it is added to the allocated-objects array. This involves an atomic-add instruction to do this safely.

The sequential collector is also a mark-and-sweep collector. It first pushes all object references from the root set to the to-do array and increments a mark-phase-counter. Next it starts a single kernel on the GPU (as it is a sequential collector) to mark objects that are reachable from the to-do array. Whenever an object reference inside an object is found it is pushed to the to-do list and the object's mark-phase is set to the next mark-phase-counter's value. This continues until all reachable objects have been marked.

The collector uses a single Cuda kernel to traverse the allocated-objects array. If an object is found that still has the old mark-phase, it is recycled.

Note that the sequential collector has two advantages over the parallel collector: (1) there are no atomic instructions required in the mark or sweep phases; (2) it does not look at references that are not yet proven to be live during marking.

6. Performance

In the collector and in the allocator there are a number of switches and constants that can be varied to change their behavior. The switches are:

- Parallel mark-sweep of immediately **A**djacent **S**egments (AS), default: enabled (Sec. 5.4.1).
- **R**eference **C**ounted segments (RC), default: enabled (Sec. 5.4.2).
- **D**elayed **M**arking of large arrays (DM), default: enabled (Sec. 5.4.3).

The constants are:

- **REC**ursive mark depth (REC) (triggered after 10 mark iterations), default: 8 (Sec. 5.4.4).
- The size of an object-id **M**ark-**S**egment in the collector (MS), default: 256 (see Sec. 5.4.5).
- The size of an object-id **S**weep-**S**egment in the collector (SS), default: 32 (see Sec. 5.4.5).
- The number of **B**ig-object **B**uckets in the allocator (BB), default: 16 (see Sec. 4).
- The number of **S**mall-object **F**ree-**L**ists in the allocator (SFL), default: 1024 (see Sec. 4)

The minimum object size is fixed to 128 bytes. The Cuda work group size of the marker is fixed to 256 Cuda threads and for the sweeper to 8 Cuda threads. The sweeper's work group size is so small because we expect many concurrent accesses to the free-list to recycle objects which can involve many conflicting atomic compare-and-exchange instructions. A larger value would only cause more serialization in this case while a smaller value can potentially allow more parallel work groups.

In the following measurements, we take the default values of the above switches and constants and change a single variable each time to see its effect. The defaults, however, are already reasonable to not exaggerate effects.

All measurements were performed on a Xeon 5550 "Nehalem" chip (8 cores + SMT) running at 2.66 GHz with 8 MB shared cache per chip and 24 GB of RAM (DDR3-1333). The GPU used is an nVidia Tesla M2070 GPU Board which has 6 GByte of GDDR5 memory and offers 448 Cuda cores. To further strain the collector, we allocate a maximum 512 MByte heap for SOOC programs. The machine runs Linux kernel 2.6.18.

All benchmarks were written in SOOC which is translated to a combination of C++ and CUDA. Final compilation is performed by CUDA 3.2 and GNU G++ 4.3.3.

In the following measurements, all options are set to their defaults and only one variable is changed to see its effects.

6.1 Microbenchmarks

Since GPU code is often data-parallel, we study the performance of flat arrays of objects where each kernel operates on a different object. Other data-structures that work well are hash tables, maps, vectors, and B+ trees with large fan-outs. Because on a GPU, divergence is a problem, we do not expect large linked lists to be used where each kernel operates on a different list element. After all, each kernel would have to first traverse the list to get to its element. That would take a different number of loop iterations for each list node so that all kernels would inevitably diverge and cause sequential execution.

We first examine the allocation and collector performance for large single-linked lists which demonstrates our worst case behavior. See the top chart of Fig. 9. Concurrently 16 Cuda kernels allocate lists with 8192 elements each. One list is kept, the other 15 lists become collectable. This is repeated 8 times.

As shown in the first two bars, the sequential collector's mark phase is faster than the parallel collector's mark phase as it does not have to repeatedly flip control from CPU to GPU to mark seg-

ments. Since the sweep phase of the parallel collector is far superior, the parallel collector wins overall. As this benchmark allocates almost solely small objects, the work per sweep-segment is large. The effect of this is that the overhead of a parallel-call to sweep a segment becomes negligible making AS less effective. Even though RC can skip sweeping over 15% of sweep segments this causes only a very slight performance increase. Delayed marking (DM) has little influence in this benchmark as there are no large arrays. When recursive marking is disabled (REC 0) the performance of the parallel collector drops so that we can conclude that this is an important optimization. A too small mark segment size (MS) causes a drop in performance as not enough parallelism is extracted (a single segment containing no live objects breaks AS's segment merging of mark-segments). Because AS already merges many sweep-segments, changing the sweep segment size has little influence. The allocator constant SFL should be set to at least 64 to eliminate contention.

The bottom chart of Fig. 9 shows the results of repeatedly allocating large arrays of references to fresh objects. This benchmark has 1024 parallel kernels each of which creates arrays filled with 1024 small objects. The arrays of only 64 kernels are kept. The other 960 arrays (and pointed to objects) become garbage.

The parallel collector is faster than the sequential collector because all segments with allocated objects are swept in parallel by removing some parallel-call Cuda overheads. The slight drop in sweep performance when disabling parallel mark/sweep of adjacent segments (AS) again shows its importance. Even though RC causes approx. 10% fewer segments to be swept, this does not result in much less run time as sweeping segments where all objects are already marked is very efficient. The mark phase is also slightly faster because all elements of the kept arrays are marked in parallel (disabling DM causes a small performance drop). Changing REC does not show any change as the benchmark has no data-structure that reaches deeper than 10 pointers. The benchmark is also insensitive to SS and MS which indicates that very little kernel divergence occurs in either marking or sweeping (the heap has little fragmentation) and AS is very successful in merging segments. Again, the allocator constant SFL should be set to at least 64 to eliminate contention. With increasing sizes of BB, performance slightly worsens as the system's allocator will have more buckets to search for free memory once its own bucket runs empty.

6.2 Application Benchmarks

Without looking into each individual application's results, we can say the following things.

For all benchmarks below, RC is able to consistently sweep at least 10% fewer segments (skipping segments where all objects therein are kept alive). However, this does not result in much better performance as the sweeper is very fast at skipping these objects in parallel anyway. Furthermore, the sweeper is already very fast so that even a 10% speedup of the sweeper has little influence overall. This confirms our hypothesis that the simpler version that only keeps a boolean per segment suffices.

Changing the sweep segment size has too little influence to see its effects. The effect is small mainly because little divergence occurs, involves only one GPU to CPU memory copy, and the sweep pass is short.

None of the applications repeatedly allocates large arrays. They all allocate some large arrays at startup and keep them around. The applications also do not allocate very large linked lists so that the worst case behavior requiring recursive marking does not occur.

For these reasons and to not overwhelm, we do not show the corresponding measurements in the charts (RC, SS *, REC *, and BB *) as they are all flat.

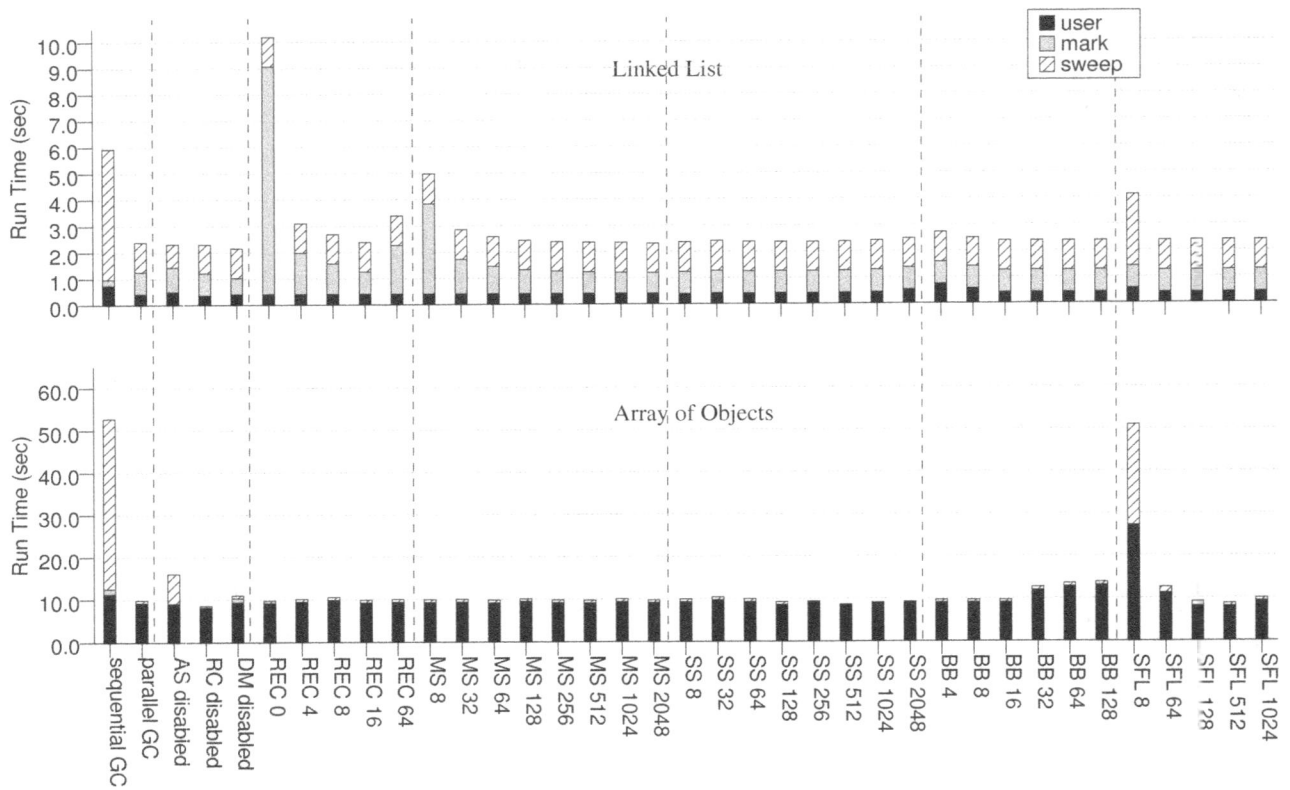

Figure 9. Microbenchmarks.

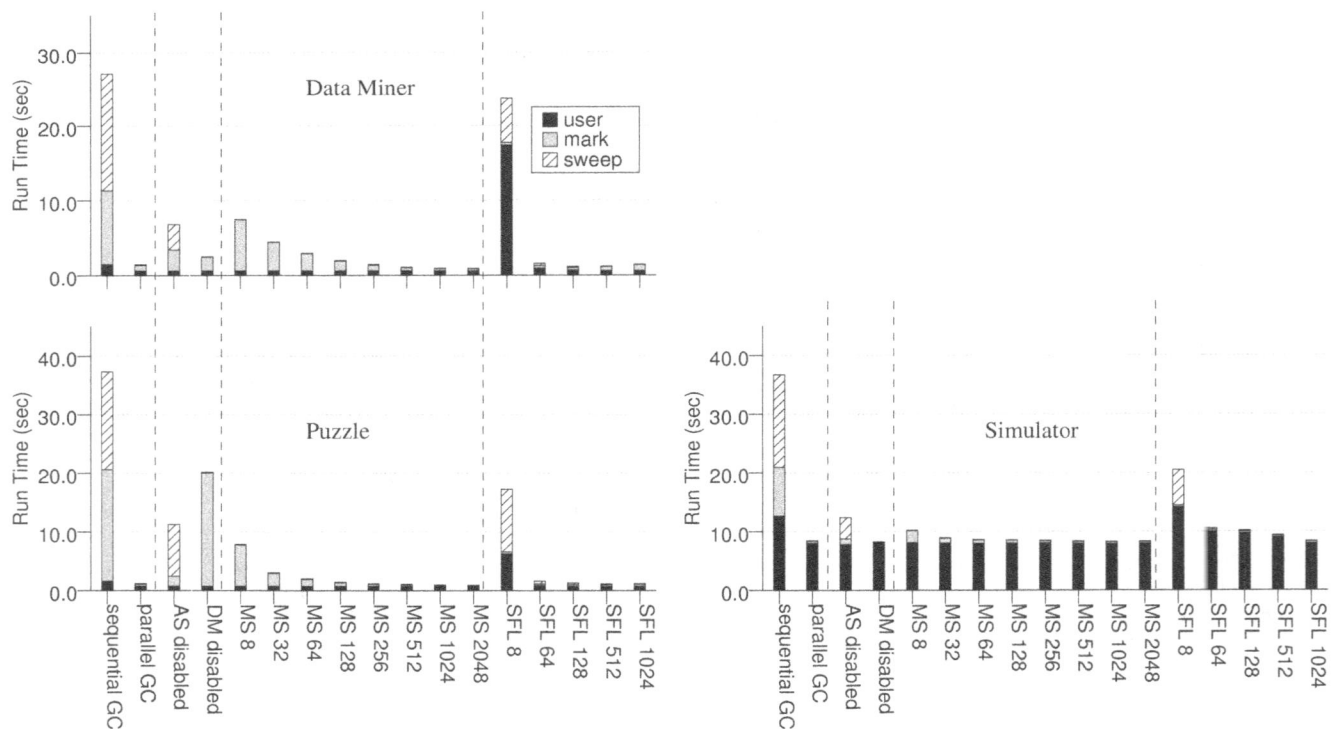

Figure 10. Application performance.

6.2.1 Parallel Data Miner for Supermarket receipts

A large set of receipts of sold items is stored on the GPU. The benchmark determines how often two items were sold together. The code uses a large flat array of references to receipt objects. Each receipt object holds a small linked list of items bought. The code in parallel builds a frequency list of items sold where kernel K is responsible for all combinations that start with item K. Every iteration of the code operates on a new set of receipts that renders the previous receipts garbage.

As shown in the top chart of Fig.10, a lot of time is spent in the collector as in each iteration all previous receipts (which is most of the data of this application) can be recycled. The parallel collector is much faster than the sequential collector. Disabling AS (one parallel call for adjacent live/allocated segments) causes many GPU $\leftrightarrow$ CPU context switches which kill performance for marking the linked-lists of items sold inside of receipts. Disabling delayed marking (DM) also causes a performance drop as the elements of the large array of receipts are not processed in parallel.

If the mark segment size is too small, i.e. below 512 elements, performance degrades as too many context switches are performed.

When the number of free-lists becomes too small, the contention is of course very high which degrades performance enormously.

6.2.2 Puzzle - Parallel Game Tree Search

This application solves the 5x5 sliding puzzle problem by searching through all permutations of a 5x5 matrix to find a sorted sequence. The application itself maintains a number of to-do lists from where each kernel picks a puzzle and shifts its blank in (up-to) four directions to create four new puzzles. The new puzzles are again pushed into one of the to-do lists where the blank can be moved around some more. To reduce the probability of the blank moving back-and-forth over the same positions, the last position of the blank is recorded.

Each time a puzzle's blank is shifted, it is tested against a large hash-table to see if it has been seen before. In that case, the puzzle is discarded and can be collected. Because the search space is so large, the to-do lists have a fixed size so that sometimes a puzzle must be discarded because no space exists for it on a to-do list.

As the bottom-left chart of Fig. 10 shows, again, the parallel collector is much faster than the sequential collector.

Scanning adjacent segments (AS) that also require marking or sweeping in parallel markedly increases parallelism and decreases the number of context switches. Delayed parallel marking (DM) of large arrays is also important in this benchmark. Here the to-do list and the hash-table of already seen puzzles are both implemented with large arrays whose elements are best traced in parallel. After all their elements have been marked live, control returns to the CPU where all newly marked live segments are scanned in parallel (the objects pointed to from the large arrays).

With increasing mark-segment sizes, the amount of parallelism in the mark phase increases (all elements in a mark-segment are processed in parallel). A side-effect is also that the arrays that are used to store per-segment information are slightly smaller. This causes the CPU to have slightly less work in scanning and copying them from GPU to CPU.

The free-list (SFL) of the marker should be at least 64 to combat congestion.

6.2.3 Particle Simulator

This application simulates a set of 16384 particles that interact using Newtonian physics. To reduce the number of particle-to-particle interactions that need to be computed, the particles are first put into boxes wherein every particle's exerted force on every other particle is computed. Afterwards, the center of mass and total mass are computed for each box and the box's gravitational effect is computed for every particle in every other box.

The application's data is structured as an array of box objects where each box contains an array of particle objects. Each particle object contains references to 3D vector objects that store the particle's position, velocity, and acceleration. Additionally, each particle object contains a field holding its mass.

In each iteration, the exuded forces are computed and new position, velocity, and acceleration objects are created and inserted into a new particle object to hold the new data. This new particle overwrites the old particle. Also, during computation, new temporary vectors are created to hold, for example, the difference between two particle positions. Together this generates many objects to be collected after every iteration of the simulation.

This application performs a lot of computation in user code and in the allocator compared to time in the collector (Fig. 10, bottom-right chart). However, the parallel collector is again decidedly faster than the sequential collector. The collector itself spends little time doing marking and most in the sweeper. When the collector starts, all boxes and all particles in them are marked in parallel so that mark-time becomes very low. When sweeping, the collectable particles and vector objects are very near to each other in memory so that sweeping performance is near optimal (very little divergence).

Scanning adjacent segments (AS) that also require marking or sweeping in parallel again shows its usefulness by both increasing parallelism and decreasing the number of context switches. Delayed marking (DM) of the array that holds the references to all boxes does not improve performance much as the array is relatively small and exists only once. The arrays of particles inside each box are also fairly small (and there are many of them) which causes some overhead in recording them for delayed marking. Changing the mark segment size (MS) does not change much which proves that there is not much divergence.

7. Related Work

A good introduction to garbage collection is given in [9] and indexes[2] are available to give a general introduction to the field.

The work closest to ours is that of [6] and that of [11]. In both papers the authors examine theoretical collector performance for multi-core machines when using up to 1024 processors on the SPECjvm and DeCapo Java benchmarks. They notice that some applications do indeed use deep pointer hierarchies and as such do not scale well unchanged. To optimize collector scalability the authors of [6] propose two techniques: (1) to change data-structures to add dummy pointers to elements of lists or trees that point further into the list or tree. This artificially makes the list or tree a little flatter and so more amenable to parallel traversal during marking. (2) to speculatively pick a random object from the heap and start tracing from it in parallel. If the random root is later proven reachable, the objects found reachable can then be added to the actual set of marked objects.

Both techniques to add more parallelism to the collector are orthogonal to the collector presented in this paper. However, parallel codes written for a GPU will be structured differently from those for a CPU such that given the opportunity of automatic memory management they will most certainly require different data structures. The Java benchmarks for CPU-based systems therefore do not apply to a GPU-based collector (although they would work when translated to SOOC, they would not work very efficiently on a GPU).

Instead of stopping the world and then performing a collection, it is also possible to collect concurrently while the mutators (the user's kernels) continue to work. This is for example implemented

---

[2] http://www.cs.kent.ac.uk/people/staff/rej/gcbib/gcbib.html

for a mark-and-sweep collector in [2]. This and other concurrent collectors typically use a write-barrier to maintain collector safety. Such a write-barrier consists of a few 'if' statements inserted before every reference assignments to a field of an object or array. These 'if's can cause significant overhead on GPUs (no branch prediction). Alternatively, the CPU's memory management unit (MMU) has been used to track page usage as is done in [5, 7]. However, since present GPUs do not use an MMU, this will not work.

Instead of mark-and-sweep, [3] uses reference counting of objects to find collectable objects. Here the reference counting operations are first locally queued, and then they are stolen by the collector thread that performs the actual increments and decrements of the reference counters. If a reference count falls to zero, the object is reclaimed. Because work stealing of locally-queued counting operations requires critical sections, divergence of control on GPUs is hard to avoid.

Instead of marking all objects on segments in parallel, parallelism could also be managed by means of work-stealing. Here, whenever a live object is discovered, it is put onto a stack from where some other thread can steal it to trace its references. See for example [4, 12]. However, work stealing (or pushing) does not work well on a GPU because each successful stealing attempt would cause divergence from all those concurrent stealers that fail.

A parallel mark-and-sweep collector that uses work-stealing for a normal CPU is presented in [8]. They determined that load-imbalance quickly becomes an issue. In their system, large arrays are partitioned into small chunks that are marked in parallel. Our system goes a little further by marking every single array element in parallel while task distribution is managed differently so that less load-imbalance occurs.

Another popular GC technique is a copying-GC. In general, a copying GC copies live objects away to a 'to'-space leaving the garbage objects in the 'from'-space. A comparison of parallel copying vs. mark-and-sweep collectors can be found in [1]. A recent copying collector is [10]. Many parallel copying GCs lock objects before copying. This costs performance, especially on a GPU where any threads waiting on the lock would cause divergence. Also, useful memory is halved as memory must be kept in reserve to hold both 'from' and 'to' spaces which on a limited memory GPU can be an issue.

Additionally, it is fairly slow to copy the memory in a Cuda kernel. First all kernels must reserve space on the single 'to'-space before they can start the copy which costs at least one heavily contended atomic add or subtract operation. Next each kernel must copy the bytes from its object to the allocated space which can be slow as well (no memory access coalescing).

8. Conclusions

There were four contributions presented in this paper:

- iterative data parallel mark and sweep on a GPU;
- reference counted segments to reduce sweeping work;
- delayed marking of large reference arrays for more parallelism;
- evaluation of garbage collection efficiency on a GPU.

Iterative data-parallel mark and sweep let the CPU issue parallel-calls to the GPU to mark or sweep regions of memory. The assumption that a stray non-allocated object or already marked object in a mark- or sweep segment does not overly hurt performance is confirmed by our measurements. The cost of context switching between GPU and CPU is not overly large either and using reference counted segments (using either a single boolean or a full counter) and dynamically switching to a recursive marker further reduces the context switching overheads.

There are a number of optimizations that are required for good performance for a parallel collector on a GPU. One must not only mark each object inside a segment of memory in parallel, but one must also mark the elements of each large array in parallel too. Additionally, if two or more adjacent segments hold some live objects, all elements of each segment should be scanned in parallel to reduce kernel invocation overheads. Another optimization with large effect is to switch to a recursive (sequential) marker if the pointer depth becomes high. This mitigates the costs of parallel calls. The mark-segment size should be kept large as most times a segment contains only objects of a given type (dead, live, marked, etc.) and can then be effectively processed in parallel. This is confirmed by the measurements.

Overall, data-parallel sweeping of all (potential) objects in a segment is very successful. The optimizations proposed are also very successful in reducing many of the overheads. The collector achieves a speedup of a factor of up-to 11 over a sequential collector on the same GPU, significantly reducing the GC related overheads for some very memory intensive benchmarks.

References

[1] C. Attanasio, D. Bacon, A. Cocchi, and S. Smith. A Comparative Evaluation of Parallel Garbage Collector Implementations. In *Languages and Compilers for Parallel Computing. LCPC'03*, volume 2624 of *LNCS*, pages 79–94. Springer, 2003.

[2] H. Azatchi, Y. Levanoni, H. Paz, and E. Petrank. An on-the-fly mark and sweep garbage collector based on sliding views. In *Proc. 18th ACM SIGPLAN Conf. Object-oriented Programing, Systems, Languages, and Applications*, OOPSLA'03, pages 269–281, Anaheim, CA, 2003.

[3] D.F. Bacon, C.R. Attanasio, H.B. Lee, V.T. Rajan, and S. Smith. Java without the coffee breaks: a nonintrusive multiprocessor garbage collector. In *Proc. ACM SIGPLAN 2001 Conf. Programming Language Design and Implementation*, PLDI'01, pages 92–103, Snowbird, UT, 2001.

[4] K. Barabash, O. Ben-Yitzhak, I. Goft, E.K. Kolodner, V. Leikehman, Y. Ossia, A. Owshanko, and E. Petrank. A parallel, incremental, mostly concurrent garbage collector for servers. *ACM Trans. Program. Lang. Syst.*, issue 6, 27:1097–1146, Nov. 2005.

[5] K. Barabash, Y. Ossia, and E. Petrank. Mostly concurrent garbage collection revisited. In *Proc. 18th ACM SIGPLAN Conf. Object-Oriented Programing, Systems, Languages, and Applications*, OOPSLA'03, pages 255–268, Anaheim, CA, 2003.

[6] K. Barabash and E. Petrank. Tracing garbage collection on highly parallel platforms. In *Proc. 2010 Intl. Symp. Memory Management*, ISMM'10, pages 1–10, Toronto, Canada, 2010.

[7] H.J. Boehm, A.J. Demers, and S. Shenker. Mostly parallel garbage collection. In *Proc. ACM SIGPLAN 1991 Conf. Programming Language Design and Implementation*, PLDI'91, pages 157–164, Toronto, Canada, 1991.

[8] T. Endo, K. Taura, and A. Yonezawa. A scalable mark-sweep garbage collector on large-scale shared-memory machines. In *Proc. 1997 ACM/IEEE Conf. Supercomputing*, pages 1–14, San Jose, CA, 1997.

[9] R. Jones and R. Lins. *Garbage Collection: Algorithms for Automatic Dynamic Memory Management*. Wiley, 1996.

[10] S. Marlow, T. Harris, R.P. James, and S. Peyton Jones. Parallel generational-copying garbage collection with a block-structured heap. In *Proc. 7th Intl. Symp. Memory Management*, ISMM'08, pages 11–20, Tucson, AZ, 2008.

[11] Fridtjof Siebert. Limits of parallel marking garbage collection. In *Proc. 7th Intl. Symp. on Memory Management*, ISMM'08, pages 21–29, Tucson, AZ, 2008.

[12] Ming Wu and Xiao-Feng Li. Task-pushing: a Scalable Parallel GC Marking Algorithm without Synchronization Operations. In *Proc. IEEE Parallel and Distributed Processing Symp.*, IPDPS'07, pages 1–10, Long Beach, CA, 2007.

Memory Management in NUMA Multicore Systems:

Trapped between Cache Contention and Interconnect Overhead

Zoltan Majo

Department of Computer Science
ETH Zurich, Switzerland

Thomas R. Gross

Department of Computer Science
ETH Zurich, Switzerland

Abstract

Multiprocessors based on processors with multiple cores usually include a non-uniform memory architecture (NUMA); even current 2-processor systems with 8 cores exhibit non-uniform memory access times. As the cores of a processor share a common cache, the issues of memory management and process mapping must be revisited. We find that optimizing only for data locality can counteract the benefits of cache contention avoidance and vice versa. Therefore, system software must take *both* data locality and cache contention into account to achieve good performance, and memory management cannot be decoupled from process scheduling. We present a detailed analysis of a commercially available NUMA-multicore architecture, the Intel Nehalem. We describe two scheduling algorithms: *maximum-local*, which optimizes for maximum data locality, and its extension, *N-MASS*, which reduces data locality to avoid the performance degradation caused by cache contention. N-MASS is fine-tuned to support memory management on NUMA-multicores and improves performance up to 32%, and 7% on average, over the default setup in current Linux implementations.

Categories and Subject Descriptors D.4.8 [*Performance*]: Measurements; D.4.1 [*Process Management*]: Scheduling

General Terms Performance, Algorithms, Experimentation

Keywords NUMA, multicore processors, shared resource contention, memory allocation

1. Introduction

Multicore multiprocessors create unique challenges for runtime systems and compilers. If multiple cores on a processor share a cache, contention for the shared cache memory is a major performance bottleneck. Moreover, as the number of processor cores per chip increases with every new microprocessor generation, the problems caused by limited main memory bandwidth are further aggravated.

To scale memory system bandwidth, new processors integrate a memory controller on the processor chip. Therefore, in multiprocessor systems the physical memory address space is divided between the processors, with each processor accessing its share of

the address space via its on-chip memory controller. Yet in shared-memory multiprocessors, each processor must be able to access the local memory of other processors as well. Such memory accesses happen via the cross-chip interconnect that connects the processors, and the major processor manufacturers have developed their proprietary cross-chip interconnect technology (e.g., AMD's HyperTransport, or Intel's QuickPath Interconnect). Multiprocessor configurations of these systems have a non-uniform memory architecture (NUMA) as remote memory accesses via the interconnect are subject to various overheads. The bandwidth is lower than the bandwidth provided by the (local) on-chip memory controller. The latency is higher as well: memory operations are processed by the local interface to the interconnect (arbitration may be needed if multiple cores access remote memory), a request is transmitted to another processor, and additional steps may be needed on this remote processor before the memory access can be done. Consequently, remote memory accesses suffer penalties of 1.5 to 2 times relative to local accesses. Good data locality is therefore highly desirable, i.e. the computations should take place on the processor that keeps their data. So memory management on these systems cannot be done without paying attention to process mapping, and a process scheduler that determines which processor executes a thread must consider where memory has been allocated.

There are two classes of problems that memory management and process scheduling on a NUMA-multicore must consider. First, the cores of a multicore processor share on-chip memory system resources (e.g., memory controllers, last-level caches, or prefetcher units). *Shared resource contention* can lead to severe performance degradation, as discussed in [3, 4, 9, 11, 18, 19, 23, 26, 29]. In [2, 3, 7, 12, 29] the authors show that the operating system scheduler is in a good position to reduce shared resource contention, especially contention for shared last-level caches (LLCs). Mapping memory-bound processes so that they use different last-level caches increases performance by avoiding inter-core cache misses that co-executing processes cause to each other.

The second class of problems in NUMA-multicores is related to the *data locality* in the system. There exists a large body of work on methods for improving data locality in NUMA systems, either by profile-based [14, 17] or dynamic [22, 27, 28] memory migration. However, none of the previous approaches considers increased shared resource contention that may be caused by data locality optimizations. Additionally, operating system schedulers that target shared resource contention avoidance can compromise data locality by mapping a process onto a processor that does not hold the process's data.

In this paper we argue that memory management and process scheduling must be coupled. We focus on the first and simplest part of memory management, the allocation of a process's data to a specific processor. We show that a process scheduler that aims at maximizing data locality in a system may not always obtain good performance, as contention for shared resources may degrade performance. To support our argument, we present in the first part of the paper a detailed analysis of the performance of the memory system of a commercially available NUMA-multicore architecture, the Intel Nehalem. In the second part of the paper we present a novel NUMA–Multicore-Aware Scheduling Scheme (N-MASS) that is an extension of the standard Linux scheduler. N-MASS considers *both* previously discussed performance-degrading factors (shared resource contention and data locality) when deciding on how to map processes onto the hardware. N-MASS increases performance by up to 32%, and 7% on average, relative to default operating system process scheduling.

2. Background

In this section we analyze the performance impact of mapping processes onto a NUMA-multicore computer with data locality constraints with a simple example: mapping two memory-bound processes. For this example we select two programs from the SPEC CPU2006 benchmark suite, mcf and lbm. Both programs have a high last-level cache (LLC) miss rate, therefore the performance of both programs is highly dependent on efficiently using the memory system of the machine.

For the discussion of the example we assume that the two programs are executed on a NUMA-multicore machine similar to the one shown in Figure 1. The machine has two processors. Each processor is multicore, and the cores of each processor share an LLC. Moreover, the machine is NUMA: each processor is directly connected to a part of the physical memory, and the processors are connected to each other with a cross-chip interconnect.

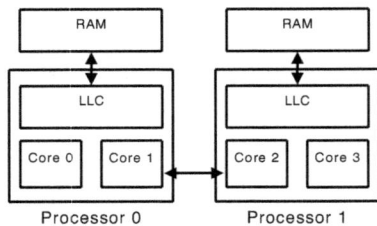

Figure 1: Example NUMA-multicore machine.

In a NUMA system a process's data can be allocated in the memory of any processor in the system. We say that a process p is *homed* on Processor i of the system if the process's data was allocated only on Processor i. If a process runs on its home processor, it is executed *locally*. Similarly, if a process runs on a processor different from its home processor, it is executed *remotely*. For our example we assume that both processes (executing mcf resp. lbm) are homed on Processor 0 of the machine (we relax this constraint in the evaluation presented in Section 4.3). Because both programs are single-threaded, there are four ways the processes executing the two programs can be mapped onto the system given this memory allocation setup. Figure 2 shows all possible mappings:

(a) **Both processes executed locally.** As both processes execute on their respective home node (Processor 0), they both have fast access to main memory. As Processor 0 has only one LLC, the processes contend for the LLC capacity of Processor 0.

(b) mcf **executed locally, lbm executed remotely.** As lbm is executed remotely (on Processor 1), it accesses main memory through the cross-chip interconnect, therefore it experiences lower throughput and increased latency of memory accesses relative to local execution. Additionally, as the two processes

execute on two different processors, they do not share an LLC, therefore there is no cache contention in the system.

(c) mcf **executed remotely, lbm executed locally** This case is similar to case (b), but in this case mcf uses the cross-chip interconnect to access main memory instead of lbm.

(d) **Both processes executed remotely.** Both processes share the LLC, and both processes execute remotely. This setup is clearly the worst possible scenario for performance, therefore we exclude this case from further investigation.

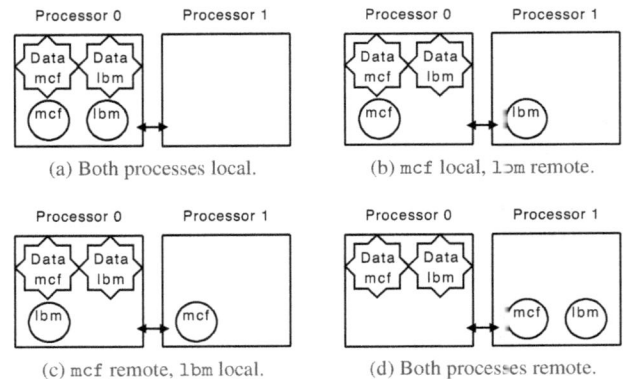

Figure 2: Possible mappings of mcf and lbm.

In this paper we use the cache miss rate per thousand instructions executed (MPKI) to characterize the memory-boundedness of programs. Figure 3.(a) shows the increase of the MPKI of mcf and lbm relative to each program's execution in *single-process mode* (executed alone and locally on the system, also referred to as *solo mode*). In case (a) (both processes locally executed), the MPKI increases by 47% resp. 62% due to cache contention. In cases (b) and (c) (when the processes are mapped onto different processors, therefore different LLCs), the MPKI increases by at most 4% relative to solo mode. The reason for this small increase is the contention on the memory controller relative to solo mode.

Good data locality is crucial for obtaining good performance in NUMA systems. Figure 3.(b) shows the distribution of bandwidth over the interfaces of the system. In case (a), when both processes are executed locally, the system has good data locality: 100% of the memory bandwidth in the system is provided by the local memory interface of Processor 0. In cases (b) and (c), when one of the two processes executes on Processor 1, data is transferred also on the cross-chip interconnect of the system: 56% (resp. 33%) of the generated bandwidth is due to one of the two processes executing remotely. Figure 3.(b) also shows the total bandwidth measured on the interfaces in the system. If the processes execute locally and thus share the cache (case (a)), the total bandwidth is approximately 50% more than in cases (b) and (c) (when caches are not shared).

In this paper we investigate which mapping leads to best performance: when cache contention is minimized (cases (b) and (c)), or when data locality is maximized (case (a)). Figure 3.(c) shows the individual and average performance degradation of mcf and lbm in all three mapping scenarios. The performance degradation of a program is calculated as the percent slowdown in wall clock execution time relative to the solo mode execution of the program. (Generally, if not qualified, performance means wall-clock execution time in this paper.) The average performance of the workload consisting of mcf and lbm is better in cases (b) and (c) than in case (a). Case (b) shows only a minor improvement over case (a) because remote execution slows down lbm by almost 30%. However, in case (c) the degradation is reduced relative to case (a); mcf

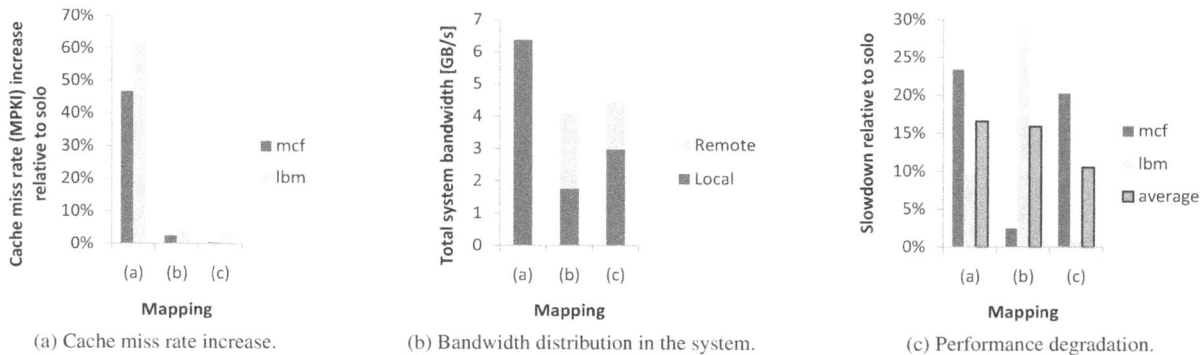

(a) Cache miss rate increase.

(b) Bandwidth distribution in the system.

(c) Performance degradation.

Figure 3: Performance of `mcf` and `lbm` in different mapping scenarios.

sees a small improvement, `lbm`'s slowdown is reduced from 11% to 1%, so the average degradation is reduced from 17% to 11%.

In conclusion, in a NUMA-multicore system we must find a compromise between favoring data locality and avoiding cache contention. Good data locality is beneficial in most cases, however when the memory pressure on LLCs is high, it is beneficial to avoid cache contention, even at the cost of compromising data locality in the system. In this paper we show that an architecture-aware process scheduler that is also aware of the memory allocation setup in the system can significantly increase performance relative to default operating system scheduling.

To simplify the discussion, we focus on a setup with 2 processors. We also assume that all the cores of a processor share an LLC. There are systems that do not support this assumption (see multi-socket implementations like the AMD Magny-Cours). In this case you should consider all the cores that share a cache to form a "processor". We consider only the memory allocation aspect of memory management. We restrict our attention as even this simple issue has many interesting aspects. Garbage collectors without doubt add additional complexity (and require more space for a detailed discussion). We assume that all the data of a process is allocated to one processor. This assumption includes scenarios when co-executing processes have their memory allocated on specific, possibly different, processors. We assume only that a single process's memory is not scattered around in the system. We also assume that the home processor of a process cannot be changed (i.e., data cannot be migrated). These limitations are discussed in Section 5.

3. Cache-conscious scheduling in NUMAs

3.1 Principles

In general, the tradeoff between local cache contention and remote execution can be observed with memory-bound programs. We focus in the presentation on the `soplex` benchmark from the SPEC CPU2006 benchmark suite. This program stores large amounts of data in the caches, and its performance is hurt if the available cache capacity is reduced because of other memory-bound programs using the same caches. There are several other memory-bound programs in the SPEC suite that show this behavior (see [25] for details), and the principles we discuss here are valid for these programs as well. We construct a multiprogrammed workload that consists of four identical copies (clones) of `soplex`. We allocate the memory of all clones on Processor 0 of a 2-processor NUMA-multicore system (details about the machine in Section 4.1). We execute the multiprogrammed workload in various mapping configurations with a different number of clones executed locally respectively remotely. The mapping configurations range from all four clones executed locally (on Processor 0) to the configuration where

all four clones execute remotely. If a clone finishes earlier than the other clones in the workload, we restart it. We run the experiment until all clones execute at least once.

Figure 4 shows the average MPKI increase of all `soplex` clones relative to the solo mode MPKI of `soplex`. Remember that the MPKI of a program increases if in its execution the program contends for LLC capacity with other programs using the same LLC. When the data locality is maximal in the system (100% of the references are local), the average increase of MPKI peaks at 35% because all clones execute on the same processor and thus use the same LLC. When the data locality in the system is 57%, cache contention is minimal as the MPKI increase is also minimal (19%).

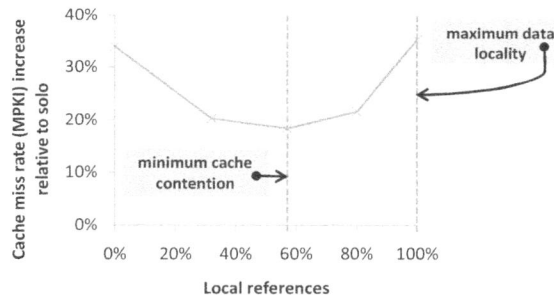

Figure 4: Increase in MPKI vs. data locality of `soplex`.

Figure 5 shows the slowdown of the locally resp. remotely executing `soplex` clones. The slowdown is calculated relative to the solo mode execution of `soplex`. We also plot the average degradation of the clones. Clearly, neither the mapping with minimum cache contention, nor the mapping with maximum data locality performs best. The average slowdown (and also the individual slowdown) of the clones is minimal if there is 80% data locality in the system. Therefore, process scheduling on NUMA-multicores must target a tradeoff between data locality and cache contention avoidance (the optimum performance point on Figure 5).

Our approach builds upon the idea of cache-balancing algorithms for SMPs ([12, 29]). The basic principle of these algorithms is illustrated in Figure 6 (for a system with two LLCs). If the difference D between the pressure on the two caches of the system is large (Figure 6.(a)), some processes (with a pressure of $D/2$) are scheduled onto the cache with the smaller pressure, therefore the difference between the pressure on the two caches is minimized (Figure 6.(b)). Our approach is similar to cache-balancing algorithms in SMPs and relies on two principles. First, we also distribute pressure across caches, however not evenly as in an SMP

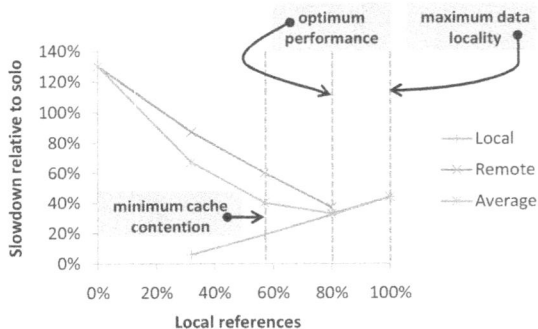

Figure 5: Performance vs. data locality of `soplex`.

performance monitoring unit (PMU) of modern CPUs. Knauerhase et al. [12] use the LLC misses per elapsed CPU cycle to estimate cache pressure, Blagodurov et al. [29] use the MPKI. Other synthetic metrics like stack-distance profiles [4, 25] or miss-rate curves [26] can offer better precision in estimating cache behavior, but generating these metrics might result in higher runtime overhead than low-overhead PMU-based measurements, therefore we estimate cache pressure based on the MPKI of programs.

The second parameter we want to estimate is the *NUMA penalty* of a program. This parameter quantifies the slowdown of a remote execution of a program relative to the program's local execution. Let CPI_{local} denote the CPI (cycles per instruction) of a program executing locally, and let CPI_{remote} denote the CPI of the same program executing remotely. Given this notation, the NUMA penalty is defined as:

$$\text{NUMA penalty} = CPI_{remote}/CPI_{local} \qquad (1)$$

The NUMA penalty is a lower-is-better metric, and its minimum value is 1 (if a program does not slow down in its remote execution). E.g., if a program has a NUMA penalty equal to 1.3, the program slows down 30% on remote execution. We measure the NUMA penalty of a program by executing the program twice, once locally and once remotely. During the measurements all cores are inactive, except the core that executes the program. Figure 7 plots the NUMA penalty of all programs of the SPEC CPU2006 suite against their MPKI. The chart also plots the linear model fitted onto the data. Although the two parameters are positively correlated (the NUMA penalty increases with the MPKI), the coefficient of determination (R^2) is relatively low, 0.64.

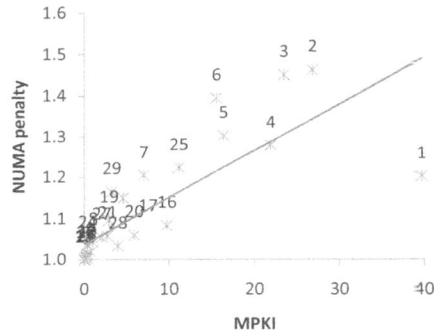

system: The amount of cache pressure transferred to Cache 1 is less than $D/2$ (the half of the difference) – as illustrated in Figure 6.(c). If mapping processes onto a different LLC results in the remote execution of the re-mapped process, then we account also for the performance penalty of remote execution. The pressure on the caches is equal if this penalty is also considered. The second principle of our approach states that overloading the cross-chip interconnect with too many remotely executing processes must be avoided. Therefore, if the pressure on the remote cache is above a threshold, we do not re-map processes for remote execution. Section 3.3 presents the N-MASS algorithm that implements these two principles; Section 3.2 discusses how we calculate LLC pressure.

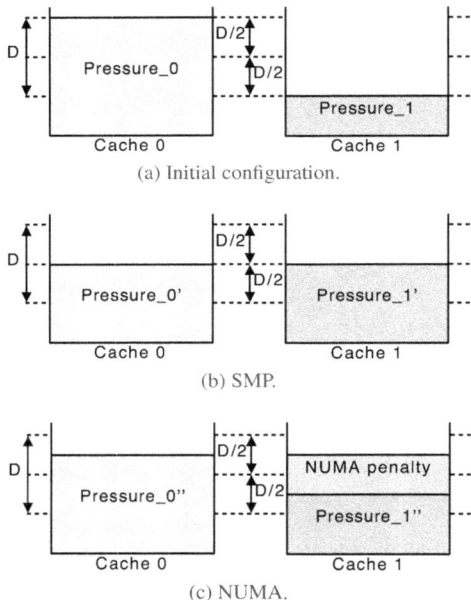

(a) Initial configuration.

(b) SMP.

(c) NUMA.

Figure 6: Cache balancing in SMP and NUMA context.

Figure 7: NUMA penalty vs. MPKI.

3.3 The N-MASS algorithm

The NUMA–Multicore-Aware Scheduling Scheme (N-MASS) implements the two principles of cache-aware scheduling in NUMA systems described in Section 3.1. Algorithm 1 presents an outline of N-MASS. The algorithm is designed for a 2-processor NUMA system, but it can be easily extended to handle a higher number of processors as well. The algorithm is invoked after a scheduler epoch has elapsed, and it calculates the mapping M_{final} : Processes $\mapsto$ Cores of processes onto cores. The number of scheduled processes n equals at most the number of cores in the system (this limitation is discussed later in this section). The algorithm uses the following performance data about each scheduled process i: the process's *cache pressure* ($mpki_i$) and an estimate of the process's *NUMA penalty* (np_i). The N-MASS algorithm has three steps. First, for each processor, it sorts the list of processes homed on the processor in descending order of the processes' NUMA penalty (lines 2-3). Second, it maps the processes onto the system using the *maximum-local* policy (line 5). If the

3.2 Program characterization

A scheduling algorithm targeting memory system optimizations must be able to quickly estimate the memory behavior of the scheduled programs on runtime. There are two parameters that we want to estimate: the cache pressure of programs, and the performance penalty they experience due to remote execution.

The cache pressure of programs can be estimated with reasonable precision by performance metrics available at runtime via the pressure on the memory system of the two-processor system is unbalanced, then in the third step the algorithm refines the mapping decision produced by the maximum-local mapping (line 7). In the following paragraphs we describe Step 2 and Step 3 of N-MASS.

Algorithm 1 N-MASS: maps n processes onto a 2-processor NUMA-multicore system.

Input: List of processes P_0 and P_1 homed on Processor 0 resp. Processor 1.
Output: A mapping M_{final} of processes to processor cores.
1: // Step 1: Sort list of processes by NUMA penalty
2: $P_{sorted_0} \leftarrow sort\_descending\_by\_np(P_0)$
3: $P_{sorted_1} \leftarrow sort\_descending\_by\_np(P_1)$
4: // Step 2: Calculate maximum-local mapping
5: $M_{maxlocal} \leftarrow map\_maxlocal(P_{sorted_0}, P_{sorted_1})$
6: // Step 3: Refine maximum-local mapping
7: $M_{final} \leftarrow refine\_mapping(M_{maxlocal})$

Step 2: Maximum-local mapping The maximum-local scheme (described in detail by Algorithm 2) maximizes data locality in the system by mapping processes onto their home nodes in descending order of their NUMA penalty. The algorithm has as its input two lists of processes, P_0 and P_1. The processes in list P_0 (P_1) are homed on Processor 0 (Processor 1). The lists are sorted in descending order of the NUMA penalty of the processes they contain. The algorithm merges the two lists. During the merge, the algorithm determines which core each process is mapped onto. The algorithm guarantees that processes with a high NUMA penalty are mapped onto a core of their home node with higher priority than processes with a lower NUMA penalty that are homed on the same processor. The lists P_0 and P_1, and the mapping $M_{maxlocal}$ of processes are double-ended queues. The function $pop\_front(l)$ removes the element from the front of the list l; the function $push\_back(l, e)$ inserts element e at the back of the list l. The function $get\_next\_available\_core(p)$ returns the next free core, preferably from processor p. If there are no free cores on processor p, the function returns a free core from a different processor.

Algorithm 2 map_maxlocal: maps n processes onto a 2-processor system NUMA system so that data locality is maximized.

Input: List of processes P_{sorted_0} and P_{sorted_1} homed on Processor 0 respectively Processor 1. The lists are sorted in descending order of the processes' NUMA penalty (np).
Output: A mapping $M_{maxlocal}$ of processes to processor cores.
1: $M_{maxlocal} \leftarrow \emptyset$
2: $p_0 \leftarrow pop\_front(P_{sorted_0}); p_1 \leftarrow pop\_front(P_{sorted_1})$
3: **while** $p_0 \neq NULL$ or $p_1 \neq NULL$ **do**
4:   **if** $p_1 = NULL$ or $np_{p_0} > np_{p_1}$ **then**
5:     $core \leftarrow get\_next\_available\_core(\text{Processor } 0)$
6:     $push\_back(M_{maxlocal}, (p_0, core))$
7:     $p_0 \leftarrow pop\_front(P_{sorted_0})$
8:   **else if** $p_0 = NULL$ or $np_{p_0} \leq np_{p_1}$ **then**
9:     $core \leftarrow get\_next\_available\_core(\text{Processor } 1)$
10:     $push\_back(M_{maxlocal}, (p_1, core))$
11:     $p_1 \leftarrow pop\_front(P_{sorted_1})$
12:   **end if**
13: **end while**

Step 3: Cache-aware refinement If the maximum-local mapping results in increased contention on the caches of the system, Step 3 of the N-MASS algorithm refines the mapping produced by the maximum-local scheme in Step 2. This step implements the two principles of scheduling in NUMA-multicores previously discussed in Section 3.1, and is described in detail in Algorithm 3. First, the algorithm accounts for the performance penalty of remote execution by multiplying the MPKI of remotely mapped processes with their respective NUMA penalty (lines 8, 9, 12). Second, the algorithm avoids overloading the cross-chip interconnect by moving processes only if the pressure on the remote cache is less than a predefined threshold (line 14). We discuss in Section 3.4 how the threshold is determined. By construction (line 6 and 10 of Algorithm 2) $M_{maxlocal}$ contains pairs $(process, core)$ ordered in descending order of the processes' NUMA penalty. The function $back(l)$ returns the last element of list l without removing it from the list; $push\_front(l, e)$ inserts element e to the front of list l.

Algorithm 3 refine_mapping: refines the maximum-local mapping of n processes to reduce cache contention.

Input: Maximum-local mapping of processes $M_{maxlocal}$. For each process i the NUMA penalty respectively the MPKI of the last scheduler epoch is available in np_i respectively $mpki_i$.
Output: A mapping M_{final} of processes to processor cores.
1: $M_0 = \{(p, core) \in M_{maxlocal} \mid core \in \text{Processor } 0\}$
2: $M_1 = \{(p, core) \in M_{maxlocal} \mid core \in \text{Processor } 1\}$
3: $pressure_0 = \sum\{mpki_p \mid (p, core) \in M_0\}$
4: $pressure_1 = \sum\{mpki_p \mid (p, core) \in M_1\}$
5: **repeat**
6:   $\Delta \leftarrow |pressure_1 - pressure_0|$
7:   $(p_0, core_0) \leftarrow back(M_0); (p_1, core_1) \leftarrow back(M_1)$
8:   $\Delta_{\text{MOVE}_{0 \rightarrow 1}} \leftarrow mpki_{p_0} \cdot np_{p_0}$
9:   $\Delta_{\text{MOVE}_{1 \rightarrow 0}} \leftarrow mpki_{p_1} \cdot np_{p_1}$
10:   **if** $\Delta_{\text{MOVE}_{0 \rightarrow 1}} < \Delta_{\text{MOVE}_{1 \rightarrow 0}}$ **then**
11:     $pressure_0 \leftarrow pressure_0 - mpki_{p_0}$
12:     $pressure_1 \leftarrow pressure_1 + mpki_{p_0} \cdot np_{p_0}$
13:     $core \leftarrow get\_next\_available\_core(\text{Processor } 1)$
14:     // Could be on Processor 0 if $\nexists$ free core on Processor 1
15:     **if** $core \notin \text{Processor } 0$
    and $pressure_1 < \text{THRESHOLD}$ **then**
16:       $pop\_back(M_0, (p_0, core_0))$
17:       $push\_front(M_1, (p_0, core))$
18:       $decision \leftarrow \text{MOVE}_{0 \rightarrow 1}$
19:     **else**
20:       $decision \leftarrow \text{CURRENT}$
21:     **end if**
22:   **end if**
23:   **if** $\Delta_{\text{MOVE}_{0 \rightarrow 1}} \geq \Delta_{\text{MOVE}_{1 \rightarrow 0}}$
  or $decision = \text{CURRENT}$ **then**
24:     // Similar to the $\text{MOVE}_{0 \rightarrow 1}$ case
25:   **end if**
26: **until** $decision \neq \text{CURRENT}$
27: $M_{final} \leftarrow M_0 \cup M_1$

Limitations The N-MASS algorithm requires the number of processes n to be at most the total number of cores on the system, therefore it can only decide on spatial multiplexing of processes (and not on temporal multiplexing). Nevertheless, if the OS scheduler decides on the temporal multiplexing (the set of processes that will be executed in the next scheduler epoch), N-MASS can refine this mapping so that the memory allocation setup in the system is accounted for, and the memory system is efficiently used.

3.4 Implementation

To verify that N-MASS is capable of finding the tradeoff between cache contention avoidance and optimizing for data locality, we implemented a prototype version of N-MASS as a user-mode extension to the Linux scheduler. We design N-MASS to adapt to program phase changes. N-MASS samples the PMU to characterize applications at runtime. The length of the sampling interval is determined adaptively to bound the sampling overhead. Each sample includes the MPKI of a process. The scheduler is invoked if a process's MPKI changes by more than 20% relative to the previous scheduler epoch. The costs of re-schedules (moving a process to a different core) can be high. We select an epoch length of 1s. This epoch length almost completely eliminates the costs of re-schedules, while the scheduler is still able to quickly react to program phase changes. We select 60 MPKI for the threshold used by the refinement step of the N-MASS algorithm (line 14 of Algorithm 3). We base our selection on a detailed empirical evaluation of the memory system performance of the STREAM and SPEC CPU2006 benchmarks. We have found that a cache pressure of around 60 MPKI corresponds to the saturation limit of the cross-chip interconnect of our evaluation machine. We omit details of this evaluation because of a lack of space.

The N-MASS algorithm relies on an estimate of the NUMA penalty of processes (in lines 8, 9 and 12 of Algorithm 3). In the first part of our evaluation, we look at performance of N-MASS with perfect information available about the NUMA penalty of scheduled programs. We simulate the availability of the NUMA penalty to the scheduler by using program traces generated on separate profiling runs (for each sample we compute the NUMA penalty using Formula 1). In Section 4.5 we also evaluate N-MASS with an on-line estimation of the NUMA penalty. In our evaluation machine the number of local and remote LLC misses generated by a process cannot be measured at the same time. Therefore, when a process is re-mapped from its home node to a remote node, the PMU must be reconfigured, which results in unacceptably large overhead. Hence we also include the MPKI of programs in the trace file. Nevertheless, the performance measurements of N-MASS include the overhead of performance monitoring, as we sample the number of instructions executed by each process to keep track of the process's execution in the trace file. We also record the number of elapsed processor cycles to measure performance.

4. Evaluation

4.1 Experimental setup

We use a 2-processor system based on the Intel Nehalem microarchitecture. The machine is multicore: each processor has four cores that share an LLC. The machine is NUMA because it has two types of memory controllers: Each processor has half of the physical memory directly connected through an on-chip memory controller (IMC), and cross-processor communication is handled by the QuickPath Interconnect (QPI). Table 1 shows the detailed parameters of the machine. The bandwidth of the IMC and QPI are approximately the same, but while there are two IMCs in the system (one on each processor), there is only one QPI link connecting the two processors. Therefore, if there is good data locality in the system, the full throughput of the two IMCs can be exploited. But if most memory accesses are remote, the QPI link is a performance bottleneck. The latencies of local resp. remote memory accesses also differ significantly, as shown in Table 1 (values based on [10]).

The evaluation machine runs Linux 2.6.30 patched with perfmon2 to allow access to the PMU. We disable frequency scaling, simultaneous multithreading, and the Turbo Boost feature of the machine to avoid measurement variance. We use standard Linux APIs to control the CPU affinity of processes and also to set their preferred memory allocation policy.

Our evaluation methodology is very similar to the methodology used in [2, 3, 6, 7, 12, 29]. We use a subset of the SPEC CPU2006 benchmark suite (14 programs out of the total 29 in the suite). Our selection includes programs 1–14 in Figure 7. We select the subset

Processor:	2 x Intel Xeon E5520
Cores per processor:	4
L3 cache size:	8 MB
Main memory:	12 GB DDR3
IMC bandwidth:	25.6 GB/s
QPI bandwidth:	23.44 GB/s
Local DRAM access latency:	∼50 ns
Remote DRAM access latency:	∼90 ns

Table 1: Parameters of the evaluation machine.

so that it includes programs with a broad range of memory pressure. The MPKI of a program (the x-axis in Figure 7) roughly characterizes the memory boundedness of the program. The selection includes both CPU- and memory-bound programs. Some memory-bound programs saturate the IMC of the evaluation machine even in solo mode. The programs in the subset have also a broad range of NUMA penalties (between 1.0 and 1.46).

We are interested in multiprocessor performance therefore we construct multiprogrammed workloads with the programs of the SPEC CPU2006 benchmark suite. Like [12], we run each multiprogrammed workload exactly one hour. If a program terminates before the other programs in a workload do, we restart the program that terminated early. We use the reference data set and follow the guidelines described in [21] to minimize measurement variance. This setup usually gives us three measurable runs for each workload within the one hour limit. For each run we report the average slowdown of each constituent program relative to its solo mode performance. We also report the average slowdown of the whole workload, as suggested by Eyerman et al. [5].

4.2 Dimensions of the evaluation

There are two dimensions that must be considered to evaluate the interaction between memory allocation and process scheduling in a NUMA-multicore system. The two dimensions (shown in Figure 8) are the memory boundedness of the workloads (y-axis) and the balance of memory allocation in the system (x-axis).

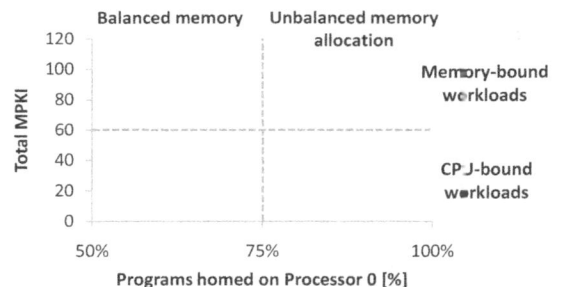

Figure 8: Dimensions of the evaluation.

To show that N-MASS can handle workloads with different memory-boundedness, we use 11 different multiprogrammed workloads (WL1 to WL11). This setup corresponds to evaluating N-MASS along the first dimension (the y-axis in Figure 8). The workloads are composed of different number of compute-bound (C) resp. memory-bound (M) programs. The memory-boundedness of a workload is characterized by the sum of the MPKIs of its constituent programs (measured in solo mode for each program). The total MPKI of each multiprogrammed workload we use is shown in Figure 9. The composition of the multiprogrammed workloads is shown in Table 2. The workloads in the set of 4-process workloads (WL1 to WL9) contain one to four memory-bound programs. The 8-process workloads (WL10 and WL11) contain three, resp. four, memory-bound programs. In the case of all 11 workloads we add CPU-bound programs so that at the end there are four (resp. eight) programs in each workload.

Figure 9: Total MPKI of multiprogrammed workloads.

#	Programs				Type
1	soplex	sphinx	gamess	namd	1M, 3C
2	soplex	mcf	gamess	gobmk	2M, 2C
3	mcf	libquantum	povray	gamess	2M, 2C
4	mcf	omnetpp	h264	namd	2M, 2C
5	milc	libquantum	povray	perlbench	2M, 2C
6	sphinx	gcc	namd	gamess	1M, 3C
7	lbm	milc	sphinx	gobmk	2M, 2C
8	lbm	milc	mcf	namd	3M, 1C
9	mcf	milc	soplex	lbm	4M
10	lbm	milc	mcf	namd	3M, 5C
	gobmk	perlbench	h264	povray	
11	mcf	milc	soplex	lbm	4M, 4C
	gobmk	perlbench	namd	povray	

Table 2: Multiprogrammed workloads.

As the performance of process scheduling closely depends on the memory allocation setup in the system, for each workload we consider several ways memory is allocated in the 2-processor evaluation machine. The second dimension of our evaluation (the x-axis in Figure 8) is the percentage of the processes of a multiprogrammed workload homed on Processor 0 of the system. (Ideally we would like to vary the percentage of memory references to local resp. remote memory, but as we can map only complete processes, we vary along this dimension by mapping processes.) The left extreme point of the x-axis represents the configuration with balanced memory allocation (50% of the processes homed on Processor 0). On the other end of the x-axis we find the most unbalanced configuration (100% of the processes homed on Processor 0). Because of the symmetries of the system there is no need to extend the range to the case with 0% of the processes' memory allocated on Processor 0. This corresponds to 100% of the processes homed on Processor 1, which is equivalent to all processes homed on Processor 0.

In Section 4.3 we evaluate N-MASS with different memory allocation setups (along the x-axis of Figure 8). Then we focus on unbalanced memory allocation setups in Section 4.4.

4.3 Influence of data locality

The second dimension of our evaluation is defined as the percentage of the processes homed on Processor 0 of the system. This percentage however does not specify *which* constituent processes of a multiprogrammed workload are homed on each processor in the system. We define the concept of *allocation maps*. An allocation map is a sequence $M = (m_0, m_1, \ldots, m_n)$, where n is the number of processes in the workload executing on the system, and

$$m_i = \begin{cases} 0, & \text{if the } i^{th} \text{ process is homed on Processor 0;} \\ 1, & \text{if the } i^{th} \text{ process is homed on Processor 1.} \end{cases} \quad (2)$$

There are $\sum_{i=0}^{4} \binom{4}{i} = 2^4 = 16$ ways to allocate memory for a 4-process workload on the Nehalem system (assuming each program's memory is allocated entirely on one of the two processors of the system). Because of the symmetries of the system the number of combinations is reduced to 8. These allocation maps are shown in Table 3. For example, if 50% of the processes are homed on Processor 0 we must consider three different possibilities. If we look at the performance of a mapping algorithm with a multiprogrammed workload that has a composition (M, M, C, C) (first two processes are memory-bound, the last two compute-bound), then the 50%-allocation maps 1100 and 1010 are different from the point of view of the maximum-local scheduling scheme. Remember that the maximum-local scheme maps processes onto their home nodes if possible. In the case of the 1100 allocation map maximum-local maps the two memory-bound processes onto the same processor, therefore the *same* LLC. This setup results in good data locality but also produces high cache contention. In the case of the 1010 allocation map maximum-local maps the memory-bound processes onto *separate* LLCs. Therefore, the maximum-local policy maximizes data locality and minimizes cache contention in this case.

Processes homed on Processor 0	Allocation maps
50%	1100, 1010, 1001
75%	1000, 0100, 0010, 0001
100%	0000

Table 3: Allocation maps for 4-process workloads.

For clarity of presentation we use two workloads from opposite ends of the memory-boundedness spectrum to evaluate the performance of N-MASS with different allocation maps: the compute-bound WL1, and the memory-bound WL9. We compare the performance of three mapping schemes: *default*, *maximum-local* and *N-MASS*. If not stated otherwise, in our evaluation *N-MASS* denotes the version of the algorithm that has perfect information about the NUMA penalty of the programs from profile-based program traces. The *maximum-local* policy is similar to N-MASS, except it does not include the cache-aware refinement step of N-MASS (Step 3 of Algorithm 1). We evaluate this scheme to quantify the improvement of the cache-aware refinement step over maximum-local mapping.

The performance of multiprogrammed workloads varies largely with the default Linux scheduler, and simple factors like the order in which workloads are started influence the performance readings. Because operating system schedulers (including the Linux scheduler) balance only the CPU load and do not account for data locality or cache contention, processes might be mapped so that they use the memory system in the most inefficient way possible. To avoid measurement bias, we account for all schedules that an OS scheduler that balances CPU load would consider. E.g., in the case of 4-process workloads the default Linux scheduler always maps two processes onto each processor so that each processor is allocated half the total CPU load. For each 4-process workload there are $\binom{4}{2} = 6$ equally probable different schedules with the CPU load evenly distributed in the system. Running a single workload in all these schedules takes 6 hours execution time with our evaluation methodology, which is tolerable. Therefore, for each workload we run the workload in each schedule possible for the default scheduler, and then we report the average degradation of the workload in all schedules as the performance of *default* scheduling.

17

(a) Performance degradation (WL9).

(b) Performance degradation (WL1).

(c) N-MASS improvement over default (WL9).

(d) N-MASS improvement over default (WL1).

(e) N-MASS compared to *maximum-local* (WL9).

(f) N-MASS compared to *maximum-local* (WL1).

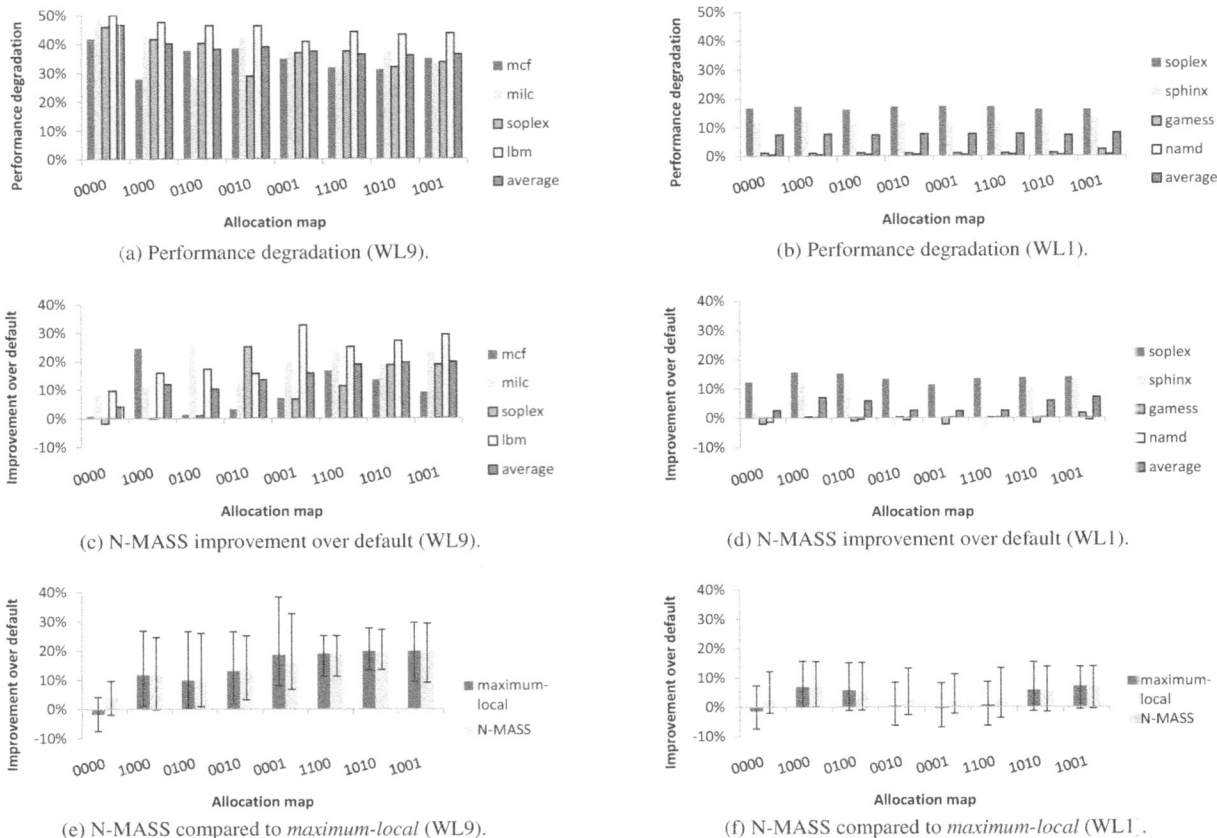

Figure 10: Performance evaluation of the *maximum-local* and N-MASS schemes.

Figure 10.(a) (resp. Figure 10.(b)) shows the performance degradation of the programs of WL9 (WL1) with the default scheduler. The degradations are calculated relative to the solo mode performance of the programs. WL9 is composed of more memory-bound programs than WL1, therefore the degradations experienced by WL9 programs are higher (up to 50% vs. 18%). Figure 10.(c) (resp. Figure 10.(d)) shows the performance improvement of N-MASS relative to default scheduling. Performance improvements of individual programs up to 32% are possible.

An interesting question is how much improvement is due to the maximum-local scheme, and how much benefit is due to the final refinement step of N-MASS. In Figure 10.(e) and Figure 10.(f) we compare the average performance improvement of N-MASS versus the maximum-local scheme. The bars show the maximum and performance improvement of the constituent programs of the workloads; these bars do not show the "standard error". A negative performance improvement means performance degradation. N-MASS performs approximately the same as maximum-local in most of the cases. However, when the memory allocation in the system is unbalanced (allocation map 0000 for both workloads, allocation maps 0001, 0010, and 1100 for WL1), the additional cache-balancing of the N-MASS scheme improves performance relative to maximum-local. In these cases maximum-local results in a performance degradation relative to default, because cache contention on the LLCs cancels the benefit of good data locality. There are also some cases when N-MASS performs slightly worse than maximum-local, but its average performance is never worse than the performance of default scheduling.

4.4 A detailed look

In the previous section we have shown that in case of unbalanced memory allocation maps the cache-aware refinement step of N-MASS improves performance over maximum-local. In this section we look in detail at the performance of the N-MASS and maximum-local policies in case of unbalanced memory allocation maps, and extend our measurements to the 8-process workloads. Figures 11 and 12 show the performance for each of the programs in the various workload sets (WL1 to WL11). In many cases the maximum-local mapping scheme performs well, and the final refinement step of N-MASS brings only small benefits. However, in the case of WL1, WL7, WL8, WL9, and WL11 individual programs of the workloads experience up to 10% less performance degradation with N-MASS than with maximum-local. Performance degradations relative to default scheduling are also reduced from 12% to at most 3%.

4.5 Estimating the NUMA penalty

Figures 11 and 12 also show the effect of estimating the NUMA penalty through linear regression. For this evaluation, we do not use the profile-based information about the NUMA-penalty of programs (as this number may be difficult to obtain in current multi-core systems). Instead, we estimate the NUMA penalty based on the MPKI rate, fitting a simple linear model onto the data shown in Figure 7. Before fitting the model we remove the outlier mcf (data point "1" on Figure 7) as well as all non–memory-bound programs (programs with a MPKI smaller than 1). The resulting model's slope intercept and slope are 0.015 and 1.05 respectively.

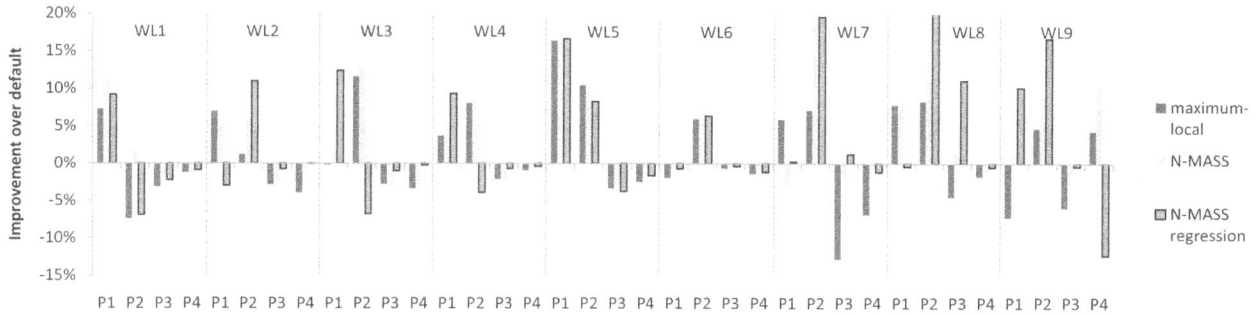

Figure 11: Performance improvement of 4-process workloads.

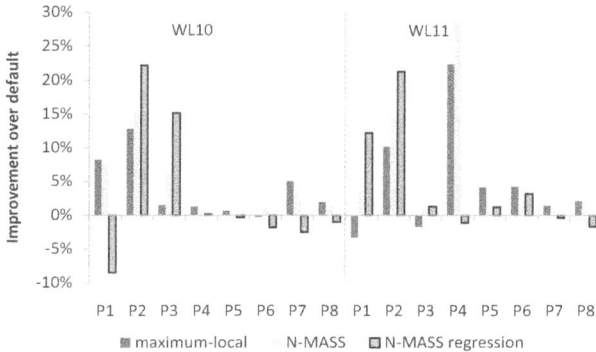

Figure 12: Performance improvement of 8-process workloads.

For the measurements the memory of all processes of the multiprogrammed workloads was allocated on the same processor, Processor 0 (allocation maps 0000 and 00000000).

Regression-based N-MASS also improves performance over the maximum-local scheme, but in the case of four workloads it results in a performance degradation of individual programs of more than 5% relative to the default scheduler (but on average not more degradation than the maximum-local scheme). The degradation is due to the imprecision of the MPKI-based estimates of the NUMA penalty. On-line techniques to estimate the NUMA penalty are difficult to construct with the PMU of current CPU models. We hope that future PMUs will provide events that can be used to estimate NUMA penalty better. If the NUMA penalty cannot be obtained directly, the MPKI offers a reasonable approximation.

5. Discussion

In summary, if the memory allocation in the system is balanced, then maximum-local scheduling provides large performance benefits. If the memory allocation setup of the system unbalanced, the mapping given by the maximum-local scheme needs adjustment, otherwise it causes performance degradation even relative to default scheduling.

In cases with unbalanced memory allocation, the refinement step of N-MASS can re-map processes onto a different LLC to reduce cache contention. When memory allocation in the system is balanced, maximum-local mapping is performed, and cache contention within a processor is minimized as in an SMP context, using existing approaches [12, 29]. Our scheme is orthogonal to these schemes: the cache-aware step of N-MASS kicks in only if the memory allocation map in the system is unbalanced, and additional cross-processor cache balancing is required.

Memory migration is an alternative technique to improve data locality in NUMA systems. We limit the discussion to process scheduling because of two issues: (1) it is difficult to estimate the cost of memory migration, and (2) memory migration is not always possible because there is not always enough free memory available on the destination processor. In these cases the process scheduler is the only part of the system software that can optimize performance.

We do not consider multithreaded programs with a shared address space. For these programs sharing caches can be beneficial, therefore finding a tradeoff between data locality and cache contention is difficult. To limit the number of cases that must be evaluated, we restrict memory allocation of a process to a single processor. OSs provide information about the distribution of pages in the system. This information can be used to determine a program's preferred home processor if the program's memory is scattered around.

6. Related work

Memory system analysis Molka et al. [20] analyze the memory system of an Intel Nehalem-based machine. They use sophisticated synthetic benchmarks to determine the bandwidth and latency of memory accesses to different levels of the memory hierarchy. Hackenberg et al. [8] compare the memory system of different NUMA architectures using these synthetic benchmarks. Majo et al. [16] use synthetic benchmarks to evaluate the fairness of bandwidth sharing of the Intel Nehalem. Here we focus on more realistic programs and also consider caching effects. Blagodurov et al. [3] describe the sources of performance degradation that cause slowdowns to programs co-executing on NUMA systems (the remote latency and interconnect degradation). The NUMA penalty used in this paper quantifies the slowdown that a single program experiences due to both factors.

Shared resource contention Chandra et al. [4] use analytical models to predict the inter-thread cache contention of co-executing programs. Jiang et al. [11] prove that the complexity of optimal co-scheduling on chip multiprocessor systems is NP-complete. Mars et al. [18] describe a system that characterizes resource contention on runtime. Zhuravlev et al. [29] compare the accuracy of different models used to characterize the interference of co-executing programs. They find that the MPKI is reasonably accurate.

There are several methods to mitigate shared resource contention. Qureshi et al. [23] partition caches between concurrently executing processes. Tam et al. [26] identify the size of cache partitions on runtime. Mars et al. [19] halt low priority processes when contention is detected. Herdrich et al. [9] analyze the effectiveness of frequency scaling and clock modulation to reduce shared resource contention. Awasthi et al. [1] show that data migration and adaptive memory allocation can be used to reduce memory controller overhead in systems with multiple memory controllers (such as NUMAs). OS process scheduling is also well suited for reducing contention on shared caches, as described by Fedorova et al. [6].

Process scheduling for contention avoidance Fedorova et al. present an OS scheduling algorithm that reduces the performance degradation of programs co-executed on multicore systems [7]. Banikazemi et al. [2] describe a cache model for a process scheduler that estimates the performance impact of program-to-core mapping in multicore systems. The process scheduler mechanism described by Knauerhase et al. [12] and Zhuravlev et al. [29] is most closely related to the N-MASS scheme presented in this work. The schemes presented by both groups schedule processes so that each LLC must handle approximately equal memory pressure. These approaches were evaluated on SMPs with uniform memory access times. We show that cache balancing algorithms do not work well in NUMA systems if the memory allocation setup of the system is not considered.

Performance-asymmetric multicore architectures Recent research proposed performance-asymmetric multicore processors (AMPs). In contrast to AMPs the cores of a NUMA system have the same performance, but the memory system is asymmetric, and programs have different performance on remote execution. Li et al. present an OS scheduler for AMPs [15]. They evaluate their system also on NUMA systems, but they do not account for cache contention. Saez et al. [24] and Koufaty et al. [13] independently describe a scheduler for AMPS based on the efficiency specialization principle. Their schedulers implement a strategy similar to the maximum-local policy presented in this paper, but their system targets performance asymmetry instead of memory system asymmetry (compute-bound processes are scheduled onto high performance cores with larger priority than memory-bound processes).

7. Conclusions

We have shown that operating system scheduling fails to obtain good performance in NUMA-multicores if it does not consider the structure of the memory system, and the allocation of physical memory in the system. If memory allocation in a NUMA-multicore system is balanced (the cumulative memory demand of processes homed on each processor in the system is approximately the same), then it is beneficial to simply map processes onto the architecture so that data locality is favored, and avoiding cache contention does not bring any benefits. Nonetheless, when the memory allocation in the system is unbalanced (the sum of the memory demands of processes homed on each processor in the system is different), then mapping processes so that data locality is maximized can lead to severe cache contention. In these cases refining the maximum-local mapping so that cache contention is reduced improves performance, even with the cost of some processes executing remotely. The N-MASS scheme described in this paper successfully combines memory management and process scheduling to better exploit the potential of NUMA-multicore processors.

Acknowledgments

We thank Albert Noll, Michael Pradel, Oliver Trachsel, Faheem Ullah and the anonymous referees for their helpful comments.

References

[1] M. Awasthi, D. W. Nellans, K. Sudan, R. Balasubramonian, and A. Davis. Handling the problems and opportunities posed by multiple on-chip memory controllers. In *PACT'10*.

[2] M. Banikazemi, D. Poff, and B. Abali. PAM: a novel performance/power aware meta-scheduler for multi-core systems. In *SC'08*.

[3] S. Blagodurov, S. Zhuravlev, and A. Fedorova. Contention-aware scheduling on multicore systems. *ACM Trans. Comput. Syst.*, 2010.

[4] D. Chandra, F. Guo, S. Kim, and Y. Solihin. Predicting inter-thread cache contention on a chip multi-processor architecture. In *HPCA'05*.

[5] S. Eyerman and L. Eeckhout. System-level performance metrics for multiprogram workloads. *IEEE Micro*, 2008.

[6] A. Fedorova, M. Seltzer, C. Small, and D. Nussbaum. Performance of multithreaded chip multiprocessors and implications for operating system design. In *ATEC'05*.

[7] A. Fedorova, M. Seltzer, and M. D. Smith. Improving performance isolation on chip multiprocessors via an operating system scheduler. In *PACT'07*.

[8] D. Hackenberg, D. Molka, and W. E. Nagel. Comparing cache architectures and coherency protocols on x86-64 multicore SMP systems. In *MICRO 42*, 2009.

[9] A. Herdrich, R. Illikkal, R. Iyer, D. Newell, V. Chadha, and J. Moses. Rate-based QoS techniques for cache/memory in CMP platforms. In *ICS'09*.

[10] Intel Corporation. *Intel 64 and IA-32 Architectures Optimization Reference Manual*, January 2011.

[11] Y. Jiang, X. Shen, J. Chen, and R. Tripathi. Analysis and approximation of optimal co-scheduling on chip multiprocessors. In *PACT'08*.

[12] R. Knauerhase, P. Brett, B. Hohlt, T. Li, and S. Hahn. Using OS observations to improve performance in multicore systems. *IEEE Micro*, 2008.

[13] D. Koufaty, D. Reddy, and S. Hahn. Bias scheduling in heterogeneous multi-core architectures. In *EuroSys'10*.

[14] H. Li, H. L. Sudarsan, M. Stumm, and K. C. Sevcik. Locality and loop scheduling on NUMA multiprocessors. In *ICPP'93*

[15] T. Li, D. Baumberger, D. A. Koufaty, and S. Hahn. Efficient operating system scheduling for performance-asymmetric multi-core architectures. In *SC'07*.

[16] Z. Majo and T. R. Gross. Memory system performance in a NUMA multicore multiprocessor. In *SYSTOR'11*.

[17] J. Marathe and F. Mueller. Hardware profile-guided automatic page placement for ccNUMA systems. In *PPoPP'06*.

[18] J. Mars, L. Tang, and M. L. Soffa. Directly characterizing cross core interference through contention synthesis. In *HiPEAC'11*.

[19] J. Mars, N. Vachharajani, M. L. Soffa, and R. Hundt. Contention aware execution: Online contention detection and response. In *CGO'10*.

[20] D. Molka, D. Hackenberg, R. Schne, and M. S. Müller. Memory performance and cache coherency effects on an Intel Nehalem multiprocessor system. In *PACT'09*.

[21] T. Mytkowicz, A. Diwan, M. Hauswirth, and P. F. Sweeney. Producing wrong data without doing anything obviously wrong! In *ASPLOS'09*.

[22] T. Ogasawara. NUMA-aware memory manager with dominant-thread-based copying GC. In *OOPSLA'09*.

[23] M. K. Qureshi and Y. N. Patt. Utility-based cache partitioning: A low-overhead, high-performance, runtime mechanism to partition shared caches. In *MICRO 39*, 2006.

[24] J. C. Saez, M. Prieto, A. Fedorova, and S. Blagodurov. A comprehensive scheduler for asymmetric multicore processors. In *EuroSys'10*.

[25] A. Sandberg, D. Eklöv, and E. Hagersten. Reducing cache pollution through detection and elimination of non-temporal memory accesses. In *SC'10*.

[26] D. K. Tam, R. Azimi, L. B. Soares, and M. Stumm. RapidMRC: approximating L2 miss rate curves on commodity systems for online optimizations. In *ASPLOS '09*.

[27] M. M. Tikir and J. K. Hollingsworth. Hardware monitors for dynamic page migration. *Journal of Parallel and Distributed Computing*, 2008.

[28] B. Verghese, S. Devine, A. Gupta, and M. Rosenblum. Operating system support for improving data locality on CC-NUMA compute servers. In *ASPLOS'96*.

[29] S. Zhuralev, S. Blagodurov, and A. Fedorova. Addressing shared resource contention in multicore processors via scheduling. In *ASPLOS'10*.

Multicore Garbage Collection with Local Heaps

Simon Marlow

Microsoft Research, Cambridge, U.K.
simonmar@microsoft.com

Simon Peyton Jones

Microsoft Research, Cambridge, U.K.
simonpj@microsoft.com

Abstract

In a parallel, shared-memory, language with a garbage collected heap, it is desirable for each processor to perform minor garbage collections independently. Although obvious, it is difficult to make this idea pay off in practice, especially in languages where mutation is common. We present several techniques that substantially improve the state of the art. We describe these techniques in the context of a full-scale implementation of Haskell, and demonstrate that our local-heap collector substantially improves scaling, peak performance, and robustness.

Categories and Subject Descriptors D.3.4 [*Programming Languages*]: Processors—Memory management (garbage collection)

General Terms Languages, Performance

1. Introduction

In a garbage collected environment, multithreaded programs can run into an "allocation wall" (Zhao et al. 2009), in which performance is limited by the rate at which newly allocated data can be written to main memory, and adding more cores does not improve performance once the limit is reached. One way to avoid the allocation wall is to use a generational collector with per-thread nurseries each smaller than the size of the L2 cache, so that most memory accesses hit the cache rather than main memory. However, such a small nursery size entails very frequent collections, and with a stop-the-world collector this requires frequent synchronisation across processors, which also hurts performance as the number of processors increases. Moreover, performance becomes more fragile at scale, because latency in a single core can halt the whole system — and that is exactly what happens if the operating system deschedules the language runtime in favour of another process running on that core.

To avoid the synchronisation inherent in stop-the-world collection, one might turn to concurrent GC. However, running the collector on a separate core from the mutator is also suboptimal from a cache perspective. Concurrent GC is therefore not likely to solve the problem of scaling nursery allocation, but is more appropriate for collecting a large old generation. In this work we focus on throughput rather than latency and pause-times, and hence we do not consider concurrent GC further.

To address the cost of frequent stop-the-world synchronisation while still maintaining locality, there have been several attempts

to design collectors in which each processor has a private heap that can be collected independently without synchronising with the other processors; there is also a global heap for shared data. Some of the existing designs are based on static analyses to identify objects whose references never escape the current thread and can therefore be allocated in the local heap (Jones and King 2005; Steensgaard 2000), while others employ a dynamic approach in which objects are allocated in the local heap, but may subsequently be moved to the global heap if necessary (Anderson 2010; Doligez and Leroy 1993; Domani et al. 2002). In this paper we present a new garbage collector of the latter kind, with some novel techniques that improve on the existing designs. Specifically, our contributions are as follows:

- We present data quantifying the principal shortcoming of existing techniques, namely the costs associated with writing to global heap objects (Section 3).

  Handling mutation (writes) well is important: Java-like languages make heavy use of *explicit* mutation in the form of writes to object fields, but even in a pure language (Haskell in our case) there is a great deal of *implicit* mutation of heap objects due to lazy evaluation.

- We present two new ideas that together help alleviate the penalty for mutation in a local-heap collector (Section 4):

  - Our heap structure allows pointers from the global heap to the local heap, protected by a read barrier. This technique reduces the cost of the write barrier by avoiding premature promotion of mutable objects into the global heap.

  - We use a combination of moving and non-moving collection in the local heap, which allows both mutable and immutable objects to be allocated in the local heap, while retaining the efficiency of bump-pointer allocation in the common case.

- Our new design gives rise to a family of policy decisions, concerning exactly when and how much to promote from the local heap to the global heap. We explore these designs, and shed some light on where the most effective solutions probably lie (Section 6.3).

- We have implemented our collector in the Glasgow Haskell Compiler (a state-of-the-art optimising compiler for Haskell), and we demonstrate that our new collector yields improved scaling and peak throughput on a substantial collection of parallel Haskell benchmarks, on average improving performance by 15% at 24 cores, compared to the baseline parallel generational copying collector (Section 6.2). Moreover, the performance is less sensitive to having exclusive access to a fixed number of cores; performance drops less sharply when cores are removed compared with the stop-the-world collector (Section 6.2.3).

While our work is motivated by a desire to make parallel Haskell programs go faster, throughout the paper we delimit the parts of our design that are specific to Haskell and the GHC compiler, and those that should apply in other settings. In particular, we believe that our main results related to mutation should also apply in settings such as .NET and Java.

2. Garbage collection with processor-local heaps

The overall memory architecture is this. Each processor has its own *local heap*, in which it allocates, and which (crucially) it can garbage-collect independently of other processors. In addition there is a shared *global heap* which is visible to all processors, and which is only collected when all processors synchronise and cooperate in a (parallel) global garbage collection. We call this a *local heap collector*. Other terms have been used in the literature, notably *private nursery*, *thread-local* or *thread-specific heap*, and *on-the-fly collection*.

There are two established approaches to organising the heap in a local-heap collector:

- In the Doligez and Leroy (1993) design, and the later Anderson (2010) design, the local heap is collected with a copying collector. The global and local parts of the heap are segregated by address.
- In the Domani et al. (2002) design, the local heap is collected with a non-moving algorithm (mark-sweep). This allows objects to be relocated from the local heap to the global heap without physically copying them; a separate bitmap indicates which objects in the local heap are global. Local and global objects are therefore intermingled in the address space.

In both of these designs, the key invariant is that *the processor that owns the local heap has exclusive access to its contents*. The owning processor is therefore free to do local garbage collection without disturbing objects that are being read or modified by other processors.

The invariant is maintained by banning pointers from the global heap to the local heap, because one of these would allow a mutator to follow a pointer into a foreign local heap. To maintain the invariant, whenever a local-heap pointer is written into a global-heap object, or is communicated to another processor, a *write barrier* must detect the potential breakage, and somehow fix it up.

The existing designs take different approaches to this write barrier. In the original Doligez-Leroy design, before writing a local-heap pointer into a global mutable object we first *globalise* the local-heap object by copying it from the local heap to the global heap. Since it may contain further local-heap pointers, they too must be globalised, so the net effect is to globalise the transitive closure of the local heap pointer. (Globalisation is a bit like the *promotion* of generational GC, but its timing and purpose are different, so a different term is useful.)

Mutable objects complicate globalisation. Since mutable objects have identity and cannot be copied[1], mutable objects are always allocated directly in the global heap. Hence mutable objects and mutation are likely to be costly; the setting for this design was a strict functional language in which mutation was rare, which explains the choices made here.

In the Anderson variant of Doligez-Leroy, the write barrier triggers a local collection, with a refinement to catch some common cases where the full local GC is not necessary. This design allows mutable objects to be allocated in the local heap, but at a substantial cost: the write barrier may trigger a complete local GC, which in

---

[1] without using a replicating write barrier or suchlike

turn will tend to cause global GC to happen more frequently than it would otherwise have.

The Manticore system (Fluet et al. 2008), implements a variant of the Doligez-Leroy design in which each local heap is a separate Appel-style generational collector. Manticore does not provide mutation in any form to the programmer, however.

The Domani et. al. design is similar to Doligez-Leroy in that objects in the transitive closure of the local heap pointer are made global, but since the collector is non-moving, these objects are simply marked as being global and left in place. Again, this design allows mutable objects to be allocated in the local heap, which was important in this case because the setting was Java in which *all* heap objects are potentially mutable. A disadvantage is that the local heap must be collected with mark-sweep, which is known to have an impact on allocation performance (Blackburn et al. 2004).

3. The problem of mutation

Although the collectors described in the previous section allow mutation in the heap, a problem common to all of the existing designs is that a mutable object in the global heap has considerable cost: *every mutation of that object causes retention of the entire transitive closure of the pointer written, until the next global GC*. What is particularly annoying is that

1. Mutable objects are often repeatedly mutated. The write barrier preserves the transitive closure of *every single value written* into a global mutable object until the next global GC, even though these values may be overwritten almost immediately.

2. The effect is viral. If the value written into a global mutable object M1 contains (transitively) a currently-local, mutable object M2, then M2 must be globalised. Hence M2 is subject to the write barrier, and anything written to it must be globalised, and so on.

The first effect is unavoidable: if the value is written into a global mutable location, another processor might read it before it is overwritten, so the value must be preserved[2]. The trick is to stop the mutable object becoming global in the first place — but the viral consequences of transitive promotion make that hard.

Intuitively, these effects seem likely to lead to a great deal of ultimately-fruitless globalisation, reducing locality, and triggering expensive global GC more often than necessary. We set out to quantify this effect in the context of Haskell. In Haskell, *explicitly* mutable objects are usually far less common than immutable objects. Nevertheless, *implicit* mutation of heap objects is rife at runtime, thanks to the implementation of lazy evaluation[3]. A lazy computation is represented by a *thunk*: a closure of the code to compute the value together with its free variables. When the value of a thunk is demanded, its value is computed and then the thunk is overwritten with an indirection to the value. This write operation is called an *update*, and is a frequent source of mutation in the Haskell heap.

3.1 Quantifying the effect of transitive globalisation

We measured the cost of transitive globalisation by modifying a conventional, single-threaded, two-generation collector. Table 1 shows the performance of several single-threaded benchmarks with three different configurations for the old-generation write barrier (there is no barrier for writes to the young generation):

---

[2] This is worse than the promotion semantics of most generational collectors, which only retain the data of the last update preceding a minor collection. However "snapshot-at-the-beginning" concurrent collectors (Pirinen 1998) also have the property that they retain all values written until the next GC cycle.

[3] which, we admit, is somewhat ironic.

Program	% change in wall-clock time	
	promote transitive	promote immutable
circsim	+43.9	+3.7
constraints	+124.0	+2.0
fibheaps	+46.7	-0.6
fulsom	+49.6	+6.6
gc_bench	-63.0	-64.4
happy	+10.9	-0.1
lcss	+82.0	-0.3
mutstore1	-2.1	-2.4
mutstore2	+0.0	+0.2
power	+7.8	+15.7
spellcheck	+218.8	-0.8
Min	-63.0	-64.4
Max	+218.8	+15.7
Geometric Mean	+29.9	-7.1

Table 1. Comparison of write barrier promotion policies

- The baseline: standard generational collection, where writes to the old-generation are recorded in a remembered set.

- "Promote transitive": a write to the old generation immediately promotes the transitive closure of the pointer written. This models the invariant of Doligez-Leroy and Domani *et al.*

- "Promote immutable": a write to the old generation promotes the object it points to recursively, but avoids promoting mutable objects (in our case, thunks). Mutable objects are left in the young generation and an entry in the remembered set is created for the pointer.

The "promote transitive" policy incurs a significant overhead: 29.9% on average, while "promote immutable" provides similar performance to the baseline (with one outlier that performs significantly better with eager promotion, `gc_bench`, which we discuss below). This suggests that the premature promotion caused by effect (2) above, and its knock-on effects, have a significant impact on performance.

In `gc_bench`, promoting writes eagerly has a huge benefit, because performing the promotion avoids having to extend the remembered set. This is a GC microbenchmark and we would be unlikely to see the effect on this scale in a real program.

The bottom line is this: the viral globalisation of mutable objects into the global heap carries a significant cost. These costs are almost certainly under-stated in Table 1, which is derived from modifying a *single-threaded* generational collector. Our real goal is to allow independent local-heap garbage collection in a *parallel* machine.

4. Our design: improving support for mutation

Our design has two main novelties, both focussed on improving the performance of mutation in a local heap collector.

- **Allow pointers from the global heap to a local heap, protected by a read barrier.** We replace the invariant that objects in the global heap may not point to objects in the local heap, with a read barrier that checks for global-to-local pointers. Such pointers may only be followed directly by the processor that owns the appropriate local heap. Other processors that attempt to read the pointer are required to communicate with the owning processor to request that the data be moved into the global heap.

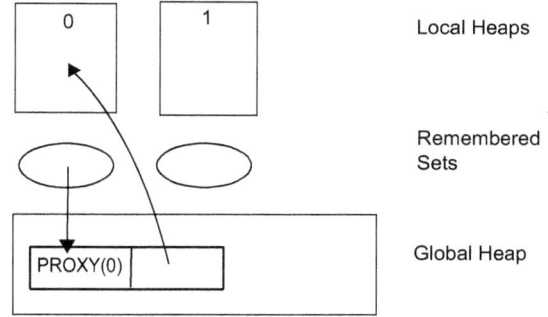

Figure 1. Heap architecture showing a proxy indirection

Admitting pointers from the global heap to the local heap allows us to avoid globalising the transitive closure of every write into the global heap, and thus avoid the performance penalty measured in the previous section.

- **The sticky heap: no read barrier.** We divide the local heap into two parts[4]. The first is a traditional nursery in which objects are allocated using bump-pointer allocation and memory is reclaimed using copying GC, as in typical generational-copying designs. A separate part of the local heap, that we call the *sticky heap*, is where we allocate objects that lack a read barrier, and hence must be immovable (Section 4.4), including mutable objects and objects with identity. The sticky heap is collected using mark-sweep GC.

This aspect of our design is a combination of the Doligez-Leroy design (immutable objects with copying GC), with the Domani et. al. approach (mutable objects with mark-sweep GC). It allows us to retain fast allocation and collection in the common case, while allowing both mutable and immutable objects to be allocated and reclaimed in the local heap.

To summarise, the read-barrier allows us to globalise fewer objects, while the sticky heap allows us to selectively choose to omit the read barrier for some objects while mostly retaining efficient bump-pointer allocation. These are the two key aspects of our design; the following sections discusses the implementation of these ideas.

4.1 Implementing the read barrier: proxy indirections

The read barrier must perform the following operations when dereferencing any pointer stored in a global heap object:

- If the pointer points to a local heap, and it is not the local heap of the current processor, then send a message to the owning processor requesting that the pointer's referent be moved to the global heap. Block the current thread until a response is received.

In GHC[5], *every pointer dereference already has a read-barrier*, because an object could be represented by an unevaluated thunk. Whenever a pointer is dereferenced, we test tag bits in the pointer to determine whether the pointer points to a value or not; if not, then the caller jumps to the code for the object, which is expected to perform whatever computation is necessary and eventually return the value.

The existing read barrier identifies a property of the object pointed to, whereas in our local-heap implementation we need to

---

[4] In fact, there is also a large-object area (Section 5.6)

[5] The Glasgow Haskel Compiler, http://www.haskell.org/ghc/

distinguish pointers into the global heap from pointers into a local heap. Nevertheless, we would like to use the same read barrier, so as to avoid adding new overhead to every pointer dereference. The technique we use is to represent global-to-local pointers by a new kind of heap object in the global heap that we call a *proxy indirection*, or just proxy. A proxy has two fields: the pointer to the local object, and an integer identifying the processor that owns that local heap. Figure 1 shows a diagram of our heap architecture including a proxy indirection.

Pointers from the global heap to the local heap are always represented by proxies. To the existing read barrier, a proxy looks like a thunk, so the caller will jump to its code, which in the case of a proxy implements the rest of the read barrier for global-to-local pointers:

- If the owner of the proxy is the current processor, continue; otherwise

- Send a message to the owner containing the addresses of the proxy and the current thread, and block the current thread until a reply is received. The details of the message communication between processors is described later in Section 5.7.

In GHC the read barrier on global-to-local pointers therefore carries no additional overhead, except that we need to create proxy objects as necessary. In other systems, a suitable read barrier would need to be used, and that would necessarily impose some overhead. It has been shown that with careful optimisation a read barrier in Java can be implemented with only 4-10% overhead (Bacon et al. 2003); this compares favourably with the 30% overhead we found for promoting mutable objects too early (previous section).

4.2 The write barrier

As in other local heap designs, our collector requires a write barrier. Fortunately the write barrier can be piggy-backed on the existing generational write barrier, since it only applies to writes to objects in the old generation (i.e. the global heap). The write barrier maintains the following invariant:

- There are no pointers from the global heap to the local heap, except for proxy indirections.

The write barrier must track the proxy indirections so that they can be treated as roots and updated by local GC. Our implementation uses remembered sets, one per processor, each containing the set of proxy indirections pointing to that processor's local heap.

The write barrier must catch a write of a local pointer into a global object. When this action occurs, the write barrier is free to implement a range of policies, provided it establishes the invariant. We have implemented the following policies:

- Create a single new proxy indirection in the global heap, containing the local pointer.

- Globalise some or all of the data referred to by the local pointer into the global heap. At any point we can elect to stop globalising and create a proxy indirection.

We present measurements comparing these policies in Section 6.3.

4.3 Globalising an object

Making a local object global is called *globalising* it. Exactly how we globalise an object depends on the kind of object:

- **Immutable objects** (constructors and functions) reside in the movable portion of the local heap, and are copied into the global heap to globalise them. There may be other pointers to the local copy, so we overwrite the header of the local copy with a *forwarding pointer* to the global object, so that the local copy will be collected at the next local collection.

The object header is used mainly by the garbage collector, and is seldom read by the mutator (Marlow et al. 2007). However, if the mutator does need to read the object header, it must be careful to dereference a forwarding pointer.

- **Mutable objects**, such as mutable variables and arrays, cannot be copied, and so (following Domani et al. (2002)) we allocate them in immovable storage: the sticky heap (we describe the sticky heap below, Section 4.4).

- **Thunks** are objects that represent an unevaluated computation (and are thus specific to lazy evaluation). A thunk is a closure over an expression, and therefore contains pointers to the free variables of the expression. After evaluation, the thunk is overwritten with an indirection to its value: this is a one-time mutation, replacing the fields pointing to the free variables with a single field pointing to the value.

Strictly speaking, thunks are mutable objects, but we treat them specially because they come with a built-in read barrier. When the value of an object is required, the mutator already has to check whether the object has been evaluated or not; if it is not a value, then it has to be evaluated, and that is achieved by jumping to the object's code. Normally the object is a thunk, and jumping to its code causes its evaluation. However, an object may also be an indirection to another object, and evaluating an indirection is equivalent to evaluating the object it points to.

Hence, we can allocate thunks in the movable nursery, and to globalise a thunk, we can *move* the thunk to the global heap, replacing it in the local heap with an indirection to its new location in the global heap.

4.4 The sticky heap

The sticky heap is a part of the local heap used to store objects that cannot move. Most objects are movable: immutable objects can be copied, and thunks have a read-barrier that enables them to be replaced by indirections. The remaining class of objects, mutable objects, could only be made movable by adding a new read-barrier to their operations, and to do so would add overhead and complexity. Since these objects tend to be in the minority in Haskell, we opted for an alternative approach: mutable objects are immovable while in the local heap.

As we argued earlier, generally we would like to avoid globalising mutable objects if possible. However sometimes it is unavoidable: if a mutable object is really shared between multiple processors, it must be globalised.

Each processor therefore has its own *sticky heap*, where it allocates mutable objects. Objects in the sticky heap are born local, and can be reclaimed by local GC. However, if necessary they can be globalised without changing their address, by flipping a *global bit* attached to each sticky object (details in Section 5.5). Once a sticky object is thus globalised it becomes part of the global heap, and can only be recovered by global GC.

Note that the lack of read barriers on sticky objects means that whenever we encounter one during globalisation we have no option but to globalise it. This seems counter to our policy of not globalising mutable objects, and indeed it is – although in our setting it is far more important that the policy applies to thunks than to these explicitly-mutable objects.

Strictly speaking the sticky heap is an optional part of our design. The alternative is to use a read barrier consistently; whether this is the right choice depends on the particular costs involved. One should think of the design space as continuous, with the Domani et al. (2002) design at one end in which the entire heap is sticky, and at the other end there is no sticky heap but a read barrier is used consistently. In between are points in the design space in which heap objects are divided into those with a read barrier and those that are sticky. We contend that the read barrier is necessary to avoid the effects described in Section 3.1, and therefore the read barrier should be used for the majority of objects; however it may also make sense to omit the read barrier for certain objects and store them in a sticky heap instead. We cannot speculate on what the appropriate tradeoff for a different language might be, but if a read barrier is being added then it would make sense to measure the impact of that first, before deciding whether to reduce the read barrier costs by classifying certain objects as sticky.

4.5 Managing the parallel work queues

To provide load-balancing in the Parallel Haskell implementation, each processor has a *spark pool*: a circular array of pointers to heap objects supporting lock-free work-stealing (Marlow et al. 2009). Each processor may put work items in its spark pool, and processors may take work items from the local spark pool or *steal* them from other processors' spark pools.

This approach works nicely in a completely shared heap, because adding an entry to the spark pool is a straightforward write into the circular buffer. However, in the local-heap setting we must treat the spark pool as a global object where writes are subject to the write barrier, because other processors may steal from it, and they may only steal global pointers.

As with other writes to the global heap, we have to decide how much data to globalise for each write (see Section 4.2). In the case of a spark pool write, globalising more data would make stealing cheaper at the expense of greater overhead when adding sparks to the pool. Conventional wisdom is to load costs onto the steal rather than the spark, but doing so uncritically risks increasing startup latency, because a stealing processor must first ask the originating processor to globalise the spark before it can get to work. If we can arrange to have relatively few large-granularity sparks – using lazy tree-splitting, for example (Bergstrom et al. 2010) – eager globalisation of sparked work might be a better policy.

In our system, by changing the write barrier policy, we can simulate a range of alternatives, from an approach in which sparks are cheap but every steal incurs a message exchange, to a system which has completely asynchronous steals but where sparks are relatively expensive because they have to copy data to the global heap. We present some measurements in Section 6.3.2 to compare these approaches.

5. Implementation Details

In this section we describe our implementation in greater detail.

5.1 The block layer

The lowest layer of the GHC garbage collector is the *block allocator* (Marlow et al. 2008). The block allocator's API allows memory *blocks* to be allocated and freed, where each block is a multiple of 4Kbytes in size. Internally the block allocator requests memory from the OS in large units (typically a megabyte), and uses an efficient free-list of blocks in which most operations are O(1).

Every area of memory that the garbage collector manages, including the nursery, is represented as a linked list of (possibly discontiguous) blocks. Hence, the garbage collector is completely insensitive to address-space layout, which is good for portability, and it can easily manage multiple regions (for different generations, say) whose size varies over time.

Each block has a small amount of metadata associated with it, called the *block descriptor*. A simple calculation maps an arbitrary memory address to its block descriptor. The block descriptor contains a link field for chaining blocks together, other information

such as which generation the block belongs to, and some flags. Our sticky heap, for example, is represented by a chain of blocks that each have the STICKY flag set in the block descriptor.

5.2 Virtual processors

The runtime system uses a number of virtual processors that we call HECs (Haskell Execution Context). The number of HECs is chosen at startup time, and cannot currently be changed during the run of a program. Typically the number of HECs is chosen to be the same as the number of hardware cores; the reader should think of a HEC as being approximately equivalent to a processor.

Each HEC is "animated" by an OS thread. In fact there may be many such OS threads for a single HEC, because our runtime creates extra OS threads on demand, to handle blocking system calls (Marlow et al. 2004). However, the scheduler allows only one OS thread per HEC to run at any one time. The OS threads (and hence the HEC) can be pinned to hardware cores using the OS's affinity APIs, although we find in practice that this makes little difference to performance and in some cases actually degrades it.

Each HEC runs its own scheduler, and has its own queue of runnable Haskell threads, and its own local heap. A HEC may create new Haskell threads to run parallel sparks stolen from other HECs.

5.3 Local heap collections

Our collector supports *aging* in the local heap: objects have to survive at least one garbage collection in the local heap before being moved to the global heap. We found that aging objects at least one GC cycle was important for performance, because we avoid some premature promotion, but aging more than one GC cycle is a pessimisation due to the extra copying entailed. Aging is implemented by grouping objects by age: all live objects in the nursery are copied to a separate area containing objects that have survived one GC, and live objects in this area are copied to the global heap.

The sticky heap has to be collected using mark-sweep: we cannot move any of the global objects in it, because other processors may be accessing them concurrently. However, we could move *local* objects in the sticky heap to reduce fragmentation; currently our implementation does not do this (though the Domani et al. (2002) collector does).

Our sweeping reclamation algorithm is based on the Immix mark-region strategy (Blackburn and McKinley 2008), in which memory is reclaimed at a granularity larger than a single object in order to speed up sweeping and allocation. GHC's block-based memory allocation scheme (Section 5.1) is a perfect fit: when mark-sweep finds a complete block with no live objects, it can simply return it to the block allocator. The granularity at which we can free memory is somewhat larger than that used by Immix, which may lead to fragmentation. However, in our case this is not a serious problem, since at the next global GC we will compact the sticky heap anyway, and fragmentation will simply cause the global GC to happen a bit sooner. The sweeping algorithm therefore classifies blocks in the sticky heap as

- **Free**: the block has no live objects at all, and can be immediately reclaimed.

- **Global**: a block that contains at least one global object is marked global, and never swept again. We do not attempt to reclaim unused memory in these blocks until the next global GC, when live objects in the block will be copied out and the block can be re-used. We found that this optimisation was particularly important for programs that make heavy use of mutable objects, otherwise each local collection sweeps an ever-growing immovable region.

- **Local**: the block has live local objects in it; we aggregate free space in the block into extents, in order to speed up future sweeps, but otherwise do not attempt to re-use it.

We cannot age objects in the sticky heap, because the aging implementation relies on copying in order to group objects by age. A variety of policies are possible but our current policy is this: sticky objects are never promoted by local GC but are always promoted by global GC. So after global GC all the sticky heaps are empty.

5.4 Global heap collections

The global heap is collected with stop-the-world parallel collection, exactly as described in Marlow et al. (2008). In the default configuration, the global heap is collected when it has doubled in size since the last global collection, with a minimum of 1 MB. This provides a reasonable tradeoff between collection frequency and memory usage. However, for the purposes of comparative measurements between collectors in Section 6, we use a fixed heap size configuration and collect the global heap when the total heap size has grown to half of this size (to allow for copying).

5.5 Where to store the "global" bit in the sticky heap

Each object in the sticky heap needs to have an associated flag to indicate whether it belongs to the local or the global heap. The approach we chose is to allocate an extra word *before* each object in the sticky heap, which is zero if the object is local and non-zero otherwise. We considered two alternative approaches:

- Store the global bit in the object itself: either a bit in the object's header, or a bit in the object's metadata (which is pointed to by the header). This would be more complex than the approach we took: we would either need to modify code that inspects object headers to mask out the bit, or we would need to change an object's metadata when we globalise it, which would be dependent on the kind of object being globalised.

- Store the global bit in a separate bitmap. This is the approach taken in Domani et al. (2002). This would be slower than the approach we took, although it would waste less memory. We considered this to be an appropriate tradeoff, given that in our setting we expect objects in the sticky heap to be in the minority. The wasted memory in our case only applies while the object is in the sticky heap; there are no extra words once a global collection has taken place and the objects are moved to the global heap proper.

5.6 Large objects

Objects larger than a certain threshold (currently about 3KB) are classed as "large objects" and are never copied by the GC. Instead they are allocated in a contiguous region of blocks, and stored in a linked list associated with the heap to which they belong. Moving a large object from the local heap to the global heap therefore consists of removing it from the linked list in the local heap, and adding it to the global heap's list.

The fact that large objects are immovable is useful, because it means that a large mutable object (such as an array) does not need to be allocated in the sticky heap, and it can be managed in the same way as other large objects.

5.7 Requesting private data from another processor

When one processor encounters a proxy indirection that belongs to another processor, it sends a message to the other processor to request globalisation of the data referred to by the proxy. The (Haskell) thread making the request is placed into a blocked state until the other processor replies; meanwhile the HEC runs some other thread.

On receipt of the message, the owner of the proxy globalises the data. Just as for the write barrier in Section 4.2, there is a policy decision to make about how far to globalise, but in this case the owner must globalise at least *some* of the data because it is required by the other processor.

Having globalised the data, the owner then overwrites the proxy with a plain indirection to the now-global object, and sends a reply to wake up the blocked thread on the original processor.

As a special case, if the other processor is idle, then the processor that encountered the proxy can simply take control of the other processor's local heap temporarily in order to perform the globalisation without the need to incur the cost of the message exchange and waking up the idle OS thread. This is quite an important optimisation: we found that in some of our benchmarks it was common for a processor to run out of work and become idle while holding data in the local heap needed by other processors. We experimented with having idle processors do a local GC before sleeping, but found that this lead to a large number of local GCs and thrashing in some cases.

6. Measurements

Our measurements were made on a 24-core machine consisting of 4 Intel Xeon E7450 processors (2.4GHz), running Windows Server 2008. We compiled our benchmarks to 32-bit code. The results for 64-bit code are broadly similar, but differences in performance tend to be amplified at 64 bits due to the greater stress put on the memory system.

As our baseline for comparison we use GHC HEAD as of 21 January 2011, and our implementation of the local-heap GC is based directly on this GHC version.

6.1 Benchmarks

Our benchmarks are a collection of parallel Haskell programs. They are all deterministically parallel, and use the internal spark mechanism for parallelism, rather than explicit threads.

- `blackscholes`: An implementation of the Black-Scholes algorithm for modelling financial contracts.
- `coins`: computes the list of ways in which a set of coins can be combined to make an amount of money.
- `gray`: a ray-tracer with an interpretive mini-language for specifying the scene. Only the rendering part of the computation is parallelised, so we do not expect to achieve full speedup here.
- `mandel`: a mandelbrot set renderer.
- `matmult`: matrix multiplication (unoptimised using a list-of-lists representation for the matrices).
- `minimax`: a program to find the best move in a game of 4×4 noughts-and-crosses, using alpha-beta searching of the game tree to a depth of 7 moves.
- `nbody`: calculate the forces due to gravity between a collection of bodies in 3-dimensional space.
- `parfib`: the standard nfib microbenchmark in which the tree of recursive calls is evaluated in parallel down to a fixed depth, beyond which the calls are evaluated sequentially.
- `partree`: build a tree in which each node contains an expensive computation, and evaluate it in parallel.
- `prsa`: perform an RSA encoding in parallel.
- `queens`: calculate the number of solutions to the N-queens problem for 14 queens on a 14x14 board.

Program	Allocated (MB)	Rate (MB/s) 24-core	Heap size (MB)
blackscholes	4014	919	700
coins	2509	2669	500
gray	1937	1655	48
mandel	6510	3720	64
matmult	95	61	90
minimax	28465	6859	64
nbody	11777	12267	48
parfib	287	251	32
partree	2106	2106	512
prsa	2754	2899	32
queens	1794	1602	128
ray	6721	2721	32
sumeuler	4642	3439	32
transclos	4304	5448	32

Table 2. Memory usage of benchmark programs

- `ray`: a basic ray-tracer with a very fine granularity (each pixel is a separate spark). This benchmark is included mainly to test how well the system copes with fine-grained parallelism; it is not expected to achieve optimal performance for a ray tracer.

- `sumeuler`: compute the sum of the value of Euler's function applied to each integer up to a given bound.

- `transclos`: computes the transitive closure of a relation over an initial set of values.

The programs vary in size with the smallest being 18 lines of non-comment code (`parfib`) and the largest 1738 lines (`gray`); most are around 100 non-comment lines.

In two cases (**blackscholes** and **nbody**) the benchmark code is taken from the suite of examples that comes with the Haskell CnC distribution[6], and adapted to use the standard Parallel Haskell API instead of Haskell CnC. The code differences are minimal, but our versions of the benchmarks perform slightly better than the Haskell CnC originals[7]. In the case of `nbody`, we deliberately de-optimised the program because in its fully optimised form it does no allocation in its inner loop and hence virtually no GC, which made it a poor benchmark for our purposes (we already have a benchmark like this: `parfib`). To de-optimise the program we avoided using some specialised versions of overloaded numerical functions in the inner loop, which lead to some temporary allocation being required, which in turn exercises the young-generation GC.

Table 2 summarises the memory requirements of these benchmarks. These figures reflect the memory requirements on a 32-bit platform; requirements when compiled for a 64-bit platform are approximately double.

The first column shows the total amount of memory allocated over the benchmark run; these results hardly change when running in parallel, so we give only the 1-core figures. Some of our benchmarks allocate relatively little (`parfib`, `matmult`, `queens`), while others allocate over 10GB during the run (`mandel`, `minimax`, `ray`).

The second column of Table 2 gives the allocation *rate* that the benchmarks achieve, using our local heap collector on 24 cores. The main memory write bandwidth on this machine for sequential writes is approximately 1.5GB/s, and yet we see that many of these benchmarks are exceeding that, in one case by a factor of 8 (`nbody`). This indicates that our collector is successfully avoiding

---

[6] http://hackage.haskell.org/package/haskell-cnc

[7] the Haskell CnC versions of these algorithms are competitive with the C++ implementations

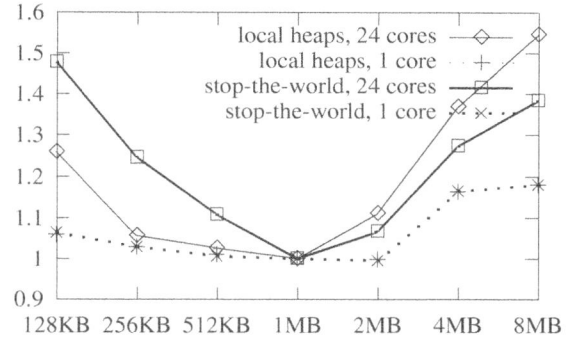

Figure 2. Comparison of nursery sizes

the "allocation wall" of the main memory bandwidth by making effective use of the caches.

The final column shows the heap size we used for each benchmark. Our collector normally runs with a variable heap size, but for the purposes of obtaining a like-for-like comparison we ran both collectors with a fixed heap size. The heap size in each case was chosen to be approximately 3-4 times the maximum residency, plus additional space for 24 nurseries at 1MB (24MB). This gives enough space for each program not to encounter slowdowns due to memory starvation and excessive collection of the global heap. In practice the memory requirements of our local heap collector are very similar to those of our baseline stop-the-world collector.

Many of these programs use lazy streams to run in constant heap space, while generating large output files, and hence do not have large residencies. So for the most part our measurements are not significantly dependent on the performance of the global GC; the one notable exception being `coins` which generates a large list of results in memory (we included this benchmark deliberately because it had a large residency). The use of parallelism does cause an increase in residency, but in most cases it is not significant, and in one case (`coins`) the residency is actually decreased; we believe this is merely an accident due to the timing of global collections.

6.1.1 Choosing the nursery size

In order to determine the fixed nursery size that would give the best performance on average for our benchmarks, we measured the relative performance of the benchmark suite with different nursery sizes (Figure **??**). We plotted geometric means of normalised run-times across all benchmarks, for combinations of stop-the-world and local heaps with 1 and 24 cores. For each configuration we arbitrarily normalised against the 1MB result set.

Note that these results are averaged over all benchmarks, and as such should not be considered to be representative of the behaviour for any one benchmark. Nevertheless, we do find that on average there is a local minimum around 1MB on this hardware. The dip is more pronounced when running on multiple cores, as we might expect: staying within the cache becomes more beneficial as contention for main memory increases. Interestingly, the results for the local heap collector show that it favours slightly smaller nurseries than the stop-the-world collector, indicating perhaps that it is able to benefit from the greater locality.

Our results contradict those of Zhao et al. (2009), which found no local maximum in the performance of different young-generation sizes for multithreaded Java programs. Accounting for this discrepancy is beyond the scope of this paper, but we conjecture that it may be due to a different lifetime distribution.

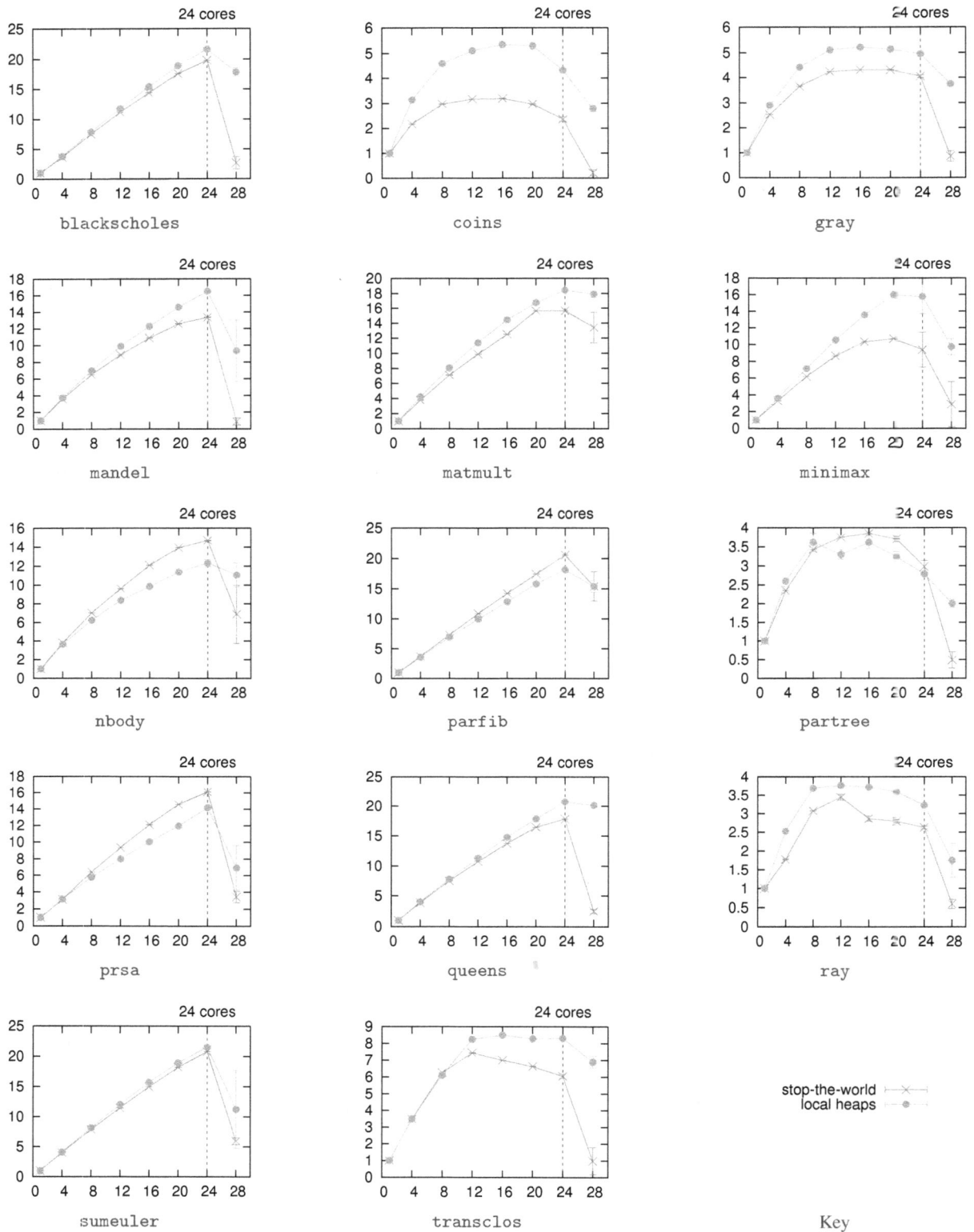

Figure 3. Speedup results on 24 cores (Y axis is speedup, X axis is number of OS threads)

6.2 Scaling

Figure 3 shows the scaling results for our benchmarks on the 24-core 32-bit hardware, comparing GHC's existing stop-the-world parallel collector against the new local heap implementation. The 1-core baseline in all cases was the stock GHC compiling for single-threaded execution. We measured the wall-clock elapsed time to run each benchmark, averaged over 5 runs. Error bars are shown at one standard deviation.

Note that although our machine has 24 cores, we took measurements up to 28 OS threads. Normally the runtime system would be configured to use no more OS threads than there are hardware threads, but here we wanted to simulate the behaviour of the system when hardware resources are being shared with other processes on the machine (we discuss the 28-core results below in Section 6.2.3).

6.2.1 Analysis of scaling results

At 24 cores, the local heap collector delivers better performance in 10 out of 14 benchmarks. The median improvement across all benchmarks was 15%.

We expect performance differences between the two collectors to be attributable to some combination of the following effects:

1. **Synchronisation.** The local heap collector does not have to synchronise all processors to perform a local collection.

2. **Locality.** Although the stop-the-world collector achieves good locality by not load-balancing during young-generation collections (Marlow et al. 2009), there may be benefits to managing explicit processor-local heaps.

3. **Single-threaded copying.** Local GC can use a single-threaded algorithm with no atomic memory instructions, unlike the parallel collector which must use atomic instructions to avoid duplicating objects. However, our base parallel collector already forgoes atomic copying for immutable objects, so we expect the difference here to be small.

4. **Fewer young-generation collections.** A local GC is only performed when the local nursery is full, whereas the stop-the-world collector performs a young-generation collection whenever *any* nursery is full. The latter policy could cause premature promotion and extra copying, particularly if different processors are allocating at different rates.

5. **Sharing requires copying.** The local heap collector is required to copy data into the global heap whenever it is shared between processors, and to maintain the global-heap invariant. This will cause the local-heap collector to copy more data in general.

We collected additional metrics to provide some insight into the extent to which each of the above factors affect the results. Unfortunately it is not possible to measure the proportion of the wall-clock elapsed time of the benchmark spent in local heap collections, because local collections are overlapped with mutator activity. Moreover, the local heap collector performs globalisation on demand, so mutator activity is interleaved with GC at a fine granularity. However, the metrics that we can measure are summarised below.

6.2.1.1 Number of collections.
We used the same fixed nursery size in both collectors (1MB), and a fixed total heap size. Table 3 shows the number of young-generation collections performed by each collector at 1 and 24 cores, with the 1-core stop-the-world results as the baseline.

At 1-core the local-heap collector performs almost exactly the same number of young-generation collections as the stop-the-world collector, as we expect; this is a good sanity-check that the local-heap collector has similar allocation behaviour.

The stop-the-world collector performs 87% more young-generation collections than it does at 1 core, due to effect (4) above.

Program	stop-the-world		local heaps	
	1 core	24 cores	1 core	24 cores
blackscholes	3758	+78.8	+0.0	+0.3
coins	2506	+64.7	+0.0	+0.5
gray	1950	+347.7	+0.0	-0.7
mandel	6519	+108.0	+0.0	+0.7
matmult	96	+1100.0	+0.0	+18.8
minimax	28499	-0.6	-0.0	-2.8
nbody	11789	+9.0	+0.0	-0.1
parfib	281	+17.8	+0.0	-67.3
partree	2033	+44.2	+0.0	-0.2
prsa	2789	+30.1	+0.1	-15.0
queens	1800	+22.4	+0.0	+8.3
ray	6741	+136.1	-0.0	-6.8
sumeuler	4660	+15.7	+0.0	-0.8
transclos	4284	+159.3	+0.0	+0.8
Min		-0.6	-0.0	-67.3
Max		+1100.0	+0.1	+18.8
Geometric Mean		+87.9	+0.0	-7.7

Table 3. Number of young-generation collections

Program	stop-the-world	local heaps
	24 cores	24 cores
blackscholes	0.16	-6.4
coins	0.15	+36.5
gray	1.61	-8.8
mandel	0.92	-31.8
matmult	0.22	+25.0
minimax	3.38	+126.6
nbody	0.28	+121.8
parfib	0.00	+0.0
partree	2.59	+126.5
prsa	0.94	+90.4
queens	0.52	-80.9
ray	0.55	+166.7
sumeuler	0.07	+136.4
transclos	0.36	-54.9
Min		-80.9
Max		+166.7
Geometric Mean		+19.2

Table 4. Wall-clock time spent in old-generation collections

The local-heap collector, however, actually performed 8% *fewer* on average. The reduction is because a global collection collects the local heaps too, so depending on the timing of global collections we may need fewer local collections.

The number of old-generation collections is too small to gain any useful insight from (single figures in most cases). Table 4 shows the difference in wall-clock time spent in old-generation collections between the stop-the-world and local-heap collectors. The time spent in old-generation collections increased by 19% on average with the local-heap collector, although the variability across the benchmark set was very high and this may not be a robust effect.

6.2.1.2 Amount of data copied by GC
The amount of data copied by GC is a reasonable proxy for the cost of GC, and hence GC time. We expect there to be less copying due to there being fewer young-generation collections, but balanced against that is the need to do more copying to globalise data that is shared between processors, and to maintain the global-heap invariant.

Program	stop-the-world		local heaps	
	1 core	24 cores	1 core	24 cores
blackscholes	1997188	+85.7	+9.1	+48.6
coins	402911340	+0.2	+0.0	+0.1
gray	53900792	+38.0	+0.0	+31.8
mandel	50358496	-25.8	+0.3	-25.3
matmult	32577184	-28.1	+0.1	+1.4
minimax	2288432768	-19.6	+0.3	-9.2
nbody	2389432	+701.1	+10.7	+1694.8
parfib	58752	+1046.4	-0.4	+378602.4
partree	301763736	+6.4	+0.1	+17.6
prsa	26268076	+5.9	+0.8	+52.4
queens	53848299	+11.8	+24.0	+28.3
ray	145387572	-57.7	+16.7	+21.5
sumeuler	2077124	+1.3	+0.1	+209.4
transclos	9043744	+23.9	+0.9	+3.2
Min		-57.7	-0.4	-25.3
Max		+1046.4	+24.0	+378602.4
Geometric Mean		+35.1	+4.2	+164.4

Table 5. Total data copied by GC (bytes)

Table 5 shows the total amount of data copied by each collector (including globalisation in the local-heap collector) at 1 and 24 cores, with the 1-core stop-the-world results as the baseline.

The amount of data copied increased in the local-heap collector compared with stop-the-world. Discounting two outliers: parfib, where the amount of copying increased by $32,000\%$, and sumeuler, where the amount of copying was small but highly variable, the average over the rest of the benchmarks was a **23% increase** (ranging from -20% to +187%).

6.2.1.3 Summary To summarise these results, it seems that although the local heap collector performs many fewer young-generation collections and fewer synchronisations, the benefits are offset to some extent by the extra work being done by the collector to maintain the global-heap invariant. These results are by no means conclusive; in future work we plan to gain further insights into the performance differences between the two collectors by measuring additional metrics. For example, measuring the time spent at synchronisation barriers would give some insight into effect (1), measuring cache misses would quantify effect (2), and effect (3) could be measured by turning on atomic copying in the local-heap collector.

6.2.2 Individual benchmarks

Some benchmarks exhibit worse performance with the local-heap collector. We examined these with our ThreadScope profiling tool, and found:

- nbody incurs a message-passing overhead when the main thread requests results from the other processors. In contrast, the stop-the-world collector just shares the data directly.

- partree develops some threads with deep stacks. Migrating a thread from one processor to another in the local-heap collector takes time proportional to the depth of the stack, because the thread's local data must first be globalised, whereas in the stop-the-world collector migration was a constant-time operation. The scheduler's load-balancing heuristics are currently not sophisticated enough to avoid expensive migration. We can improve performance on partree by disabling automatic migration, but we felt it was important to highlight the issue and raise it as a topic for future work.

- prsa appears to be slower with the local-heap collector due to imperfect load-balancing, perhaps related to communication overhead as with nbody.

- parfib incurs overhead in the local heap collector due to the requirement to globalise data when creating sparks in the spark pool.

6.2.3 Robustness to processor unavailability

In a shared computing environment such as a modern desktop OS, it is highly unlikely that a program will have uninterrupted access to all the processors cores during its runtime. A parallel program should degrade gracefully when the OS deschedules one or more of its threads so as to run other processes.

With a stop-the-world collector, the cost of synchronisation imposes a severe performance penalty when one or more of the HECs is descheduled by the OS, because when all the other HECs want to garbage collect they stall until the sleeping HEC is reawakened by the OS. We expect that processor-independent GC should ameliorate this effect considerably, by reducing the frequency of synchronisation. We modelled this by running 28 HECs on 24 hardware cores, where it is certain that four will be descheduled at any one moment.

Our results in Figure 3 show that in all cases our local-heap collector outperforms the stop-the-world collector when using 28 threads on the 24-core machine. The median improvement was **73%**.

All benchmarks incur some dropoff in performance with 28 HECs even with the local heap collector, and we believe this is accounted for largely by cache and OS scheduling effects.

6.3 Globalisation policies

A key decision is the globalisation policy: when globalising a pointer, how much of the transitive closure should we globalise? There are a range of possibilities, including:

1. Globalise nothing; just create a new proxy indirection for each write (optimising the case where the pointer written is to a global object).

2. Globalise recursively, but do not globalise mutable objects - leave proxy indirections instead.

Program	Elapsed time ($\Delta\%$)	
	globalise nothing	globalise transitive
blackscholes	-0.8	+0.1
coins	-1.6	-1.0
gray	+2.0	+415.9
mandel	-0.9	+158.3
matmult	+5.1	+2.3
minimax	-0.2	+93.9
nbody	-0.4	-6.8
parfib	-1.8	-0.4
partree	+34.4	+127.6
prsa	+0.3	+536.7
queens	+0.3	+10.7
ray	+21.1	+283.1
sumeuler	-0.2	-4.8
transclos	+4.9	+576.9
Min	-1.8	-6.8
Max	+34.4	+576.9
Geometric Mean	+4.0	+92.6

Table 6. Comparison of write barrier promotion policies on 8 cores

3. Globalise recursively, up to a maximum amount of data. Since globalisation is naturally breadth-first (as with copying GC), appling a cut-off to the amount of data copied is similar to a depth-bound. Once the limit has been reached, new proxies would be created for any remaining unglobalised references. (To date we have not implemented this strategy, but mention it here for completeness.)

4. Globalise the full transitive closure.

We can make an independent choice for different write barriers; for example, updating a thunk could use a different policy than writes to a mutable array.

The tradeoff is not straightforward. From our measurements in Section 3 we know that promoting the full transitive closure incurs a significant overhead for single-threaded programs. However, in a parallel program there is a countervailing effect: when data is needed by multiple processors, it is important that it is moved to the global heap quickly, to avoid latency and excessive communication.

6.3.1 Thunk updates

We measured the effect of modifying the globalisation policy for thunk updates at 8 cores; Table 6 gives the results. To summarise the table:

- Globalising only immutable data was the best (the baseline in the table).

- Globalising nothing at all was on average 4% slower.

- Globalising the entire transitive closure was on average 93% slower, and results ranged from 7% faster to 577% slower.

These results mirror those that we found for single-threaded programs in Section 3, but we find that the negative effect of promoting mutable objects is more extreme when running in parallel.

6.3.2 Spark pool writes

Recall from Section 4.5 that the spark pool (our parallel work queue) is a global heap object and is subject to a globalisation policy in the same way as other writes to the global heap.

We measured the difference between the three different globalisation policies for spark pool writes, and to our surprise there was very little difference. Globalising the full transitive closure was very slightly better on average, but the difference was less than 2% and hence difficult to measure accurately.

Why should there be so little difference, while we see a significant difference in the policies for thunk updates? We believe this is due to several reasons:

- spark pool writes are much less frequent than thunk updates;

- sparks are by their nature unevaluated computations, so globalising thunks referred to by a spark is likely to be the right choice;

- spark pool writes tend to be more persistent: the spark pool entry will typically remain live until it is evaluated; the only way a spark pool entry could become garbage is if the spark was speculative, and our benchmarks here do not use speculation for the most part (`minimax` has a little);

- reducing communication latency is worthwhile, so globalising early is a good idea.

7. Conclusion

A garbage collector with local per-processor heaps can outperform a stop-the-world parallel garbage collector in raw parallel throughput, and exhibits more robust performance through having fewer all-core synchronisations. Our collector performs best with a small (1MB) nursery size, and does not suffer from the "allocation wall" imposed by main-memory bandwidth.

Our scaling results are not as dramatic as we had hoped when embarking on this line of research, and if we consider parallel throughput alone, it is not clear whether the improvements are worth the (substantial) increase in complexity imposed by the local-heap collector over a stop-the-world implementation. However, the reduction in synchronisation frequency leads to a more significant improvement when the machine is being shared with other processes. Furthermore, although we have not measured pause times here, we believe that the local heap collector together with an incremental or concurrent old-generation collector could be an effective way to control pause times.

Throughout the paper we have identified the aspects of the design that are specific to our particular setting, although it remains unclear whether similar results could be obtained in, say, Java. We firmly believe that a read barrier is necessary for local heap collection in a mutation-rich environment. The sticky-heap aspect of our design is strictly speaking optional, but allows the read barrier to be omitted for some objects, in exchange for not moving them between global collections. A Java implementation could choose to use a read barrier consistently and no sticky heap, or it could identify a class of objects (e.g. arrays) that it is not important to move between global collections and would benefit from having no read barrier.

In future work, we would like to generalise the heap structure to allow multiple generations both local and global.

Acknowledgements

We would like to thank John Reppy and Mike Rainey for several useful discussions about the GC architectures of Manticore and GHC, and we thank the anonymous reviewers of earlier versions of this paper for many helpful insights.

References

Todd A. Anderson. Optimizations in a private nursery-based garbage collector. In *ISMM '10: Proceedings of the 2010 international symposium on Memory management*, pages 21–30. ACM, 2010.

David F. Bacon, Perry Cheng, and V. T. Rajan. A real-time garbage collector with low overhead and consistent utilization. In *Proceedings of the*

30th ACM SIGPLAN-SIGACT symposium on Principles of programming languages, POPL '03, pages 285–298, 2003.

Lars Bergstrom, Mike Rainey, John Reppy, Adam Shaw, and Matthew Fluet. Lazy tree splitting. In *Proceedings of the 15th ACM SIGPLAN international conference on Functional programming*, ICFP '10, pages 93–104, 2010.

Stephen M. Blackburn and Kathryn S. McKinley. Immix: a mark-region garbage collector with space efficiency, fast collection, and mutator performance. In *Proceedings of the 2008 ACM SIGPLAN conference on Programming language design and implementation*, PLDI '08, pages 22–32, 2008.

Stephen M. Blackburn, Perry Cheng, and Kathryn S. McKinley. Myths and realities: the performance impact of garbage collection. In *Proceedings of the joint international conference on Measurement and modeling of computer systems*, SIGMETRICS '04/Performance '04, pages 25–36. ACM, 2004.

Damien Doligez and Xavier Leroy. A concurrent, generational garbage collector for a multithreaded implementation of ML. In *POPL '93: Proceedings of the 20th ACM SIGPLAN-SIGACT symposium on Principles of programming languages*, pages 113–123, 1993.

Tamar Domani, Gal Goldshtein, Elliot K. Kolodner, Ethan Lewis, Erez Petrank, and Dafna Sheinwald. Thread-local heaps for java. In *ISMM '02: Proceedings of the 3rd international symposium on Memory management*, pages 76–87. ACM, 2002.

Matthew Fluet, Mike Rainey, John Reppy, and Adam Shaw. Implicitly-threaded parallelism in manticore. In *Proceeding of the 13th ACM SIGPLAN international conference on Functional programming*, ICFP '08, pages 119–130, 2008.

Richard Jones and Andy C. King. A fast analysis for thread-local garbage collection with dynamic class loading. In *Proceedings of the Fifth IEEE International Workshop on Source Code Analysis and Manipulation*, pages 129–138, Washington, DC, USA, 2005. IEEE Computer Society.

Simon Marlow, Simon Peyton Jones, and Wolfgang Thaller. Extending the haskell foreign function interface with concurrency. In *Proceedings of the 2004 ACM SIGPLAN workshop on Haskell*, Haskell '04, pages 22–32, 2004.

Simon Marlow, Alexey Rodriguez Yakushev, and Simon Peyton Jones. Faster laziness using dynamic pointer tagging. In *Proceedings of the 12th ACM SIGPLAN international conference on Functional programming*, ICFP '07, pages 277–288, 2007.

Simon Marlow, Tim Harris, Roshan P. James, and Simon Peyton Jones. Parallel generational-copying garbage collection with a block-structured heap. In *Proceedings of the 7th international symposium on Memory management*, ISMM '08, pages 11–20. ACM, 2008.

Simon Marlow, Simon Peyton Jones, and Satnam Singh. Runtime support for multicore haskell. In *Proceedings of the 14th ACM SIGPLAN international conference on Functional programming*, ICFP '09, pages 65–78, 2009.

Pekka P. Pirinen. Barrier techniques for incremental tracing. In *Proceedings of the 1st international symposium on Memory management*, ISMM '98, pages 20–25. ACM, 1998.

Bjarne Steensgaard. Thread-specific heaps for multi-threaded programs. In *ISMM '00: Proceedings of the 2nd international symposium on Memory management*, pages 18–24. ACM, 2000.

Yi Zhao, Jin Shi, Kai Zheng, Haichuan Wang, Haibo Lin, and Ling Shao. Allocation wall: a limiting factor of java applications on emerging multicore platforms. In *Proceeding of the 24th ACM SIGPLAN conference on Object oriented programming systems languages and applications*, OOPSLA '09, pages 361–376, 2009.

A Comprehensive Evaluation of Object Scanning Techniques *

Robin Garner   Stephen M Blackburn   Daniel Frampton

Research School of Computer Science
Australian National University
Canberra, ACT, 0200, Australia
{Robin.Garner,Steve.Blackburn,Daniel.Frampton}@anu.edu.au

Abstract

At the heart of all garbage collectors lies the process of identifying and processing reference fields within an object. Despite its key role, and evidence of many different implementation approaches, to our knowledge no comprehensive quantitative study of this design space exists. The lack of such a study means that implementers must rely on 'conventional wisdom', hearsay, and their own costly analysis. Starting with mechanisms described in the literature and a variety of permutations of these, we explore the impact of a number of dimensions including: a) the choice of data structure, b) levels of indirection from object to metadata, and c) specialization of scanning code. We perform a comprehensive examination of these tradeoffs on four different architectures using eighteen benchmarks and hardware performance counters. We inform the choice of mechanism with a detailed study of heap composition and object structure as seen by the garbage collector on these benchmarks. Our results show that choice of scanning mechanism is important. We find that a careful choice of scanning mechanism alone can improve garbage collection performance by 16% and total time by 2.5%, on average, over a well tuned baseline. We observe substantial variation in performance among architectures, and find that some mechanisms–particularly specialization, layout of reference fields in objects, and encoding metadata in object headers–yield consistent, significant advantages.

Categories and Subject Descriptors   D.3.4 [*Programming Languages*]: Processors—Memory management (garbage collection)

General Terms   Design, Performance, Algorithms

Keywords   Java, Mark-Sweep

1. Introduction

Enumerating object reference fields is key to all precise garbage collectors. For tracing collectors, liveness is established via a transitive closure from some set of roots. This requires the collector to identify and then follow all reference fields within every reachable object. For reference counting collectors, once an object's reference count falls to zero, each of its referents must be identified and have its reference count decremented. The process of reference field identification is known as *object scanning*. In order to be *precise* in the absence of hardware support, object scanning requires assistance from the language runtime. Otherwise, tracing must *conservatively* assume all fields are references [6, 7, 14]. This paper quantitatively explores the design tradeoffs for object scanning in precise garbage collectors.

Object scanning is performance-critical since it constitutes the backbone of the tracing mechanism, and therefore may be executed millions of times for each garbage collection. The extensive literature on garbage collection records a variety of object scanning mechanisms, but despite its performance-critical role, to our knowledge there has been no prior study quantitatively evaluating the various approaches. As we show here, a detailed understanding of these tradeoffs informs the design of the best performing object scanning mechanisms.

The mechanism for scanning an object typically involves parsing metadata that is explicitly or implicitly associated with the object. The means of parsing and the form of the metadata can vary widely from one implementation to another. We identify four major dimensions in the design space: i) compiled versus interpreted evaluation of metadata, ii) encoding and packing of metadata, iii) levels of indirection between each object and its metadata, and iv) variations in object layout.

To inform our study of design tradeoffs, we first perform a detailed analysis of heap composition and object structure as seen by the garbage collector. We conduct our study within Jikes RVM [1], a high performance research JVM with a well tuned garbage collection infrastructure [4]. First, to characterize the workload seen by any scanning mechanism, we execute eighteen benchmarks from the DaCapo [5] and SPEC [16, 17] suites, and at regular intervals examine the heap and establish the distribution of object layouts among traced objects. We were not surprised to find that a relatively small number of object layout patterns account for the vast majority of scanned objects. We include in this study the extent to which packing of reference fields within objects changes the distribution of layout patterns.

Guided by this information, we conduct a performance analysis of various object scanning implementation alternatives. We evaluate each alternative on four architectures against the DaCapo and SPEC suites. We observe substantial variation in performance among architectures but find that some mechanisms yield consistent, significant advantages, averaging 16% or more relative to a well tuned baseline. Specifically, we find that metadata encoding offers consistent modest advantages, object field reordering gives little measurable advantage (but improves the effectiveness of other optimizations), and that specialized compiled scanning code for

---

* This work is supported by ARC DP0452011 and DP0666059. Any opinions, findings and conclusions expressed herein are those of the authors and do not necessarily reflect those of the sponsors.

common cases significantly outperforms interpretation of metadata. The most effective scheme uses a small amount of metadata encoded cheaply into the object header to encode the most common object patterns.

We also implement and evaluate the bidirectional object layout used by SableVM [9] and find that it performs well compared to orthodox object layout schemes. The Sable object model combined with specialization of object scanning code outperforms the alternatives in almost all benchmarks. There is however a small but consistent overhead in mutator time for this object model, giving it an advantage in overall time when the heap is small, and a slight disadvantage in large heaps.

This study is the first in-depth evaluation of object scanning techniques and the tradeoffs they are exposed to. As far as we know, our findings are the first to provide a quantitative foundation for the design and implementation of tracing, the performance-critical mechanism at the heart of all modern garbage collection implementations.

2. Related Work

Sansom [15] appears to have been the first to propose compiling specialized code for scanning objects (see Section 4.2), although he did not perform a performance analysis of the benefits of this technique. Jones and Lins [14], authors of the standard text on garbage collection, make reference to Sansom's work and subsequent work, but do not directly discuss the question of design options for scanning mechanisms. Grove and Cheng did a proof-of-concept implementation of scanning specialization for Jikes RVM and concluded that it was a profitable idea, but did not publish this work or incorporate it into the main code base [12]. David Grove kindly provided us with their implementation, which we forward-ported and used as the basis for our implementation of specialization. This implementation has been the default scanning mechanism in Jikes RVM since 2007.

Gagnon carefully examined the question of object layout and garbage collection efficiency in his PhD thesis [8]. He proposed the bidirectional object layout, where reference and non-reference fields are laid out on opposite sides of the object header. SableVM implements this object layout [9]. This design has two significant properties: a) it maintains separation of reference and non-reference fields in spite of accretion of fields due to inheritance, and b) object scanning logic is trivial since reference fields are always contiguous. Since SableVM did not have an optimizing compiler, it was hard for Gagnon to perform a detailed performance evaluation of this design. More recently Gu, Verbrugge and Gagnon [13] set out to compare the performance of this layout in Jikes RVM but concluded that it was difficult to accurately evaluate such design choices in the context of a complex, non-deterministic JVM. Dayong Gu generously made available to us his port to Jikes RVM of the SableVM bidirectional object model, which we forward-ported, tuned, and used in our evaluation of the bidirectional object model reported here. We use replay compilation to remove the non-determinism of the adaptive optimization system and found significant, repeatable results across four architectures.

3. Analysis of Scanning Patterns

To ground our study of scanning mechanisms, we begin with a comprehensive analysis of the distribution of object layout patterns, as seen at garbage collection (GC) time for a large suite of benchmarks. Since scanning consists of identifying and then acting on the reference fields of objects transitively in the heap, understanding the distribution of the patterns in which reference fields occur is important to the design decisions.

We use the term *reference* to describe a language-level reference to an object. The live object graph is defined as the set of objects that are transitively *referenced* from some set of roots. By contrast, we use the term *pointer* as an implementation-level address ('`void *`') which may or may not point to an object. We define the *reference pattern* of an object to be the number and location of reference fields within the object. All objects of a given class have the same reference pattern, and two classes may have the same pattern even though they differ in such aspects as size (in bytes), number of fields, or inheritance depth.

Because the policy for the layout of references within an object will affect the distribution of reference patterns, we consider two key object layout regimes; *declaration order*, and *references first*. These alternatives are straightforward design choices and were described in Etienne Gagnon's PhD work as 'naive' and 'traditional' layouts respectively [8]. In the first case object fields appear within the object in the order in which they are statically declared (with minor adjustments to ensure efficient packing in the face of alignment requirements). This is the approach used by Jikes RVM. In the second case, references are packed together before non-reference fields, at *each* level of the inheritance tree for each class. Note that for efficiency reasons, language implementations generally require that field offsets are *fixed* across an inheritance hierarchy, allowing the same code to access fields of a class and all of its subclasses. So in practice, the field layout for any subclass may only be additive with respect to its super class. Thus the 'references first' layout will typically result in alternating regions of references and non-references corresponding to levels of inheritance for the given type. Gagnon's *bidirectional* object layout [8] avoids this problem by growing the object layout in two directions, with references on one side and non-references on the other. Thus references will always be packed on one side of the object header regardless of inheritance.

A minor variant on the 'references first' scheme involves alternating the packing of reference fields first or last in an attempt to maximize the opportunity for contiguous groups of reference fields, and could in principle lead to further speedups. In practice we found that such schemes perform almost identically to the 'references first' scheme, and in the interests of space we omit any further discussion.

3.1 Analysis Methodology

In order to conduct our analysis of scanning patterns we instrument Jikes RVM to identify and then record the reference pattern for each object that it scans at collection time. At the end of the execution of each benchmark, the collector prints a histogram indicating the frequency with which each reference pattern was seen by the scanning mechanism throughout the execution of the benchmark. We hold the collection workload constant by setting a fixed heap of $2\times$ the minimum heap size for each benchmark. This is a moderate heap size and is same size as we use in our performance study in Section 6. We chose $2\times$ as representative of a 'reasonable' heap, although our analysis is largely insensitive to heap size. If the heap were made significantly tighter, very short lived objects may be slightly more prominent, and of course if the heap were made considerably larger collections would happen less frequently or not at all, making our analysis more difficult.

Encoding and Counting Patterns We study the frequency distribution of reference layout patterns in objects. Since the number of different possible reference layouts is enormous, to make the study tractable, we consider a fixed set of $2^{16}+4$ layouts. We exhaustively consider all 2^{16} layouts possible for non-array reference patterns of up to 16 words in length. We bound the set by grouping together all non-array reference patterns of 17-32 words in length, and all non-array reference patterns greater than 32 words in length.

Table 1 header columns: rank, reference pattern, mean, cumulative mean, 202_less, 201_compress, 205_raytrace, 209_db, 213_javac, 222_mpegaudio, 227_mtrt, 228_jack, antlr, bloat, fop, hsqldb, jython, lusearch, luindex, pmd, xalan, pseudojbb

rank	reference pattern	mean	cumulative mean	202_less	201_compress	205_raytrace	209_db	213_javac	222_mpegaudio	227_mtrt	228_jack	antlr	bloat	fop	hsqldb	jython	lusearch	luindex	pmd	xalan	pseudojbb
1	no references	33.02	33.02	30.28	33.01	44.09	37.44	31.41	33.94	46.36	32.36	30.01	27.88	26.67	39.16	27.42	31.34	29.96	18.85	32.70	41.54
2	00 0000 0000 0001	18.19	51.21	21.65	20.32	15.93	33.10	19.05	19.14	15.01	20.15	18.85	18.62	11.99	1.53	12.79	20.72	19.24	16.97	15.27	27.05
3	00 0000 0000 0111	16.99	68.20	20.17	22.42	11.60	11.72	21.63	22.05	9.30	20.92	21.41	21.72	17.13	1.94	19.97	20.40	21.59	17.98	19.89	4.00
4	00 0000 0011 1111	10.95	79.15	13.54	17.96	8.78	9.31	12.13	16.36	7.00	14.69	13.04	13.00	7.41	1.03	5.85	13.41	13.74	18.67	8.63	2.53
5	00 0000 0000 0011	7.14	86.29	4.16	3.07	6.96	1.60	7.70	3.74	7.63	4.09	7.86	7.19	10.16	19.00	12.92	7.89	6.57	6.41	10.55	1.00
6	refarray	5.55	91.84	5.86	0.70	2.96	2.96	1.68	1.21	10.90	2.36	2.21	2.82	9.64	18.42	6.28	1.83	2.17	13.97	3.92	3.76
7	00 0000 0011 1101	1.03	92.88													18.22					0.41
8	00 0000 0111 0111	0.92	93.80	0.78	0.37	0.25	0.22	0.97	0.66	0.21	0.57	1.31	1.19	1.35	0.17	3.13	1.02	1.11	1.27	1.82	0.18
9	00 0000 0001 1011	0.80	94.59	0.89	0.82	0.40	0.44	0.79	0.80	0.32	0.90	1.21	0.85	1.13	0.12	2.58	0.63	0.88	0.59	0.86	0.15
10	00 0111 1001 1111	0.73	95.32	0.72	0.33	0.23	0.20	0.91	0.54	0.19	0.52	0.99	0.91	1.03	0.12	2.23	0.76	0.85	0.94	1.42	0.17
11	00 0000 0001 1101	0.66	95.98									0.02									11.93
12	00 0000 0001 1111	0.64	96.63	0.28	0.17	1.04	0.12	0.29	0.24	1.21	1.04	0.31	0.96	0.93	0.04	1.98	0.37	0.44	1.13	0.98	0.04
13	00 0000 0000 0010	0.47	97.10	0.16	0.01		2.51	0.01	0.01		0.52	0.01	0.14	3.50		0.57	0.06	0.37	0.26	0.40	
14	00 0001 0110 0001	0.40	97.50	0.01	0.01	0.50		0.11		0.96		0.54	1.81	1.98			0.01	0.85		0.28	0.12
15	00 0000 0001 1111	0.40	97.90	0.31	0.21	0.13	0.09	0.62	0.38	0.10	0.72	0.48	0.45	0.60	0.09	0.77	0.38	0.46	0.43	0.81	0.10
16	00 0000 0011 0111	0.36	98.26	0.30	0.19	0.11	0.08	0.60	0.35	0.09	0.32	0.52	0.46	0.66	0.09	0.87	0.36	0.42	0.40	0.64	0.10
17	00 0111 1100 0011	0.30	98.56	0.39	0.14	0.12	0.09	0.47	0.23	0.09	0.29	0.47	0.40	0.47	0.03	0.90	0.18	0.29	0.38	0.47	
18	00 0000 1111 1101	0.22	98.78																		4.00
19	> 31 bits	0.14	98.92	0.15	0.06	0.04	0.04	0.14	0.10	0.03	0.10	0.16	0.13	0.20	0.02	0.62	0.16	0.17	0.15	0.25	0.02
20	00 0000 0000 1101	0.13	99.06					0.39												0.01	2.00
21	00 0000 0000 0110	0.12	99.18	0.02	0.08	0.01	0.02	0.76	0.03	0.01	0.06	0.11	0.50	0.01			0.18	0.05	0.15	0.03	0.07
22	> 16 bits	0.11	99.29										0.03	1.77			0.02			0.14	
23	01 0000 0011 1111	0.07	99.36																1.31		
24	00 0001 1111 1111	0.06	99.42	0.01	0.01	0.01	0.01	0.01	0.01	0.01	0.01	0.03	0.01	0.79			0.07	0.02	0.05	0.01	0.01
25	00 0000 1001 1111	0.06	99.47	0.02	0.01	0.01	0.01	0.01	0.05	0.01	0.02	0.09	0.09	0.10	0.02	0.05	0.09	0.09		0.15	0.19
26	00 1110 0110 1111	0.05	99.53			0.43				0.52											
27	11 1111 0000 1111	0.04	99.57											0.78							
28	00 0000 0100 0011	0.03	99.60														0.12	0.40			
29	00 1110 1100 0011	0.03	99.63	0.02	0.01	0.02		0.10	0.05	0.02	0.03	0.04	0.02	0.01		0.04	0.03	0.03	0.02	0.07	0.01
30	00 0000 1101 1111	0.03	99.65													0.50					
31	01 1100 0001 1111	0.02	99.68											0.44							
32	00 0000 0000 0101	0.02	99.70	0.10				0.16		0.07											0.08

Table 1. Detailed *reference layout pattern* distributions for 'references first' object layout (all numbers expressed as percentages).

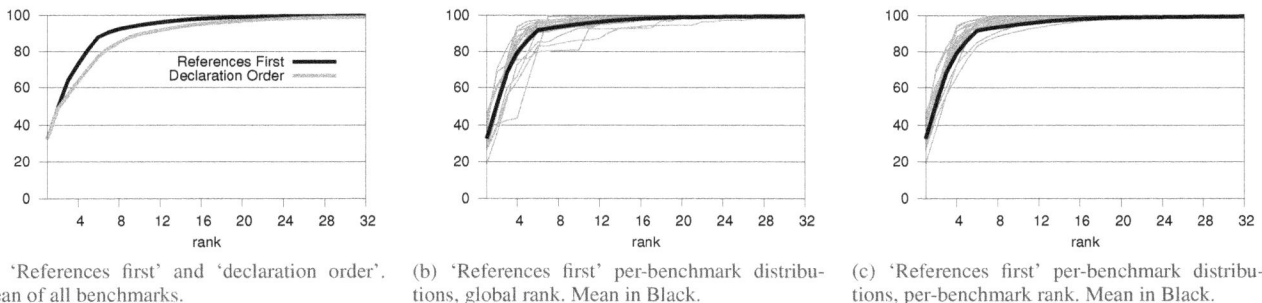

(a) 'References first' and 'declaration order'. Mean of all benchmarks.

(b) 'References first' per-benchmark distributions, global rank. Mean in Black.

(c) 'References first' per-benchmark distributions, per-benchmark rank. Mean in Black.

Figure 1. Cumulative frequency distribution curves for *reference layout patterns*. Each graph plots cumulative percentage of all objects (y-axis) covered by the N most common patterns (x-axis).

In practice, such patterns comprise just 0.58% and 0.10% of all objects respectively. Because all other patterns are counted precisely, our study is precise with respect to 99.32% of all objects for the benchmarks we study. The relative size of the pattern groups is as follows: a) objects with no references (29.60%), b) arrays of references (6.17%, 35.77% cumulatively), c) the 2^{16} reference layout patterns that can potentially arise in objects with up to 16 words in length (63.55%, 99.32% cumulatively), d) non-array objects with references that are 17–32 words in length (0.58%, 99.90% cumulatively), and e) non-array objects with references that are larger than 32 words in length (0.10%, 100% cumulatively).

Our instrumentation works as follows. We modify Jikes RVM to encode each non-array object's reference pattern as a 32 bit vector in the per-class metadata. Each bit maps to a word in the object and identifies whether that word is a reference or not. For example, an object which contained (only) two references, in its first and third words, would be encoded as `0...0101` (0x5). An object with references (only) in the first, third and sixth fields would be encoded as `0...0100101` (0x25). We create a histogram with $2^{16} + 4$

bins (to account for each of our fixed set of reference layouts) and initialize the bins to zero at the start of execution. As each object is scanned during each garbage collection, we determine its pattern either as one of the four special cases, or by using the low 16 bits of the object's encoding. We then increment the appropriate bin in the histogram. At the end of execution we print out the histogram.

We also inform our study of the Sable object layout by counting the number of reference fields in each object.

Jikes RVM We use Jikes RVM and MMTk for all of our experiments. Jikes RVM [1] is an open source high performance Java virtual machine (VM) written almost entirely in a slightly extended Java. Jikes RVM *does not have* a bytecode interpreter. Instead, a fast template-driven baseline compiler produces machine code when the VM first encounters each Java method. The adaptive compilation system then judiciously optimizes the most frequently executed methods [2]. Using a timer-based approach, it schedules periodic interrupts. At each interrupt, the adaptive system records the currently executing method. Using a threshold, it

rank	pointer count	mean	cumulative mean	202_jess	201_compress	205_raytrace	209_db	213_javac	222_mpegaudio	227_mtrt	228_jack	antlr	bloat	fop	hsqldb	jython	lusearch	luindex	pmd	xalan	pseudojbb
1	0	33.02	33.02	30.31	33.01	44.09	37.44	31.41	33.94	46.36	32.35	29.96	27.88	26.65	39.16	27.42	31.37	29.97	18.83	32.35	41.54
2	1	18.68	51.70	21.79	20.34	15.94	35.61	19.06	19.15	15.01	20.70	18.94	18.81	15.57	1.53	13.44	20.79	19.59	17.27	15.70	27.05
3	3	17.17	68.87	20.18	22.43	11.60	11.72	22.02	22.05	9.30	20.91	21.37	21.81	17.10	1.94	19.97	20.51	22.16	18.06	19.91	6.01
4	6	11.97	80.85	14.37	18.34	9.07	9.54	13.21	17.11	7.24	15.29	14.47	14.41	8.87	1.22	9.06	14.53	14.90	20.09	10.74	3.08
5	2	7.31	88.16	4.31	3.18	6.99	1.64	8.64	3.81	7.65	4.24	7.90	7.85	10.25	19.00	13.10	8.02	6.85	6.44	10.37	1.09
6	refarray	5.56	93.72	5.83	0.70	9.28	2.96	1.68	1.21	10.90	2.38	2.30	2.82	9.67	18.42	6.27	1.83	2.15	13.95	3.91	3.77
7	4	2.50	96.22	1.23	1.00	1.95	0.56	1.19	1.04	2.48	1.97	2.07	3.62	4.04	0.16	4.56	1.01	2.14	1.72	2.11	12.25
8	5	1.84	98.06	0.62	0.41	0.25	0.18	1.22	0.74	0.20	1.21	1.04	1.19	1.49	18.39	1.64	0.75	0.88	0.83	1.48	0.61
9	9	0.87	98.93	0.74	0.34	0.67	0.20	0.92	0.56	0.71	0.53	1.02	0.92	1.96	0.13	2.30	0.78	0.89	0.95	1.45	0.52
10	7	0.67	99.59	0.45	0.16	0.13	0.10	0.48	0.25	0.10	0.31	0.72	0.46	0.47	0.03	1.51	0.21	0.26	1.70	0.57	4.06
11	32	0.14	99.73	0.15	0.06	0.04	0.04	0.14	0.10	0.03	0.09	0.16	0.13	0.20	0.02	0.62	0.16	0.16	0.15	0.21	0.01
12	12	0.10	99.83											1.60		0.02				0.11	
13	10	0.04	99.87											0.78							
14	8	0.04	99.91				0.02						0.05	0.44		0.07				0.09	
15	15	0.02	99.93											0.33			0.02	0.04		0.06	

Table 2. Detailed reference *field count* distributions (all numbers expressed as percentages).

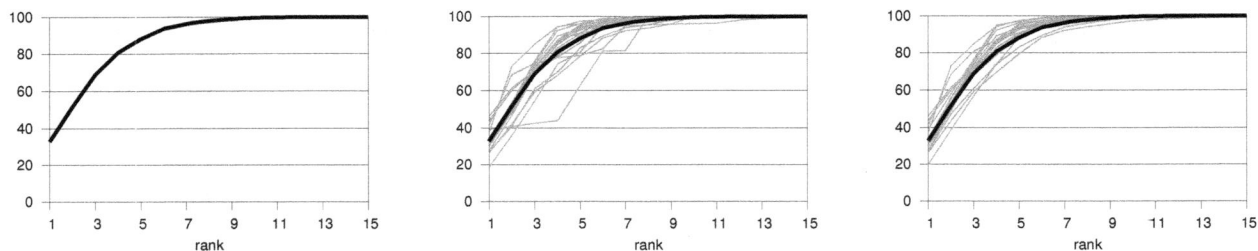

(a) Reference fields per object. Mean of all benchmarks.

(b) Reference fields per object, per-benchmark distributions, global rank. Mean in black.

(c) Reference fields per object, per-benchmark distributions, per-benchmark rank. Mean in black.

Figure 2. Cumulative frequency distribution curves for reference *field counts*. Each graph plots cumulative percentage of all objects (y-axis) covered by the N most common reference field counts (x-axis).

then selects frequently executing methods to optimize. Finally, the optimizing compiler thread re-compiles these methods at increasing levels of optimizations. All of our experiments were run using Jikes RVM's *replay compilation* feature, which provides deterministic hot method compilation using adaptive compilation profiles gathered on previous runs.

MMTk MMTk is Jikes RVM's memory management sub-system. It is a composable memory management toolkit that implements a wide variety of collectors that reuse shared components [3]. Any full heap tracing collector could be used to perform this analysis; we use MMTk's mark-sweep collector (*MarkSweep*). To perform our analysis of reference patterns, we instrument MarkSweep to gather information on the distribution of reference patterns in objects scanned at GC time. This instrumentation does not affect the garbage collection workload (the exact same set of objects are scanned with or without the instrumentation). The instrumentation slows the collector down considerably, but since our analysis of scanning patterns is simply concerned with demographics, not collector performance, this slowdown is irrelevant. We remove the instrumentation for our subsequent performance study (Section 6).

Benchmarks We use the DaCapo and SPECjvm98 benchmark suites, and pseudojbb in all of the measurements taken in this paper. The DaCapo suite [5] is a suite of non-trivial real-world open source Java applications. We use version dacapo-2006-10-MR2. We did not use eclipse because its use of classloaders is incompatible with Jikes RVM's replay mechanism. We did not use chart because of problems on 64-bit Ubuntu with the Java libraries that (only) chart depends on. pseudojbb is a variant of SPEC JBB2000 [16, 17] that executes a fixed number of transactions to perform comparisons under a fixed garbage collection load.

3.2 Reference Pattern Distributions

Table 1 and Figure 1 summarize the results of our study of scanning pattern distribution.

Figure 1(a) shows a cumulative frequency plot of scanning patterns. In this graph, the y-axis represents the percentage of all scanned objects covered by the number of patterns on the x-axis. The patterns are ordered from most to least coverage, so from left to right each additional pattern has a diminishing impact on the total coverage. The two curves in Figure 1(a) each plot the mean of all eighteen DaCapo and SPEC benchmarks. We show curves for both 'references first' and 'declaration order' object layouts.

Table 1 shows the 32 'reference first' patterns which, when averaged over all eighteen benchmarks, have the highest coverage of object scans. The first column gives the rank importance, the second column shows a binary representation of the reference pattern (or identifies the special case), the third column states the percentage of scanned objects covered by the pattern (the mean of the per-benchmark percentages) and the fourth column gives the cumulative value of column three. Columns one and four correspond to the x and y axes of Figure 1(a). The remaining columns give the percentage coverage for the pattern on each benchmark.

Figure 1(a) shows that by packing references together as much as possible, 'references first' requires significantly fewer patterns to cover a given number of objects. We find that of the large space of possible reference patterns, remarkably few are needed to cover the vast majority of scanned objects. Specifically, 6 (11) patterns cover 90% of scanned objects, 10 (16) patterns cover 95%, and 20 (30) patterns cover 99% for 'references first' and 'declaration order' object layouts respectively.

Figure 1(b) and columns five onward of Table 1 show the frequency distribution for each of the eighteen benchmarks using the

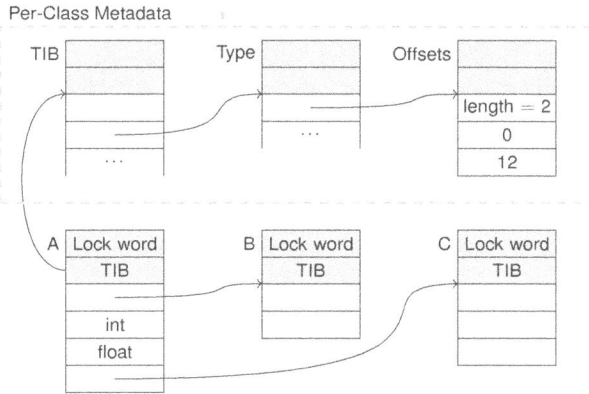

Figure 3. Objects and Per-Class Metadata Structure in Jikes RVM.

'references first' object layout. In Figure 1(c), the cumulative total is separately calculated for each benchmark with respect to that benchmark's ordering of pattern importance. On the other hand, Table 1 and Figure 1(b) present the data using a single global ordering of patterns. Here we see that on a benchmark-by-benchmark basis, the situation is accentuated further, with very few patterns required to cover most scanning cases. The left-most curve at the 80th percentile is for _209_db, and the two left most at the 95th percentile are for _201_compress and hsqldb. _209_db requires just 4, 6, and 8 patterns to cover 90%, 95% and 99% of all scanned objects respectively. Only four benchmarks fall significantly below the mean, namely fop, jython, pmd and xalan. The most prominent outlier is fop, which requires 9, 14, and 21 patterns to cover 90%, 95% and 99% of scanned objects. Thus even at worst, very few patterns are required to cover the vast bulk of scanned objects.

The data in Figure 1 and Table 1 show that a few special cases and a small number of patterns cover the vast majority of objects scanned, and furthermore that these common patterns are very simple. This suggests that object scanning mechanisms which can optimize for these few scenarios may be very effective.

3.3 Reference Field Count Distributions

The bidirectional Sable object layout depends only on the *number* of reference fields in an object, since the pattern of references and non-references is fixed. Table 2 and Figure 2 show the frequency distribution of number of reference fields among our benchmarks. This data shows that the vast majority of objects in all benchmarks have a small number of reference fields. 93% or more of objects in all benchmarks have 6 or fewer reference fields or are reference arrays, and 99% of all objects have 12 or fewer reference fields. There are however some outliers: the xalan benchmark has some scalar objects with 46 reference fields. Figure 2(b) highlights the variation in frequency between benchmarks even in the most common patterns.

These figures demonstrate that optimizations that focus on objects with a small number of reference fields have significant potential, especially in the bi-directional object model where reference fields are contiguous.

4. Design Alternatives

We now discuss the primary design dimensions for object scanning. We begin our discussion with a description of the object scanning mechanism in Jikes RVM (as at version 3.1.0).

The Jikes RVM Scanning Mechanism   Figure 3 shows three user objects, A, B, and C, and Jikes RVM metadata associated with

```
1  void scan(Object object) {
2    TIB tib = getTIB(object);
3    RVMType type = tib.getObjectType();
4    int[] offsets = type.getReferenceOffsets();
5    if (offsets != null) {
6      Address base = objectAsAddress(object);
7      for (int i=0; i < offsets.length; i++) {
8        processEdge(object,base.plus(offsets[i]));
9      }
10   } else { /* scan reference array */ }
11 }
```

Figure 4. The default scanning loop in Jikes RVM.

object A (metadata for B and C is omitted for clarity). If A and C were of the same type, they would both have pointers to the same metadata. Each object has a two-word header, one of which is a pointer to a *TIB* (type information block) for the object's class. The TIB incorporates a dispatch table, a pointer to a type (class) object and some other per-type metadata. The type object points to an array of *offsets*, indicating the location of reference fields within each instance of the type (class). Thus to scan A, the garbage collector must follow three indirections to reach the offsets array for A, which identifies the location of each reference field. Figure 4 shows pseudocode for the default scanning code in Jikes RVM. [1]

During tracing, Jikes RVM *'interprets'* each object's reference field layout by scanning the offset array. The offset array contains an entry for each reference field in a type, and encodes the offset (in bytes) to the given field from the object header. Jikes RVM makes no special effort to optimize object layouts for improved object scanning time.

4.1 Inlining Common Cases

```
1  int[] offsets = type.getOffsets();
2  for (int i=0; i < offsets.length; i++) {
3    trace(obj, obj.plus(offsets[i]));
4  }
```

(a) Unoptimized scanning loop (using offset arrays).

```
1  static final int[] OFFSETS_ZERO = new int[0];
2  static final int[] OFFSETS_1 = new int[]{0};
3  static final int[] OFFSETS_7 = new int[]{0,4,8};
4  ...
5  int[] offsets = type.getOffsets();
6  // Optimized code for the frequent case
7  if (offsets == OFFSETS_ZERO) {
8    // Do nothing
9  } else if (offsets == OFFSETS_1) {
10   trace(obj,obj.plus(0));
11 } else if (offsets == OFFSETS_7) {
12   trace(obj,obj.plus(0));
13   trace(obj,obj.plus(4));
14   trace(obj,obj.plus(8));
15 } else {
16   for (int i=0; i < offsets.length; i++) {
17     trace(obj, obj.plus(offsets[i]));
18   } ...
```

(b) Optimized loop with hand-inlined code for patterns 0, 1 and 7.

Figure 5. Unoptimized and optimized versions of scanning code.

---

[1] Jikes RVM now uses a version of specialized scanning implemented for an early version of this study, but falls back to this array-of-offsets 'interpreted' metadata scheme.

One simple optimization is to hand-inline special case code for the most frequently executed patterns. This trades additional branches and code size for rare cases against faster execution of common cases. An example of this optimization when using offset arrays for scanning is given in Figure 5. Similar optimizations are possible alongside other design choices in scanning mechanism and object layout.

4.2 Compiled vs. Interpreted Evaluation

Sansom [15] realized that a compiler could statically generate specialized code for scanning each type. This idea allows the garbage collector to use the standard dispatch method on each scanned object to execute code optimized for scanning that particular type, rather than interpreting metadata attached to the object. Advantages of this approach include a lower data cache footprint by removing the memory accesses to per-instance metadata, and avoiding branches associated with iteratively interpreting the metadata. On the other hand, this approach incurs a dynamic dispatch overhead and has a greater instruction cache footprint than interpreting. Variations on this approach may include specialization by object layout pattern rather than object type (removing redundancy and reducing instruction cache footprint), and limiting compilation to a modest number of common patterns (falling back to interpretation in all other cases).

4.3 Encoding and Packing of Metadata

The Jikes RVM mechanism uses a simple array of offsets to encode the location of reference fields in each type. Alternative encodings could be used, including a bitmap indicating which words are references. Hybrids are also possible, whereby a fixed size bitmap is used in common cases, with a fallback to an offset array for types unable to fit in the bitmap. Packed representations may allow the metadata to be directly encoded in the object header in many cases, thereby avoiding any indirection to the metadata data structure for those objects whose metadata could fit in the header.

In any virtual machine implementation, space in the object header is generally at a premium. Adding a word to the object header for GC metadata is an option, but the performance cost due to increased heap pressure and decreased cache locality outweigh any possible gains. JikesRVM makes eight bits available to MMTk, which uses four of those bits for the mark state (see [10] for details). Our implementation of the bi-directional object model uses an additional bit to identify the word as a non-pointer in order to allow the object header to be found when scanning the object (as per [8]), which leaves three bits for encoding metadata in our case.

There is an alternative approach (which we use in this study) that allows us to obtain these metadata bits for 'free'. We exploit the fact that the GC metadata is constant across all objects of a given class. By selectively aligning the TIB (vtable) of each class, we effectively encode metadata into the header field that stores the TIB pointer. We achieve this quite simply: when allocating a TIB and encoding n bits of metadata, we allocate a block of memory 2^n words larger than the TIB itself. Then we choose a start location within this chunk of memory that puts our metadata value into bits $w \ldots w + n - 1$, where w is the number of bits required to naturally align a pointer (i.e. $w = 2$ in a 32-bit machine). This scheme also has the advantage that it doesn't require an additional initializing store to the object header when an object is allocated. On a 32-bit machine we incur a space cost of 32 bytes per loaded class, which is insignificant.

4.4 Indirection to Metadata

The example of the Jikes RVM scanning mechanism (Figure 3) indicates the potential to shorten the level of indirection from the object to its metadata. We look at the effects of removing one of these levels of indirection by allocating an additional field in the TIB for holding a pointer to the reference offsets array. We evaluate the cost of this in Section 6. Schemes where metadata is encoded into the object header also benefit from the absence of indirection, although we don't directly study the effects of this.

4.5 Object Layout Optimizations

In addition to increasing opportunities for commonality among distinct types (Section 3), object layout strategies can more directly impact object scanning performance. The bidirectional object layout proposed by Gagnon [8] and used in SableVM [9] arranges every object so that reference fields are packed on one side of the object header, while non-reference fields are packed on the other. SableVM itself encodes the number of references into the object header, and in this study we look at the effects of the object layout separately from the effect of the header metadata optimization. As discussed in Section 3, an important property of the bidirectional layout is that it maintains reference packing in the face of inheritance. Unidirectional field packing may offer some benefits, but sub-types must strictly append their declared fields, potentially interrupting any grouping of reference and non-reference fields inherited from the parent class. Unidirectional field packing may be profitable in hybrid schemes where common cases are handled differently. In these scenarios, a field packing algorithm such as 'references first' will increase the coverage of a given set of special cases (Section 3, Figure 1 and Table 1), thereby improving the efficacy of the special cases.

The potential drawback of the bi-directional object model is that there is no longer a fixed offset from the start of the memory region occupied by an object and its header/object pointer. Lazy sweeping in particular can be adversely affected by this, and we see this in our total time results in Section 6.6.

5. Methodology

The methodology used for our analysis work is described in Section 3.1. We extend that here to describe the methodology used to evaluate the performance of the various scanning mechanisms.

We implement each scanning mechanism in Jikes RVM's memory management toolkit, MMTk [4]. We isolate and measure the time spent in the garbage collector's *scanning phase* (transitive closure), thereby excluding the time taken to establish roots etc, which is unaffected by the scanning mechanism we evaluate here. On average, scanning takes up ∼80% of total garbage collection time, and takes time proportional to the size of the heap. In Section 6.6 we also evaluate the effect on total time. We measure each of the DaCapo and SPEC benchmarks, timing the second benchmark iteration in a 2× heap as described in Section 3.1, and using replay compilation to avoid non-determinism due to adaptive compilation. We use MMTk's inbuilt timers which separately report total time spent in each of the major GC phases, including scanning. We use Jikes RVM's 'FastAdaptive' builds, which remove assertion checks and fully optimize all code for the virtual machine (and hence the garbage collector), and incorporate execution profile data to further optimize the code in the virtual machine. Experiments were performed 6 times for each benchmark, with the average for each benchmark normalized to the performance of the base configuration on that benchmark. We report the geometric mean of this normalized value across all benchmarks. The graphs show error bars for a 90% confidence interval using Student's t-distribution as outlined in [11].

We use as a baseline an optimized version of the original MMTk implementation described in Section 4 (see Figure 3, and which we refer to in the remainder of the paper as **Off-3/Decl**. This configuration has three levels of indirection from the object to the offset array and uses the 'declaration order' object layout. Because this

Platform	Clock	DRAM	L1 D	L1 I	LLC
Atom D510	1.8GHz	4GB	32KB	32KB	1MB
Core i5 670	3.4GHz	4GB	64KB	64KB	4MB
Core 2 Duo E7600	3.1GHz	4GB	32KB	32KB	3MB
AMD Phenom II X6 1055T	2.8GHz	4GB	64KB	64KB	6MB

Table 3. Hardware platforms.

Name	Primary Metadata	Indirections	Hand-inlining	Layout
Off-2/Decl	Offset Array	2	N	Decl
Off-3/Decl[a]	*Offset Array*	*3*	*N*	*Decl*
Off-3/Ref	Offset Array	3	N	Ref
Off-3+Inl/Ref	Offset Array	3	N	Ref
Off-3/Sable	Offset Array	3	N	Sable
Hdr[1R]/Ref	1-bit Header	1	Y	Ref
Hdr[1Z]/Ref	1-bit Header	1	Y	Ref
Hdr[2]/Ref	2-bit Header	1	Y	Ref
Hdr[3]/Decl	3-bit Header	1	Y	Decl
Hdr[3]/Ref	3-bit Header	1	Y	Ref
Hdr[3]+Spec/Ref	3-bit Header[b]	1	Y	Ref
Hdr[3]/Sable	3-bit Header	1	Y	Sable
Spec/Decl	Specialization	2	N	Decl
Spec/Ref	Specialization	2	N	Ref
Spec/Sable	Specialization	2	N	Sable
Count-3/Sable	32-bit count[c]	3	Y	Sable
Bmp-3/Decl	32-bit bitmap	3	Y	Decl
Bmp-3/Ref	32-bit bitmap	3	Y	Ref

[a] Baseline configuration.
[b] Falls back to specialization, and then to Offset-3.
[c] Only possible with the Sable object layout.

Table 4. Configurations evaluated.

is the configuration to which all others are normalized, it does not appear explicitly in the graphs.

Hardware Platforms We use four different hardware platforms in our analysis, described in detail in Table 3. The systems were running Linux 2.6.32 kernels with Ubuntu 10.04.1 LTS. All CPUs were operated in 64-bit mode, although JikesRVM is a 32-bit application.

Configurations For our performance results we evaluate 18 configurations combining features from the design space outlined in Section 4. The specific configurations evaluated are summarised in Table 4. The metadata representations we use are:

- An array of 32-bit offsets.
- A 32-bit count field (only applicable to the Sable object model).
- A 32-bit bitmap. Two special values indicate that the object is a reference array or cannot be described in 32 bits. This is necessarily held outside the object header.
- A 3-bit field in the object header. We use this to encode the six most common patterns in Table 1, interpreting results with a series of 'if' statements in the scanning code. The seventh value indicates a fallback to the more general case. When using the bi-directional object model we use this field to encode the five most frequent reference field counts. The coverage of this scheme for both object models is shown in Table 5.
- A 2-bit field in the object header, indicating whether the object is a reference array, has zero references, a single reference in position 1, or the fallback case. The coverage of this scheme for both object models is shown in Table 5.
- A 1-bit header field indicating whether the object is a reference array ('1R').
- A 1-bit header field indicating whether the object has no reference fields ('1Z').

In the declaration order and references first object layouts, our specialization implementation compiles 66 specialized methods, covering all objects with reference fields in the first six positions, with an additional method for reference arrays and a fallback method for the fallback case. In the Sable object layout, we compile 18 specialized methods, covering objects with up to 16 reference fields plus reference arrays and the fallback case.

Bits	Layout Scheme	Patterns	% Objects Min.	% Objects Mean	% Objects Max.
3	Ref-first	6 most common	79.9	91.8	97.5
3	Sable	5 most common	81.0	93.0	98.9
2	Ref-first	0, 1, refarray	46.5	56.8	73.5
2	Sable	0, 1, refarray	47.1	57.3	76.0

Table 5. Header encoding: Percentage of objects covered by the schemes evaluated.

6. Results

We now evaluate the performance of the design space described in Section 4. Since our focus is on the scanning mechanism, and the designs we explore have little or no impact outside of the scanning loop (which typically dominates garbage collection performance), unless otherwise stated, we present the relative performance of the scanning loop alone. Since many of the design dimensions are independent, we evaluate many combinations of the design choices in order to help understand which combinations of choices are most profitable. In total we implemented and evaluated around twenty five which combine multiple optimizations. We only report results for the most significant of these.

This section concludes with a summary of the best performing designs, and their impact on scanning time and total execution time.

6.1 Inlining Common Cases

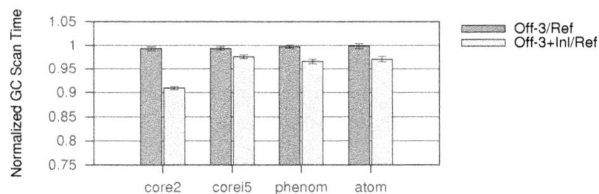

Figure 6. The effect of inlining common cases. Geometric mean of 18 benchmarks.

The speedup gained by hand-inlining the most frequently executed patterns (as described in Section 4.1) is illustrated in Figure 6, using Off-3/Ref and Off-3+Inl/Ref. The Off-3+Inl/Ref configuration uses the technique illustrated in Figure 5 to avoid interpreting the offset array for the most common object patterns. This shows that inlining common cases delivers a clear performance advantage. We use this technique in most of the configurations evaluated (the exceptions are identified in column four of Table 4).

6.2 Compiled vs. Interpreted Evaluation

In Figure 7 we compare specialized scanning (Section 4.2) across the three object layout schemes. Specialization performs well on average compared to the baseline Off-3/Decl configuration, but as we show in Section 6.6, not as well as three bits of header metadata. The reason is clear: for the 90% of objects that can be encoded by the 3-bit header field, scanning requires a load and then on average three conditional branches to the specialized code for scanning that

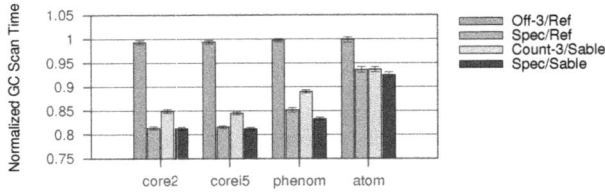

Figure 7. The effect of specialization. Geometric mean of 18 benchmarks.

object. Specialization requires two (dependent) loads and a jump, and on the Core i5 processor where an L1 cache hit costs four cycles, it is not difficult to see how this can be more expensive than the header metadata approach.

On the Atom processor, specialization offers less advantage. While header metadata obtains an average 15% speedup, specialization only yields a 7% speedup. The out-of-order processors appear to be able to absorb more of the stall time caused by the indirect jump than the in-order Atom.

6.3 Encoding and Packing of Metadata

We now explore the header metadata design space described in Section 4.3. Where not otherwise specified we use the 'references first' object layout.

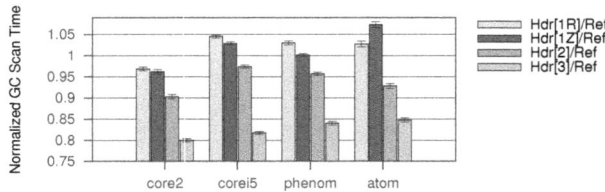

Figure 8. Effect of varying header encodings. Geometric mean of 18 benchmarks.

Figure 8 shows results for four configurations that use one, two, or three bits of header metadata. In each case we use the 'references first' object layout, and when optimizing special cases in the code we only optimize for the cases covered by the metadata. The 1-bit header fields reduce performance on all architectures except the Core 2. The 3-bit header field performs best, significantly outperforming the 2-bit header field, as predicted by the coverage figures given in Section 4.3.

6.4 Indirection to Metadata

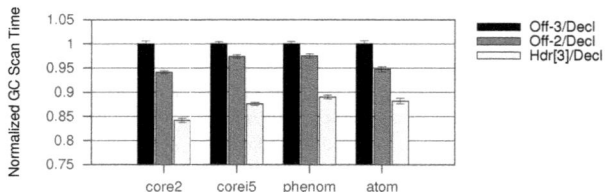

Figure 9. Effect of different levels of indirection. Geometric mean of 18 benchmarks.

In Figure 9 we explore the impact of indirection to metadata. The Off-2/Decl configuration differs only from the base Off-3/Decl configuration by one level of indirection. Since we can't practically

build an Off-1/Decl configuration without adding a word to the object header, the graph also includes Hdr[3]/Decl which while not directly comparable, only uses one indirection to its metadata before applying its specific optimization.

The results show that shortening the path to the metadata achieves a modest 3–6% speedup, with the largest gain on the in-order Atom processor. Since Hdr[3]/Decl is the result of removing one further level of indirection before applying the optimization evaluated in Section 6.1, we can see that the majority of Hdr[3]/Decl's speedup over Off-3/Decl is due to the elimination of indirection versus hand-inlining.

6.5 Object Layout Optimizations

In this section we investigate the effect of changing the object layouts, both in the context of the default scanning mechanism, as well as interactions with design choices across the other dimensions. Figure 10 compares ten configurations, illustrating the effect of object layout on four different schemes.

Figure 10(a) shows that for the most part, the choice of 'references first' or Sable object layout has very little impact on performance in the absence of any other optimizations. The slight improvement in performance on the out-of-order processors might be explained by small locality improvements.

The graphs in Figures 10(b), (c) and (d) show that where another optimization is used, object layout has a significant impact on the effectiveness of the optimization. In all these cases the 'references first' layout improves significantly over the 'declaration order' object layout, while the Sable layout provides a small improvement over 'references first'.

6.6 Summary

Figures 11(a)–11(g) show the scan time and total time performance of six of the best performing designs. The performance of some design choices is highly affected by architecture. A bitmap performs poorly on the in-order Atom processor, as does specialized scanning. The combination Hdr[3]+Spec/Ref performs best on all architectures (taking into account experimental error). The 3-bit field in the object header is a universally beneficial optimization when coupled with an object model that enhances its effectiveness. However, Figures 11(e)–11(g) show that for benchmarks like hsqldb—where the object demographics are not a good match for the assumptions underlying the Hdr[3]/Decl configuration—Spec/Ref has a measurable advantage due its more comprehensive coverage of object patterns. Hdr[3]+Spec/Ref also performs well in this case as its less expensive fallback provides a 'soft landing' for these edge cases.

Figure 11(b) shows the effect of optimizations on total time. While the magnitude of the improvement is modest due to our choice of heap size, the Sable object model is less effective than the others due to a slight increase in mutator time. Nonetheless, these results show clearly that the choice of scanning design has a measurable effect on total execution time.

The important features of a high performance scanning mechanism (at least on the architectures we have benchmarked) are: a) the elimination of memory loads, both through indirection to metadata and in the metadata itself (see the performance of Bmp-3/Decl vs. Off-3/Decl); b) good choice of object layout, to facilitate the performance of the optimizations used; and c) good coverage of reference patterns.

The Hdr[3]+Spec/Ref design combines the best effects of all the optimizations discussed here. The 3-bit header field eliminates loads for the majority of objects, while 64 specialized patterns as a fallback provide good performance for benchmarks like hsqldb which are a poor match for the 3-bit field. This configuration achieves speedups in scan time of over 25% on several benchmarks, at no cost to mutator performance.

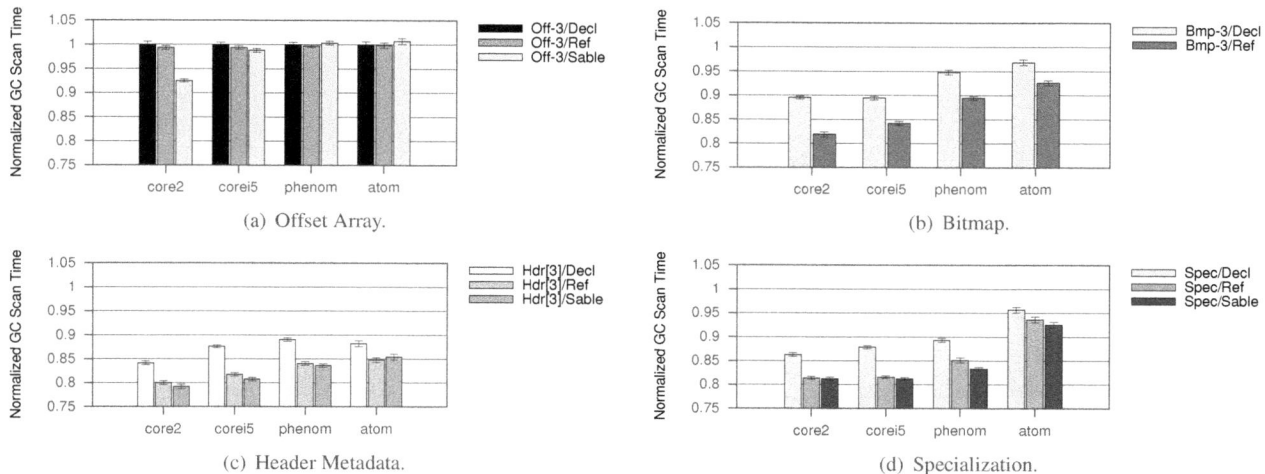

(a) Offset Array.

(b) Bitmap.

(c) Header Metadata.

(d) Specialization.

Figure 10. Effect of various object layout optimizations. Geometric mean of 18 benchmarks.

7. Conclusion

Object scanning is the mechanism at the heart of tracing garbage collectors. A number of object scanning mechanisms have been described in the literature, but—despite their performance-critical role—we are unaware of any prior work that provides a comprehensive study of their performance. In this paper we outline the design space for object scanning mechanisms, and then use a comprehensive analysis of heap composition and object structure as seen by the garbage collector to inform key design decisions. We implement a large number of object scanning mechanisms, and measure their performance across a wide range of benchmarks. We include an implementation and evaluation of the bidirectional object layout used by SableVM [9], and find that it performs well at collection time (although not significantly better than the more orthodox 'references first' optimized layout) but comes at a small but measurable cost to mutator performance. Our study shows that careful choice of object scanning mechanism alone can improve average scanning performance against a well tuned baseline by 21%, leading to a 16% reduction in GC time and an improvement of 2.5% in total application time in a moderate sized heap.

Acknowledgments

We would like to thank David Grove and Perry Cheng of IBM Research for their initial implementation of scan method specialization, and Dayong Gu for his port of the Sable object model to JikesRVM.

References

[1] B. Alpern et al. The Jalapeño virtual machine. *IBM Systems Journal*, 39(1):211–238, February 2000.

[2] M. Arnold, S. J. Fink, D. Grove, M. Hind, and P. Sweeney. Adaptive optimization in the Jalapeño JVM. In *ACM Conference on Object-Oriented Programming Systems, Languages, and Applications*, pages 47–65, Minneapolis, MN, October 2000.

[3] S. M. Blackburn, P. Cheng, and K. S. McKinley. Myths and realities: The performance impact of garbage collection. In *ACM SIGMETRICS Conference on Measurement & Modeling Computer Systems*, pages 25–36, NY, NY, June 2004.

[4] S. M. Blackburn, P. Cheng, and K. S. McKinley. Oil and water? High performance garbage collection in Java with MMTk. In *ICSE 2004, 26th International Conference on Software Engineering*, May 2004.

[5] S. M. Blackburn, R. Garner, C. Hoffman, A. M. Khan, K. S. McKinley, R. Bentzur, A. Diwan, D. Feinberg, D. Frampton, S. Z. Guyer, M. Hirzel, A. Hosking, M. Jump, H. Lee, J. E. B. Moss, A. Phansalkar, D. Stefanović, T. VanDrunen, D. von Dincklage, and B. Wiedermann. The DaCapo benchmarks: Java benchmarking development and analysis. In *ACM Conference on Object-Oriented Programming Systems, Languages, and Applications*, New York, NY, USA, Oct. 2006. ACM Press.

[6] H.-J. Boehm. Space efficient conservative garbage collection. In *PLDI '93: Proceedings of the ACM SIGPLAN 1993 conference on Programming language design and implementation*, pages 197–206, New York, NY, USA, 1993. ACM Press.

[7] H.-J. Boehm and M. Weiser. Garbage collection in an uncooperative environment. *Softw. Pract. Exper.*, 18(9):807–820, 1988.

[8] E. Gagnon. *A Portable Research Framework for the Execution of Java Bytecode*. PhD thesis, McGill University, Montreal, 2002.

[9] E. Gagnon and L. Hendren. SableVM: A research framework for the efficient execution of Java bytecode. In *Proceedings of the 1st Java Virtual Machine Research and Technology Symposium, April 23-24, Monterey, CA, USA*, pages 27–40. USENIX, Apr. 2001.

[10] R. Garner, S. M. Blackburn, and D. Frampton. Effective prefetch for mark-sweep garbage collection. In *The 2007 International Symposium on Memory Management*. ACM Press, Oct. 2007.

[11] A. Georges, D. Buytaert, and L. Eeckhout. Statistically rigorous Java performance evaluation. In *ACM Conference on Object-Oriented Programming Systems, Languages, and Applications*, OOPSLA '07, pages 57–76, New York, NY, USA, 2007. ACM.

[12] D. Grove and P. Cheng. Private communication, 2005.

[13] D. Gu, C. Verbrugge, and E. M. Gagnon. Relative factors in performance analysis of Java virtual machines. In *VEE '06: Proceedings of the Second International Conference on Virtual Execution Environments*, pages 111–121, New York, NY, USA, 2006. ACM Press.

[14] R. Jones and R. Lins. *Garbage Collection: Algorithms for Automatic Dynamic Memory Management*. John Wiley and Sons, 1996.

[15] P. Sansom. Dual-mode garbage collection. In H. Glaser and P. H. Hartel, editors, *Proceedings of the Workshop on the Parallel Implementation of Functional Languages*, pages 283–310, Southampton, UK, 1991. Department of Electronics and Computer Science, University of Southampton.

[16] Standard Performance Evaluation Corporation. *SPECjvm98 Documentation*, release 1.03 edition, March 1999.

[17] Standard Performance Evaluation Corporation. *SPECjbb2000 (Java Business Benchmark) Documentation*, release 1.01 edition, 2001.

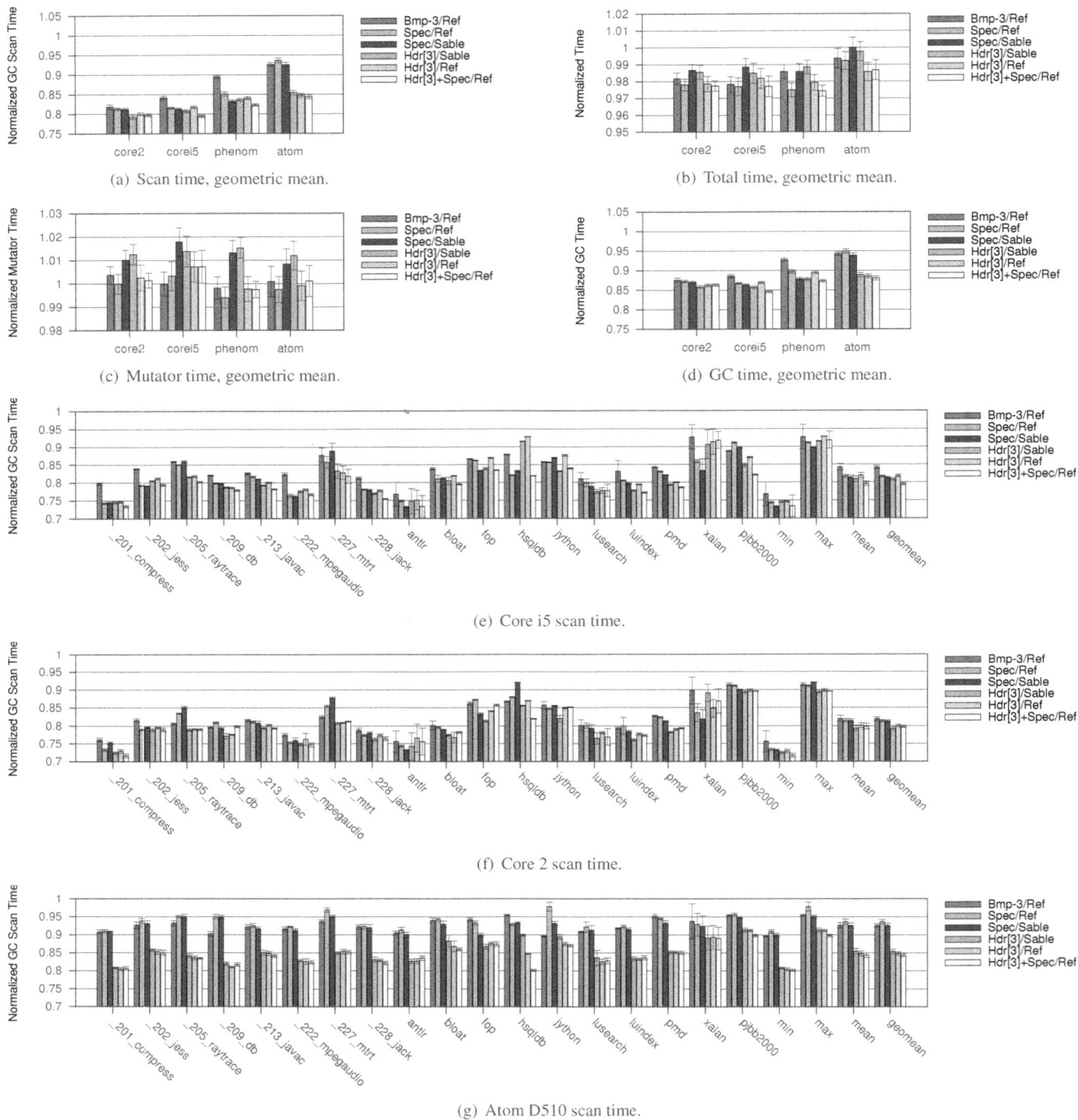

(a) Scan time, geometric mean.

(b) Total time, geometric mean.

(c) Mutator time, geometric mean.

(d) GC time, geometric mean.

(e) Core i5 scan time.

(f) Core 2 scan time.

(g) Atom D510 scan time.

Figure 11. Summary, showing six well-performing designs.

On the Theory and Potential of LRU-MRU Collaborative Cache Management

Xiaoming Gu   Chen Ding

Department of Computer Science
University of Rochester
Rochester, New York, USA
{xiaoming, cding}@cs.rochester.edu

Abstract

The goal of cache management is to maximize data reuse. Collaborative caching provides an interface for software to communicate access information to hardware. In theory, it can obtain optimal cache performance.

In this paper, we study a collaborative caching system that allows a program to choose different caching methods for its data. As an interface, it may be used in arbitrary ways, sometimes optimal but probably suboptimal most times and even counter productive. We develop a theoretical foundation for collaborative caches to show the inclusion principle and the existence of a distance metric we call LRU-MRU stack distance. The new stack distance is important for program analysis and transformation to target a hierarchical collaborative cache system rather than a single cache configuration. We use 10 benchmark programs to show that optimal caching may reduce the average miss ratio by 24%, and a simple feedback-driven compilation technique can utilize collaborative cache to realize 50% of the optimal improvement.

Categories and Subject Descriptors   D.3.4 [*PROGRAMMING LANGUAGES*]: Processors - Compilers, Memory management

General Terms   Algorithms, Measurement, Performance

Keywords   collaborative caching, bipartite cache, cache replacement algorithm, LRU, MRU, OPT

1. Introduction

Cache management is increasingly important on multicore systems since the available cache space is shared by an increasing number of cores. Optimal caching is generally impossible at the system or hardware level for lack of program information. At the program level, optimal caching requires solving NP-hard problems and is not yet practical [14, 20, 25].

A number of hardware systems have been built or proposed to provide an interface for software to influence cache management. Examples include cache hints on Intel Itanium [9], bypassing access on IBM Power series [27], and evict-me bit [31]. Our earlier work showed a theoretical result that two extensions of LRU cache

may be managed optimally by a program [17]. Wang et al. called a combined software-hardware solution *collaborative caching* [31].

In this paper, we study the formal properties of collaborative cache management. We define a model called *bipartite cache*. It supports two types of accesses: the normal LRU access and the special MRU access. Data loaded by an MRU access is managed by MRU replacement. At a miss, it selects the most recently used data for eviction. It is equivalent to tagging the loaded data with an evict-me flag [31], setting the MRU data for eviction before any LRU data. With bipartite cache, a program influences the cache management by selecting which data to be accessed by which type.

In comparison, conventional cache uses a variant of the LRU strategy. More significantly, a conventional cache uses a single interface for all data access. The use of software control makes hybrid management inevitable. The LRU-MRU combination in one cache warrants a re-examination of the fundamental properties of caching.

A foremost property of memory (and storage) hierarchy is what Mattson et al. termed the *inclusion principle*, which says that the content of a smaller cache is always contained in larger caches [23]. The inclusion principle has important benefits. In theory, the miss ratio is a monotone function of cache size. There is no Belady anomaly [7]. In practice, the miss ratio of caches of all sizes can be evaluated using one-pass simulation over a program trace.

More importantly for software, a machine-independent metric called stack distance can be defined for each access [23]. Software techniques are developed to minimize the stack distance and improve performance for a cache hierarchy rather than targeting a particular cache level. A type of stack distance called reuse distance has been used to improve memory management including garbage collection techniques [34, 36].

The inclusion principle is intuitive for LRU cache. Data is ranked by the last access time. The most recent data enters from the top of the cache stack and gradually steps down as it ages over time. Bipartite cache, however, stores data in two parts and ranks data in opposite ways. The MRU data is placed at the bottom of the cache. The placement depends on cache size. As Mattson et al. have cautioned, it goes against the inclusion principle to base a caching decision on cache capacity [23].

In this paper, we analyze the general LRU-MRU bipartite cache. Interestingly, the inclusion property still holds. We give a proof first and then an efficient one-pass simulation algorithm to compute the miss ratio for fully associative caches of all sizes. The algorithm defines and measures the *LRU-MRU stack distance* for each access. An access is a hit in bipartite cache if and only if its LRU-MRU stack distance is no greater than the cache size.

To demonstrate the potential benefit of bipartite cache, we describe a simple method called *PACMAN* for Program-Assisted

Cache MANagement. PACMAN shows how much a program can reduce the miss ratio under a number of simplifying assumptions. It shows the potential of collaborative cache management but it is not yet a practical solution.

In practice, caches are set associative rather than fully associative. For theoretical analysis, fully associative cache is more interesting (and difficult) since the associativity changes with the cache size. Its properties and results have practical significance. First, the inclusion property holds for each set of set-associative cache and for most real cache hierarchies. Second, modern cache has high associativity, i.e. 8-way and up, which means similar performance as fully associative cache [18]. The empirical results in the paper show the general effect of bipartite cache of all sizes, regardless of the specific implementation. Finally, important for software research, the LRU-MRU stack distance provides a machine-independent target for program analysis and transformation, as we explain in Section 5.

2. Background

LRU The data in cache is sorted by the last use time. If x is a miss and the cache is full, the datum in the LRU (least recently used) position is evicted. LRU can be costly when the set associativity is high. Pseudo-LRU is the one usually used in practice [29]. The performance of fully associative LRU cache can be measured in one pass for all cache sizes using reuse distance analysis in near linear time [37].

OPT The *optimal replacement algorithm (OPT)* was invented by Belady [6]. At a replacement, the victim is the datum that will be reused in the farthest future. Mattson et al. showed its inclusion property and gave a two-pass algorithm to measure the OPT stack distance [23]. Sugumar and Abraham invented an efficient one-pass algorithm [30]. OPT is not practical purely in hardware as it would require infinite ahead. However, it has a vital theoretical value since it shows the limit of caching.

Stack algorithm and stack distance As defined by Mattson et al., if the content of a smaller cache is always a subset of the content of a larger cache, the cache management algorithm obeys the *inclusion property* and is considered a *stack algorithm* [23]. In stack algorithms each access has a *stack distance*, the minimum cache size, to make the access become a hit. The miss rate is a monotone (non-increasing) function of cache size, and there is no Belady's anomaly [7]. The paper proved the inclusion property for LRU, LFU (least frequently used), OPT, and a form of random replacement. The inclusion property is beneficial in evaluation, when we can evaluate all cache sizes in one simulation, and in analysis, when we can target the stack distance and all cache sizes instead of a single cache size.

Two characteristics of the LRU-OPT gap As an example, we show the difference between LRU and OPT cache replacement algorithms using a workload of Jacobi Successive Over-relaxation (SOR) from SciMark 2.0 [2]. We use currently the fastest one-pass analysis methods for LRU [37] and OPT [30]. The LRU and OPT miss rate curves of an execution of SOR are shown in Figure 1 for cache sizes ranging between 1KB and 8MB (twice the size of the program data). The cache line size is 8 bytes.

Figure 1 shows two interesting aspects of optimal caching compared with LRU.

- *Non-uniform improvement.* OPT is not uniformly better than LRU. The improvement varies greatly between cache sizes.

- *Gradual miss-ratio change.* The miss ratio of OPT decreases gradually as the size of cache increases.

We observe that the curves of OPT and LRU diverge first, converge at size 16KB and then diverge again before both dropping to near zero at 4MB (with only cold-start misses). The difference depends on the cache size. In 16KB or 32KB cache, there is little or no improvement. In 8KB and 2MB cache, the improvement is more than 60% and 90% respectively. It is important to evaluate across all cache sizes.

The OPT miss ratio changes gradually, while the LRU miss ratio either stays the same or drops sharply. The sharp drops mark the size of working sets—each steep descent happens when the cache is large enough to hold the next working set. SOR has mainly two working sets: one at 8KB and one at 2MB. The smooth curvature of OPT shows that it caches a partial working set if the whole set is too large.

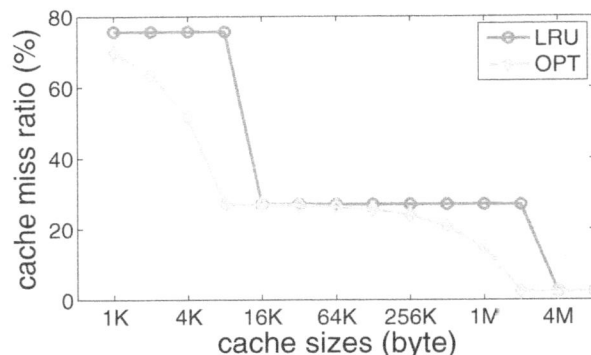

Figure 1. The gap between LRU and OPT in SOR

Collaborative caching In collaborative caching, a program designates some of its references to make MRU accesses. Figure 2 shows the kernel SOR whose miss rates are just shown in Figure 1. It is typical of stencil algorithms. Consider the data access in the loop body. Array G is traversed in each iteration of the outermost loop. If M*N is larger than cache size, array G cannot fit entirely in the cache. The streaming access of G would lose all data reuse because LRU evicts the least recently used datum, which is actually the datum that will be reused in the nearest future. OPT, however, would evict the most recently used datum. To obtain the same effect, we can tag the last access to each datum as an MRU access. A bipartite cache of size C would keep the first C bytes of G in cache and reuse them across loop iterations.

Require: G is a 2-dimensional double array with the size M*N
```
1:  for p = 1; p < NUM_STEPS; p++ do
2:      for i = 1; i < M-1; i++ do
3:          Gi = G[i];
4:          Gim1 = G[i-1];
5:          Gip1 = G[i+1];
6:          for j = 1; j < N-1; j++ do
7:              Gi[j]      =      0.3125*(Gim1[j]+Gip1[j]+Gi[j-1]+Gi[j+1])-
                0.25*Gi[j];
8:          end for
9:      end for
10: end for
```

Figure 2. The SOR kernel computation

3. Properties of Collaborative Cache

We first define the LRU and MRU memory accesses and then prove that bipartite cache has the inclusion property and can be evaluated efficiently using one-pass simulation.

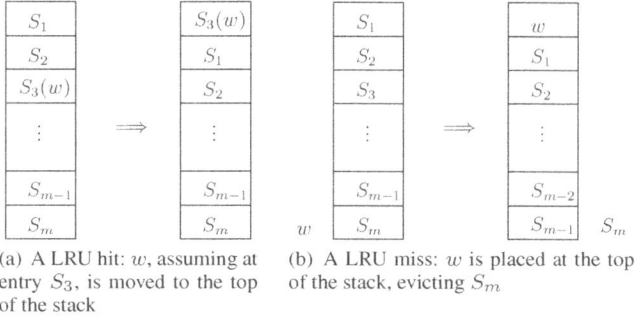

(a) A LRU hit: w, assuming at entry S_3, is moved to the top of the stack

(b) A LRU miss: w is placed at the top of the stack, evicting S_m

Figure 3. A LRU memory access

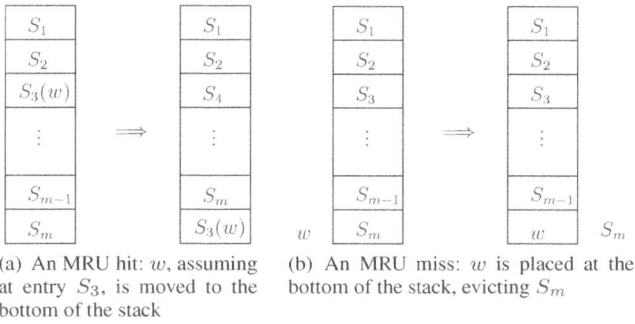

(a) An MRU hit: w, assuming at entry S_3, is moved to the bottom of the stack

(b) An MRU miss: w is placed at the bottom of the stack, evicting S_m

Figure 4. An MRU memory access

3.1 Bipartite LRU-MRU Cache

The collaborative cache provides two instructions for accessing memory: the normal LRU access and the special MRU access. LRU is a standard concept defined in textbooks. For comparison with MRU, we show a diagram in Figure 3. LRU cache can be thought of as organized in a stack. The newly accessed data is at the top—the MRU position—and the rest of LRU data is ordered top-down based on the recency of access. In an actual implementation, the order of recency is maintained or approximated efficiently without moving cache entries.

In comparison, Figure 4 shows the handling of an MRU access. If it is a miss, the new data is replaced at the LRU position at the bottom of the stack. If it is a hit, the accessed data is moved to the bottom of the stack. Multiple MRU elements may gather at the bottom after a series of MRU access hits.

The LRU-MRU interface can be used to obtain optimal cache performance [17], yet it is simple to implement. The implementation of the MRU instruction is not much harder than a normal LRU instruction. In a real hardware design, the cycles required to execute an MRU access should be similar to the cost of a normal LRU cache access.

Bipartite cache differs from conventional cache in three ways:

- *Bipartite content.* The cache stack is divided into two parts: the upper part for LRU data and the lower part for MRU data. Either part may be missing, and the cache is entirely LRU or MRU.

- *Capacity dependent placement.* The MRU data is placed at the bottom. The location depends on the size of the cache.

- *Hybrid priority.* The LRU part is prioritized by the LRU order, that is, the last accessed is last replaced. The MRU part is by the MRU order, that is, the last accessed is first replaced.

In comparison, conventional, non-collaborative cache manages data using a single priority order, e.g. LRU by the last access time and OPT by the next access time. The placement depends on the priority order and not on cache size. The single priority naturally gives rise to the inclusion property and its practical benefits. To understand collaborative caching, we must understand its bipartite nature.

3.2 The Inclusion Property

If the collaborative cache is used optimally, the performance is the same as OPT [17]. In general, however, the cache may not be used optimally. The selection of MRU accesses may be arbitrary. The following proof is for all uses of bipartite cache, including the extreme cases (when all accesses are normal, i.e. LRU caching, and when all accesses are special, i.e. MRU caching), the optimal use, and everything in between. In a sense, the proof subsumes the individual conclusions for LRU, MRU, and OPT [23].

We prove that for any sequence of LRU and MRU accesses, the bipartite cache obeys the inclusion principle.

LEMMA 1. *If the bottom element in the bipartite cache stack is last accessed by a normal LRU access, then all elements in cache are last accessed by normal LRU accesses.*

The Lemma 1 follows from the fact that MRU data are placed at the bottom of the stack and only replaced by LRU data (never pushed up except by other MRU data). There is a formal proof of Lemma 1 in our workshop paper [17]. Next we prove the inclusion property.

THEOREM 1. *A trace P is being executed on two bipartite caches of sizes $|C_1|$ and $|C_2|$ ($|C_1| < |C_2|$). At every access, the content of cache C_1 is always a subset of the content of cache C_2.*

Proof Let the access trace be $P = (x_1, x_2, ..., x_n)$. Let $C_1(x_t)$ and $C_2(x_t)$ be the set of elements in cache C_1 and C_2 after access x_t. The initial cache contents are $C_1(0) = C_2(0) = \emptyset$. The inclusion property holds. We now prove the theorem by induction on t.

Assume $C_1(x_t) \subseteq C_2(x_t)$ ($1 \le t \le n - 1$). It is easy to see that if x_{t+1} is a hit in C_2 ($x_{t+1} \in C_2(x_t)$), the inclusion property holds. We now consider the case that x_{t+1} is a miss in C_2. Since C_1 is included in C_2, x_{t+1} is also a miss in C_1.

Let the evicted elements be last accessed at x_p in C_1 and x_q in C_2. After the cache miss, we have $C_1(x_{t+1}) = C_1(x_t) - x_p + x_{t+1}$ and $C_2(x_{t+1}) = C_2(x_t) - x_q + x_{t+1}$. Since $C_1(x_t) \subseteq C_2(x_t)$, the only possibility for $C_1(x_{t+1}) \not\subseteq C_2(x_{t+1})$ is that C_2 evicts x_q, and C_1 has x_q but does not evict it, so $x_q \in C_1(x_{t+1})$ but $x_q \notin C_2(x_{t+1})$.

First we assume x_p exists (a cache miss does not mean a cache eviction—see the next case). The eviction in C_1 happens at the LRU position regardless whether x_p is a LRU or MRU access. x_p is at the bottom in C_1 before access x_{t+1}. At the same time, x_q is at the bottom in C_2. To violate the inclusion property, we must have $x_q \in C_1(x_t)$ in a position over x_p. From the inductive assumption, $x_p \in C_2(x_t)$ and it is in a position over x_q. Therefore, both C_1 and C_2 contain x_p and x_q but in an opposite order.

The two accesses, x_p and x_q, may be LRU or MRU accesses. There are four cases:

I x_p and x_q are both LRU accesses. Because x_q is at a higher position than x_p in C_1, we have $p < q$. Similar reasoning from C_2 requires $q < p$, which makes this case impossible.

II x_p is normal, and x_q is a MRU access. Using Lemma 1 on C_1, we see that this case is impossible—x_q has to be normal because it resides over a normal access x_p in C_1.

45

III x_p is a MRU access, and x_q is normal. Using Lemma 1 on C_2, we see that this case is impossible—x_p has to be normal because it resides over a normal access x_q in C_2.

IV x_p and x_q are both MRU accesses. Because x_q is at a higher position than x_p in C_1, we have $p > q$. Similar reasoning from C_2 requires $q > p$, which makes the last case impossible.

There is no eviction in C_1 if the bottom cache line is unoccupied when x_{t+1} is accessed. x_q is at the bottom of C_2. Regardless of whether x_q is LRU or MRU, C_2 is filled. Since $|C_2| > |C_1|$, there must have been enough data access to fill C_1, making it impossible for its bottom spot to remain unoccupied. Hence, by induction, the inclusion property holds for every access in the trace. ■

The inclusion property holds for any access trace with mixed LRU and MRU accesses, regardless how these two types of accesses are interleaved.

3.3 The LRU-MRU Stack Distance

The inclusion property implies the existence of the LRU-MRU stack distance. An access has a distance k if it is a cache hit in caches of sizes k and up and a miss in caches of size $k-1$ and down. Given a program trace with mixed LRU-MRU accesses, Algorithm 1 computes the stack distance for each access. Effectively the algorithm simulates LRU-MRU caches of *all* sizes—top C elements in the priority list are always the content of a cache with size C. We call the algorithm *bi-sim* in short for bipartite cache simulation.

Algorithm 1 Bi-sim: computing the stack distance of bipartite cache

---

Require: x is accessed at time t with flag $f = \{LRU, MRU\}$. The cache is organized as a priority list, with data d_i and priority p_i, $i = 1, \ldots, M$. No two priorities are the same, i.e. $\forall i$ and j, $p_i \neq p_j$ if $i \neq j$. The list may not have been sorted.

Ensure: It returns the LRU-MRU stack distance and updates the priority p_x of x (first adding it to the priority list if it was not included). The priority p_x is unique.

```
1:  if f = LRU then
2:      p_x = t
3:  else
4:      p_x = -t
5:  end if
6:  /* process x */
7:  if x ∉ {d_i : i = 1, . . . , M} then
8:      /* x is a miss */
9:      for i = 1; i < M; i++ do
10:         if p_i < p_{i+1} then
11:             swap d_i and d_{i+1}
12:         end if
13:     end for
14:     /* d_m is the bottom of the cache */
15:     if p_M < 0 then
16:         remove d_M from the list
17:     end if
18:     insert x at the front of the list
19:     return ∞
20: else
21:     /* x is a hit */
22:     find out d_k = x
23:     for i = 1; i < k; i++ do
24:         if p_i < p_{i+1} then
25:             swap d_i and d_{i+1}
26:         end if
27:     end for
28:     move x to the front of the list
29:     return k
30: end if
```

For access x at time t, Algorithm 1 computes the stack distance and updates the priority list. The algorithm has three parts:

- The first part, lines 1 to 5, sets the priority for x to be t or $-t$ depending on whether x is LRU or MRU. The purpose is to handle mixed priority. By negating t, the priority of MRU data is reverse to the access order. The MRU in the access order becomes LRU in the priority order. In addition, the negative priority means that all MRU data has a lower priority than every LRU data. Finally, all priority numbers remain distinct. As a result, all data in the cache are prioritized with no ties.

- The second part, lines 9 to 19, handles cache replacement at a miss when x is not in the priority list. The element with the lowest priority is shifted down to the bottom. It is removed if its priority is negative (an MRU datum). x is inserted to become the new head of the list.

- The third part, lines 22 to 29, handles a hit at location k, that is, $d_k = x$. The element of the lowest priority in $d_1, \ldots, d_k$ is shifted down to replace d_k. x is added to the front of the list as in the second part.

The update process, swapping and then insertion, is similar to Mattson et el. [23] but with two notable qualities. First, the priority list of bi-sim is not completely sorted, and the victim may or may not be d_M or d_k. In comparison, the priority list in LRU simulation is always totally sorted, and the victim can always be found at d_M or d_k. Second, bi-sim may remove an element from the priority list (line 16), even if it is simulating cache of an infinite size. The stack simulation of previous caching methods such as LRU and OPT never removes elements (when simulating for all cache sizes).

An example An example depicting bi-sim in action is given in Table 1. The access trace and the access types are listed in the second and third columns. The priority list (after each access) is shown in the next column. The last column is the stack distance returned by Algorithm 1: ∞ always means a miss, and k means a cache hit if cache size $C \geq k$ and a miss otherwise. The priority lists in the table show only the priority numbers p_x. A reader can find the datum from the p_xth row of the table (the p_xth access in the trace).

The example shows two notable characteristics of the bi-sim algorithm. The priority list is not completely sorted because of the negative priority numbers of MRU accesses. An MRU element may be removed from cache even when there is space, as happened at access 2. These are necessary to measure the miss ratios of all cache sizes in a single pass.

The cost and its reduction The asymptotic cost of Algorithm 1 is $O(M)$ in time and space for each access, where M is the number of distinct data elements in the input trace. The main time overhead comes from the two swap loops at lines 9-13 and 23-27. To improve performance, we divide the priority list into partially sorted groups. For example, there are 4 windows at the 25th access in the example in Table 1: [25], [21, -22], [19, -22,-23], and [16,13,10, 0] [1]. The swap loops are charged to iterate over the groups. The minimal element of a group is simply the last element. Grouping in priority lists was first invented by Sugumar and Abraham for simulating OPT [30]. A difference between OPT and bi-sim is that the accessed datum can be in the middle of a group in bi-sim. For OPT, the accessed datum always stays at the front of a group.

3.4 The Equivalence Proof

So far we have presented the bipartite cache and its simulation. We now show that the simulation algorithm is correct, that is, the

---

[1] For convenience, the top element is always put into a separate window.

access no.	the access trace	LRU?	the priority list (top → bottom)										stack distance
0	h	y	0										∞
1	f	n	-1	0									∞
2	i	y	2	0									∞
3	i	n	-3	0									1
4	c	y	4	0									∞
5	b	y	5	4	0								∞
6	b	n	-6	4	0								1
7	e	n	-7	4	0								∞
8	d	n	-8	4	0								∞
9	b	y	9	4	0								∞
10	g	y	10	9	4	0							∞
11	b	y	11	10	4	0							2
12	e	y	12	11	10	4	0						∞
13	d	y	13	12	11	10	4	0					∞
14	a	y	14	13	12	11	10	4	0				∞
15	c	y	15	14	13	12	11	10	0				6
16	e	y	16	15	14	13	11	10	0				4
17	a	y	17	16	15	13	11	10	0				3
18	c	y	18	17	16	13	11	10	0				3
19	i	y	19	18	17	16	13	11	10	0			∞
20	f	y	20	19	18	17	16	13	11	10	0		∞
21	b	y	21	20	19	18	17	16	13	10	0		7
22	a	n	-22	21	20	19	18	16	13	10	0		5
23	f	n	-23	21	-22	19	18	16	13	10	0		3
24	c	n	-24	21	-22	19	-23	16	13	10	0		5
25	c	y	25	21	-22	19	-23	16	13	10	0		1
26	e	n	-26	25	21	19	-22	-23	13	10	0		6
27	i	n	-27	25	21	-26	-22	-23	13	10	0		4
28	c	y	28	-27	21	-26	-22	-23	13	10	0		2
29	f	y	29	28	21	-26	-22	-27	13	10	0		6

Table 1. Example one-pass simulation of bipartite cache

elements of the priority list $d_1, d_2, \ldots, d_C$ in the algorithm are indeed the content of the LRU-MRU cache of size C. We show the equivalence in two steps. First, we show that the algorithm observes the inclusion property. Then we show that the two are equivalent at each cache size.

Proving the inclusion property is easier for the algorithm than for bipartite cache because we can use its algorithmic design directly. We first define a property in cache replacement. Let two caches of size $s, s + 1$ be C_s, C_{s+1}. Assume that C_s, C_{s+1} are filled with data, and z is the element in C_{s+1} but not in C_s. At a cache miss, C_s evicts element y_s, and C_{s+1} evicts y_{s+1}. The *eviction invariance* is a property that requires

$$y_{s+1} = y_s \lor y_{s+1} = z$$

Mattson et al. [23] showed the following result:

LEMMA 2. *Eviction invariance is a necessary and sufficient condition for maintaining the inclusion property.*

Proof First, we show the necessity. If $y_{s+1} \neq y_s \land y_{s+1} \neq z$, y_{s+1} must be in C_s. Its eviction would mean that $C_s \not\subseteq C_{s+1}$ and would break the inclusion property. The property is also sufficient. At each eviction, if $y_{s+1} = y_s$, we have $C_{s+1} = C_s + z$; otherwise, we have $y_{s+1} = z$ and $C_{s+1} = C_s + y_s$. In both cases, $C_s \subseteq C_{s+1}$. ∎

The simulation algorithm observes the eviction invariance. The "stack" is embodied in a priority list. Each element has a numerical priority distinct from others. Therefore, the caches it simulates have the inclusion property.

LEMMA 3. *Algorithm 1 observes the eviction invariance and is therefore a stack algorithm.*

Proof Algorithm 1 identifies a victim for replacement using one of the two swap loops at lines 9-13 and 23-27. Consider two caches C_s, C_{s+1} of sizes $s, s + 1$. Let z be the element in C_{s+1} but not in C_s. Let y be the element in C_s that has the lowest priority. When a cache replacement is needed in C_{s+1}, the swap loops would choose as the victim y if $p_y < p_z$ and z otherwise. The eviction invariance is therefore observed. ∎

Intuitively, the simulation is a stack algorithm because the simulated caches of all sizes share a single priority list. It is obvious that sharing a priority list implies eviction invariance. Next we show that Algorithm 1 computes the right stack distance. First we have the following lemma. We omit the proof, which is straightforward based on the handling of LRU and MRU accesses.

LEMMA 4. *At a miss in bipartite cache, the victim is always the data with the lowest priority.*

THEOREM 2. *Given an execution on bipartite cache of size C, an access is a cache hit if and only if the stack distance returned by Algorithm 1 is no greater than C.*

Proof The case for infinite distances is easy to verify, we only prove the case when the distance is of a finite value. Specifically, Algorithm 1 always stores the data in the priority list such that a cache of size C would contain and only contain the first C elements in the list, $d_1, d_2, \cdots, d_C$. This is equivalent to showing that for each data d_i, we have $d_i \in C_i$ and $d_i \notin C_{i-1}$, where $i > 0$ and C_i, C_{i-1} are the sets of data in caches of sizes $i, i - 1$ respectively.

Let the memory trace be $(x_1, x_2, \cdots, x_n)$. We prove by induction on x_j.

47

I After accessing x_1, x_1 becomes d_1 in the priority list. The base case holds since $d_1 \in C_1$ and $d_1 \notin C_0$.

II Assume the theorem holds after accessing x_j $(1 \leq j \leq n-1)$. Let the element at position d_i be d_i^j and the content of caches of size $i-1, i$ be C_{i-1}^j, C_i^j. From the inductive hypothesis, we have $d_i^j \in C_i^j$ and $d_i^j \notin C_{i-1}^j$. There are two cases after accessing x_{j+1}:

(a) x_{j+1} is a (compulsory) miss. Each element of the priority list is updated from d_i^j to d_i^{j+1} $(1 \leq i \leq M$ or $1 \leq i \leq M+1)$.

  i. $d_1^{j+1} = x_{j+1}$ and satisfies $d_1^{j+1} \in C_1^{j+1}$ and $d_1^{j+1} \notin C_0^{j+1}$.

  ii. For d_i^{j+1} $(2 \leq i \leq M)$, the swap loop (lines 9 to 13) moves the datum d_h^j $(1 \leq h \leq i)$ with the lowest priority in C_i^j out of the priority list. According to Lemma 4, after evicting d_h from C_i^j, the top i elements in the priority list are still in C_i^{j+1}, so $d_i^{j+1} \in C_i^{j+1}$. In the same way, we can show that d_i^{j+1} is either d_i^j or the victim (of C_{i-1}^j), so $d_i^{j+1} \notin C_{i-1}^{j+1}$.

  iii. If d_M^j has a positive priority, d_{M+1}^{j+1} is at the new bottom and must be the victim of C_i^j, so $d_{M+1}^{j+1} \notin C_M^{j+1}$. $d_{M+1}^{j+1} \in C_{M+1}^{j+1}$ follows from Lemma 1.

  iv. If d_M^j has a negative priority, the stack distance would be infinite. It is a miss in all finite-size bipartite cache.

(b) x_{j+1} is a hit. Let the hit location be $d_k^j = x_{j+1}$. Each element of the priority list is updated from d_i^j to d_i^{j+1} $(1 \leq i \leq M)$.

  i. Consider d_i^{j+1} $(1 \leq i \leq k-1)$. The access is a miss in caches $C_1^j, \cdots, C_{k-1}^j$, so the inference of the (previous) miss case can be reused here. The swap loop in lines 23 to 27 is identical to the swap loop in lines 9 to 13.

  ii. Consider d_k^{j+1}. Since $C_k^j = C_k^{j+1}$, we have $d_k^{j+1} \in C_k^{j+1}$. From the inference of the miss case, $d_k^{j+1} \notin C_{k-1}^{j+1}$.

  iii. Finally consider d_i^{j+1} $(k+1 \leq i \leq M)$, $d_i^{j+1} = d_i^j$ since there is no change made by the algorithm. From $x_{j+1} = d_k^j \in C_k^j$, we have x_{j+1} is a cache hit in C_i^j $(i \geq k+1)$ and $C_i^j = C_i^{j+1}$ $(k+1 \leq i \leq M)$. From the induction assumption, we have $d_i^{j+1} \in C_i^{j+1}$ and $d_i^{j+1} \notin C_{i-1}^{j+1}$ $(k+1 \leq i \leq M)$.

For all accesses, the cache of size C would contain and only contain the first C elements in the priority list, $d_1, d_2, \cdots, d_C$. Hence the relation is established between the stack distance and the cache hit/miss as stated in the theorem. ∎

4. Potential of Collaborative Caching

PACMAN uses OPT training analysis to select MRU memory references in a program. We first show a simple design and then use it to evaluate the potential benefit of collaborative caching.

4.1 PACMAN Design

PACMAN is a feedback-based compiler technique. As a study of the performance potential rather than a practical solution, we analyze one execution of a target program on bipartite cache of one size. The first step is OPT training, which uses an efficient OPT implementation to identify MRU accesses at the trace level and the program instructions that make these accesses. When an eviction happens in the OPT simulation, the most recent access to the victim is MRU [17]. After training, each reference in program code has a

unique indicator values—the *MRU ratio*. An MRU ratio of y means that y fraction of its accesses were selected as MRU in the optimal solution. We use a simple heuristic to select MRU references: a reference is MRU if at least half of its accesses were MRU in the training run.

Once a reference is selected, all its accesses in execution will be MRU. This is most likely suboptimal. For example, if the MRU ratio of a reference is 50%, the reference will be selected and half of the accesses will be issued as MRU while they should be normal (LRU) accesses. Other heuristics may be used. Regardless of the selection method, bipartite cache will always observe the inclusion property as we have shown.

4.2 Experimental Setup

The PACMAN tool is implemented as follows. We use the gold plugin of LLVM 2.8 [1] with -O4 option to generate executables. To collect memory accesses, a profiling pass is added at the end of the link-time optimization (LTO) passes. The OPT cache simulation uses the OPT* algorithm presented in [17]. The same profiling pass is used to measure the performance of LRU and OPT caches using the fastest analyzers available [30, 37].

We examined the floating-point code in three benchmark suites—SciMark 2.0, SPEC 2000, and SPEC 2006 [2–4]—and selected those for which we can reduce the input size so the numbers of accesses are in tens of millions. We increased the number of time steps in SOR to reduce the effect of its initialization code. As mentioned earlier, as a feasibility study, we use the same input size and cache size in training and in testing. We will relax these two restrictions later.

The ten test programs are listed in Table 2. As the table shows, the programs have between 51 to 37,313 lines of C/Fortran code. There are between 12 to 10,746 static references in the programs. The length of their executions is between 100 and 800 million accesses.

We simulate fully associative bipartite cache with 8-byte cache blocks. An actual cache is always set associative, but the set associativity on modern systems is high: 4-way L1D, 10-way L2, and 12-way L3 on IBM Power 5; 8-way L1D and L2 and 16-way L3 on Intel Nehalem; and 4-way L1D and 16-way L2 on Niagara II. Hill and Smith showed that for sequential code, 8-way associative cache incurs about 5% more misses than fully-associative cache, consistently across cache sizes and cache block sizes [18]. We use fully-associative cache, so the results represent the effect of set-associative cache without being specific to particular cache parameters. As a limit study, we use 8-byte cache-line size to exclude the effect of cache spatial reuse, which depends on data layout in addition to cache management. The OPT result is the best possible (but possibly not realizable) for all data layouts.

4.3 The LRU-OPT Gap

Let $miss_{LRU}(C), miss_{OPT}(C)$ be the number of cache misses incurred by LRU and OPT cache of size C. We define the LRU-OPT gap as:

$$gap(C) = \frac{miss_{LRU}(C) - miss_{OPT}(C)}{miss_{LRU}(C)}$$

The gap is between 0 and 100%. We have simulated the LRU-OPT gap for the ten test programs for cache sizes from 1KB up to program data size (before all misses are cold-start misses). The results are summarized in Table 3.

The 2nd column of the table shows the average LRU-OPT gap for all measured cache sizes. The highest average gaps are 34% in *lucas* and 31% in *mgrid* and *milc*. The first two have hierarchical computations. The least gaps are 12% in *zeusmp* and 17% in *applu*. Both are computational fluid dynamics simulation

workload name	benchmark suite	programming language	#lines of source code	#memory references	#run-time accesses
SOR	SciMark 2.0	C	51	12	1.07E+7
171.swim	CPU2000	Fortran	435	307	1.02E+7
172.mgrid	CPU2000	Fortran	489	451	4.13E+7
173.applu	CPU2000	Fortran	3980	2515	1.50E+7
183.equake	CPU2000	C	1513	853	8.12E+7
189.lucas	CPU2000	Fortran	2999	1419	4.26E+7
410.bwaves	CPU2006	Fortran	918	755	5.30E+7
433.milc	CPU2006	C	15042	4163	8.43E+7
434.zeusmp	CPU2006	Fortran	37313	10746	3.75E+7
437.leslie3d	CPU2006	Fortran	3807	4403	3.80E+7

Table 2. The ten test programs

	the OPT imprv. over LRU		the PACMAN imprv. over LRU	
	average	largest	average	largest
SOR	25%	91%	15%	91%
171.swim	19%	64%	12%	59%
172.mgrid	31%	60%	13%	46%
173.applu	17%	50%	8.2%	19%
183.equake	22%	54%	17%	54%
189.lucas	34%	67%	26%	64%
410.bwaves	25%	80%	12%	60%
433.milc	31%	62%	8.8%	22%
434.zeusmp	12%	79%	1.4%	3.9%
437.leslie3d	27%	50%	10%	29%
average	24%	66%	12%	45%

Table 3. The LRU-OPT gap and the PACMAN improvement. The average improvement is the arithmetic mean of the improvement for all cache sizes between 1KB and data size.

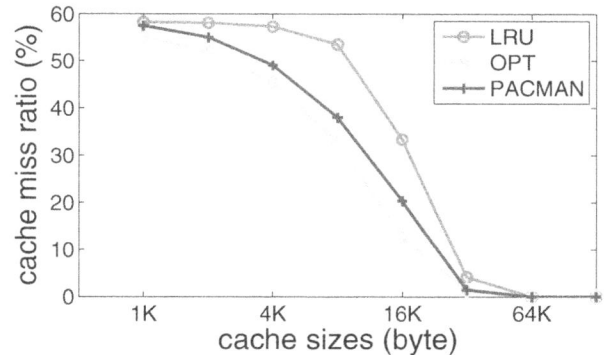

Figure 5. The miss curves of 189.lucas on fully-associative caches

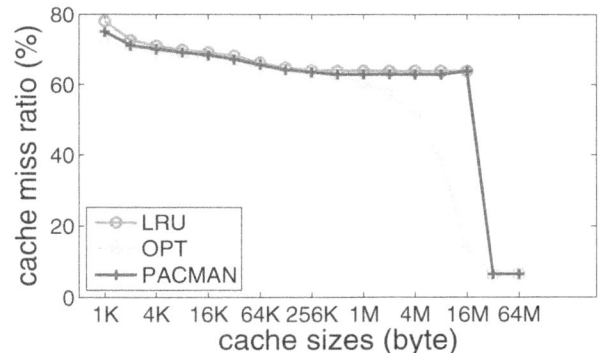

Figure 6. The miss curves of 434.zeusmp on fully-associative caches

programs. Across all ten programs, OPT incurs on average 24% fewer misses than LRU does on every cache size.

The improvement from LRU to OPT is not uniform. The gap can be much larger at some cache sizes. The 3rd column of the table shows that the best improvement is between 50% and 91% in all programs. In other words, for every program there is a cache size for which at least half of the misses in LRU cache can be eliminated by optimal caching. These results show a significant potential for improving cache utilization.

4.4 The Improvement by PACMAN

Let $miss_{PACMAN}(C)$ be the number of cache misses incurred by a program after the PACMAN transformation. We define the PACMAN improvement as:

$$\frac{miss_{LRU}(C) - miss_{PACMAN}(C)}{miss_{LRU}(C)}$$

The improvement may be negative if the number of misses is increased by PACMAN. We have measured the improvement for the ten test programs for all cache sizes from 1KB to the program data size. The results are in Table 3.

The 4th column of the table shows the average improvement for each program by PACMAN. Seven programs, *SOR*, *lucas*, *equake*, *mgrid*, *swim*, *bwaves*, and *leslie3d*, show 10% or more average improvements across all cache sizes. Two programs, *milc* and *applu*, show near 8% average improvements. The remaining one, *zeusmp*, does not show a significant improvement (1.4%).

The effect of PACMAN can be plotted for all cache sizes using a miss ratio curve. In this section, we show the plots first for *lucas* and *zeusmp*, which have the most and the least improvement in our test set by PACMAN; and then for *SOR*, *swim*, and *applu* to show

the effects of data size, MRU ratio threshold, and cache line size. The same type graphs for the other 5 programs are included in the appendix.

Three miss ratio curves are shown in Figure 5 for *lucas* when executed with LRU caching, OPT caching, and collaborative caching. The differences between LRU and OPT curves show a large potential for improvement, on average 34% and up to 67%. The collaborative caching by PACMAN realizes over two-thirds of the potential, reducing the miss ratio by 26% on average and up to 64% in 32KB size cache.

The miss ratio curves of *zeusmp* are shown in Figure 6. There is a significant room for improvement over LRU, 12% on average and up to 79%. While PACMAN reduces the miss ratio for almost all cache sizes, the reduction is very small (1.4% on average).

The PACMAN performance for other programs is somewhere between *lucas* and *zeusmp*, as shown by the summary in Table 3. On average, PACMAN reduces the miss ratio by 12% for each program and each cache size. Optimal caching reduces the miss ratio by 24% on average. Hence, under idealized conditions used in this study, PACMAN realizes one half of the improvement potential of optimal caching.

4.5 The Effect of Program Input

So far we train and test PACMAN on the same input. A comprehensive study on the effect of input is outside the scope of this paper (our concern here is mainly the theoretical properties and the potential). But we show that for at least one program, PACMAN shows similar improvment with different input sizes. In *swim*, the matrix size determines the program data size. We compare the results of the matrix sizes 128×128 and 256×256.

The miss ratio curves of the two executions of *swim* are shown in Figure 7. The PACMAN curve has an identical shape in both graphs, showing identical improvements over LRU. But because of the difference in input size, the improvements happen for different cache sizes—4KB, 8KB, 512KB, and 1MB for the smaller input and 8KB, 16KB, 2MB, and 4MB for the larger input. An LRU curve shows the size of working sets in an execution. Comparing the two LRU curves, we can see two working sets in this program. The first working set doubles in size in the larger input, and the second working set quadruples in size. PACMAN improves the two working sets by the same degree regardless of the input size.

4.6 The Impact of the MRU Ratio Threshold

Currently PACMAN sets the MRU ratio threshold to 50%. A program reference is designated as MRU if 50% of its run-time accesses are MRU in the optimal solution. The benefit of PACMAN depends on the choice of the threshold. Figure 9 shows one example, *173.applu* on a 512KB cache, for which different threshold values have a significant effect on performance. When the threshold is 0, all memory references become MRU. The miss ratio jumps to 99%. When the threshold is 100%, only memory references without LRU accesses are selected as MRU. The effect on this program is very close to LRU. When the threshold is 50%, the improvement over LRU is 4.6% (shown for all cache sizes in Figure 8). By choosing the threshold 30% or 35%, the miss ratio is further reduced to 20%. This suggests a higher potential if PACMAN can properly use different threshold values for different programs.

4.7 A Closer Look at SOR

All the previous evaluations are based on 8-byte cache line size for limit study. However, real cache systems usually use much larger cache line size such as 64-byte. We change to use 64-byte cache line size to make a more realistic test with SOR.

Figure 10 shows the SSA-form [13] of the SOR loop kernel (for original code see Figure 2). The loop indexes into array G to create three virtual arrays $Gi, Gim1, Gip1$ for use in the innermost loop.

The innermost loop has 4 array references. The MRU ratio changes with cache sizes, as shown by Figure 11 as a curve for each reference. The ratio for $Gim1[j]$ is clearly higher than the other three. For cache size between 8KB and 512KB, the MRU ratio is from over 12.5% to 63% for $Gim1[j]$ but near 0 for the other three. PACMAN chooses this reference as an MRU reference.

The MRU ratio is a factor of 8 lower because of spatial reuse. To separate the last touch of a cache block, we transform line 9 to an if-else block (line 9.1 to 9.5) in Figure 10. In actual implementation, we use loop unrolling instead of branching. In LLVM, we adapt the available loop unrolling pass and put it at the end of the LTO passes

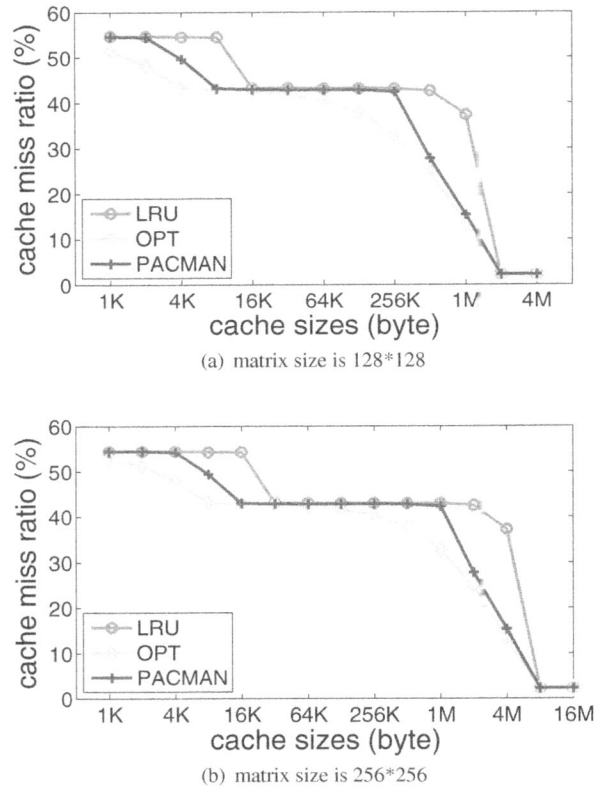

(a) matrix size is 128*128

(b) matrix size is 256*256

Figure 7. The miss curves of 171.swim on two different inputs. The curves have an identical shape but cover different cache-size ranges: between 1KB and 4MB in the upper graph and between 1KB and 16MB in the lower graph.

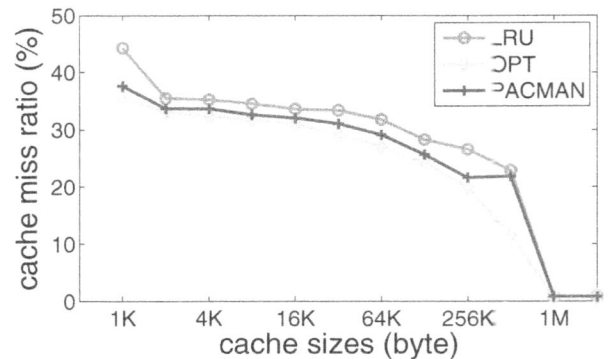

Figure 8. The miss curves of 173.applu on fully-associative caches

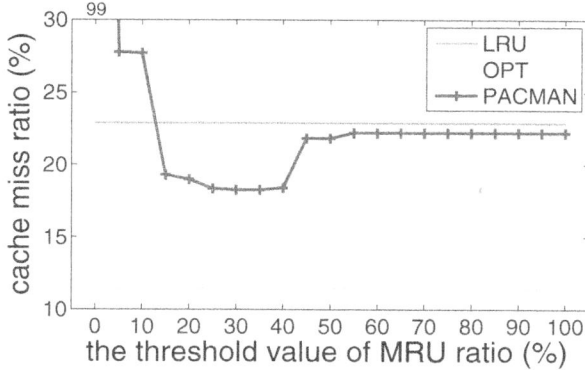

Figure 9. The impact of the MRU ratio threshold for 173.applu at 512KB

Require: G is a 2-dimensional double array with the size M*N
```
 1:  for p = 1; p < NUM_STEPS; p++ do
 2:    for i = 1; i < M-1; i++ do
 3:      Gi = G[i];
 4:      Gim1 = G[i-1];
 5:      Gip1 = G[i+1];
 6:      Gijm1 = Gi[0];
 7:      Gij = Gi[1];
 8:      for j = 1; j < N-1; j++ do
 9:        Gim1j = Gim1[j];      ⟹    9.1: if j%8 == 7 then
10:        Gip1j = Gip1[j];             9.2:   Gim1j =
11:        Gijp1 = Gi[j+1];                       MRU_load(Gim1[j]);
12:        tmp1 = Gim1j + Gip1j;        9.3: else
13:        tmp1 += Gijm1;               9.4:   Gim1j = Gim1[j];
14:        tmp1 += Gijp1;               9.5: end if
15:        tmp1 *= 0.3125;
16:        tmp2 = -0.25 * Gij;
17:        tmp1 += tmp2;
18:        Gi[j] = tmp1;
19:        Gijm1 = tmp1;
20:        Gij = Gijp1;
21:      end for
22:    end for
23:  end for
```

Figure 10. The SOR kernel loop in SSA form with PACMAN transformation. M = N = 512 and NUM_STEPS = 10.

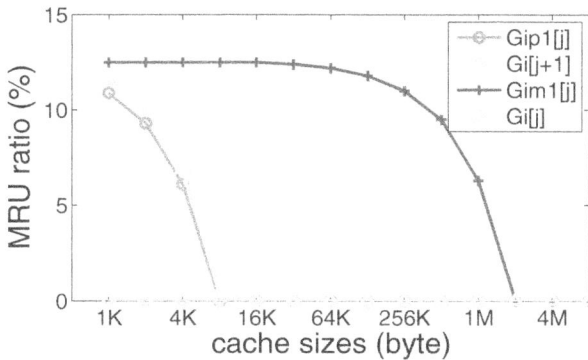

Figure 11. The MRU ratio curves of SOR on fully-associative caches with cache line size 64B

but before the profiling pass. We also change to use `memalign()`

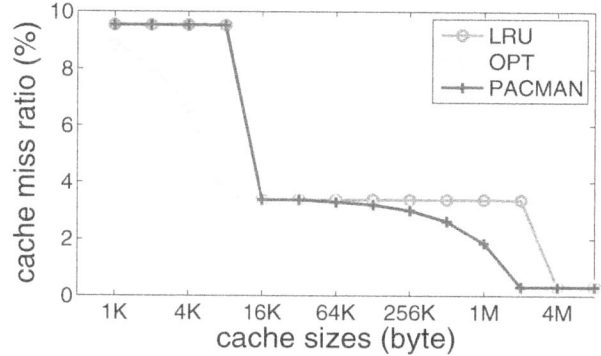

Figure 12. The miss curves of SOR on fully-associative caches with cache line size 64B

instead of `malloc()` to make array G 64-byte aligned. After loop unrolling, the load in line 9.2 has an MRU ratio of 75% at 512KB.

The miss ratio curves of Figure 12 show that PACMAN produces almost identical results as OPT for cache sizes over 64KB (up to 2MB). The improvements are significant—2.3%, 5.2%, 10.8%, 22.2%, 44.9%, and 90.7% respectively between 64KB to 2MB. The average improvement is 15%, as reported in Table 3. It is worth mentioning that at cache size 2MB, OPT training found 704 MRU accesses out of more than ten million accesses. These MRU accesses reduced the miss ratio by an order of magnitude from 3.3% to 0.3%.

5. Related Work

Cache hints The ISA of Intel Itanium extends the interface of the memory instruction to provide source and target hints [5]. The source hint suggests where data is expected, and the target hint suggests which level cache the data should be kept. The target hint changes the cache replacement decisions in hardware. IBM Power processors support bypass memory access that do not keep the accessed data in cache [27]. Wang et al. proposed an interface to tag cache data with evict-me bits [31]. Recently, Ding et al. developed ULCC which uses page coloring to partition cache to separately store high locality and low locality data [15]. It may be used to approximate LRU-MRU cache management in software on existing machines. The bipartite cache interface in this paper can imitate the effect of the target hints, cache bypasses, and evict-me bits. Consequently, the theoretical properties such as the inclusion principle and bipartite stack distance are valid for these existing designs of collaborative cache.

Collaborative caching Collaborative caching was pioneered by Wang et al. [31] and Beyls and D'Hollander [8, 9]. The studies were based on a common idea, which is to evict data whose forward reuse distance is larger than the cache size. Wang et al. used compiler analysis to identify self and group reuse in loops [24, 31, 32] and select array references to tag with the evict-me bit. They showed that collaborative caching can be combined with prefetching to further improve performance.

Beyls and D'Hollander used profiling analysis to measure the reuse distance distribution for each program reference. They added cache hint specifiers on Intel Itanium and improved average performance by 10% for scientific code and 4% for integer code [8]. Profiling analysis is input specific. Fang et al. showed a technique that accurately predicts how the reuse distances of a memory reference change across inputs [16]. Beyls and D'Hollander later developed static analysis called reuse-distance equations and obtained similar improvements without profiling [9]. Compiler analysis of reuse distance was also studied by Cascaval and Padua for scientific code [10] and Chauhan and Shei for Matlab programs [11].

In this paper, we show the theoretical potential of collaborative caching. With bipartite cache, these techniques may be extended to achieve optimal cache performance. OPT analysis is a possible extension. It is more precise. Recall an example in Section 4.7 where a few hundred MRU accesses can reduce the miss ratio of a ten-million long trace by an order of magnitude. Such OPT training can be used to evaluate and improve compiler and profiling-based techniques.

Virtual machine, operating system and hardware memory management   Garbage collectors may benefit from the knowledge of application working set size and the affinity between memory objects. For LRU cache, reuse distance has been used by virtual machine systems to estimate the working set size [34] and to group simultaneously used objects [36]. There have been much research in operating systems to improve beyond LRU. A number of techniques used last reuse distance instead of last access time in virtual memory management [12,28,38] and file caching [19]. The idea of evicting dead data early has been extensively studied in hardware cache design, including deadblock predictor [22], adaptive cache insertion [26], less reuse filter [33], virtual victim cache [21], and globalized placement [35].

Hardware based techniques improve memory and cache performance without changing software. On the flip side, they do not allow software to communicate information about its data usage. This communication is the goal of collaborative cache. We believe the idea is also interesting for heap and virtual memory management. A basic problem in collaborative systems is that the interface may be misused. We have shown the theoretical properties of this interface under all uses. Particularly important for software is that the LRU-MRU stack distance exists and may be used to estimate the working set size and reference affinity in collaborative cache as reuse distance has been used for conventional cache.

Optimal caching   Optimal caching is difficult purely at the program level. Kennedy and McKinley [20] and Ding and Kennedy [14] showed that optimal loop fusion is NP hard. Petrank and Rawitz showed that given the order of data access and cache management, the problem of optimal data layout is intractable unless P=NP [25]. Our earlier workshop paper showed that collaborative caching can be used to obtain optimal cache performance [17]. It described two extensions to LRU called bypass LRU and trespass LRU and gave an counter example showing bypass LRU does not observe the inclusion principle. The paper gave an efficient algorithm for simulating OPT cache replacement, which we use in this paper for PACMAN training analysis. The previous study assumed that a program could be optimally transformed. In this paper, we study the properties of collaborative caching in all uses, not just optimal uses.

6.   Summary

In this paper, we have characterized the difference between current LRU-style cache management and optimal cache management. To approximate optimal solution on real cache systems, we have formalized the interface of bipartite LRU-MRU cache and shown that it obeys the inclusion principle. We give a one-pass simulation algorithm to measure the LRU-MRU stack distance. We have measured the potential of collaborative caching using a simple algorithm based on OPT training analysis. The evaluation on 10 SciMark and SPEC CPU benchmarks show that optimal caching can reduce the miss ratio by 24% on average per program per cache size, and collaborative caching has the potential to realize 50% of the optimal performance improvement.

Acknowledgments

We wish to thank Luke K. Dalessandro for help with LLVM. We also wish to thank Tongxin Bai, Bin Bao, Arrvindh Shriraman, Xiaoya Xiang, and the anonymous reviewers for their comments and/or proofreading.

The research is supported by the National Science Foundation (Contract No. CCF-0963759, CNS- 0834566, CNS-0720796) and IBM CAS Faculty Fellowships. Any opinions, findings, and conclusions or recommendations expressed in this material are those of the authors and do not necessarily reflect the views of the funding organizations.

References

[1] The LLVM Compiler Infrastructure. http://llvm.org/.

[2] SciMark2.0. http://math.nist.gov/scimark2/

[3] SPEC CPU2000. http://www.spec.org/cpu2000.

[4] SPEC CPU2006. http://www.spec.org/cpu2006.

[5] *IA-64 Application Developer's Architecture Guide*. May 1999.

[6] L. A. Belady. A study of replacement algorithms for a virtual-storage computer. *IBM Systems Journal*, 1966.

[7] L. A. Belady, R. A. Nelson, and G. S. Shedler. An anomaly in space-time characteristics of certain programs running in a paging machine. *Communications of ACM*, 1969.

[8] K. Beyls and E. D'Hollander. Reuse distance-based cache hint selection. In *Proceedings of the 8th International Euro-Par Conference*, 2002.

[9] K. Beyls and E. D'Hollander. Generating cache hints for improved program efficiency. *Journal of Systems Architecture*, 2005.

[10] C. Cascaval and D. A. Padua. Estimating cache misses and locality using stack distances. In *International Conference on Supercomputing*, 2003.

[11] A. Chauhan and C.-Y. Shei. Static reuse distances for locality-based optimizations in MATLAB. In *International Conference on Supercomputing*, 2010.

[12] F. Chen, S. Jiang, and X. Zhang. CLOCK-Pro: an effective improvement of the CLOCK replacement. In *Proceedings of USENIX Annual Technical Conference*, 2005.

[13] R. Cytron, J. Ferrante, B. K. Rosen, M. N. Wegman, and F. K. Zadeck. Efficiently computing static single assignment form and the control dependence graph. *ACM Transactions on Programming Languages and Systems*, 1991.

[14] C. Ding and K. Kennedy. Improving effective bandwidth through compiler enhancement of global cache reuse. *Journal of Parallel and Distributed Computing*, 2004.

[15] X. Ding, K. Wang, and X. Zhang. ULCC: a user-level facility for optimizing shared cache performance on multicores. In *Proceedings of the ACM SIGPLAN Symposium on Principles and Practice of Parallel Programming*, 2011.

[16] C. Fang, S. Carr, S. Önder, and Z. Wang. Instruction based memory distance analysis and its application. In *Proceedings of the International Conference on Parallel Architecture and Compilation Techniques*, 2005.

[17] X. Gu, T. Bai, Y. Gao, C. Zhang, R. Archambault, and C. Ding. P-OPT: Program-directed optimal cache management. In *Proceedings of the Workshop on Languages and Compilers for Parallel Computing*, 2008.

[18] M. D. Hill and A. J. Smith. Evaluating associativity in CPU caches. *IEEE Transactions on Computers*, 1989.

[19] S. Jiang and X. Zhang. LIRS: an efficient low inter-reference recency set replacement to improve buffer cache performance. In *Proceedings of the International Conference on Measurement and Modeling of Computer Systems*, 2002.

[20] K. Kennedy and K. S. McKinley. Typed fusion with applications to parallel and sequential code generation. Technical Report TR93-208, Dept. of Computer Science, Rice University, 1993.

[21] S. M. Khan, D. A. Jiménez, D. Burger, and B. Falsafi. Using dead blocks as a virtual victim cache. In *Proceedings of the 19th international conference on Parallel architectures and compilation techniques*, 2010.

[22] A.-C. Lai, C. Fide, and B. Falsafi. Dead-block prediction & dead-block correlating prefetchers. In *Proceedings of the International*

Symposium on Computer Architecture, 2001.

[23] R. L. Mattson, J. Gecsei, D. Slutz, and I. L. Traiger. Evaluation techniques for storage hierarchies. *IBM System Journal*, 1970.

[24] K. S. McKinley, S. Carr, and C.-W. Tseng. Improving data locality with loop transformations. *ACM Transactions on Programming Languages and Systems*, 1996.

[25] E. Petrank and D. Rawitz. The hardness of cache conscious data placement. In *Proceedings of the ACM SIGPLAN-SIGACT Symposium on Principles of Programming Languages*, 2002.

[26] M. K. Qureshi, A. Jaleel, Y. N. Patt, S. C. S. Jr., and J. S. Emer. Adaptive insertion policies for high performance caching. In *Proceedings of the International Symposium on Computer Architecture*, 2007.

[27] B. Sinharoy, R. N. Kalla, J. M. Tendler, R. J. Eickemeyer, and J. B. Joyner. Power5 system microarchitecture. *IBM J. Res. Dev.*, 2005.

[28] Y. Smaragdakis, S. Kaplan, and P. Wilson. The EELRU adaptive replacement algorithm. *Perform. Eval.*, 2003.

[29] K. So and R. N. Rechtschaffen. Cache operations by MRU change. *IEEE Transactions on Computers*, 1988.

[30] R. A. Sugumar and S. G. Abraham. Efficient simulation of caches under optimal replacement with applications to miss characterization. In *Proceedings of the ACM SIGMETRICS Conference on Measurement & Modeling Computer Systems*, 1993.

[31] Z. Wang, K. S. McKinley, A. L.Rosenberg, and C. C. Weems. Using the compiler to improve cache replacement decisions. In *Proceedings of the International Conference on Parallel Architecture and Compilation Techniques*, 2002.

[32] M. E. Wolf and M. Lam. A data locality optimizing algorithm. In *Proceedings of the SIGPLAN '91 Conference on Programming Language Design and Implementation*, 1991.

[33] L. Xiang, T. Chen, Q. Shi, and W. Hu. Less reused filter: improving L2 cache performance via filtering less reused lines. In *Proceedings of the 23rd international conference on Supercomputing*, 2009.

[34] T. Yang, E. D. Berger, S. F. Kaplan, and J. E. B. Moss. Cramm: Virtual memory support for garbage-collected applications. In *Proceedings of the Symposium on Operating Systems Design and Implementation*, 2006.

[35] M. Zahran and S. A. McKee. Global management of cache hierarchies. In *Proceedings of the 7th ACM international conference on Computing frontiers*, 2010.

[36] C. Zhang and M. Hirzel. Online phase-adaptive data layout selection. In *Proceedings of the European Conference on Object-Oriented Programming*, 2008.

[37] Y. Zhong, X. Shen, and C. Ding. Program locality analysis using reuse distance. *ACM Transactions on Programming Languages and Systems*, 2009.

[38] P. Zhou, V. Pandey, J. Sundaresan, A. Raghuraman, Y. Zhou, and S. Kumar. Dynamic tracking of page miss ratio curve for memory management. In *Proceedings of the International Conference on Architectural Support for Programming Languages and Operating Systems*, 2004.

A. The Miss Ratio Curves of LRU, OPT, and PACMAN

Figure 13 to 17 shows the miss-ratio curves of the rest of the test programs (in addition to programs already shown in Section 4).

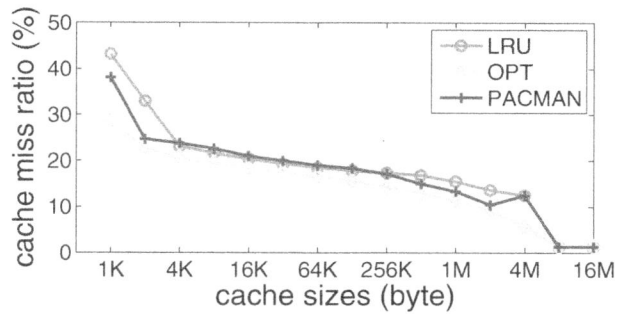

Figure 14. 183.equake

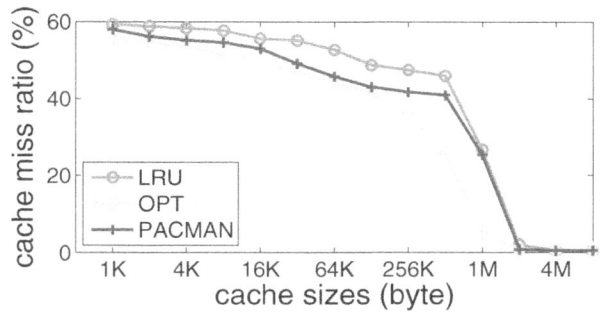

Figure 15. 410.bwaves

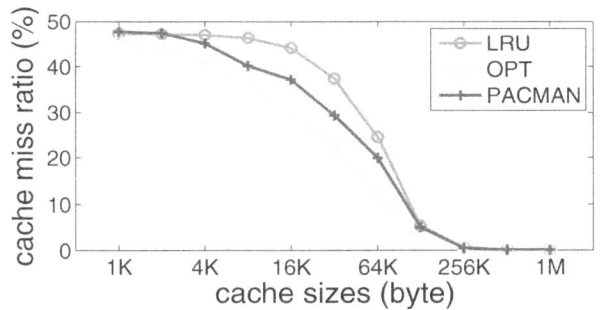

Figure 16. 433.milc

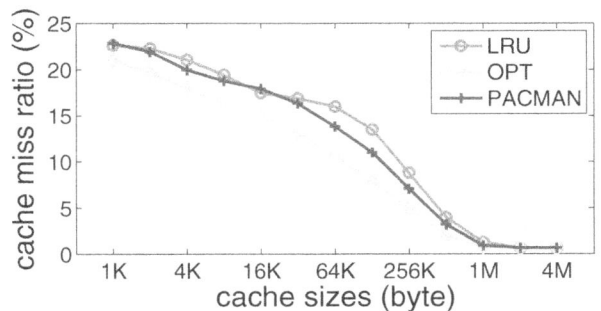

Figure 13. 172.mgrid

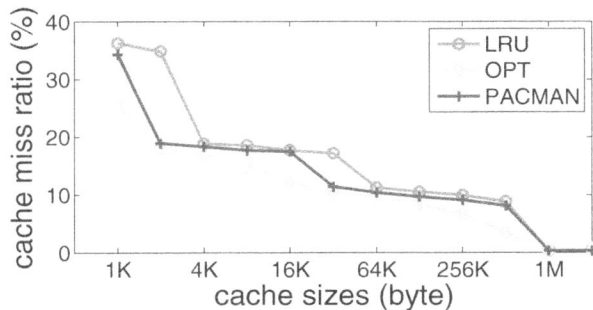

Figure 17. 437.leslie3d

Cache Index-Aware Memory Allocation

Yehuda Afek

School of Computer Science, Tel Aviv
University
afek@post.tau.ac.il

Dave Dice

SunLabs at Oracle
dave.dice@oracle.com

Adam Morrison

School of Computer Science, Tel Aviv
University
adamx@post.tau.ac.il

Abstract

Poor placement of data blocks in memory may negatively impact application performance because of an increase in the cache *conflict miss* rate [18]. For dynamically allocated structures this placement is typically determined by the memory allocator. Cache *index-oblivious* allocators may inadvertently place blocks on a restricted fraction of the available cache indexes, artificially and needlessly increasing the conflict miss rate. While some allocators are less vulnerable to this phenomena, no general-purpose `malloc` allocator is index-aware and methodologically addresses this concern. We demonstrate that many existing state-of-the-art allocators are index-oblivious, admitting performance pathologies for certain block sizes. We show that a simple adjustment within the allocator to control the spacing of blocks can provide better index coverage, which in turn reduces the superfluous conflict miss rate in various applications, improving performance with no observed negative consequences. The result is an *index-aware* allocator. Our technique is general and can easily be applied to most memory allocators and to various processor architectures.

Furthermore, we can reduce inter-thread and inter-process conflict misses for processors where threads concurrently share the level-1 cache such as the Sun UltraSPARC-T2™and Intel "Nehalem" by coloring the placement of blocks so that allocations for different threads and processes start on different cache indexes.

Categories and Subject Descriptors D.4.2 [*Operating Systems*]: Allocation/Deallocation Strategies

General Terms Performance,experiments,algorithms

Keywords Dynamic storage allocators, memory allocation, malloc, caches, shared caches, conflict misses, placement policies

1. Introduction

Modern `malloc` memory allocator designs tend to focus first on the performance of the allocator itself, often ignoring the performance of the application code that accesses blocks returned by the allocator. The design and policies of the allocator can, for instance, have a significant influence on the data TLB (translation look-aside buffer - a cache of virtual to physical page translations) and data cache miss rates of applications accessing blocks returned from that allocator. We identify key aspects of allocator performance as follows:

- **Latency** and **Scalability** of the allocator itself
- **Memory footprint** – space-efficiency
  - **Peak memory usage** - capacity and consumption of system resources
  - **Data Cache and data TLB locality and span** - reflecting the density of the set of allocated blocks as measured by the number of pages and cache lines underlying those blocks. This measure also includes wastage, fragmentation and the overheads imposed by the allocator such as block headers (metadata - if present), `malloc` size quantization and heap layout.
- Inter-block **false sharing** in concurrent environments
- **Cache line relative block address alignment** – the placement of blocks by the allocator with respect to cache line boundaries
- **Cache index placement**

Our paper focuses on the final aspect – cache index placement. In particular our concern is how blocks returned by `malloc` are distributed over the set of possible cache indices. If the distribution is imbalanced or non-uniform then repetitive access to those blocks by the application might incur excessive conflict misses, which in turn may degrade overall system performance.

As a concrete illustration of the problem consider a `malloc` allocator that maintains arrays of 128-byte blocks – inclusive of both header data (allocator metadata, if any) and the data area – that may be used to satisfy `malloc` requests of sizes suitably close to 128 bytes. These arrays are private to the allocator implementation and opaque to applications. As blocks are packed densely in the array we find blocks starting every 128 bytes. If the base of the array is B then the block addresses will be B, $B + 128$, $B + 256$, and so on. Consider a data cache with 16-byte blocks and 128 indices. Crucially, the set of level-1 data cache (L1D) indices associated with the base addresses of the blocks within such arrays is restricted to just 16 instead of the full complement of 128. That is, given the way virtual addresses map to cache indices and because of the regular consecutive spacing of the blocks in the array, blocks of that particular *size-class* (128 bytes) can start on only 16 of the 128 possible indices. If an application allocates a set of such blocks and then repeatedly accesses just a few fields in a group of blocks then it may suffer excessive conflict misses as some cache indices are "hot" and others underutilized and "cold". Conflict misses, which arise from lack of cache associativity, cause the application accessing blocks returned by interfaces such as `malloc` to underutilize the data cache, robbing the application of potential performance.

One aspect of our solution is to insert small *spacer* regions into the array of blocks to better distribute the block indices, forming a *punctuated array* and disrupting the regular ordering of block addresses. We show that this approach is both effective and simple to implement.

While we describe our techniques in terms of the implementation of a specific malloc allocator, it is general and can easily be applied in other environments such as pool allocators [24] or to the object allocators found in managed run-time environments with automatic garbage collection. Furthermore, while we explain our technique in terms of the Sun UltraSPARC-T2™processor, it carries to other architectures as well.

This paper starts with a discussion of modern malloc allocator design and show how such allocators can easily cause cache index imbalance – a poor distribution of blocks over the set of possible cache indexes. We then proceed to describe a simple solution that involves inserting *spacers* into the block arrays to provide a better distribution, yielding an index-aware allocator. We provide experimental data to support our claim. Next, we describe other varieties of index conflicts and provide insight on how they can also be easily avoided, followed by a survey of related work and conclude with a discussion of future research directions related to our topic.

2. Modern malloc allocator design

The default Solaris™libc allocator uses a single global heap protected by one mutex. Memory is allocated from the operating system by means of the sbrk system call. The global free list is organized as a splay tree [33] ordered by size and allocation requests are serviced via a best-fit policy. The heap is augmented by a small set of segregated free lists of bounded capacity, allowing many common requests to operate in constant-time. This results in an allocator with excellent heap density, reasonable single-threaded latency, but poor scalability. Furthermore, applications using the libc allocator may be subject to excessive allocator-induced false sharing, where blocks allocated to different threads happen to abut in the midst of a cache line.

Modern state-of-the-art allocators include Hoard [8], CLFMalloc [27], LFMalloc [14], libumem [9], jemalloc [16] and tcmalloc [6]. They are broadly categorized as *segregated free-list* [19] allocators as they maintain distinct free lists based on block size. Such allocators round requested allocation sizes up to the nearest *size-class* where a size-class is simply an interval of block sizes and without ambiguity we can refer to a size-class by its upper bound. The set of size-classes forms a partition on the set of possible allocation sizes. The choice of size-classes is largely arbitrary and defined at the whim of the implementor, although a step size of 1.2x between adjacent size-classes is common [8] as the worst-case internal fragmentation is constrained to 20%.

We will use Hoard as a representative example of modern allocator design. Hoard uses multiple heaps to reduce contention. Specifically, Hoard attempts to diffuse contention and improve scalability by satisfying potentially concurrent malloc requests from multiple local heaps – this strategy also mitigates the allocated-induced false sharing problem. Each heap consists of an array of references to *superblocks*, with one slot for each possible size-class. A superblock is simply an array of blocks of a certain size class. Superblocks are all the same size, a multiple of the system page size, and are allocated from the system via the mmap interface which allocates virtual address pages and associates physical pages to those addresses. Mmap is used instead of the more traditional sbrk operator as pages allocated through mmap may later be returned to the system, if desired, through munmap. The superblock is the fundamental unit of allocator for Hoard. Each superblock has a local singly-linked free list threaded through the free blocks and maintained in LIFO order to promote TLB and data cache locality. A small superblock header at the base of the array contains the head of the superblock-local free list. Superblocks and heaps are opaque to the application that uses the allocator. The Hoard implementation

places superblocks on highly aligned addresses. The free operator then uses address arithmetic – simple masking – on the block address to locate the header of the enclosing superblock, which in turn allows the operator to quickly push the block onto the superblock's free list. As such, in-use blocks do not require a header field. If a superblock becomes depleted it can be detached from a heap and moved to a global heap. The local heap can be reprovisioned from either the global heap, assuming a superblock with sufficient free space is available, or by allocating a new superblock from the system. Superblocks can circulate between various local heaps and the global heap, but will be associated with at most one local heap at any one time. Allocator metadata is minimal, consisting of the heap structures and superblock headers. The implementation associates a malloc request with a heap by hashing the identity of the current thread. To reduce collisions Hoard overprovisions the number of heaps to be twice the number of processors. Concurrency control is provided by per-heap locks.

Hoard's malloc operator first quantizes the requested size to an appropriate size-class, identifies a heap, locks the heap, locates a superblock of the appropriate size-class in that heap, unlinks a block from that superblock's free list, unlocks the heap, and finally returns the address of the block's data area. As Hoard employs segregated free lists (segregated by size), in the common case finding a free block of a given size is a simple constant-time operation. Given this allocation policy the returned addresses for a given size-class may be regular in a manner that results in *interblock cache index conflicts* and excessive conflict misses if a group of blocks of a size-class are accessed frequently by the application. More generally, array-based superblock allocators coupled with inopportune index-oblivious block sizes can easily result in patterns of block addresses that map to only a few cache indices.

Superblock-based allocators of this design allow for good scaling although their footprint is often somewhat larger than that of libc as they attempt to diffuse contention by distributing requests over multiple heaps. Latency varies but usually reflects path length through malloc and free and metadata access costs, which are properties of the implementation and not fundamental to the category of segregated free list allocators.

CLFMalloc is structurally similar to Hoard, differing mostly in the policy by which it associates malloc requests with heap instances and in that CLFMalloc is lock-free.

Libumem and tcmalloc use a central heap but diffuse contention via multiple local free lists. In the case of tcmalloc the central heap uses segregated free lists which are populated by allocating runs of pages and then splitting those pages into contiguous arrays of the desired size-class.

3. CIF : Improving index distribution – Punctuated arrays

We introduce a new index-aware segregated-free list allocator, CIF (Cache-Index Friendly), which was derived from LFMalloc. CIF and LFMalloc are structurally similar to Hoard. LFMalloc used hardware transactional memory [15] or restartable critical sections for concurrency control but for the sake of portability CIF uses simple mutual exclusion locks. CIF is easily portable and currently runs on Solaris SPARC and Linux x86 (32-bit and 64-bit).

In CIF each processor is associated with a processor-private heap. A superblock consists of a coloring region (described below), a header containing metadata and an array of blocks of the given size-class. As in Hoard the superblock header contains a pointer to the head of a LIFO free list of available blocks within that superblock. All blocks in a superblock are of the same length. Superblocks are 64KB in length.

CIF does not explicitly request *large pages* for superblocks. Large pages, if supported by the processor and operating system, can improve performance by decreasing TLB miss rates. Solaris attempts to provision mappings with large pages as a best-effort optimization. On SPARC large pages must be physically contiguous and both physically and virtually aligned to the large page size. The UltraSPARC-T2 supports 8KB, 64KB, 4MB and 256MB pages.

Concurrency control in CIF is implemented by heap-specific locks. Contention is rare and arises only by way of preemption. The impact of contention can be reduced by using techniques such as the Solaris `schedctl` mechanism [1] to advise the scheduler to defer involuntary preemption by time slicing for threads holding the heap lock.

Threads use the `schedctl` facility to efficiently identify the processor on which the thread is running, thus enabling the use of processor-specific heaps. On Linux/x86 CIF can be configured to use the CPUID or RDTSCP instructions to select a heap.

In CIF threads instantiate superblocks via `mmap`. On CC-NUMA systems that use a "first touch" page placement policy this means that the pages in a superblock will tend to be local to the node where the thread is running, improving performance.

All the allocators except Hoard, `tcmalloc` and `jemalloc` require at least a word-size metadata header field for in-use blocks. In CIF, for instance, an in-use block consists of a header word – a pointer to the enclosing superblock – followed by the data area. `Malloc` returns the address of the data area, which by convention must aligned on at least an 8-byte address boundary. The `free` operator consults this header to locate the free list in the superblock's header. CIF places the header word on the last word of the cache line preceding the address returned by `malloc` so the address returned by `malloc` is always aligned on 16-byte boundaries.

In CIF the size-classes inclusive of the header are simple powers-of-two starting at 16 bytes. We intentionally selected powers-of-two for the purposes of comparison against other allocators, whereas a production-quality allocator would use finer-grained size-classes.

To avoid undesirable index distributions and reduce the rate of inter-block cache conflicts the CIF allocator inserts a cache line-sized and aligned *spacer* into the superblock array when indices start to repeat, yielding a *punctuated array*. This allows the allocator to retain its existing size-classes. Say we have a superblock with 768-byte blocks and a sequence of blocks within that superblock that fall on addresses B, $B + 768$, $B + 1536$, $B + 2304$, $B + 3072$, $B + 3840$, $B + 4608$, $B + 5376$, $B + 6144$, etc. The UltraSPARC-T2 has 16-byte lines, 128 possible indices, and a 2048-byte cache page size. (Refer to Appendix A for details on the UltraSPARC-T2 cache organization). Our blocks would fall on indices I, $I + 48$, $I + 96$, $I + 16$, $I + 64$, $I + 112$, $I + 32$, $I + 80$ and I, respectively, where I is the cache index associated with block address B. If block address B falls on index I then the N-th block beyond B falls on address $B + (768*N)$ having index $I + (((768*N)/16) mod 128)$. In our example the indices repeat after just 8 blocks or 6144 bytes as the least common multiple of 2048 (the cache page size) and 768 (the block size) is 6144 bytes. If an implementation inserts a spacer after every 8 blocks, however, then a punctuated array of such blocks will land on the full set of 128 indices. A more naive implementation could simply insert a spacer after each contiguous run of blocks totaling at least 2048 bytes. The implementation in CIF uses this latter policy. In the worst case punctuated arrays require just one cache line of spacer per cache page within the superblock, putting a tight bound on wastage. Furthermore, the spacer lines are never accessed, so while they might increase TLB pressure and physical RAM usage, they do not influence L1D pressure. Finally, we note that we only need to employ spacers in superblocks that have index-unfriendly size-classes, where a simple unpunctuated array

of blocks would otherwise land on only a subset of the possible indices.

As an alternative to the punctuated array, changing the set of size-classes to be index-aware can also provide relief by ensuring that the block addresses within a superblock array fall on the full complement of indices. We discuss this approach in more detail in Appendix B.

To derive benefit from an index-aware allocator we presume an access model where multiple instances of a structure type are accessed repetitively and frequently, some fields in the type are "hot" (accessed frequently relative to other fields) and those hot fields tend to be clustered. Furthermore each instance is allocated separately. That is, we assume temporal locality for blocks and temporal and spatial locality within individual blocks. Such an access pattern is not atypical. Bonwick et al. [9] calls out the kernel `inode` construct as an example. The pattern is common in object graphs with intrusive linkage where the linkage fields reside in a "header" that precedes the body of the object.

CIF can also be configured by means of an environment variable to use a simple "flat" array of blocks with no spacers. We refer to this form as CIU – Cache-Index Unfriendly. This form yields extremely poor cache index distribution similar to that which would be achieved with a binary buddy allocator [23]. It serves as a useful measure of cache index sensitivity.

4. Index placement survey

Using a simple program we show that a number of popular allocators are index-oblivious and that index-oblivious block placement can result in performance pathologies.

In Figure 1 each point in the graph represents a distinct run of a simple single-threaded benchmark program **mcache** that `mallocs` 256 blocks of size B byte. The program then reports the cache index of the base address for each of the blocks. The index can be computed with simple address arithmetic. On the X-axis we vary the block size B with a step of 16 bytes. The Y-axis values are the number of distinct UltraSPARC-T2 L1D indices on which those blocks were placed, reflecting cache index distribution. A value of 128 – the number of L1D indices – is ideal. (See Appendix A). Each UltraSPARC-T2 core has a 128-way fully associative data TLB and thus more than sufficient capacity to cover 1024 blocks of 256 bytes for a reasonable heap layout without incurring TLB misses. Other more descriptive statistics might better reflect index distribution, such as a histogram, standard deviation or spread between maximum and minimum of the index population, but a simple count of the number of distinct indices serves to illustrate our assertion that many allocators have non-uniform index distribution.

The various allocators were configured by way of the LD_PRELOAD dynamic linking facility. Data was collected under actual execution, not simulation. `Libumem` and `libc` are provided with Solaris. Hoard version 3.8 was obtained from [2] and CLFMalloc version 0.5.3 was obtained from [3]. We used `jemalloc` version 2.0.1 and `tcmalloc` version 1.6 in the `tcmalloc-minimal` configuration without call-site profiling. Where SPARC executables were not available, source code was compiled with `gcc` version 4.4.1 at optimization level -O3. Unless otherwise noted all data in this paper was collected with 32-bit programs under the Solaris 10 operating system on a UltraSPARC-T2 processor model T5120 which has 8 cores and which exposes 64 logical processors.

As can be seen in Figure 1, all of the allocators except CIF have one or more size values where blocks fall on only a fraction of the 128 possible indices, potentially limiting the performance of an application that repeatedly accesses a few "hot" fields (fields exhibiting strong temporal locality) in a set of such blocks. CIF gives an ideal uniform index distribution over all sizes.

The same experiment on a Linux/x64 Nehalem system revealed index imbalance under the default `libc` allocator, itself based on Lea's `dlmalloc` [5], although the situation was not as dire for mid-sized blocks as the cache has higher associativity. (The Nehalem processor has an L1D with 64 indices, 8 ways, and 64-byte lines. The cache page is 4KB so page coloring is not possible).

In Figure 2 we configure `mcache` so that the 256 blocks are configured in a ring by ascending virtual address. The first field in the block contains a pointer to the next block in the ring. The remainder of the block is not accessed during the run. Our program runs for 10 seconds, traversing the ring and then reports the number of steps per millisecond on the Y-axis. Again, we vary the block size on the X-axis. The only activity during the measurement interval is "pointer chasing" over the ring of allocated nodes. As can be seen, block placement greatly impacts performance. Note that we selected 256 blocks intentionally, as the L1D can contain 512 distinct lines and, ideally, with uniform index distribution, could accommodate all 256 blocks in cache without incurring any cache misses. As expected, when we collect CPU performance counter data when running `mcache` under the various allocators we see that the L1D miss rate correlates strongly with the performance reported by the application, supporting our claim that the slow-down, when present, arises from cache misses.

5. Conflict varieties and remediation

This section provides a partial taxonomy of index conflict varieties and enumerates various ways to lessen the rate of such conflicts.

Simple **inter-block** index conflicts, described above, may be inter-superblock or intra-superblock. We can address and often reduce the degree of intra-superblock conflicts by choosing index-aware size-classes or insertion of spacers but note that such approaches also provide benefit against inter-superblock conflicts simply by making index access more uniform and diluting hot spots.

Inter-thread conflicts arise with the advent of shared level-1 caches. Assume for instance that threads *T1* and *T2* run concurrently on the same *core* and share the L1D. Both threads `malloc(100)` immediately after they start. Each thread will typically access distinct CPU-private heaps and within those heaps, superblock instances of the size-class appropriate for 100 bytes. The superblocks will be instantiated via `mmap` which returns addresses that will be at least page-aligned and in practice often have much higher alignment. Thus, if the allocator creates the superblock at the address returned from `mmap` it is very likely that the blocks returned from the `malloc` requests by *T1* and *T2* will collide at the same cache indices. We have *intra-core*, inter-thread, inter-superblock, inter-heap index conflicts. One way to reduce the odds of such inter-thread conflicts is to insert a randomly sized variable length *coloring* area at the start of each superblock. We initially placed the superblock header on the address returned by `mmap` and then inserted the coloring region after the superblock header and before the array of blocks, but noticed that the superblock header itself was vulnerable to index conflicts. We ultimately placed the coloring area before the header, providing better index distribution for the cache lines underlying the superblock headers.

With shared level-1 caches, applications can also encounter **inter-process** index conflicts where different processes have threads running concurrently on the same core. One way to mitigate such conflicts is to seed the pseudo-random number generator – used to generate superblock colorings – differently for each process, perhaps based on the time-of-day, process-ID, or a system random number generator. Absent per-process seeding of the random number generator used for superblock coloring, allocations in similar but distinct processes may fall on precisely the same virtual addresses, increasing the likelihood of inter-process conflicts. This effect can be easily demonstrated by spawning a number of concurrently executing single-threaded processes, each of which iterates over a small ring of `malloc`-ed blocks. Without seeding we can find destructive interference in the L1D and degraded performance. All of the allocators except `CIF` exhibited this problem.

We note that Solaris randomly colors the offset of the stack for a process's primordial thread, in part to lessen the odds of inter-process conflict between stacks. Similarly, the HotSpot Java[TM] Virtual Machine explicitly colors the stacks for threads created by the JVM.

The `CIF` and `CIU` allocators employ random superblock coloring – 16 possible colors in the interval [0,15] with the length of the coloring region taken as the color times the L1D line length -– and process-specific seeding of the random number generator. Ideally an implementation would provide one color for each of the 128 possible indices. Recall, however, that the coloring region is never allocated from and never accessed. It exists solely to control the offset of the array of blocks. As a practical concern to bound wastage from the coloring area we restrict ourselves to just 16 colors.

6. Experimental results

We first establish the existence of index-sensitive applications, and then show the efficacy of index-aware allocation on that set of benchmarks. Next, we show the benefits of coloring on system where multiple threads concurrently share caches. Finally, we report on the scalability of various allocators.

While not shown for lack of space, we have tested various allocators on a wide set of pointer-intensive benchmarks and found the index-aware size-classes or punctuated arrays do no harm and that no particular trade offs are required. `CIF` is competitive with the current best-of-breed allocators.

We ran each benchmark 5 times and took the median result, observing extremely low variation between runs.

6.1 Index-sensitive applications

In Figure 3 we report results from a set of single-threaded cache index-sensitive applications. Formally, cache index sensitivity is an aspect of application performance determined both by application structure and allocator design choices. We define an application as index sensitive *under an allocator* if it suffers excessive conflict misses because of poor index distribution. Index distribution, in turn, is largely determined by the allocator policies and design choices. These applications are sensitive because of the block sizes requested and access patterns to those blocks. Excluding `CIF`, no one allocator is best over all the applications as each exhibits different pathological index-unfriendly sizes as was previously seen in Figure 1.

We intentionally selected the applications below as (a) they were insensitive to `malloc-free` performance with such operations typically confined to a brief initialization phase; (b) they were cache index-sensitive; (c) they were insensitive to cache line relative block alignment, and (d) they were sufficiently simple so as to be amenable to direct analysis, allowing us to establish that the benefit arose solely from index-aware allocation.

Regarding (c), above, during our investigation we discovered that some applications were extremely sensitive to how allocators placed blocks with respect to cache line boundaries - whether, for instance, the blocks were always aligned, never aligned, or sometimes aligned for a given size. Our set of allocators used various policies. By default `CIF` always returns blocks aligned on cache line boundaries, but, as a test of sensitivity can be configured otherwise. We only reported on applications that were not sensitive to cache line relative block alignment.

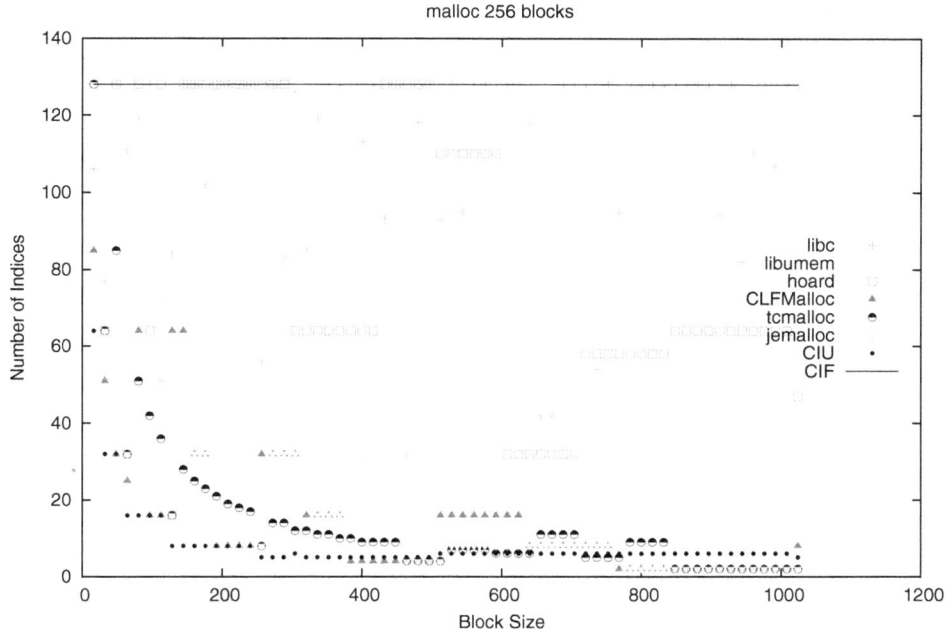

Figure 1. Index distribution over 256 allocated blocks

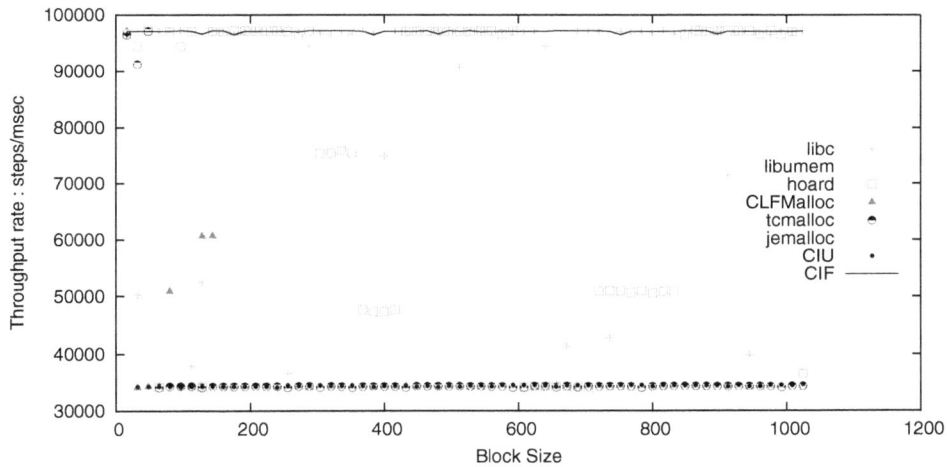

Figure 2. Pointer chasing performance : traversal rate over a list of 256 blocks

- **llubenchmark** [36] allocates groups of nodes and then iterates over those nodes during the benchmark interval. We used the version of `llubenchmark` found in the LLVM test suite version 2.7, and augmented it to report cache index distribution and allow for variable-length node sizes. The original form from Zilles allowed the node size to be specified on the command line but used a custom allocator while the form in the LLVM test suite used `malloc` but with a fixed node size. Our form `malloc`s each node and allows the node size to be specified on the command line. We used a command line of "-i 2000000 -n 1 -l 341 -g 0.0 -s 250" which specifies one list of 341 nodes of 250 bytes and 2000000 iterations over the list. As configured by the command line, all allocation is performed at startup time, so differences in reported performance reflect the rate at which

the thread iterates over the list. We collect the elapsed time by running the program under the `time` command. We note that `llubenchmark` behaves similarly to our own `mcache`.

- **egrep** is GNU grep version 2.6.3, a regular expression search utility based on deterministic finite automata. We timed the search of a 500Mb text file containing nucleotide sequences. The key block size `malloc`-ed by the application is 1024 bytes, which represents arrays of 256 `int`s which serve as transition tables for the state machine. Only a few indices are actually accessed, however. All significant allocation occurs at startup time and the run is dominated by pointer chasing operations over the DFA graph structures. The performance differences in the figure are almost entirely attributable to `malloc` placement policies in the different allocators. All the other benchmarks report elapsed time, but for `egrep` we report user-mode CPU time to factor out the IO-time required to read the file. (For reference, the run under `libc` took 11.2 seconds elapsed time with 2.01 seconds IO time. An IO time of 2.01 seconds is constant over the various allocators). Similar results were seen with the Google `RE2` regular expression package which is also index-sensitive.

- **dnapenny**[7] is benchmark in the "phylip" Phylogenic Inference Package component of the BioPerf bioinformatics benchmark suite. It uses a branch-and-bound algorithm to compute parsimonious trees. The source code was obtained from [4]. When starting, the application allocates 16 "tip" nodes. Each contains 4 buffers of size 6872 which are allocated separately. In the main loop there is an iteration that accesses a single buffer in each tip node. The program is moderately long-running, requiring more than 8 minutes under `libc`. Other phylip components such as `promlk` are similarly index-sensitive.

- **stdmap** creates a `std::map<int,int>` standard template library collection at startup. The benchmark then times the collection's iterator. The key-space is [0,499] and is approximately half populated. `std::map<>` is implemented as a red-black tree. The tree nodes are 40 bytes in length which some allocators round up to 64 bytes – a size that is cache index-unfriendly. The benchmark is written in C++ and produces a 64-bit executable. By default the C++ `new` and `delete` operators map directly to `malloc` and `free`. The tree implementation and nodes are opaque to the application so we were unable to directly report node addresses and indices, but instead used the Solaris `dtrace` and `truss -fl -t\!all -u ::malloc` commands to observe the allocation patterns.

- **Xml** is a 64-bit microbenchmark written in C that constructs an in-memory XML document tree via the Solaris `libxml2` package and then repeatedly iterates over the tree, reporting iteration times. The `xmlNode` instances are individually allocated by `malloc` and 120 bytes in length although only a few fields are accessed by the iterator. The `libxml2` library package parses the XML document and directly allocates the nodes which form the internal representation of the document.

- **Gauss** performs Gaussian elimination on $200x200$ matrices of 64-bit floating point numbers using the partial-pivot method. Each row is individually allocated.

- **DotProduct** computes the dot-product of a 200 vectors each of 200 elements.

Both Gauss and DotProduct have array accesses of the form $a[I][J]$ where an inner loop advances I and an outer loop advances J and each row is individually allocated. (That is, the outer loop varies column and the inner loop varies row). There is no temporal locality as each element is accessed just once, although spatial locality is potentially available between iterations. While processing index I the inner loop may access a cache line underlying a row at address A only to find that same line subsequently evicted later in the inner loop because of conflict displacement. On the next iteration of the outer loop the code will access index $I + 1$ adjacent to I in that same line underlying A, incurring a conflict miss. In this case our code is iterating over multiple arrays simultaneously, in lock-step, and there are no hot fields. Because of avoidable index conflicts, the application may fail to leverage potential spatial locality. Cache index-aware allocation can often avoid this problem.

This is a fundamentally different mode of benefit than is seen in the other applications, where index aware allocation leverages temporal locality in a small number of "hot" fields.

6.2 Superblock coloring

In Figure 4 we use `mcache` to demonstrate the efficacy of superblock coloring to reduce inter-thread index conflicts. Each thread `malloc`s two blocks of 100 bytes at startup and configures them as a ring via intrusive "next" pointers. (The choice of size is largely irrelevant in this benchmark). All the threads are completely independent. During the 10 second measurement interval each thread iterates over its private ring, visiting the two nodes in turn. When finished, the program reports the aggregate throughput rate of the threads. Figure 4 reports that throughput rate on the Y-axis in steps per millisecond while varying the number of threads on the X-axis. `CIF-NoColor` represents `CIF` configured with superblock coloring disabled. In an ideal system we would see perfect linear scaling but our real system has shared resources such as the pipeline (2 per core), caches, memory channel, etc. [34]. Beyond 8 threads, assuming ideal dispersion of those threads by the scheduler [13], threads start sharing the L D. At 32 threads we have 4 threads per core. Recall that the L1C is 4-way set associative, so above 32 threads index collisions start to manifest as misses and impede scaling, even to the extent of actually reducing performance in some cases. As we can see the application scales reasonably up to 32 threads under all the allocators. Beyond 32 threads we see that performance bifurcates: we still find reasonable scaling under `libc`, `tcmalloc`, `CIF` and `libumem`, while under `Hoard`, `CLFMalloc`, `jemalloc` and `CIF-NoColor` we find that scaling fades. `libc`, `tcmalloc` and `libumem` are not vulnerable as the blocks distributed to the various threads come from a centralized heap instead of per-thread `mmap`-ed heaps.

We encountered an interesting performance phenomenon where access performance dropped precipitously under `jemalloc` at thread counts above 32. The problem manifested both under `mmicro` and `mcache`. We observed that only a fraction of the currently executing threads were afflicted, and those threads suffered extremely high level-2 cache (L2) miss rates. Investigation revealed that `jemalloc` requests memory in units of 4MB chunks via `mmap` – each thread that invokes `malloc` will have at least one such thread-private 4MB region. 4MB happens to precisely coincide with a large page size on our platform. Indeed, the `pmap -s` command confirmed that Solaris was placing those 4MB regions on 4MB pages. `jemalloc` does not provide any type of superblock coloring, so when a homogeneous set of threads invoke `malloc` they will obtain addresses that are the same offset from the base of their 4MB block. 4MB pages must start on 4MB physical address boundaries. Thus the physical addresses underlying the 4MB blocks are extremely regular, differing in only a small number of bits between threads. The set of addresses returned by `malloc` to the threads thus tend to conflict as they select only a small set of the possible L2 banks and L2 indices, resulting in conflict misses in the L2. The UltraSPARC-T2 applies an XOR-based hash to physical addresses to avoid such behavior, but in our case the physical addresses were so regular that the hash did not avoid the problem. We confirmed our suspicion by using an unsupported Solaris API to translate virtual addresses to physical addresses within our benchmark program, allowing us to analyze the distribution of physical addresses underlying the blocks allocated within the 4MB regions. Once the problem was understood we could avoid the issue by setting the `MALLOC_CONF` environment variable to "lg_chunk:20" which directs `jemalloc` to use 1MB regions instead of its default 4MB regions. All `jemalloc` data in this paper was collected in this mode (1MB). We could also induce the same performance problem under `CIF` by forcing the superblock size to 4MB and disabling superblock coloring, further illustrating the benefits of coloring.

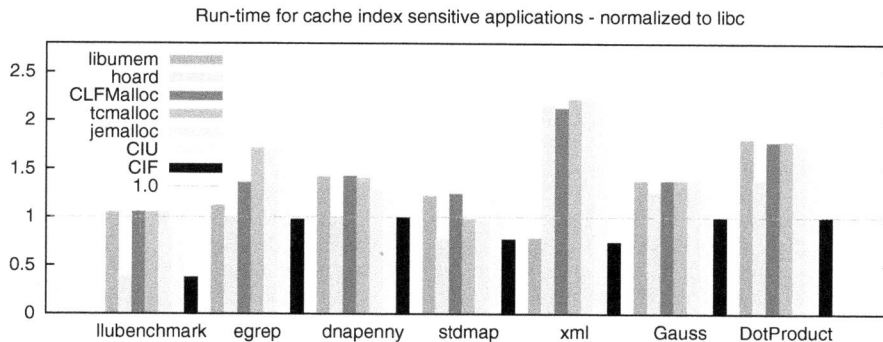

Figure 3. Cache index-sensitive applications

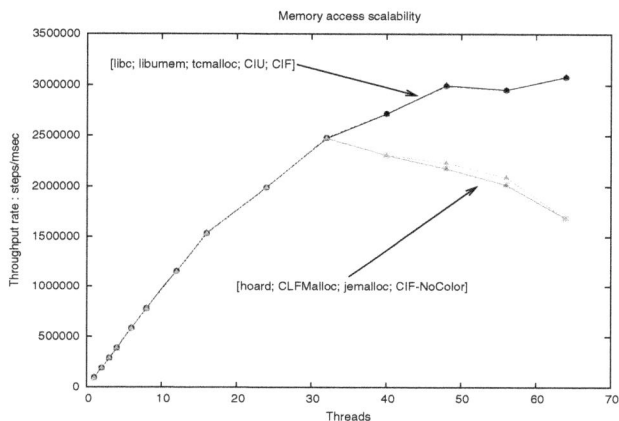

Figure 4. Impact of superblock coloring on memory access scalability

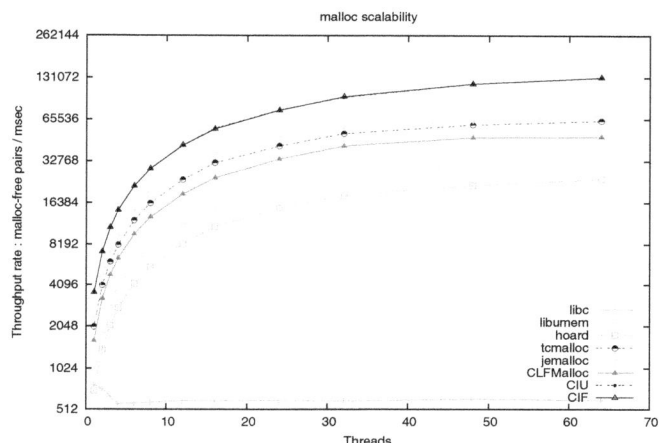

Figure 5. Malloc scalability varying thread count and allocators

6.3 Allocator Scalability

Here, we show that making an allocator index-aware does not affect its performance or scalability. In Figure 5 we use the `mmicro` benchmark from [15] and [14] which runs concurrent threads within a single process, each of which invokes `malloc` and `free` repetitively over a 50 second measurement interval, reporting the aggregate throughput rate of the threads in `malloc-free` pairs per millisecond. The threads are completely independent and do not communicate or write to any shared data. The UltraSPARC-T2 has only two pipelines per core, so scaling above 16 threads is modest and arises largely from memory-level parallelism [12]. As we can see from the graph all the allocators scale well except `libc`, which uses a single heap with a centralized lock. Broadly, the ratio of performance between the allocators observed at 1 thread holds as the number of threads increases, suggesting that path length through the `malloc` and `free` dominates multithreaded performance, and that the allocators have no substantial scaling impediments. As is made obvious in the graph, the application is insensitive to cache index placement as CIU effectively yields the same results as CIF.

7. Related work

The literature is rich with studies that show how layout and placement can influence cache behavior and impact performance for pointer-based programs [25][37]. Petrank [29] shows that cache-conscious data placement is, in the general case, NP-hard. By exploiting common access patterns and behavior found in applications we can still, however, provide benefit in many circumstances. Broadly, the optimization techniques involve changing the access pattern; intra-object field layout changes; and inter-object placement policies. Calder et al. [10] introduce *cache conscious data placement* which reduces cache misses by profiling an application, building a temporal relationship graph of data accessed, and finally using the temporal access patterns discovered in the profiling stage to refine data placement. Kistler et al. [22] develop an algorithm that clusters data members to promote and enhance spatial locality. Chilimbi et al. [11] show the benefit of cache-conscious data layout and field placement. Their allocator interface is non-standard, however, and does not allow drop-in binary replacement under the standard `malloc-free` interface.

Lvin et al. [26] use object-per-page allocation in the `archipelago` allocator to probabilistically detect errors in the heap arising from software flaws. Naively, if all objects were to start on page-aligned virtual address boundaries then applications accessing such objects could suffer from excessive conflict misses. To reduce the conflict miss rate their allocator randomly colors the offset of the object with the page. Coloring was used to salve the impact of page alignment, and not applied in a general and principled fashion that minimizes wastage. Furthermore, an object-per-page allocator may impose high TLB pressure.

Bonwick et al. [9] (section 4.1-4.3) also suggested superblock coloring, but only as remedy for *inter-superblock* intra-thread cache index conflicts and to relieve bus and bank imbalance for systems with multiple memory channels. Their paper predates commodity CMT (chip multithreading) systems with shared caches. We believe that index-aware size-classes or punctuated block arrays largely obviate and supersede the use of superblock coloring for the purpose of addressing inter-superblock intra-thread conflicts. That is, index-aware size-classes or punctuated arrays reduce both intra- and inter-superblock conflicts for a given thread accessing a set of superblocks. Superblock coloring remains useful, however, as it provides a new mode of benefit for intra-core inter-thread inter-superblock conflicts on modern shared cache CMT platforms. Bonwick also noted that binary buddy allocators are pessimal with respect to cache index distribution. We concur and generalize to sizes other than simple powers-of-two. We also note that facilities such as `memalign` should be used judiciously as excessive unneeded alignment can induce conflict misses.

Page coloring [30] operates at the level of the operating system or virtual machine monitor by influencing the choice of physical pages to assign to virtual addresses. The color of a physical page is just the value in the intersection of the physical page number field and the cache index field of the page address. Page coloring attempts to provide a uniform distribution of page colors for the physical pages assigned to a set of virtual pages, which in turn promotes balanced utilization of the set of available cache indices. Say that in the physical address layout we find that the page number field overlaps the cache index field by 2 bits, giving 4 possible page colors. If the kernel does not provide ideal page coloring and inadvertently mapped virtual pages V0, V1, V2 and V3 to physical pages P0, P1, P2 and P3, respectively, and those physical pages happened to be of the same page color, then cache lines underlying V0, V1, V2 and V3 would be able to reside in just one quarter of the available cache indices, possibly underutilizing parts of the cache and creating a "hot spot" in other sectors. Page coloring attempts to avoid such unfavorable assignments of physical pages to virtual addresses.

Hardware-based means of reducing the rate of conflict misses were suggested Seznec [32] (skew-associative caches) and later by by Gonzales [17] and Wang [35]. All entail changes to the hash function that maps addresses to cache indices and none is currently available in commodity processors. Min and Hu [28] suggest completely decoupling memory addresses from cache addresses in order to reduce conflict misses while Sanchez and Kozyrakis [31] subsequently suggest decoupling ways and associativity.

Our approach is most similar to that of page coloring except that it is implemented entirely in user-space within the virtual address `malloc` allocator and operates only on low-order bits of the cache index field of addresses that are not part of the physical page number field. Page coloring and cache index-aware allocation are complementary optimizations. Like page coloring our approach is non-intrusive in that it operates without any need to profile the application or modify the application's source code. If the `malloc` library is implemented as a separately deliverable dynamically loadable module, as is the case on most platforms, then our approach can be used by simply substituting a new `malloc` library, eliminating the need to recompile and providing benefit to legacy binary applications. In addition, our technique is orthogonal to but benefits from complementary mechanisms that change field layout to promote spatial locality [22]. Instead of specifically increasing locality it simply leverages ambient locality already present in the application.

8. Conclusion

Optimal index placement - like optimal field placement – is NP-hard. Techniques such index-aware allocation can, however, still benefit index-sensitive applications, avoiding a performance pitfall. Not all applications will benefit from an index-aware allocator but our approach is benign and has no observed negative impact. We make no general claims or guarantees about performance but note that all other factors being equal, balanced index distribution, like balanced page coloring, is preferable, given that it is relatively easy to avoid the vagaries of index-oblivious allocators. Finally, in most allocators, application of our technique requires extremely simple modifications, often changing just a few lines of code.

The phenomena of index sensitivity has been noticed before, and solutions along similar lines have been proposed but here we approach the issue methodologically, providing guidelines to future designers and developers. We clarify, explain and analyze the behavior and provide general solutions.

8.1 Contributions of this paper

- We identify the problem of *inter-block cache index conflicts* arising from excessive regularity in addresses returned by memory allocators. We show that the placement policies of `malloc` and related allocators, by virtue of conflict miss rates, can have a significant impact on application performance.

- We provide a simple solution to inter-block conflicts through index-aware size-classes or punctuated superblocks arrays with interspersed spacers. While not all applications are cache index-sensitive and thus show no benefit from an index-aware allocator, we claim our solution has no observed negative consequences reflecting the principle of "first, no harm" and argue that it should be used in new and existing allocators.

- We note that superblock coloring provides new benefits for CMT systems with shared caches, reducing both intra-thread and inter-thread inter-superblock index conflicts.

- We propose process-specific color seeding to avoid inter-process cache index conflicts that can come to be on CMT systems where concurrently executing threads share a data cache.

- We provide a partial taxonomy for allocator-based index conflicts.

- Taken collectively index-aware size-classes, punctuated block arrays, superblock coloring, and process-specific color randomization provide index-aware block placement and allow the construction of index-aware allocators.

We note that cache line relative block alignment has an impact on performance but is largely neglected in the literature. We found many applications to be sensitive to whether blocks were returned on addresses that coincide with cache line boundaries. The least significant nibble of addresses returned by `malloc` must be either 0 or 8. Some allocators always return addresses of the latter form for certain size-classes. We recommend that allocators should, to the extent possible and reasonable, return addresses aligned on cache line boundaries – this policy minimizes the number of cache lines underlying an object and decreases cache pressure, as well as reducing the odds of allocator-induced false sharing.

8.2 Future work

We plan to further explore using our techniques in other `malloc` allocators as well as in a Java Virtual Machine, where we can enforce index-aware size-classes in the object layout manager and provide random coloring either at the start of or within thread local allocation buffers (TLABs), which are contiguous thread-local object allocation regions managed by a simple *bump pointer*. Initial testing with `mcache` transliterated to Java has shown that the HotSpot JVM exhibits index unfriendly placement for certain object sizes with reduced performance and increased L1D miss rates.

We believe that cache index-aware allocation should be particularly helpful for hardware transactional memory implementations where the address-sets are tracked in the L1D and where conflict misses cause transaction aborts.

When multiple processors share a cache it may be useful to modify the hardware to mark cache lines with the identity of the processor that inserted a given line into the cache. It is possible that identity could be inferred from the tag value, depending on the address space layout. New performance counters and performance sampling facilities could be implemented that could differentiate *intrinsic* (intra-processor) and *extrinsic* (inter-processor) cache line displacement. If processor 1 displaced a line that was installed by processor 2 then we have extrinsic eviction, for instance. That information, in turn, could be useful to the developer or perhaps to the operating system scheduler in order to better place threads within the system topology in order to reduce miss rates. If the index and CPU ID (or tag) were made visible to a sampling facility then software could also measure rates of intra-core inter-thread conflict misses.

We hope to extend our analysis to the level-2 cache and also to determine if our approach might yield better DRAM bank and channel balance, admitting more parallelism in the memory subsystem for accesses that miss in caches.

Instead of using random number generators to assign color, it may be profitable to track the population of superblock colors and assign the least used color when creating a superblock.

A source of surprise was that, holding all other parameters fixed, using widely-spaced size-classes (2x) often yielded better performance than the more traditional 1.2x stepping recommended in the literature, which bounds fragmentation at 20%. For a given set of `malloc` requests, a coarse 2x set of size-classes may result in fewer underlying pages but more intra-block fragmentation. This suggests that TLB span might be more important in some cases than the wastage and increased data cache span arising from using coarse-grained size-classes. We hope to investigate this effect - – the tensions between wastage and data cache-span versus TLB span - in the future, possibly implementing size-class schemes that adaptively refine the set of size-classes and superblock sizes at runtime.

8.3 Observations

We note that address-space randomization (ASR), while often used for security purposes to make programs less vulnerable to exploits such as buffer overrun attacks, may have a beneficial effect as it provides implicit coloring.

Caches with much higher levels of associativity largely obviate our approach of index-aware size-classes, but the trend of platform design is not toward such complex implementations. Similarly, *victim caches* [20] would provide relief, but these are not found in commodity systems.

The UltraSPARC-T2 has 8 replicated *L2 Banks*. Each L2 bank has 512 indices with 64-byte lines and is 16-way set associative. The L2 cache line is the unit of coherence. L2 banks are physically-indexed and physically tagged. The L2 is unified, caching both code and data. Pairs of L2 banks share a DRAM channel. A central cross-bar resides between the cores and the L2 banks and routes physical addresses from cores to the appropriate L2 bank based on the value of physical address bits [8:6]. To help improve L2 index distribution the cross-bar applies a hash to the physical address by XORing high-order physical address bits into bits [17:11], which overlap the L2 index field. Physical address bits [17:9] constitute the L2 index field. Virtual address bits [10:0] pass through verbatim into the physical address. As such, the L2 bank select field of the physical address is a sub-field of the L1 index field, and the low 2 bits of the L2 cache index field overlap the 2 highest of the L1 index field. Thus, better and more uniform L1 index distribution yields better L2 bank distribution (inter-bank benefit) and better L2 index distribution within a bank (intra-bank benefit). Better L2 bank balance may admit more memory-level parallelism by reducing contention on the channel or path between the cores and L2 banks. Better L2 index distribution within a bank may lower the L2 miss rate. Cache index-aware allocation reduces L1 conflict misses, but accesses that miss in the L1 may also enjoy benefits from index-aware allocation.

References

[1] *The Solaris Schedctl Facility*. US Patent #5937187.

[2] *hoard.org*, 2010 (accessed 2010-1-14). hoard.org.

[3] *Amino-CBBS*, 2010 (accessed 2010-1-5). amino-cbbs.sourceforge.net.

[4] *BioPerf*, 2010 (accessed 2010-5-19). http://www.bioperf.org/.

[5] *dlmalloc*, 2010 (accessed 2010-7-2). http://gee.cs.oswego.edu/dl/html/malloc.html.

[6] *tcmalloc : version 1.6*, 2010 (accessed November 9, 2010). http://code.google.com/p/google-perftools/.

[7] D. Bader, Y. Li, T. Li, and V. Sachdeva. Bioperf: a benchmark suite to evaluate high-performance computer architecture on bioinformatics applications. *IEEE Workload Characterization Symposium*, 0:163–173, 2005.

[8] E. D. Berger, K. S. McKinley, R. D. Blumofe, and P. R. Wilson. Hoard: a scalable memory allocator for multithreaded applications. In *Proc. ninth international conference on Architectural Support for Programming Languages and Operating Systems*, pages 117–128, New York, NY, USA, 2000. ACM.

[9] J. Bonwick. The slab allocator: an object-caching kernel memory allocator. In *USTC'94: Proceedings of the USENIX Summer 1994 Technical Conference on USENIX Summer 1994 Technical Conference*, pages 6–6, Berkeley, CA, USA, 1994. USENIX Association.

[10] B. Calder, C. Krintz, S. John, and T. Austin. Cache-conscious data placement. *SIGPLAN Not.*, 33(11):139–149, 1998.

[11] T. M. Chilimbi, M. D. Hill, and J. R. Larus. Making pointer-based data structures cache conscious. *Computer*, 33(12):67–74, 2000.

[12] Y. Chou, B. Fahs, and S. Abraham. Microarchitecture optimizations for exploiting memory-level parallelism. *SIGARCH Comput. Archit. News*, 32(2):76, 2004.

[13] D. Dice. *Dave Dice's blog*, 2010 (accessed 2010-7-21). http://blogs.sun.com/dave/entry/solaris_scheduling_and_cpuids.

[14] D. Dice and A. Garthwaite. Mostly lock-free malloc. In *Proc. 3rd International Symposium on Memory Management*, pages 163–174, New York, NY, USA, 2002. ACM.

[15] D. Dice, Y. Lev, V. J. Marathe, M. Moir, D. Nussbaum, and M. Oleszewski. Simplifying concurrent algorithms by exploiting hardware transactional memory. In *SPAA '10: Proceedings of the 22nd ACM symposium on Parallelism in algorithms and architectures*, pages 325–334, New York, NY, USA, 2010. ACM.

[16] J. Evans. A scalable concurrent malloc(3) implementation for freebsd, 2006.

[17] A. González, M. Valero, N. Topham, and J. M. Parcerisa. Eliminating cache conflict misses through xor-based placement functions. In *ICS '97: Proceedings of the 11th international conference on Supercomputing*, pages 76–83, New York, NY, USA, 1997. ACM.

[18] M. D. Hill and A. J. Smith. Evaluating associativity in cpu caches. *IEEE Trans. Comput.*, 38(12):1612–1630, 1989.

[19] M. S. Johnstone and P. R. Wilson. The memory fragmentation problem: Solved? In *ISMM*, pages 26–36, 1998.

[20] N. P. Jouppi. Improving direct-mapped cache performance by the addition of a small fully-associative cache and prefetch buffers. *SIGARCH Comput. Archit. News*, 18(3a):364–373, 1990.

[21] R. E. Kessler and M. D. Hill. Page placement algorithms for large real-indexed caches. *ACM Trans. Comput. Syst.*, 10(4):338–359, 1992.

[22] T. Kistler and M. Franz. Automated data-member layout of heap objects to improve memory-hierarchy performance. *ACM Trans. Program. Lang. Syst.*, 22(3):490–505, 2000.

[23] K. C. Knowlton. A fast storage allocator. *Commun. ACM*, 8(10):623–624, 1965.

[24] C. Lattner and V. Adve. Automatic pool allocation: improving performance by controlling data structure layout in the heap. In *PLDI '05: Proceedings of the 2005 ACM SIGPLAN conference on Programming language design and implementation*, pages 129–142, New York, NY, USA, 2005. ACM.

[25] A. R. Lebeck and D. A. Wood. Cache profiling and the spec benchmarks: A case study. *Computer*, 27(10):15–26, 1994.

[26] V. B. Lvin, G. Novark, E. D. Berger, and B. G. Zorn. Archipelago: trading address space for reliability and security. *SIGOPS Oper. Syst. Rev.*, 42(2):115–124, 2008.

[27] M. M. Michael. Scalable Lock-free Dynamic Memory Allocation. In *Proc. ACM SIGPLAN 2004 Conference on Programming Language Design and Implementation*, pages 35–46, 2004.

[28] R. Min and Y. Hu. Improving performance of large physically indexed caches by decoupling memory addresses from cache addresses. *IEEE Trans. Comput.*, 50(11):1191–1201, 2001.

[29] E. Petrank and D. Rawitz. The hardness of cache conscious data placement. In *POPL '02: Proceedings of the 29th ACM SIGPLAN-SIGACT symposium on Principles of programming languages*, pages 101–112, New York, NY, USA, 2002. ACM.

[30] T. Romer, D. Lee, B. N. Bershad, and J. B. Chen. Dynamic page mapping policies for cache conflict resolution on standard hardware. In *In 1st USENIX Symposium on Operating Systems Design and Implementation (OSDI)*, pages 255–266, 1994.

[31] D. Sanchez and K. Christos. The zcache: Decoupling ways and associativity. In *MICRO 43: Proceedings of the 43rd Annual IEEE/ACM International Symposium on Microarchitecture*. IEEE Computer Society, 2010.

[32] A. Seznec. A case for two-way skewed-associative caches. In *ISCA '93: Proceedings of the 20th annual international symposium on Computer architecture*, pages 169–178, New York, NY, USA, 1993. ACM.

[33] D. D. Sleator and R. E. Tarjan. Self-adjusting binary search trees. *J. ACM*, 32(3):652–686, 1985.

[34] V. Čakarević, P. Radojković, J. Verdú, A. Pajuelo, F. J. Cazorla, M. Nemirovsky, and M. Valero. Characterizing the resource-sharing levels in the ultrasparc t2 processor. In *MICRO 42: Proceedings of the 42nd Annual IEEE/ACM International Symposium on Microarchitecture*, pages 481–492, New York, NY, USA, 2009. ACM.

[35] Z. Wang and R. B. Lee. A novel cache architecture with enhanced performance and security. In *MICRO 41: Proceedings of the 41st annual IEEE/ACM International Symposium on Microarchitecture*, pages 83–93, Washington, DC, USA, 2008. IEEE Computer Society.

[36] C. B. Zilles. Benchmark health considered harmful. *SIGARCH Comput. Archit. News*, 29(3):4–5, 2001.

[37] M. Zukowski, S. Héman, and P. Boncz. Architecture-conscious hashing. In *DaMoN '06: Proceedings of the 2nd international workshop on Data management on new hardware*, page 6, New York, NY, USA, 2006. ACM.

A. UltraSPARC-T2 "Niagara" Level-1 Data Cache Organization

The UltraSPARC-T2 level-1 data cache is organized as follows:

- 16-byte lines
- 4-way set associative
- 128 sets per cache – 128 possible indices
- 8KB cache with 512 lines
- Shared over 8 logical processors in a core [34]
- Physically-indexed and physically-tagged : PIPT
- Physical addresses map to cache indices by way of a hash function that shifts the address 4 bits to the right and then masks off the low 7 bits to form the index. Physical addresses presented to the cache by the processor have the following format: bits [3:0] form the cache line offset; bits [10:4] form the Level-1 cache index, and the remainder form the tag.
- Addresses A and B that refer to distinct cache lines map to the same index in the L1D if and only if $(A/16)mod128 = (B/16)mod128$. We say A and B conflict in the L1D. If more than 4 addresses map to the same index then we have *index contention* and repetitive accesses to those addresses can result in conflict misses.
- 2KB *cache page* size : 128 indices * 16 bytes per line. A cache page is the set of addresses that share a common value in the tag field. Address A and $A + 2KB$ map to the same index in the L1D.
- L1D-based page coloring [21] is not applicable as there is no overlap between the physical page number and index fields. That is, the cache page size is less than the system base page size of 8KB.

B. Cache index-aware size-classes

To avoid the undesirable behavior exhibited above by index-obivious allocators we can simply choose, as an alternative to punctuated arrays, a slightly different set of size-classes that is less prone to inter-block conflicts. That is, we simply avoid block sizes that underutilize the available indices. We can apply the adjustments, below, either statically at compile-time or at run-time, to transform a set of size-classes to be index-aware, producing an index-aware allocator.

Simplifying the problem slightly for the purposes of exposition, we will assume the effective block size S inclusive of any header is always an integer multiple of 16 bytes (the cache line size). We define the cache index of a block as the index of that block's base address. Within a given superblock the constituent blocks will have addresses of the form $(S * n) + B$ where B is the base of the block array in the superblock and $n \in \mathbb{N}$ up to the number of blocks in the superblock. Given S, the number of distinct indices for blocks in a sufficiently long superblock of size-class S is $2048/GCD(2048, S)$ where 2048 is the cache page size. Equivalently, we can state the number of usable indices for S as $128/GCD(128, S/16)$. Notice that we have a cyclic subgroup $\mathbb{Z}/(128)$ where 128 is the number of indices in the cache and the cycle length of the size corresponds to the number of indices on which blocks of that size can fall. As such, to provide an ideal tessellation we want to ensure $GCD(128, S/16) = 1$. That is, $S/16$ should be coprime with 128 and thus a generator of $\mathbb{Z}(128)$, in which case blocks of size S will land uniformly on all possible indices. The following simple transformation will adjust any size S to be index-aware :

```
if GCD(2048,S) > 16 then S += 16
```

CIF can be configured to use index-aware size-classes instead of the punctuated array. And in fact the form with index-aware size-classes yields the same performance as the form that uses the punctuated array. In this mode CIF uses size-classes of the form $(2^N + 1) * 16$ for N=0,1,2,3 etc., yielding a favorable index distribution.

In the case of CLFMalloc only 4 lines of codes – an array of ints that defines the size-classes – needed change to render CLFMalloc cache index-aware. While not reported for lack of space, we constructed both an intentionally index-unfriendly form of CLFMalloc with power-of-two size-classes and an cache index-friendly form using the transformation described above. With respect to index sensitivity, the performance of these two forms parallels that of CIU and CIF but we opted to report data from CIU and CIF as those allocators show better latency and scalability than the CLFMalloc-based forms and because CLFMalloc does not expose the memalign interface, which is required by some applications.

We note that even a small change in size-classes can have a profound impact on footprint and greatly perturb the heap layout, possibly resulting in large changes in the conflict miss rate and confounding causal analysis. One set of size-classes might simply be a better fit for the choice of sizes used by the application, resulting in less wastage. Paradoxically, adjusting each size-class upward to create an index-friendly allocator might decrease footprint.

Waste Not, Want Not

Resource-based Garbage Collection in a Shared Environment

Matthew Hertz   Stephen Kane
Elizabeth Keudel

Department of Computer Science
Canisius College
Buffalo, NY 14208
{hertzm,kane8,keudele}@canisius.edu

Tongxin Bai   Chen Ding
Xiaoming Gu

Department of Computer Science
University of Rochester
Rochester, NY 14627
{bai,cding,xiaoming}@cs.rochester.edu

Jonathan E. Bard *

NYS Center for Excellence in
Bioinformatics and Life Sciences
SUNY-Buffalo
Buffalo, NY 14203
jbard@buffalo.edu

Abstract

To achieve optimal performance, garbage-collected applications must balance the sizes of their heaps dynamically. Sizing the heap too small can reduce throughput by increasing the number of garbage collections that must be performed. Too large a heap, however, can cause the system to page and drag down the overall throughput. In today's multicore, multiprocessor machines, multiple garbage-collected applications may run simultaneously. As a result, each virtual machine (VM) must adjust its memory demands to reflect not only the behavior of the application it is running, but also the behavior of the peer applications running on the system.

We present a memory management system that enables VMs to react to memory demands dynamically. Our approach allows the applications' heaps to remain small enough to avoid the negative impacts of paging, while still taking advantage of any memory that is available within the system. This memory manager, which we call *Poor Richard's Memory Manager*, focuses on optimizing overall system performance by allowing applications to share data and make system-wide decisions. We describe the design of our memory management system, show how it can be added to existing VMs with little effort, and document that it has almost no impact on performance when memory is plentiful. Using both homogenous and heterogenous Java workloads, we then show that Poor Richard's memory manager improves average performance by up to a factor 5.5 when the system is paging. We further show that this result is not specific to any garbage collection algorithm, but that this improvement is observed for every garbage collector on which we test it. We finally demonstrate the versatility of our memory manager by using it to improve the performance of a conservative whole-heap garbage collector used in executing .Net applications.

Categories and Subject Descriptors   D.3.4 [*Processors*]: Memory management (garbage collection)

General Terms   Experimentation, Measurement, Performance

---

* Work performed at Canisius College

Keywords   poor richard's memory manager, garbage collection, multiprogramming, throughput, paging

1.   Introduction

Today's developers are increasingly taking advantage of garbage collection (GC) for the many software engineering benefits it provides. Developers can do this using garbage-collected languages (e.g., Haskell, Java, ML), conservative collectors (e.g., the Boehm-Demers-Weiser collector [19]), or scripting languages executing on a garbage-collected virtual machine (VM) (e.g., JRuby or Groovy). While one study found that programs can be executed just as quickly whether they use garbage collection or explicit memory management, this performance comes only when the garbage-collected heap has been sized appropriately [27]. But keeping the heap an appropriate size is extremely difficult: collecting the heap too early increases GC overhead, but allow the heap to grow too large harms performance by decreasing data locality and increasing the number of TLB misses [13].

Even worse than decreasing locality, allowing a heap to grow too large could mean that it no longer fits in RAM and must have pages evicted to disk. Accessing memory that has been saved back to disk can require six orders of magnitude more time than if it were in main memory. Even if the mutator does not touch the evicted pages, it can still hurt performance during garbage collection. During whole-heap collections, the GC examines **all** of the reachable data. Because the mutator can only use reachable objects, the garbage collector's working set is at least as large as the mutator's, if not larger. A GC can therefore cause a massive slowdown due to paging despite the mutator not suffering any page faults. Thus selecting when to collect the heap depends on many factors: the program, the garbage collector, and the resources available.

As a result of the difficulty selecting a proper heap size, many workarounds and optimizations have been proposed. For developers, the simplest approach is to require users select a static heap size that fits into memory. Others have studied using heap and GC statistics or program profiling to determine the optimal times to collect the heap (e.g., [2, 5, 14, 20, 23, 37, 41, 43]). While these approaches can provide significant improvements when memory is plentiful, they often make poor decisions when resource-bound because they ignore paging's costs.

Other approaches have enhanced the OS to enble making *resource-based* garbage collection decisions which also factor in paging costs when selecting a heap size (e.g., [6, 7, 26, 28, 44–46]). While the scope of their changes varies greatly, all these projects require some additional OS and JVM features. The need for these features limits the ease of adopting them in new or different environments. Another problem is the multiprogrammed environments that are common today. In these situations, the amount of memory available changes dynamically and unpredictably. When these changes are observed by like-minded programs, they would choose to react similarly. Should the programs follow a conservative approach, resources may be left underutilized. More aggressive approaches, however, set a collision course to severe contention and poor performance. Unfortunately, this earlier research assumes an application was running on a dedicated machine and did not evaluate how it would perform when this was not the case.

Contributions: In this paper we address this problem of shared resource utilization by introducing *Poor Richard's Memory Manager*. Poor Richard's handles both the adjustments needed by a single process on a dedicated system and those needed to achieve good performance in the chaotic environments created by executing multiple processes. Poor Richard's provides this improvement by having each process monitor its own performance. Each process also has access to a shared *whiteboard*, in which they can each post information about their own state and read information about others' states. This allows processes to make a joint response to dynamic events and ensure that it can make a system-wide decision about this shared resource.

Following ideals espoused by its namesake, Poor Richard's uses a frugal, lightweight approach to perform its tasks. Applications monitor their state using only information already made available by most operating systems, thus avoiding any changes or additions to the OS. Similarly, Poor Richard's needs only limited interactions with the virtual machine and is entirely independent of the garbage collector being used. The code used to trigger resource-based collections in the conservative whole-heap Boehm-Demers-Weiser collector [19] is the same as the code used to trigger resource-based collection in the generational collectors defined by MMTk. This combination makes it very simple to port and adopt Poor Richard's memory manager in any system.

We present an empirical evaluation of Poor Richard's performance using multiple garbage collectors with both heterogeneous and homogeneous workloads and on two different architectures. We show that it has minimal effect on performance when there is no memory pressure. We further demonstrate that Poor Richard's provides significant performance improvements with every garbage collector we tested when memory pressure increases. Because it limits the effects of paging in an orthogonal manner to how the VM already sizes its heap, Poor Richard's enables systems to use their existing heap sizing algorithms without worrying about how they will perform if the amount of available memory suddenly changes.

The rest of the paper is organized as follows: Section 2 provides an overview of Poor Richard's Memory Manager and how it coordinates a system-wide response to memory pressure. Section 3 describes the implementation of Poor Richard's and its *whiteboard*. The results from our emprical investigation of Poor Richard's are found in Section 4. Section 5 discusses related work, and Section 6 discusses future directions for this research and concludes.

2. Overview of Poor Richard's

Poor Richard's must first be used for it to ever be useful. Adoption of this memory manager is unlikely if it required executing additional processes or adding to or modifying the OS. Even needing substantial changes to the virtual machine can limit the desire to adopt a system. We therefore made the decision that Poor Richard's would make its decisions independent of the virtual machine and that any work which needed to be performed would be done by processes using Poor Richard's only. This simplifies porting it to new environments easy as it relies only on information already available

and data common to all garbage-collected applications and requires minimal changes to the VM.

The goal of Poor Richard's memory manager is to eliminate the need to consider paging when selecting a heap size. This requires allowing processes to utilize as much main memory as they need, but not allow them to use so much that paging limits throughput. This problem is difficult on a dedicated machine since it requires balancing the mutator's and GC's working sets and adapting to changes in mutator behavior. When multiple processes are executing, the problem only gets harder. Any solutions must now account not only for changes in other processes' behavior, but also the possibility of other processes starting and stopping. Just modifying heap sizes may not be enough, since new demands may trigger paging before the next collection yields a chance to shrink the heap size. Poor Richard's solves this dilemma by working orthogonally to heap size selection. Instead it performs periodic checks and, when necessary, triggers an immediate whole-heap "resource-driven" GC. If memory suddenly becomes available, Poor Richard's will not trigger a GC and can continue using the optimal heap size previously computed.

Poor Richard's works orthogonally to systems' existing heap sizing algorithms; the resource-driven collection works like an immediate one-time shrinking of a process's heap. Because this collection is performed as soon as memory pressure is detected, it only needs to maintain the existing level of memory pressure to avoid significant slowdowns. By finding and freeing garbage objects in the heap, the collection ensures future allocations goes to pages that already contain live objects and so avoid the need to page. If the collector also performs compaction or frees pages from the heap or containing metadata, then the collection can not only prevent paging, but even reduce memory pressure. Because the prevention of paging occurs as a result of the garbage collection and does not rely on any specific algorithm, resource-driven collections should improve the performance of any system from those using whole-heap conservative collectors to those using compacting, generational collectors.

By working in multiprogrammed environments, our system must handle an additional concern. As they are running, all processes will see the same stimuli and react identically. If processes are able to react fast enough this may not be a problem, but this could lead to resources being underutilized from overly-conservative decisions or lead to contention as a result of hyper-aggressive choices. An alternative is to allow processes to work collaboratively and develop a system-wide response. As machines feed their increasing numbers of cores by execute more processes simultaneously, we feel coordination is important *if* the costs of coordinating the response can be limited. Poor Richard's therefore includes a mechanism by which processes can coordinate a strategy. To test this idea empirically, we implemented several different coordination strategies with different coordinating costs:

Selfish The simplest coordination strategy is to not coordinate at all. *Selfish* runs of Poor Richard's do not use any coordinating mechanisms and make decisions independently. When running, these processes perform a whole-heap collection whenever they detect memory pressure and do not communicate with other processes.

Communal A second approach to coordinating a response is to have processes share fully in any necessary responsibilities. When using a *Communal* strategy, processes notify all others when they detect memory pressure. When they check for memory pressure, processes also look for these notifications. Whether the process detects memory pressure itself or is notified that it was detected by another, the process performs a whole-heap collection.

If multiple cooperative applications began collecting their heap at the same time, the increased memory demands could itself trigger further paging and contention accessing the disk. Poor Richard's prevents this by using a flag placed in a shared memory buffer (the "*whiteboard*") to record whenever a process is performing resource-driven collection. While a process performs a resource-driven collection, others will continue executing normally, including performing demand-driven collections. Once the resource-driven collection completes, the process clears the shared flag and allows another to perform its resource-driven collection. Thus the need to reduce memory pressure is shared while the collections are serialized to prevent clustered collections from overloading the system.

Leadered Our third approach tries reducing the overheads of the Communal strategy while providing a more systemic solution than the Selfish strategy. Instead of all processes collecting their heaps once memory pressure is detected, a process detecting memory pressure signals a single process (the "*leader*") to perform a whole-heap collection. This ensures only one process collects its heap, thereby reducing memory demands while needing minimal overheads. How the leader is chosen can be tailored to the goals or needs of the machine. So long as some process collects their heap, memory pressure is reduced and the performance is not hurt. In this work, we evaluated selecting the process with the largest heap size as the leader.

3. Poor Richard's Memory Manager

The original Poor Richard espoused the ideals of frugality, efficiency, and unobtrusiveness. We adopted those ideals in creating a lightweight system that can easily be added to virtual machines to preserve throughput even when systems becomes resource-bound. In this section, we discuss the different techniques Poor Richard's Memory Manager employs to meet these ideals. We will initially present Poor Richard's frugality in having applications detect memory pressure only using information the operating system already provides and without knowledge of the VM or GC. We then discuss our implementation and use of the *whiteboard* to allow processes to communicate and cooperate. Finally, we document Poor Richard's interactions with the host VM and how it communicates its decisions.

3.1 Process Self-Monitoring

In Poor Richard's, each process is responsible for monitoring its own state for signs of memory pressure. In particular, processes track how many *major page faults* (evicted pages that have been read back into memory) they trigger and their *resident set sizes (RSS)* (number of pages physically residing in main memory). Poor Richard's relies upon the number of major page faults occuring since the end of the last GC as its primary indicator of memory pressure. Multiprogrammed systems running multithreaded processes can tolerate low levels of major page faults by executing the processes and threads that are not blocked by I/O. Being overly conservative, therefore, increases overheads without improving throughput. Only when the number of major page faults passes a threshold value, for this paper we used 10, will Poor Richard's report it detected increased memory pressure and take action.

As Grzegorczuk et al. correctly noted [26], however, processes seeing major page faults can tell that the system is resource-bound, but lack knowledge of the source of this contention. We further observe that major page faults can only be detected AFTER memory pressure not only caused pages with usable data on them to be evicted to disk, but that the data they contain was again needed by the mutator or GC. As Poor Richard himself noted, "the early bird catches the worm"; by reacting to memory pressure earlier, systems can avoid making the situation even worse. Towards this end, Poor Richard's also checks for changes in the process's resident set size.

```
extern "C" int checkMemoryPressure() {
  long long recentPFaults;
  long currentRSS;
  long deltaRSS;

  recentPFaults = getPageFaults() - lastPFaults;
  currentRSS = getResidentSetSize();
  deltaRSS = currentRSS - lastRSS;
  lastRSS = currentRSS;
  return ((recentPFaults >= 10) || (deltaRSS < 0));
}
```

Figure 1. Example code by which Poor Richard's memory manager determines if memory pressure warrants further action. While this assumes the VM does not relinquish pages, it could be handled by comparing deltaRSS with the number of relinquished pages.

For performance or correctness reasons, most VMs do not willingly relinquish pages; a decrease in the RSS means resources were limited enough to require evicting the process's pages.[1] Without making significant changes to the OS or VM this metric is imperfect: it fails to detect a problem when the process allocates or faults in more pages than are evicted. As we found, however, RSS frugally provides an early notification of memory pressure that would otherwise go unnoticed.

By focusing on being frugal, adopting Poor Richard's memory manager is made easier. Figure 1 shows the code it executes to check whether increased memory pressure requires further action. The only environment-specific portion of this code are the methods finding the process's current count of major page faults and resident set size. In Linux, processes can find these values among the performance statistics available in /proc/self/stat [4].[2] As part of the /proc directory, this pseudo-file can be opened and read like a normal file, but is really an interface for processes to access data from the kernel [42]. Thus Poor Richard's need not rely on any OS-specific features or modifications and can be easily ported.

3.2 *Whiteboard* Communication

In the multiprogrammed environments that are frequently used, each process's decisions about shared resources impact the other processes being executed. Consider, for example, the effect of a process performing a whole-heap collection. Whereas the mutator's working set may include only a subset of reachable data, the GC must examine all reachable objects. As a result, garbage collection will temporarily increase the memory needs of that process. Should multiple processes using resource-based collection detect increased memory pressure at the same time, their combined increased memory demands could result in severe paging and contention accessing the disk.

Were processes able to communicate, problems such as these could be avoided. As we expect memory pressure and paging to not be the common case, it is vital that collaborations be as efficient as possible. As in Wegiel and Krintz [40], Poor Richard's uses a shared memory buffer to facilitate efficient interprocess communication. Into this buffer, Poor Richard's allocates a common "*whiteboard*". Processes can then use this whiteboard to share important information and coordinate their actions. When they begin executing, processes can load the whiteboard into their address space and register themselves as a participant. As part of their registration

---

[1] This would also work with VMs that voluntarily relinquish memories (e.g., HotSpot with ergonomics [1]), by allowing the VM to specify the number of pages it gave up and returning if the RSS decreases by more than this expected amount.

[2] While /proc/*/stat exists only in Linux, these values are obtainable in Solaris, AIX, and other Unix systems using the getrusage function [3].

with the whiteboard, each process takes a space of its own on the whiteboard. At the end of each whole-heap collection, the process updates this space to specify its heap size, resident set size, and number of page faults. Each private space in the whiteboard also contains a flag that other processes can set to get that process's attention. The whiteboard also contains a shared data area in which are stored data needed for bookkeeping and to prevent data races. This shared area also contains a flag that processes can set while they perform a whole-heap collection to alert others that they will be increasing memory pressure on the system temporarily. Prior to termination, processes remove themselves from the whiteboard and make their private space available for use by another process. The whiteboard's memory demands are very limited needing only 848 bytes to hold the common values and 32 bytes for each private space.

Use of this whiteboard is therefore very efficient. Absent memory pressure, processes need only access shared areas only twice – when they register and unregister with the system – and only update their private space at the completion of each whole-heap GC. Using Poor Richard's whiteboard, processes can notify others when they detect memory pressure and allow easy implementation of any of the coordination strategies presented in Section 2. No matter the coordination strategy, Poor Richard's whiteboard enables this communication to occur efficiently and with a minimum of overhead.

3.3 Interaction with the VM

All of Poor Richard's frugality would be for naught were existing VMs required to make substantial changes to use it. The final ideal of our design was unobtrusiveness: that Poor Richard's memory manager require minimal changes and few interactions with the host VM. By doing this, we maintain all of a VM's existing optimizations and tuning to preserve their existing good performance when memory pressure is low.

These minimal changes are possible because most of the memory manager resides in a separate, fully independent, library of "C" code that gets compiled into the VM when the VM is built. Within this library resides all of its whiteboard functionality as well as the code with which a process monitors itself for signs of memory pressure. This library also contains the code which analyzes all of this data, coordinates actions with other processes, and determines the appropriate action for the VM.

To ensure Poor Richard's remain unobtrusive, code in the garbage collector is responsible for initiating all communication. The first of the calls from the GC to Poor Richard's is added to the end of the GC code responsible for reclaiming space following a whole-heap collection. When this call is made, Poor Richard's updates its baseline values of both the number of major page faults seen by this process and the process's resident set size. These are the values that the system uses to determine when a process is seeing sufficient memory pressure to warrant a response (the variables `lastPFaults` and `lastRSS` in Figure 1). During this call, Poor Richard's also updates the data stored in the process's private area of the whiteboard (i.e., the number of major page faults seen, resident set size, and the size of the heap after heap memory was reclaimed). As the purpose of this call is purely informational, no data is returned and, once complete, the GC continues as normal.

The second of the calls from the GC is where Poor Richard's can modify the behavior of the VM. This call allows Poor Richard's to check for rising memory pressure and require the GC to act when it is necessary. An example of the code executed by Poor Richard's during this call is shown in Figure 2. How the calls interacting with the whiteboard are defined depends on coordination strategy being used. For Selfish runs of Poor Richard's, these functions did not use the whiteboard, but instead checked a global variable. For other runs, they would use the whiteboard. This makes this code

```
extern "C" int consultPoorRichards() {
  int forceGC = checkWBFlags();
  if (!forceGC) {
    int memoryPressure = checkMemoryPressure();
    if (memoryPressure) {
      setWBFlags();
      forceGC = checkWBFlags();
    }
  }
  return forceGC;
}
```

Figure 2. Example of Poor Richard's code that determines if a process should perform a whole-heap collection. This initially checks if any external process has flagged this process to perform a resource-driven collection. If not, it checks for memory pressure. If memory pressure is detected, the current coordination strategy selects the process(es) chosen to perform a resource-driven collection. Finally, it checks again to see if the current process was among those selected to perform a resource-driven collection.

```
public final static boolean USING_PRMM = true;
public static int waitConsult = 100;
public static int slowPathsWait = 0;
public final boolean gcCheck() {
  int nurseryPages = nurserySpace.reservedPages();

  if (nurseryPages >= Options.nurserySize.getMaxNursery() ||
      nurseryPages >= getMatureSpacePagesAvail()) {
    return true;
  } else if (USING_PRMM && ++slowPathsWait >= waitConsult) {
    boolean forceGC = consultPoorRichards();
    waitConsult = computeNextDelay();
    slowPathsWait = 0;
    forceFullHeapCollection = forceGC;
    return forceGC;
  }
  return false;
}
```

Figure 3. Example of a collector's "slow-path" allocation code modified to also check with Poor Richard's memory manager. With this addition, the routines which already trigger demand-driven collections will also trigger any resource-driven collections.

very easy to modify and update with new coordination strategies. `consultPoorRichards` begins by checking the private area of the whiteboard to see if another process detected memory pressure and, following the active coordination strategy, determined that the current process must reduce its working set. When selected to perform a whole-heap collection, Poor Richard's returns immediately and notifies the GC of this need. If it is not notified that it must collect its heap, we perform the self-monitoring process from Figure 1. If this monitoring does not detect any memory pressure (i.e., `checkMemoryPressure()` returns false), Poor Richard's is done and allows the GC to continue as normal. When memory pressure is detected, Poor Richard's applies the active coordination strategy, notifies any processes which will need to perform a whole-heap GC, and returns if it was the selected process. How the calls interacting with the whiteboard are defined depends on coordination strategy being used.

The call in which the VM consults Poor Richard's is appended to the GC's existing "slow-path" allocation routine. Within this slow-path routine the GC already checks for demand-driven collections and so is a natural place to trigger resource-driven collections. An example of this modified slow-path routine is in Figure 3. The call to Poor Richard's is additive only and will not interfere or override any demand-driven collection decisions. When resources are plentiful, Poor Richard's never signals for a collection and so the system executes as normal. Even when resources are limited, Poor Richard's will not reject any collections or modify the preferred heap size. Instead Poor Richard's directs a process to collect its heap, thereby shrinking the working set and reducing memory pressure. If more resources become available immediately following a resource-driven collection, Poor Richard's memory manager would revert to not signalling collections and the process would continue executing as before.

Each time the VM calls Poor Richard's to check if a demand-driven collection is necessary there will need to be multiple function calls, an interaction with kernel data, and access to several buffers used only for this process. The overhead of this process is cheap relative to the cost of a hard drive access, but calling this too frequently would harm performance when memory is plentiful. Thus the VM will not perform on each slow-path allocation, but instead makes this call only periodically. This rate is determined using an additive increase/multiplicative decrease algorithm. Using this heuristic, whenever a process detects memory pressure in its self-monitoring it immediately reduces the number of slow-path allocator calls between consultations (i.e., waitConsult in Figure 3) by an order of magnitude; when no memory pressure is detected the rate is decreased by 1. This approach allows Poor Richard's to respond quickly when a response appears likely, but limit overheads when memory is plentiful.

Just as being frugal makes it easy to port our memory manager to many different environments, being unobtrusive simplifies the task of adding the system to an existing VM. The needed changes to the VM require finding where a GC releases memory at the end of a whole-heap collection and the allocation's slow path. The code within Poor Richard's cannot depend on any implementation details of the VM in which it runs and will not require any existing VM code be modified. As with the other ideals espoused by the its namesake, remaining unobtrusive keeps the implementation of Poor Richard's lightweight and ready to be included within a VM with the addition of only a few lines of code.

4. Results

We now present the results of our empirical analysis of Poor Richard's Memory Manager. We will describe our experimental methodology including the environments and garbage collectors with which we perform the majority of our experiments. We then show how Poor Richard's Memory Manager improves paging performance on multiple garbage collectors and on multiple architectures for both heterogenous and homogenous workloads. Finally, we discuss porting Poor Richard's to the Mono runtime and show how it also improves the throughput of .Net benchmarks.

4.1 Implementation

For all of our Java experiments, we used the Jikes RVM/MMTk, version 3.1.1. Nearly all of our implementation of Poor Richard's was written as a separate library of C code, however. This includes all of the code detecting memory pressure, accessing the whiteboard, and determining whether a process should perform a collection or not. Calls to Poor Richard's required using SysCall routines to support the Java-to-C transition. Only two other additions were made to the Jikes RVM/MMTk. First, we modified the slow-path allocation routines to consult with Poor Richard's and allow it to trigger resource-driven whole-heap collections. Second, we added support within the garbage collectors to allow Poor Richard's to update the process's private whiteboard space with the new heap size following each whole-heap collections. Because of the simplicity of these interactions, and despite needing each call to go from Java to C and back, these changes required under 200 LOC.

To see how well our approach would work with other systems and garbage-collection idioms, we also tested Poor Richard's using the Mono VM, an open source virtual machine which executes applications written for .Net [32]. Because Mono is already written in C, we were able to call directly into Poor Richard's functions without any overhead. As a result, we needed under *10* lines of code to enable our system in Mono and did not require any modifications to our memory manager.

4.2 Methodology

To determine how well Poor Richard's will work in multiprogramming environments, we performed our experiments on two separate machines. The first machine contains two processors each of which is a single-core, hyperthreaded 2.8GHz Intel Xeon processor with 1MB of L2 cache. For all of our unconstrained memory experiments, we used the machine's full 4GB of RAM. To create memory pressure, we used the grub loader to limit the system to only recognize 256MB of physical memory. Our second machine contained a four-core, 2.6GHz Intel Core2 processor with 4MB of L2 cache. To create memory pressure on this machine, we again used the grub loader to limit the system to 512MB of physical memory. Both system use a vanilla Linux kernel version 2.6.28. During these experiments, each machine was placed in single-user mode with all but the necessary processes stopped and the network disabled. Experiments on the first machine ran two applications concurrently while experiments on the second machine ran four applications concurrently. We ran as many application as there were machine cores, but allowed the applications to execute normally and did not limit or bind them to a core. For each experiment, we record the time required until all of the processes completed.[3]

For these experiments, we used benchmarks drawn from two sources. The first benchmark was pseudoJBB, a fixed workload variant of SPECjbb [38]. In addition, we used four benchmarks from the 2006-10-MR2 release of the DaCapo benchmark suite: *bloat*, *fop*, *pmd*, and *xalan* [15].

To limit variations between runs, these experiments used a pseudo-adaptive compilation methodology [29, 35]. Under this approach, we initially timed five separate runs of each benchmark when executing with the adaptive compiler and recorded the final optimization decisions made in each run. Using the decisions from the fastest of these five runs, all of our experiments duplicate the decisions of an adaptive compiler strategy but in an entirely repeatable manner. Compilation costs can still bias results of experiments [24]. As a result, most experiments follow a second run methodology [9]. We observed, however, that the first ("*compilation*") pass can trigger significant paging which influences the results of further passes. Since we could control or eliminate the effects of this compilation pass, we chose instead to loop the benchmark so that it ran at least five times to minimize biases introduced by the compilation costs.

Using these benchmarks we ran two sets of experiments. The first set of experiments examined system throughput when processes are executing homogeneous workloads. For these workloads, we timed how long was needed to completely execute two or four parallel instances of the benchmark. For our second set of experiments, we analyzed system performance on heterogeneous workloads using each possible pairing of DaCapo benchmarks. When running four applications, we had two processes execute one of the benchmarks and another two processes running the other. While these benchmarks would normally complete in a different amount of time, we selected the number of times each benchmark was looped so that they would complete within approximately one

---

[3] We also examined the results using the average completion time of each process. This did not change our results or conclusions and so is not presented here.

Benchmark	Bytes Alloc.	Min. Heap	# Passes	Description
pseudoJBB	0.92G	42M	1	Java server benchmark
bloat	684M	22M	5	Java bytecode optimizer
fop	66M	24M	23	Translate XSL-FO to PDF
pmd	322M	20M	7	Java program analysis
xalan	77M	99M	8	XSLT transformer

Table 1. Key Metrics for Single Pass of Each Benchmark

second of each other when run with no memory pressure. Table 1 provides important metrics for each of these benchmarks.

We ran five trials per data point and report the mean of each set of trials. Our experiments found high variances for the results of the default system. These variances decreased for Poor Richard's runs using the Collaborative strategy. For Poor Richard's runs using either the Selfish or Leadered strategy, the variances were minimal. In our results, the variance appears correlated to the amount of paging that occurs. This provides further evidence of how well Poor Richard's handles memory pressure.

4.3 Performance without Memory Pressure

While the rate with which the system consults with Poor Richard's does grow slowly, it will not go away. To maintain good performance, it was important that the processing performed by Poor Richard's be as frugal as possible. When we tested the systems using the full 4GB of RAM, we saw that this is the case. Using GenImmix and averaged across all our experiments, there is no meaningful difference between the time executing any of Poor Richard's coordinating strategies and the base Jikes RVM runs – the differences are too small to be distinguishable from the background noise. While the differences are slightly greater for GenMS, the base system averages only up to 1.6% faster than using Poor Richard's with the Leadered coordinating strategy. As Poor Richard's using the Communal strategy is nominally faster, on average, than the base Jikes RVM at the same heap size, it suggests that this result is probably within experimental error as well.

4.4 Performance with Memory Pressure

We now consider the performance of Poor Richard's Memory Manager when under memory pressure. We first examine whether Poor Richard's improves the performance of the two best performing collectors included within Jikes RVM/MMTk: generational collectors using either a mark-sweep policy ("GenMS") or the Immix algorithm [16] to collect its mature space ("GenImmix"). Figure 4 uses the dual-processor machine to compare the performance of Jikes RVM with runs with Poor Richard's using either the Selfish strategy, the Communal strategy, or a Leadered strategy. To insure that improvements are due to Poor Richard's memory manager only, these graphs (and all results in this paper) are for runs using fixed heap sizes.[4] In these graphs, the x-axis shows the fixed heap size used for the run and the y-axis shows the execution times relative to the performance of Poor Richard's memory manager using the Leadered strategy.

As soon as paging begins, the benefits of our approach become immediately apparent. The performance of runs using either the basic GenMS or GenImmix GCs quickly degrade as a result of paging. As Figure 4(a) shows, this degradation can lead to factor of 10 or more slowdowns. The results from the Poor Richard's runs, however, show that all of its strategies can reduce this slowdown

considerably. The Communal strategy is consistently the worst performing strategy for Poor Richard's. This poor performance comes about for multiple reasons. Forcing all processes to collect their heap in response to memory pressure, even with those collections being serialized, works only when executing homogeneous workloads (Figures 4(c) and 4(d)) or when both processes have heap sizes that greatly exceed the size of the live data in the heap (Figure 4(b)). When processes have very different workloads, few of the GCs triggered by the Communal strategy are needed and the short-term increase in process' working set sizes leads to greater amounts of paging. This results in performance that can be worse than the default approach (Figure 4(a)). As our results from the Leadered strategy show, only one process needs to GC to alleviate memory pressure. Second and subsequent resource-driven collections merely add GC overhead and are not needed to prevent paging.

The runs using Poor Richard's with either the Selfish or Leadered strategies, in contrast, provide very consistent results across all benchmarks. Because these results are for runs using only two processes, it is unlikely that both processes would perform simultaneous resource-driven GCs; one would expect the performance of the these strategies to be very similar on this architecture. As can be seen in Figure 5, this is the case. While the Leadered strategy was slightly better, the differences seen between these two strategies was within the variances we measured. A more interesting note is that the performance of both these collectors was largely independent of the heap size specified. At the largest heap sizes, the Leadered strategy averaged throughput a factor of 1.07 slower than at the smallest heap size using GenMS and a factor of 1.04 slower using GenImmix. For the Selfish strategy, the slowdowns were roughly similar: a factor of 1.06 for runs with GenMS and a factor of 1.05 slower for runs using GenImmix. This suggests that either of these approaches work well towards eliminating paging concerns when selecting a heap size on a dual-core machine.

In Figure 6 one can see the results from 4 simultaneous runs of pseudoJBB using the GenImmix collector. These demonstrate that the problems that arise with paging may only get worse as we use machines with ever increasing numbers of cores. As when two processes were simultaneously executed, paging causes significant slowdowns to the default Jikes RVM system. As one might expect, the overhead imposed by Communal strategy becomes increasingly more expensive as we add processes. While this system-wide solution to paging may seem attractive, its strength of involving all processes in the solution also means it is unable to respond quickly enough to avoid paging or even alleviate paging that might occur. Similarly, these results begin to show the weakness of the Selfish approach. With more processes executing, we begin to see instances where two processes perform resource-driven GCs at the same time. As we predicted, this increases the memory pressure on the system and actually causes more paging, not less. Because this event does not always happen, the results for the Selfish strategy become more erratic than before. When everything works the Selfish strategy can still match the Leadered strategy, but only if everything falls into place at the correct times. Figure 7 shows that these findings continue to hold across the board. By collaborating on a system-wide response, but without significant overheads, the Leadered strategy continues performing well at all heap sizes.

4.5 Performance in Mono

As a last experiment to see how adaptable our approach really was, we also ported Poor Richard's to the Mono [22] VM which executes .Net applications. This port was interesting because Mono uses a conservative, whole-heap collector based upon the BDW collector and is very different from the GCs on which we previously tested Poor Richard's. The differences were not hard to overcome,

---

[4] We repeated these experiments with runs using the default heap sizing algorithm and a fixed upper-bound on the heap size. These showed similar relative results and support these conclusions.

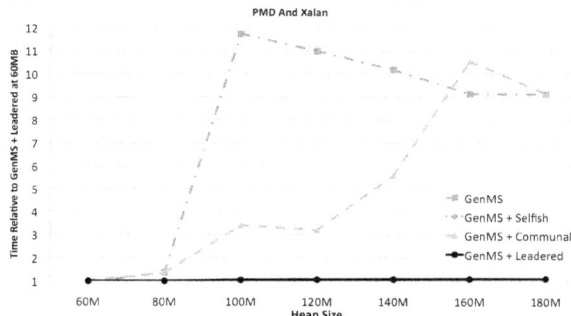

(a) Executing Xalan and PMD for GenMS and GenMS with Poor Richard's using 3 different strategies. While all runs using Poor Richard's memory manager outperforms the default system, runs using the Selfish or Leadered strategies do substantially better.

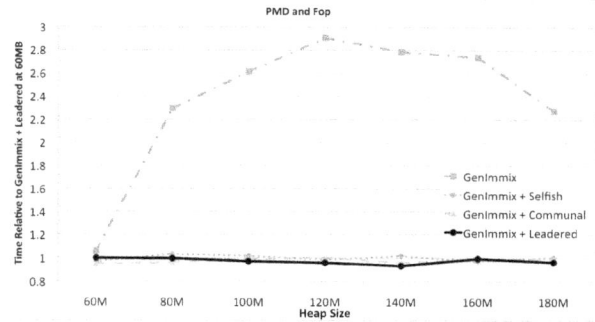

(b) Relative performance executing Fop and PMD for GenImmix with Poor Richard's using 3 different strategies. The performance of Poor Richard's memory manager does not depend on the GC being executed. When heap sizes get large enough that the number of GCs decreases substantially, the base Jikes RVM does not suffer as much from paging.

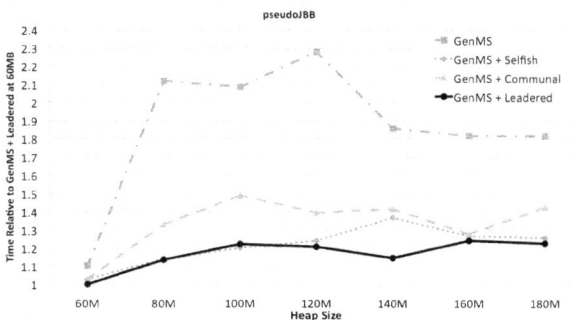

(c) Relative throughput executing pseudoJBB for GenMS and GenMS with Poor Richard's using 3 different strategies. While the Communal strategy does better with these homogeneous workloads, the Selfish and Leadered strategies continue to outperform the other approaches.

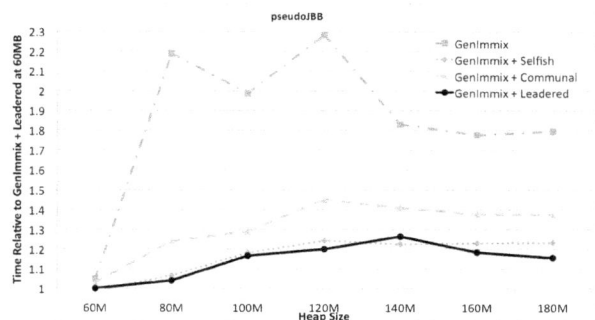

(d) Relative throughput executing pseudoJBB for GenImmix and Gen-Immix with Poor Richard's using 3 different strategies. Even with only 2 processes running in these experiments, the slight collaboration provided by the Leadered strategy can improve overall throughput.

Figure 4. Graphs showing that Poor Richard's memory manager improves the paging performance of both the GenMS and GenImmix collectors in Jikes RVM on a dual processor machine for both homogeneous and heterogeneous workloads. Because paging's impact affects all processes, a system-wide response can improve performance even when only two processes are executing.

---

however. Because of the simplicity of our interface, this port was very simple to make. Much more difficult was finding benchmarks we could run that were capable of generating a heap that could trigger paging. In the end, we relied on a port of the GCOld synthetic benchmark. We used this with several different ratios of short-to-long lived objects to test our system. Figure 8 shows that Poor Richard's memory manager was even able to improve the throughput of 2 simultaneous executions of this system, offering a speedup between 1.5 and 1.73.

5. Related work

The idea of using a lightweight approach to manage shared resources was first investigated by Zhang et al. [47]. This work investigated ways of handling threads within virtual machines executing in multiprogrammed environments. Each "friendly" virtual machine estimates system load using information already made available by the OS. Each process works selfishly, suspending threads upon determining the system is overloaded and resuming threads when it finds the system can handle an increased load. The earlier work focuses on optimizing system performance for embarrassingly parallel processes in which each thread can be treated as equal and independent. Our work investigates a more complex and dynamic environment with a far greater penalty for making the

wrong decision. While both works are motivated similarly, the research differs greatly in their environments, goals, and the means of achieving these goals.

Many early garbage collection algorithms included features designed to reduce heap sizes or the effects of paging. One common solution is to use heap compaction algorithms, which reduce the size of a program's working set and therefore the need for a system to page [10, 11, 17, 18, 22, 25]. As the size of available memory increased, algorithms were proposed to divide the heap into spaces or generations which could be collected individually [8, 12, 31, 33, 34, 39]. Our work, like these algorithms, tries to control the size of the heap to limit applications' and garbage collectors' working sets and thus reduce the need for pages to be evicted and the effects of unnecessary paging. Our work differs, however, in that it includes system-wide communication about memory pressure and is orthogonal to the specific GC algorithms being used.

Several recent approaches explored resource-based memory management and used both the operating system and virtual machine to improve paging performance. Yang et al. modified the operating system to develop approximate reuse distance histograms with which they could estimate the current available memory size. Their CRAMM system then developed collector models which enabled the JVM to select a heap size that would utilize available

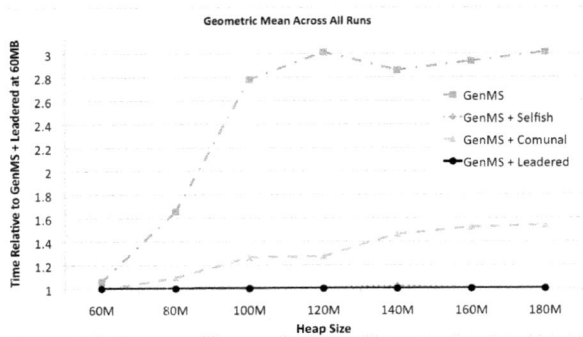

(a) Relative throughput across all runs for GenMS and GenMS with Poor Richard's using 3 different strategies. These results show that the Selfish and Leadered strategies perform well no matter the heap size.

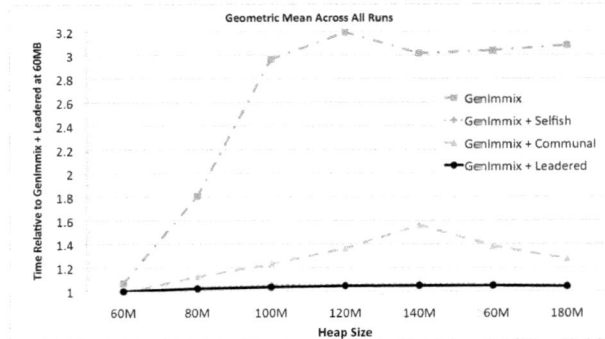

(b) Relative throughput across all runs for GenImmix and GenImmix with Poor Richard's using 3 different strategies. The Leadered approach continues to provide good performance that is largely independent of the heap size specified.

Figure 5. Graphs showing that Poor Richard's memory manager improves the paging performance of both the GenMS and GenImmix collectors in Jikes RVM on a dual processor machine for both homogeneous and heterogeneous workloads. Because paging's impact affects all processes, a system-wide response can improve performance even when only two processes are executing.

physical memory fully [44, 45]. Hertz et al. developed the Book-marking Collector (BC), a paging-aware garbage collector that worked in conjunction with a modified virtual memory manager. When used together it was able to eliminate paging costs in large heaps and greatly reduce paging costs in all situations [28]. Unlike CRAMM and BC, Poor Richard's needs no OS changes, interacts minimally with the host VM, and is independent of the GC algorithm being used.

Other studies of resource-based memory management considered ways to size the heap in response to memory pressure. Alonso and Appel presented a collector that followed each collection by consulting a process (the "advisor"). Their system could reduce the heap size to a level based on the amount of available memory [6]. More recently, Grzegorczyk et al. developed a tiny addition to Linux with which they could determine the number of page allocation stalls. Using a count of these stalls, which they showed is a good indicator of memory pressure [26], their Isla Vista system could guide a VM's heap sizing policy appropriately. Unlike these past works our approach neither modifies applications' heap sizes nor requires any additions to the OS, but instead relies on frequent polling of already available information. Our work also differs in that it explicitly considers memory sharing by mulitple JVMs and enables decision making based upon system-wide information.

Researchers have also investigated using program analysis to reduce the effects of paging on garbage-collected applications. Andreasson et al. used reinforcement learning to improve GC decisions through thousands of iterations. They assigned fixed cost for GC and paging and predicted the running time as a function of these and other parameters [7]. The average performance improvement for SPECjbb2K running on JRockit was 2% with the learning overhead and 6% otherwise. Instead of using a fixed cost and memory size, other recent work [46] adaptively monitored the number of page faults and adjusted the heap size of a program in an exclusive environment. Both of these methods relied upon manual analysis of the program. Unlike those approaches, our work is fully automated and can be applied to general programs. More importantly, Poor Richard's works in shared environments.

Many other adaptive schemes have been used for garbage collection. Several studies examined adaptation based on the program demand. Buytaert et al. use offline profiling to determine the amount of reachable data as the program runs and generate a list-

ing of program points when collecting the heap will be most favorable. At runtime, they then can collect the heap when the ratio of reachable to unreachable data is most effective [20]. Similar work by Ding et al. used a Lisp interpreter to show that limiting collections to occur only at phase boundaries reduced GC overhead and improved data locality [23]. By using allocation pauses to dynamically detect phase boundaries and limiting collections to these phase boundaries, Xian et al. improved throughput by up to 14% [43]. Soman et al. used profiling, user annotation, and a modified JVM so a program may select which garbage collector to use at the program loading time [37]. Wegiel and Krintz developed the Yield Predictor which estimated the percentage of the heap a whole-heap garbage collection would reclaim and so could be used to skip performing unproductive collections and just grow the heap initially [41]. MMTk [14] can adjust its heap size by analyzing heap and garbage collection statistics and applying a set of predetermined ratios. Similarly, HotSpot [2] and Oracle JRockit [5] can adjust their heap sizes to target a specific pause time, throughput, or heap size. Our work is orthogonal and complementary because it reacts to the changing resource in the system rather than predicting the demand of applications.

While heap management adds several new wrinkles, there are many prior works creating virtual memory managers which adapt to program behavior to reduce paging. Smaragdakis et al. developed early eviction LRU (EELRU), which made use of recency information to improve eviction decisions [36]. Last reuse distance, another recency metric, was used by Jiang and Zhang to avert thrashing [30], by Chen et al. to improve Linux VM [21], and by Zhou et al. to improve multi-programming [48]. All of these techniques try to best allocate physical memory for a fixed subset of the working set, but are of limited benefit when the total working set fits in available memory or when the available memory is too small for the subset. Resource-based memory management, on the other hand, only triggers collections upon detecting significant memory pressure. Because it does nothing in the absence of paging, the heap will grow to take full advantage of physical memory when it becomes available. Our system is therefore able to trigger more frequent collections (avoiding paging costs) dynamically without sacrificing the larger heap sizes (increased memory usage) that would otherwise provide better performance.

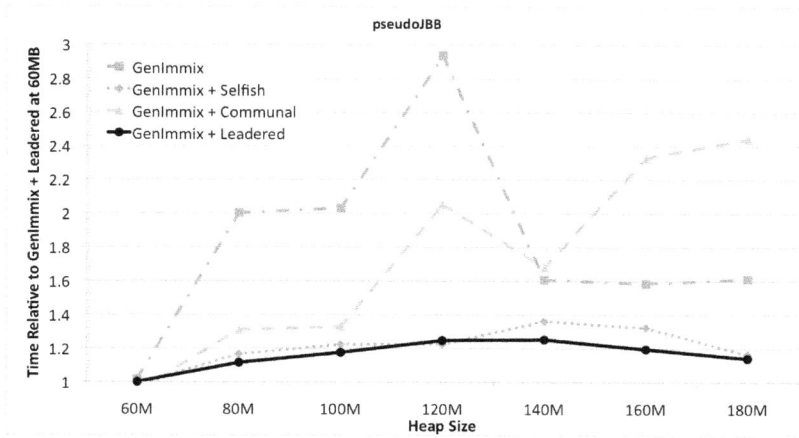

Figure 6. Results when executing 4 processes simultaneously. Only the Leadered strategy's triggering of a single resource-driven collection in response to memory pressure continues to avoid significant paging.

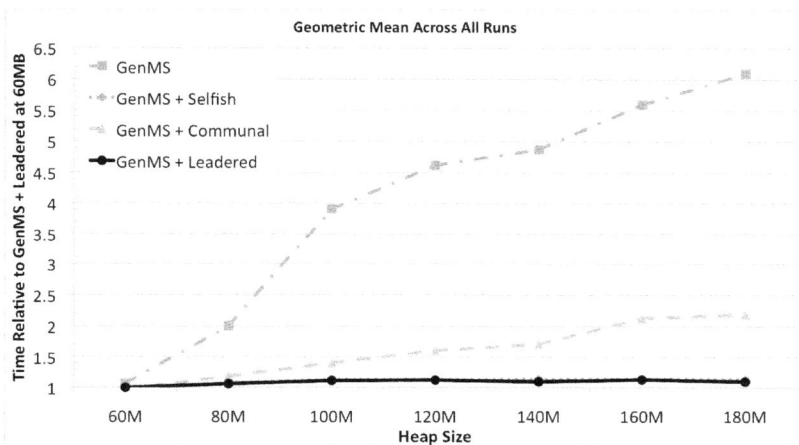

Figure 7. Average across all our runs when executing 4 process simultaneously. Poor Richard's continues to scale to this environment and the Leadered strategy's minimal collaboration increasingly outperforms all other approaches.

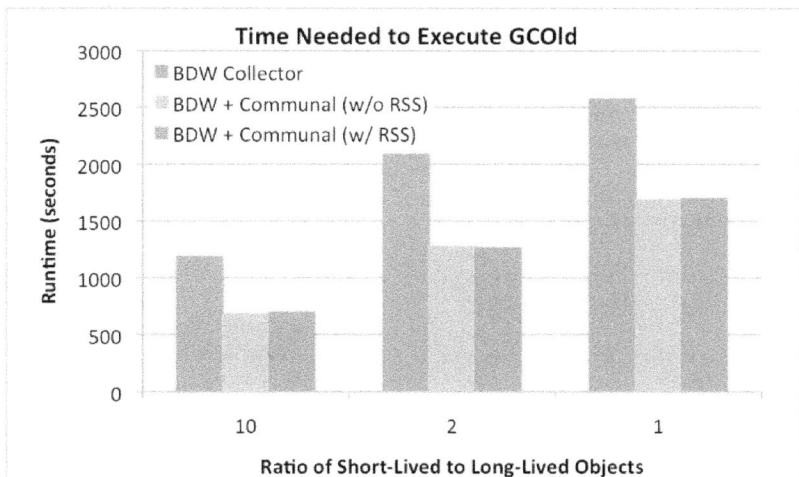

Figure 8. Graphs showing Poor Richard's memory manager improves the paging performance of the Mono runtime system. Unlike Jikes RVM, Mono uses a conservative, whole-heap collector.

6. Conclusions and Future Work

Garbage-collected applications need their heaps sized to be large enough to provide optimal performance. Sizing the heap too large, however, can lead the system to page and throughput to plummet. When executed on the multi-processor, multi-core machines that are increasingly common, this requires applications adjust their heaps dynamically and in reaction to changes brought on by other processes. Should other processes react to changes in available memory similarly, the result could lead to either increased contention as they all grab for the same resources or decreased utility as they all react too conservatively.

Poor Richard's memory manager avoids this problem by allowing each process to detect and react to increased memory pressure quickly and avoid paging. It does this in a simple, lightweight manner that requires few changes to existing systems, allowing them to keep their existing good performance when not paging, and improves the paging performance of all collectors we tried. By enabling processes to collaborate on system-wide solutions, Poor Richard's scales to multiprogramming environments easily and improves the average throughput across a range of benchmarks by up to a factor of 5.5.

As part of our future work, we plan to port Poor Richard's to additional VMs and investigate alternative methods of selecting a leader in Poor Richard's Leadered strategy. In particular, we plan on investigating approaches that would allow systems to tailor how resources are allocated to meet their particular needs. By providing a mechanism which could be used to ensure certain processes meet guaranteed performance goals, optimize throughput, or allow creation of multiple levels of priority, Poor Richard's could help ensure that the software engineering benefits of garbage collection can continue.

Acknowledgments

We are grateful to IBM Research for making the Jikes RVM system available under open source terms and for the developers of the MMTk memory management toolkit. We would also like to thank Margaret Foster and the anonymous reviewers for their excellent suggestions on this paper.

This work was supported by the Canisius Ensuring Excellence Program and the National Science Foundation under awards CSR-0834566 and CSR-0834323. Any opinions, findings, and conclusions or recommendations expressed in this material are those of the author(s) and do not necessarily reflect the views of the National Science Foundation.

References

[1] Bug ID: 4694058 Allow JRE to return unused memory to the system heap. Available at http://bugs.sun.com/bugdatabase/view_bug.do?bug_id=4694058.

[2] Garbage collector ergonomics. Available at http://download.oracle.com/javase/6/docs/technotes/guides/vm/gc-ergonomics.html.

[3] getrusage(3c) - solaris man page. Available at http://download.oracle.com/docs/cd/E19963-01/821-1465/getrusage-3c/index.html.

[4] proc(5) - process info pseudo-filesystem - Linux man page. Available at http://linux.die.net/man/5/proc.

[5] Tuning the memory management system. Available at http://download.oracle.com/docs/cd/E15289_01/doc.40/e15060/memman.htm#i1092162.

[6] R. Alonso and A. W. Appel. An advisor for flexible working sets. In *Proceedings of the 1990 Joint International Conference on Measurement and Modeling of Computer Systems*, pages 153–162, Boulder, CO, May 1990.

[7] E. Andreasson, F. Hoffmann, and O. Lindholm. To collect or not to collect? Machine learning for memory management. In *JVM '02: Proceedings of the Java Virtual Machine Research and Technology Symposium*, pages 27–39, August 2002.

[8] A. W. Appel. Simple generational garbage collection and fast allocation. *Software: Practice and Experience*, 19(2):171–183, 1989.

[9] D. F. Bacon, P. Cheng, and V. T. Rajan. A real-time garbage collecor with low overhead and consistent utilization. In *Thirtieth Annual ACM Symposium on Principles of Programming Languages*, volume 38(1), pages 285–298, New Orleans, LA, Jan. 2003.

[10] H. D. Baecker. Garbage collection for virtual memory computer systems. *Communications of the ACM*, 15(11):981–986, Nov. 1972.

[11] H. G. Baker. List processing in real-time on a serial computer. *Communications of the ACM*, 21(4):280–294, 1978.

[12] P. B. Bishop. *Computer Systems with a Very Large Address Space and Garbage Collection*. PhD thesis, MIT Laboratory for Computer Science, Cambridge, MA, May 1977.

[13] S. M. Blackburn, P. Cheng, and K. S. McKinley. Myths and reality: The performance impact of garbage collection. In *Proceedings of the 2004 Joint International Conference on Measurement and Modeling of Computer Systems*, volume 32(1), pages 25–36, June 2004.

[14] S. M. Blackburn, P. Cheng, and K. S. McKinley. Oil and water? high performance garbage collection in Java with MMTk. In *Proceedings of the 26th International Conference on Software Engineering*, pages 137–146, Edinburgh, Scotland, May 2004.

[15] S. M. Blackburn, R. Garner, C. Hoffmann, A. M. Khang, K. S. McKinley, R. Bentzur, A. Diwan, D. Feinberg, D. Frampton, S. Z. Guyer, M. Hirzel, A. Hosking, M. Jump, H. Lee, J. E. B. Moss, B. Moss, A. Phansalkar, D. Stefanović, T. VanDrunen, D. von Dincklage, and B. Wiedermann. The DaCapo benchmarks: Java benchmarking development and analysis. In *Proceedings of ACM SIGPLAN Conference on Object-Oriented Programming Systems, Languages and Applications*, volume 41(10), pages 169–190, Oct. 2006.

[16] S. M. Blackburn and K. S. McKinley. Immix: a mark-region garbage collector with space efficiency, fast collection, and mutator performance. In *Proceedings of the 2008 ACM SIGPLAN conference on Programming language design and implementation*, volume 43(6), pages 22–32, Tucson, AZ, 2008.

[17] D. G. Bobrow and D. L. Murphy. Structure of a LISP system using two-level storage. *Communications of the ACM*, 10(3):155–159, Mar. 1967.

[18] D. G. Bobrow and D. L. Murphy. A note on the efficiency of a LISP computation in a paged machine. *Communications of the ACM*, 11(8):558–560, Aug. 1968.

[19] H.-J. Boehm and M. Weiser. Garbage collection in an uncooperative environment. *Software: Practice and Experience*, 8(9):807–820, Sept. 1988.

[20] D. Buytaert, K. Venstermans, L. Eeckhout, and K. D. Bosschere. GCH: Hints for triggering garbage collections. In *Transactions on High-Performance Embedded Architectures and Compilers I*, pages 74–94, 2007.

[21] F. Chen, S. Jiang, and X. Zhang. CLOCK-Pro: an effective improvement of the CLOCK replacement. In *Proceedings of USENIX Annual Technical Conference*, 2005.

[22] C. J. Cheney. A non-recursive list compacting algorithm. *Communications of the ACM*, 13(11):677–678, Nov. 1970.

[23] C. Ding, C. Zhang, X. Shen, and M. Ogihara. Gated memory control for memory monitoring, leak detection and garbage collection. In *Proceedings of the ACM SIGPLAN Workshop on Memory System Performance*, pages 62–67, Chicago, IL, June 2005.

[24] L. Eeckhout, A. Georges, and K. D. Bosschere. How Java programs interact with virtual machines at the microarchitectural level. In *Proceedings of the 18th ACM Conference on Object-Oriented Programming, Systems, Languages, & Applications*, volume 38(11),

pages 169–186, Anaheim, CA, Oct. 2003.

[25] R. R. Fenichel and J. C. Yochelson. A Lisp garbage collector for virtual memory computer systems. *Communications of the ACM*, 12(11):611–612, Nov. 1969.

[26] C. Grzegorczyk, S. Soman, C. Krintz, and R. Wolski. Isla vista heap sizing: Using feedback to avoid paging. In *Proceedings of the International Symposium on Code Generation and Optimization*, pages 325–340, 2007.

[27] M. Hertz, Y. Feng, and E. D. Berger. Garbage collection without paging. In *Proceedings of the 2005 ACM SIGPLAN Conference on Programming Language Design and Implementation (PLDI 2005)*, volume 40(7), pages 143–153, Chicago, IL, June 2005.

[28] M. Hertz, Y. Feng, and E. D. Berger. Garbage collection without paging. In *Proceedings of the ACM SIGPLAN Conference on Programming Language Design and Implementation*, pages 143–153, Chicago, IL, June 2005.

[29] X. Huang, S. M. Blackburn, K. S. McKinley, J. E. B. Moss, Z. Wang, and P. Cheng. The garbage collection advantage: Improving program locality. In *Proceedings of the 19th ACM Conference on Object-Oriented Programming, Systems, Languages, & Applications*, volume 39(11), pages 69–80, Vancouver, BC, Canada, Oct. 2004.

[30] S. Jiang and X. Zhang. TPF: a dynamic system thrashing protection facility. *Software Practice and Experience*, 32(3), 2002.

[31] H. Lieberman and C. E. Hewitt. A real-time garbage collector based on the lifetimes of objects. *Communications of the ACM*, 26(6):419–429, June 1983.

[32] Mono Project. Mono. Available at http://www.mono-project.com/.

[33] D. A. Moon. Garbage collection in a large LISP system. In *Conference Record of the 1994 ACM Symposium on Lisp and Functional Programming*, pages 235–245, Austin, TX, Aug. 1994.

[34] J. H. Reppy. A high-performance garbage collector for Standard ML. Technical memorandum, AT&T Bell Laboratories, Murray Hill, NJ, Dec. 1993.

[35] N. Sachindran and J. E. B. Moss. Mark-Copy: Fast copying GC with less space overhead. In *Proceedings of the 18th ACM Conference on Object-Oriented Programming, Systems, Languages, & Applications*, volume 38(11), pages 326–343, Anaheim, CA, Oct. 2003.

[36] Y. Smaragdakis, S. Kaplan, and P. Wilson. The EELRU adaptive replacement algorithm. *Perform. Eval.*, 53(2):93–123, 2003.

[37] S. Soman, C. Krintz, and D. F. Bacon. Dynamic selection of application-specific garbage collectors. In *Proceedings of the International Symposium on Memory Management*, pages 49–60, Vancouver, BC, Canada, June 2004.

[38] Standard Performance Evaluation Corporation. Specjbb2000. Available at http://www.spec.org/jbb2000/docs/userguide.html.

[39] D. Ungar. Generation scavenging: A non-disruptive high performance storage reclamation algorithm. In *Proceedings of the First ASM SIGSOFT/SIGPLAN Software Engineering Symposium on Practical Software Development Environments*, volume 19(9), pages 157–167, Apr. 1984.

[40] M. Wegiel and C. Krintz. XMem: type-safe, transparent, shared memory for cross-runtime communication and coordination. In *Proceedings of the 2008 ACM SIGPLAN Conference on Programming Language Design and Implementation*, volume 43(6), pages 327–338, Tucson, AZ, June 2008.

[41] M. Wegiel and C. Krintz. Dynamic prediction of collection yield for managed runtimes. In *Proceeding of the 14th international conference on Architectural support for programming languages and operating systems*, volume 44(3), pages 289–300, Washington, DC, Mar. 2009.

[42] Wikipedia. procfs — Wikipedia, the free encyclopedia, 2011. [Online; accessed 1-Feb-2011].

[43] F. Xian, W. Seisa-an, and H. Jiang. MicroPhase: An approach to proactively invoking garbage collection for improved performance. In *Proceedings of the 22nd ACM Conference on Object-Oriented Programming, Systems, Languages, & Applications*, volume 42(10), pages 77–96, Montreal, Quebec, Canada, Oct. 2007.

[44] T. Yang, E. D. Berger, S. F. Kaplan, and J. E. B. Moss. CRAMM: virtual memory support for garbage-collected applications. In *Proceedings of the Symposium on Operating Systems Design and Implementation*, pages 103–116, Seattle, WA, Nov. 2006.

[45] T. Yang, M. Hertz, E. D. Berger, S. F. Kaplan, and J. E. B. Moss. Automatic heap sizing: taking real memory into account. In *Proceedings of the International Symposium on Memory Management*, pages 61–72, Vancouver, BC, Canada, June 2004.

[46] C. Zhang, K. Kelsey, X. Shen, C. Ding, M. Hertz, and M. Ogihara. Program-level adaptive memory management. In *Proceedings of the International Symposium on Memory Management*, pages 174–183, Ottawa, ON, Canada, June 2006.

[47] Y. Zhang, A. Bestavros, M. Guirguis, I. Matta, and R. West. Friendly virtual machines: leveraging a feedback-control model for application adaptation. In *Proceedings of the 1st ACM/USENIX international conference on Virtual execution environments*, pages 2–12, Chicago, IL, June 2005.

[48] P. Zhou, V. Pandey, J. Sundaresan, A. Raghuraman, Y. Zhou, and S. Kumar. Dynamic tracking of page miss ratio curve for memory management. In *Proceedings of the International Conference on Architectural Support for Programming Languages and Operating Systems*, volume 39(11), pages 177–188, Boston, MA, Oct. 2004.

Memory Systems in the Many-Core Era:
Challenges, Opportunities, and Solution Directions

Onur Mutlu

Carnegie Mellon University
http://www.ece.cmu.edu/~omutlu

Abstract

The memory subsystem is a fundamental performance and energy bottleneck in almost all computing systems. Recent trends towards increasingly more cores on die, consolidation of diverse workloads on a single chip, and difficulty of DRAM scaling impose new requirements and exacerbate old demands on the memory system. In particular, the need for memory bandwidth and capacity is increasing [14], applications' interference in memory system increasingly limits system performance and makes the system hard to control [12], memory energy and power are key design concerns [8], and DRAM technology consumes significant amount of energy and does not scale down easily to smaller technology nodes [7]. Fortunately, some promising solution directions exist.

In this talk, we will examine recent technology, application, and architecture trends motivating a fundamental rethinking of the memory hierarchy. Based on this motivation, we will describe requirements from an ideal memory system suitable for the many-core era. The talk will examine questions one would need to answer in approximating the ideal memory system and possible avenues that seem promising for the research community to explore. In particular, we will focus on the problem of uncontrolled inter-application interference in the memory system and draw upon our experiences in solving it by designing quality-of-service (QoS) aware memory controllers [5, 6, 9, 10, 11, 12], interconnects [1, 2, 13], and entire memory systems [3, 4]. We will make a case for application- and QoS-aware design of memory systems and integrated/cooperative design of cores, interconnects, and memory components to optimize the overall system.

Categories and Subject Descriptors C.0 [*Computer Systems Organization*]: System architectures; C.1.2 [*Computer Systems Organization*]: Multiple Data Stream Architectures

General Terms Algorithms, Design, Performance

Keywords Memory systems, multi-core, chip multiprocessors, interconnects, quality of service

References

[1] R. Das, O. Mutlu, T. Moscibroda, and C. Das. Application-aware prioritization mechanisms for on-chip networks. In *International Symposium on Microarchitecture (MICRO-42)*, 2009.

[2] R. Das, O. Mutlu, T. Moscibroda, and C. Das. Aergia: Exploiting packet latency slack in on-chip networks. In *International Symposium on Computer Architecture (ISCA-37)*, 2010.

[3] E. Ebrahimi, C. J. Lee, O. Mutlu, and Y. N. Patt. Fairness via source throttling: A configurable and high-performance fairness substrate for multi-core memory systems. In *International Conference on Architectural Support for Programming Languages and Operating Systems (ASPLOS-XV)*, 2010.

[4] E. Ebrahimi, C. J. Lee, O. Mutlu, and Y. N. Patt. Prefetch-aware shared resource management for multi-core systems. In *International Symposium on Computer Architecture (ISCA-38)*, 2011.

[5] Y. Kim, D. Han, O. Mutlu, and M. Harchol-Balter. ATLAS: a scalable and high-performance scheduling algorithm for multiple memory controllers. In *International Symposium on High-Performance Computer Architecture (HPCA-16)*, 2010.

[6] Y. Kim, M. Papamichael, O. Mutlu, and M. Harchol-Balter. Thread cluster memory scheduling: Exploiting differences in memory access behavior. In *International Symposium on Microarchitecture (MICRO-43)*, 2010.

[7] B. C. Lee, E. Ipek, O. Mutlu, and D. Burger. Architecting phase change memory as a scalable DRAM alternative. In *International Symposium on Computer Architecture (ISCA-36)*, 2009.

[8] C. Lefurgy, K. Rajamani, F. L. Rawson-III, W. M. Felter, M. Kistler, and T. W. Keller. Energy management for commercial servers. *IEEE Computer*, 36(12):39–48, 2003.

[9] T. Moscibroda and O. Mutlu. Memory performance attacks: Denial of memory service in multi-core systems. In *16th USENIX Security Symposium*, 2007.

[10] T. Moscibroda and O. Mutlu. Distributed order scheduling and its application to multi-core DRAM controllers. In *ACM Symposium on Principles of Distributed Computing (PODC-27)*, 2008.

[11] O. Mutlu and T. Moscibroda. Parallelism-aware batch scheduling: Enhancing both performance and fairness of shared DRAM systems. In *International Symposium on Computer Architecture (ISCA-35)*, 2008.

[12] O. Mutlu and T. Moscibroda. Stall-time fair memory access scheduling for chip multiprocessors. In *International Symposium on Microarchitecture (MICRO-40)*, 2007.

[13] G. Nychis, C. Fallin, T. Moscibroda, and O. Mutlu. Next generation on-chip networks: What kind of congestion control do we need? In *9th ACM Workshop on Hot Topics in Networks (HOTNETS)*, 2010.

[14] M. K. Qureshi, V. Srinivasan, and J. A. Rivers. Scalable high performance main memory system using phase-change memory technology. In *International Symposium on Computer Architecture (ISCA-36)*, 2009.

ISMM'11, June 4–5, 2011, San Jose, California, USA.
ACM 978-1-4503-0263-0/11/06.

C4: The Continuously Concurrent Compacting Collector

Gil Tene

Azul Systems Inc.
gil@azulsystems.com

Balaji Iyengar

Azul Systems Inc.
balaji@azulsystems.com

Michael Wolf

Azul Systems Inc.
wolf@azulsystems.com

Abstract

C4, the Continuously Concurrent Compacting Collector, an up-dated generational form of the Pauseless GC Algorithm [7], is introduced and described, along with details of its implementation on modern X86 hardware. It uses a read barrier to support concurrent compaction, concurrent remapping, and concurrent incremental update tracing. C4 differentiates itself from other generational garbage collectors by supporting simultaneous-generational concurrency: the different generations are collected using concurrent (non stop-the-world) mechanisms that can be simultaneously and independently active. C4 is able to continuously perform concurrent young generation collections, even during long periods of concurrent full heap collection, allowing C4 to sustain high allocation rates and maintain the efficiency typical to generational collectors, without sacrificing response times or reverting to stop-the-world operation. Azul systems has been shipping a commercial implementation of the Pauseless GC mechanism, since 2005. Three successive generations of Azul's Vega series systems relied on custom multi-core processors and a custom OS kernel to deliver both the scale and features needed to support Pauseless GC. In 2010, Azul released its first software-only commercial implementation of C4 for modern commodity X86 hardware, using Linux kernel enhancements to support the required feature set. We discuss implementation details of C4 on X86, including the Linux virtual and physical memory management enhancements that were used to support the high rate of virtual memory operations required for sustained pauseless operation. We discuss updates to the collector's management of the heap for efficient generational collection and provide throughput and pause time data while running sustained workloads.

Categories and Subject Descriptors D.3.3 [*Language Constructs and Features*]: Dynamic storage management; Concurrent programming structures; D.3.4 [*Processors*]: Memory management (garbage collection); D.4.2 [*Storage Management*]: Garbage collection; Virtual memory

General Terms Algorithms, Design, Languages, Performance.

Keywords concurrent, garbage collection, pauseless, generational, read barrier, virtual memory, Linux.

1. Introduction

Generational collectors are based on the *Weak generational hypothesis* [18] i.e. most objects die young. Therefore by focusing the GC efforts on these objects you would get the proverbial most bang for the buck. Generational focus helps GC algorithms keep up with higher allocation rates, which translates to higher throughput. Most generational collectors divide the heap into two generations, with the younger generation having a smaller, more frequently collected live set. This results in the mutators being exposed to shorter application disruptions associated with young generation collection in the common case, while allowing GC to keep up with high allocation rates. It also serves to delay old generation processing and make it more rare, reducing the frequency of the larger GC workloads and response time artifacts generally incurred in full heap collections.

Most generational collector implementations use stop-the-world, copying, parallel, young generation collectors, relying on the generally short GC pauses of parallel young generation collection to be acceptable for sustained server operations. However, while young generation stop the world pauses are generally quite short, common patterns in enterprise programs executing at current server scales can cause occasional (and sometimes frequent) large young generation GC pauses as large live sets with medium life spans appear in the young generation and are copied within it before being promoted, or as shifts in program execution phases create large amounts of new long-lived objects in rapid succession. The former case is common with in memory object caches, with fat-state session based enterprise applications (such as portals), and with replicated in-memory data and messaging systems. The latter case occurs at application phase shift times, such as during application startup, application failover, cache hydration times, and catalog or contents update or reload operations driven by higher level business processes.

The problems caused by impacts on response time, due to growing heap sizes coupled with stop-the-world-compaction old generation collectors, are well known [3, 9]. However, as Managed Runtimes continue to grow and attempt to use 10s (or even 100s) of Gigabytes of memory the lengths of occasionally long young generation stop-the-world events also grow to become unacceptable for most enterprise applications. When viewed from the perspective of current commodity server environments containing 100s of Gigabytes of cheap RAM, even "modest sized" applications would be expected to sustain live sets in the 10s of Gigabytes, with young generation live sets easily ranging into the Gigabytes and occasionally spiking into the 10s of gigabytes. Concurrent young generation collection in such environments is just as important as concurrent old generation collection was a decade ago, if not more so.

At the core of the problem lie compaction and object relocation: Object relocation is inherent to all effective generational collectors. It would be "extremely hard" to implement a generational collection scheme without supporting promotion. In order for young generation collection to be concurrent, it must support concurrent object relocation. Concurrent relocating collectors have been proposed in various works [13]. However, with the exception of Azul's JVMs, no commercially shipping concurrent compacting or concurrent relocating collectors are available as of this writing, for either Java or .NET server environments.

C4 is a Generational, Continuously Concurrent Compacting Collector algorithm. It is a throughput-friendly, multi-generational improvement to the full heap, single generation read barrier based Pauseless GC algorithm [7]. All generations in C4 use concurrent compacting collectors and avoid the use of global stop-the-world operations, maintaining concurrent mutator operation throughout all phases of each generation. The cycles and phases of the different generations can be simultaneously and concurrently executed. While current C4 implementations use two generations (young and old), the algorithm can be straightforwardly extended to an N generation system.

C4 is currently shipping as part of commercially available JVM's. These JVMs are available on Azul's custom Vega hardware platform as well as through its recently released X86 based Zing software platform. C4 has also been demonstrated within an OpenJDK based implementation as part of the Managed Runtime Initiative [2]. The C4 collector allows JVMs to smoothly scale up to 10's and 100's of Gigabytes in heap sizes and live object sets, sustain multi-Gigabyte-per-sec allocation rates, and at the same time contain the JVM's measurable jitter[1] and response time artifacts to the low 10's of msec. At the point of this writing, measured JVM jitter is no longer strongly affected by garbage collection, with scheduling and thread contention artifacts dominating.

The X86 based implementation of C4 runs on top of a modified Linux kernel that delivers a new virtual memory subsystem used to support the features and throughput needed by C4's concurrent operation and page lifecycle. The goals of this paper are to describe:

1. The basic C4 algorithm, including inter-generational concurrency and page lifecycle aspects

2. The features added to the Linux virtual memory subsystem to support C4 functionality

3. C4's updated heap management logic

2. The C4 Algorithm

C4 is generational, concurrent, and always-compacting. It uses two independently running instances of a modified Pauseless GC algorithm [7] to simultaneously collect both the young generation and old generation. Each generation's GC cycle goes through logically sequential object Mark, object Relocate and reference Remap phases. The cornerstones of C4's concurrent compacting algorithm include:

2.1 The Loaded Value Barrier (LVB)

The Loaded Value Barrier is an incarnation of Pauseless GC's read barrier. The LVB imposes a set of invariants on every object reference value as it is loaded from memory and made visible to the mutator, regardless of use. The two invariants imposed on all loaded reference values are:

- All visible loaded reference values will be safely "marked through" by the collector, if they haven't been already.

- All visible loaded reference values point to the current location of the safely accessible contents of the target objects they refer to.

An LVB can obviously encounter loaded reference value that do not meet one of these invariants, or both. In all such cases, the LVB will "trigger" and execute collector code to immediately remedy the situation and correct the reference such that it meets the required invariants, before making it visible to subsequent program operations.

LVB differs from a Brooks-style [6] indirection barrier in that, like a Baker-style [4] read barrier, it imposes invariants on references as they are loaded, rather than applying them as they are used. By applying to all loaded references, LVB guarantees no uncorrected references can be propagated by the mutator, facilitating certain single-pass guarantees.

LVB further differs from both Baker-style and Brooks-style collectors in two key ways:

1. LVB simultaneously imposes invariants both on the reference's target address and on the reference's marking state, facilitating both concurrent relocation and precise wavefront tracing in C4 [19] using a single fused barrier.

2. LVB ensures (and requires) that any trigger of either (or both) of its two invariant tests can be immediately and independently repaired by the mutator using Self Healing behavior (see below), leading to efficient and predictable fast path test execution and facilitating C4's concurrent marking, concurrent relocation, and concurrent remapping characteristics.

2.2 Self Healing

LVB is a self-healing barrier. Since the LVB is always executed at reference load time, it has access not only to the reference value being verified, but to the memory address the value was loaded from as well. When an LVB triggers and takes corrective action, modifying a reference to meet the LVB invariants, it will also "heal" the source memory location that the reference was loaded from by (atomically) storing a copy of the reference back to the source location. This allows mutators to immediately self heal the root cause of each LVB trigger as it occurs, avoiding repeated triggers on the same loaded reference, and dramatically reducing the dynamic occurrence of read barrier triggers. Each reference memory storage location will trigger "at most once" (discounting minute levels of atomicity races in the healing process). Since the number of references in the heap is finite, single pass marking and single pass reference remapping are both guaranteed in a straight forward manner.

Self healing is uniquely enabled by the LVB's semantic position in the code stream, immediately following the reference load operation, and preceding all uses or propagation of the loaded reference value. This semantic proximity to the reference load operation grants the LVB access to the loaded reference's source address, which is required in order to perform the healing actions. Through Self Healing, LVB dramatically reduces the dynamic occurrence of read barrier triggering, making LVB significantly more efficient and predictable than both Brooks style and Baker style barriers, as well as other read barriers that will continue to trigger in the hot code path during certain GC phases.

2.3 Reference metadata and the NMT state

Similarly to the single generation Pauseless GC algorithm [7], C4 tracks metadata "Not Marked Through" (NMT) state associated with all object references in the heap[2]. On modern 64 bit hardware, this metadata is tracked in bits of the object reference that are not interpreted as address bits, but are considered by the LVB. Object

---

[1] JVM jitter, in this context, refers to application observable time delays in executions, that would have been instantaneous had it not been for the behavior of the JVM and the underlying system stack. For example, a 1 msec, Thread.sleep() would be expected to wake up within 1 msec, and any observable delay beyond 1 msec can be attributed to JVM jitter

references with an NMT state that does not match the currently expected NMT value will trigger the LVB.

C4's use of NMT state differs from Pauseless [7]. Where Pauseless maintained a single, global, currently expected value of the NMT state, C4 maintains a different expected value for the NMT field for each generation. In addition, C4 uses reference metadata bits to track the reference's generation (the generation in which the object to which the reference is pointing, resides). This allows the LVB to efficiently verify the NMT value for the proper generation. Since young generation and old generation collections can proceed independent of each other, their expected NMT states will often be different. A reference's generation, however, will never change under C4 without the object it is pointing to being relocated.

If, during an active mark phase, the LVB encounters a loaded object reference value with an NMT state that does not match the current expected state for that reference's target generation, the LVB will correct the situation by changing the NMT state to the expected value, and logging the reference on the collector's work list to make sure that it is safely traversed by the collector. Through self healing, the contents of the memory location that the reference value was loaded from will be corrected as well.

2.4 Page protection and concurrent relocation

C4 uses the same underlying page protection scheme introduced in Pauseless [7]. Pages that are currently being compacted are protected, and the LVB triggers when it encounters a loaded reference value that points to a protected page. In order to correct the triggering situation, the LVB will obtain the new location of the reference's target object, correct the reference value, and heal the contents of the memory location that the reference value was loaded from. In cases where the triggering reference value points to an object that has not yet been relocated, the LVB will first cooperatively relocate the object, and then correct the reference to point to its new location.

2.5 Quick Release

C4 uses the Quick Release method, first introduced in Pauseless [7] and with later variants used in Compressor [13], to efficiently recycle physical memory resources without needing to wait for a GC cycle to complete. When relocating objects for compaction, C4 stores object forwarding information outside of the page that objects are being compacted away from ("from" pages). This forwarding information is later used by the LVB and by the collector's remap phase to correct references to relocated objects such that they point to the object's current address. Once all the objects in a "from" page have been relocated elsewhere, the contents of the "from" page are no longer needed. Quick Release leverages the fact that while the "from" page's virtual address cannot be safely recycled until all live references to objects that were relocated from it are corrected, its physical backing store can be immediately freed and recycled.

C4 uses Quick Release to support hand-over-hand compaction, using the physical memory released by each compacted page as the target resource for compacting the next page. An entire generation can be compacted in a single cycle using a single free seed page, and without requiring additional free memory. As a result, C4 does not need survivor spaces, pre-allocated "to" spaces, or an amount of free memory equal to the size of the live set in order to support single pass compaction.

Quick Release also allows memory to be recycled for mutator allocation needs without waiting for a complete heap remap to complete. This significantly reduces the time between deciding to start a GC cycle and the availability of free memory to satisfy mutator allocation, resulting in GC heuristics that are more simple and robust.

2.6 Collector Phases

Supported by the strong invariants of the LVB, the C4 mechanism is quite straightforward, with each generation's collector proceeding through three phases:

- The Mark Phase: This phase is responsible for tracing the generation's live set by starting from the roots, marking all encountered objects as live, and all encountered object references as marked through. At the beginning of a Mark phase, all live references are known to have an NMT value that matches the previous cycle's expected NMT value. As the Mark phase commences, the collector flips the expected NMT value, instantly making all live references "not marked through", arming the LVB to support single pass marking. The collector proceeds to prime its worklists with roots, and continues to mark until the work lists are exhausted, at which point all reachable objects in the generation are known to have been marked live and all reachable reference NMT states are known to be marked through.

- The Relocate Phase: This phase compacts memory by relocating live objects into contiguously populated target pages, and freeing the resources occupied by potentially sparse source pages. Per-page liveness totals, collected during the previous mark phase, are consulted in order to focus relocation on compacting the sparsest pages first. The core relocation algorithm in C4 is similar to Pauseless. Each "from" page is protected, its objects are relocated to new "to" pages, forwarding information is stored outside the "from" page, and the "from" page's physical memory is immediately recycled.

- The Remap Phase: Lazy remapping occurs as mutator threads encounter stale references to relocated objects during and after the relocate phase. However, in order to complete a GC cycle a remap pass is needed. During the remap phase, all live references in the generation will be traversed, and any stale references to objects that have been relocated will be corrected to point to the current object addresses. At the end of the remap phase, no stale references will exist, and the virtual addresses associated with "from" pages relocated in the relocate phase can be safely recycled. While the remap phase is the third and final logical step of a GC cycle, C4 is not in "a hurry" to finish it. There are not physical resources being held, and lazy remapping can continue to occur without disrupting mutator operations. As a result, C4 fuses each remap phase with the next GC cycle's mark phase for efficiency. Since both phases need to traverse the same object and reference graphs, it joins them into a combined Mark-Remap phase that performs both operations in a single combined pass. Figure 1 depicts, the interleaving of combined Mark-Remap phases across overlapping GC cycles.

3. Multi-Generational Concurrency

By leveraging the generational hypothesis [18], generational collectors tend to derive significant efficiency, and are able to support significantly higher allocation throughput than their single generation counterparts. However, since concurrent relocation of objects seems to be "hard" to do in most currently shipping collectors, their young generation collectors are inherently stop-the-world, and are exposed to significant pause time effects that arise from large transient behaviors or a significant allocation rate of mid and long lived objects.

On the other hand, concurrent single generational collectors, even when they are able to avoid or delay the use of stop-the-world

---

[2] We do not use the tricolor abstraction to represent reference traversal states. Traditional tricolor abstraction [20] applies to object traversal states and not to reference traversal states. "Not Marked Through" references that would trigger an LVB could exist in traditionally white or grey objects and could be referencing objects that are traditionally white, grey or black.

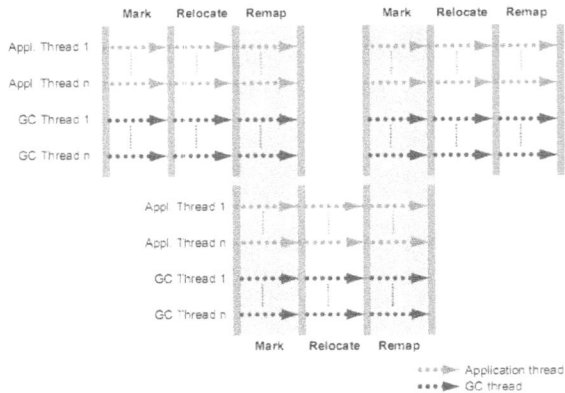

Figure 1. C4 GC cycle

object relocation, are exposed to the inefficiency issues and limited sustainable allocation rates that arise from the lack of a generational filter.

C4 eliminates this classic throughput vs. latency trade-off by supporting concurrent relocation. C4 is simultaneously concurrent in both the young and old generations, and thereby does not suffer from either of the above pathologies. C4 maintains the high throughput, efficiency and sustained allocation rates typical to generational collection while at the same time maintaining the consistent response times and robustness of concurrent compacting collectors.

Both young and old generations use the same concurrent marking, compacting, and remapping algorithm described above. C4 uses a classic card marking mechanism [12] for tracking the remembered set of references from the old generation to the young generation. C4's card marks are precise, supporting a reliably unique card mark per word in memory. C4 uses a filtering Stored Value Barrier (SVB), a write barrier that only marks cards associated with the storing of young generation references into the old generation. The SVB leverages the same generational reference metadata state used by the LVB in order to efficiently filter out unnecessary card marking operations without resorting to address range comparisons and fixed generation address ranges.

3.1 Simultaneous Young and Old generation operation

Most current generational collectors that include some level of concurrent old generation processing interleave stop-the-world young generation collector execution with longer running old generation collection. This interleaving is necessary, as without it the sustainable allocation rate during old generation collection would be equivalent to that of a non-generational collector, negating the value of having a young generation collector to begin with. Simultaneous collection of both generations is not commonly supported. Such simultaneous operation would not add value to already stop-the-world young generation collectors. When both the old and young generations use concurrent collectors, allowing concurrent young generation collection to execute during a concurrent old generation collection is similarly necessary. Straight forward interleaving may suffice for maintaining throughput. For example, the old generation collector can be "paused" while the young generation collector executes a complete cycle. However, such interleaving would limit flexibility and increase code complexity by forcing the inclusion of relatively fine grain synchronization and "safe pausing" points

in the old generation collector's mechanism, and potentially in the young generation collector's as well.

C4 supports simultaneous concurrent execution of both the old and young generation collectors, limiting cross-generational synchronization to interlocks that are used to synchronize some phase shift edges as well as access to critical data structures. Figure 2 illustrates this.

Figure 2. Simultaneous generational collection in C4

In order to facilitate continued execution of multiple young generation cycles during an old generation mark phase we avoid performing a full heap collection that would prohibit changes to the young generation's expected NMT state. Instead, we perform old generation-only marking using a set of young-to-old roots generated by a special young generation cycle that is triggered along with every old generation mark cycle. This young generation cycle hands off the young-to-old pointers it locates to the old collector for use as part of its root-set. The hand-off is done during the marking phase of the young generation cycle with the old generation collector concurrently consuming the root set produced by the young generation marker. Further young generation cycles continue to happen concurrently, and will ignore the new-to-old pointers they find during marking. While the young generation collector is mostly decoupled from the old generation collector, synchronization points around critical phase shifts are necessary. For example, the young collector does need to access objects in the old generation. If a card mark is set for a pointer in an object in the old generation, the young generation collector must read that pointer to discover which object it refers to. Similarly, Klass objects in the old generation may describe the structure of the objects in young generation memory. For the young generation collector to find the pointers in an object it needs to mark through, it must read that object's corresponding klass object to determine the layout of the object at hand. In either case, since the old collector might be in the midst of relocating the object that is of interest to the young generation, some level of synchronization around cross-generational access is necessary.

We resolve these and other issues by introducing a synchronization mechanism between the two collectors referred to as 'interlocks'. An interlock between the old and new collector, briefly halts one of the collectors, to provide safe access to the object at hand. The number of Klass objects is typically a tiny fraction of the objects in memory, and this results in a very short serialization between the young and the old generation cycles, while the mutator maintains concurrency. We similarly use the interlock mechanism to allow the young generation collector to safely scan card marks. The young generation collector waits until all old generation relocation is halted, and then performs the card mark scan. Once done, it signals the old collector that relocation may resume. The synchronization is done at page granularity, so the affected collector is delayed only for short periods of time, or the order of what it takes for the old collector to relocate the live objects in a single page.

The two collectors need to synchronize at other points as well. E.g. each collector needs exclusive access to VM internal data structures such as the system dictionary, the symbol table and the string tables. The batched memory operations described in section 5 also require the collectors to coordinate batch boundaries between them.

4. Implementation notes

The C4 *algorithm* is entirely concurrent, i.e. no global safepoints are required. We also differentiate between the notion of a global safepoint, where are all the mutator threads are stopped, and a checkpoint, where individual threads pass through a barrier function. Checkpoints have a much lower impact on application responsiveness for obvious reasons. Pizlo et al [16] also uses a similar mechanism that they refer to as ragged safepoints.

The current C4 *implementation*, however, does include some global safepoints at phase change locations. The amount of work done in these safepoints is generally independent of the size of the heap, the rate of allocation, and various other key metrics, and on modern hardware these GC phase change safepoints have already been engineered down to sub-millisecond levels. At this point, application observable jitter and responsiveness artifacts are dominated by much larger contributors, such as CPU scheduling and thread contention. The engineering efforts involved in further reducing or eliminating GC safepoint impacts will likely produce little or no observable result.

Azul has created commercial implementations of the C4 algorithm on three successive generations of its custom Vega hardware (custom processor instruction set, chip, system, and OS), as well on modern X86 hardware. While the algorithmic details are virtually identical between the platforms, the implementation of the LVB semantics varies significantly due to differences in available instruction sets, CPU features, and OS support capabilities.

Vega systems include an LVB instruction that efficiently implements the entire set of LVB invariant checks in a single cycle, and is assisted by a custom TLB mode that supports GC protected pages and fast user mode traps. The custom OS kernel in Vega systems includes support for extremely efficient virtual and physical memory management and manipulation, facilitating efficient page protection and direct support for quick release and C4's overall page lifecycle needs.

Azul's LVB implementation on modern X86 hardware maintains the same semantic set of operations and invariant checks using a set of X86 instructions, effectively "micro-coding" the LVB effect and interleaving it with other instructions in the X86 pipeline. The actual implementation of an LVB sequence varies significantly even between different parts of a single runtime. For example, LVBs appear in interpreter code, in JIT-compiled code (coming from two different levels of tiered, optimizing JIT compilers), and in a multitude of places in the C++ implementation of runtime code. While each has different implementations of slow paths, fast paths, instruction scheduling and interleaving opportunities, the same LVB semantics and invariants are maintained in all cases. For the purposes of this paper, the abstraction presented earlier and proves to be sufficient, as a full description of the various LVB implementation options and details warrants a separate research paper. However, see Appendix A for a sample implementation.

4.1 Page life cycle

Unlike most existing collectors which tend to use relatively static memory mappings, the C4 algorithm uses a dynamic page life cycle that includes continuous mapping, remapping, protection, and unmapping of memory pages as GC cycles proceed. Figure 3 depicts the various states in the life cycle of a young generation heap page (old generation heap pages go through a similar life cycle). The solid rectangles represent virtual pages with backing physical storage. The dashed rectangles represent virtual pages with no backing physical storage. The solid oval represents a physical page that hasn't been mapped to a virtual page yet. The page state is represented as a tuple: <State><Gen><Prot>.

These states map to C4's phases. Active pages start their life-cycle in the *Allocating* state, representing a virtual memory page mapped to a physical backing store, into which allocated objects are placed. *Allocating* pages transition to the *Allocated* state once their memory space is filled up with allocated objects. Pages remain in the *Allocated* state until the next relocation phase, when C4 chooses to compact pages below a certain liveness threshold. A page selected for compaction transitions to the *Relocating* state and is protected from mutator access. Each live object in a *Relocating* page is moved to a new, compacted page either by the first mutator thread to access it, or by the collector. As described in section 2.5, forwarding information that tracks new object locations is kept outside of the *Relocating* page. Once the page contents had been copied out, and the page transitions to the *Relocated* state, its physical memory can be freed. At this point, the virtual page remains in the *Relocated* state, but the physical page it was mapped to is freed and transitions to the *Free* state. We refer to this transition as Quick-Release, where physical resources are recycled well before address space can be reused. The virtual page remains in the *Relocated* state until the end of the next remap phase, at which point all the references pointing to that page would have been remapped to its new location. At that point the virtual page transitions to the *Free* state, from which it can be recycled into the *Allocating* state by mapping it to an available physical memory page.

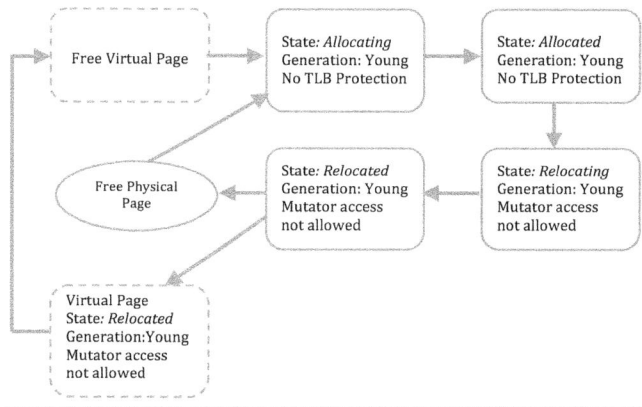

Figure 3. Life cycle of heap page

5. Operating System Support

During normal sustained operation, the C4 algorithm makes massive and rapid changes to virtual memory mappings. In a sequence that was first described in Pauseless [7], page mappings are manipulated at a rate that is directly proportional to the object allocation rate in the application. Allocation results in mapping in a new page, the page is then remapped, protected and unmapped during the course of a GC cycle, resulting in 3 or 4 different mapping changes per page-sized unit of allocation. Later works, such as Compressor [13], share this relationship between sustained allocation rates and virtual memory mapping manipulation rate. The operating system's ability to sustain virtual mapping manipulation rates directly affects the sustainable application throughput that such collectors can maintain without imposing observable application pauses.

In this section, we focus on two key metrics that are critical to sustaining continuous concurrent compaction in C4. We explain the limitations of current Linux virtual memory semantics and their performance implications, and demonstrate how virtual memory subsystem improvements achieved through new APIs and looser semantic requirements deliver several orders of magnitude in improvement for these key metrics.

Active Threads	Linux	Modified Linux	Speedup
1	3.04 GB/sec	6.50 TB/sec	>2,000×
2	1.82 GB/sec	6.09 TB/sec	>3,000×
4	1.19 GB/sec	6.08 TB/sec	>5,000×
8	897.65 MB/sec	6.29 TB/sec	>7,000×
12	736.65 MB/sec	6.39 TB/sec	>8,000×

Table 1. Comparison of sustainable mremap rates

It is typically desirable (for both stability and headroom reasons) for the GC cycles to run at a 1:5 or lower duty cycle. Furthermore, within each GC cycle, page remapping typically constitutes less than 5% of the total elapsed cycle time, with most of the cycle time consumed by marking/remapping and relocation. Together, these ratios qualities mean that the garbage collector needs to sustain a page remapping at a rate that is 100× as high as the sustained object allocation rate for comfortable operation. This places a significant stress on the virtual memory subsystem in stock Linux implementations, and would significantly limit the sustainable allocation rate on C4 unless the OS were able to support the required performance.

5.1 Supporting a high sustainable remap rate

On stock Linux, the only supported memory remapping mechanism has three key technical limitations:

- Each page remap includes an implicit TLB invalidate operation. Since TLB invalidates require multiple cross-CPU interrupts, the cost of remapping grows with the number of active CPU cores in the executing program. This reduction in remap performance with increased thread counts happens even when the active threads do not participate in the remapping, or have any interaction with the remapped memory.

- Only small (4KB on X86-64) page mappings can be remapped.

- Remap operations are single threaded within a process (grabbing a common write lock in the kernel).

To address the main remapping limitations in stock Linux and to support C4's need for sustained remapping rates, we created a new virtual memory subsystem that exposes new APIs and added features that safely support memory remaps, unmaps, and protection changes without requiring TLB invalidation (TLB invalidation can be applied at the end of a large set of remaps if needed). C4 uses these new APIs to manage page life cycles. Our new virtual memory subsystem also supports explicit and mixed mapping and remapping of large (2MB on X86-64) pages, and safely allows concurrent memory manipulation within the same process.

Table 1 has a sample comparison of sustainable remap rates between a stock, un-enhanced Linux and a Linux kernel containing our changes.

- The tests were done on a 16 core system, 4 Socket AMD Barcelona based system with 128GB of memory. The Linux kernel revision is 2.6.32.

- The tests allocate 2MB of memory, and then repeatedly remap it around a large address space for a given duration of time.

- The Active threads represent the number of additional active threads (not the remapping thread) in the test application. The active threads perform a pure integer loop workload - their sole purpose is to "exist" and allow measurement of the effect of running application threads on remap throughput (as a result of needing to send TLB invalidates to additional active CPUs).

- Stock Linux test maps the memory using mmap(), and remaps the memory using a 2MB mremap() call.

- The new virtual memory subsystem maps the memory using az_mmap() [with a flag indicating large pages are to be used], and remaps the memory using a single thread performing 2MB az_mremap() calls [with a NO_TLB_INVALIDATE flag].

- These results do not take into account the additional speedup that can be gained by using multiple remapping threads in our new virtual memory subsystem.

5.2 Supporting a high remap commit rate

For efficient implementation of large amounts of relocation, the current C4 *implementation* places an atomicity requirement on the memory remapping changes in a given relocation phase. Page protection and remapping changes need to become visible to all running application threads at the same time, and at a safe point in their execution. In order to perform a relocation of a bulk set of pages, the C4 Collector will typically bring all application threads to a common safe point, apply a massive remapping of a significant portion of the garbage collected heap, and then allow the threads to continue their normal execution. Since application code execution in all threads is stopped during this operation, a noticeable application pause would result if it cannot be applied in an extremely fast manner. The only operation supported on Stock Linux that can be used to facilitate the C4 remap commit operation is a normal remap (measured in 1). C4 would need to bring all threads to a safe point, and hold them there for the duration of time that it takes Linux to perform the remapping of the bulk page set. To address the Remap Commit Rate limitations in stock Linux, we support a batch preparation of virtual memory operations. Batch operations are performed on a shadow page table without becoming visible to the process threads, and a large batch of remap operations can be prepared without requiring any application threads to be stopped during the preparation phase. The prepared batch is then committed by the GC mechanism using a single "batch commit" operation call to the kernel virtual memory subsystem. Since a batch commit will typically be executed during a global safe point, the batch commit operation is designed to complete in a matter of microseconds, such that no perceivable application pauses will occur.

Table 2 compares stock Linux Remap Commit Rates established in previously described sustainable remap rate tests and the time it would take to perform 16GB of remaps, with the measured rate and time it takes Linux enhanced with our virtual memory subsystem to commit a 16GB batch of remap operations (prepared using az_mbatch_remap() calls) using an az_mbatch_commit() call.

Active Threads	Linux	Modified Linux	Speedup
0	43.58 GB/sec (360ms)	4734.85 TB/sec (3us)	>100,000×
1	3.04 GB/sec (5s)	1488.10 TB/sec (11us)	>480,000×
2	1.82 GB/sec (8s)	1166.04 TB/sec (14us)	>640,000×
4	1.19 GB/sec (13s)	913.74 TB/sec (18us)	>750,000×
8	897.65 MB/sec (18s)	801.28 TB/sec (20us)	>890,000×
12	736.65 MB/sec (21s)	740.52 TB/sec (22us)	>1,000,000×

Table 2. Comparison of peak mremap rates

- An Active Thread count of 0 was also included, since commits will happen during a global safepoint, and it is therefore possible that no active threads would execute during the commit operation. However, it should be noted that the number of threads that may be active during the safepoint operations can also be non-zero (which is why multiple thread counts are also modeled in the test). While Application execution is held at a safepoint during the remap commit operation, application threads may still be actively executing runtime code while logically held at the safepoint. E.g. runtime operations that occur under a single bytecode and release the safepoint lock, such as I/O system calls, long runtime calls, and JNI calls, are executed under a logical safepoint, and may keep cpu cores busy during a remap commit.

- An az_mbatch_commit() call produces a single global TLB invalidate per call.

6. Heap Management

6.1 Tiered Allocation Spaces

C4 manages the heap in 2M sized physical pages. The allocation path uses a Thread Local Allocation Buffer (TLAB) mechanism [10] found in most enterprise virtual machines. Each Java thread uses bump pointer allocation in its local allocation buffer. In supporting concurrent compaction and remapping, C4 must also adhere to a requirement for objects to not span relocation page boundaries. These allocation and relocation schemes, while being fast and supporting consistent application response times, can result in some headroom in the local buffer being wasted. The worst case headroom wastage can be as high as 50%, if a program serially allocates objects of size (N/2+1)MB's or N+1, where N is the larger of the buffer size or the relocation page size. Other work such as [16], try to deal with this waste by allocating fragmented objects while [5] addresses this issue by maintaining two levels of allocation bins. To cap the worst case physical memory waste, while at the same time containing the worst case blocking time of a mutator waiting for a single object to be copied, we bin the objects into three different size ranges, and handle the memory for each size range differently. The three tiers are:

- Small Object Space: Contains objects less than 256 KB in size. The region is managed as an array of 2 MB pages. Objects in this space must not span page boundaries, and new object allocation usually uses TLABs.
- Medium Object Space: Contains objects that are 256 KB and larger, up to a maximum of 16 MB. The region is managed as an array of 32 MB virtual blocks, physically allocated in 2MB units. Objects in this space may span 2 MB pages, but must not cross virtual block boundaries. Objects allocated within a block will be aligned to 4 KB boundaries. We explain the need for this in section 6.3.
- Large Object Space: Contains objects larger than those that would fit in Small or Medium Space (larger than 16 MB). Unlike Small Space and Medium Space where virtual memory is organized into fixed sized chunks, virtual and physical memory is allocated in multiples of 2MB to fit the size of the object being allocated. All objects in this space are allocated on 2MB aligned boundaries, with no two objects sharing a common 2MB page.

The Small and Medium tiers are managed using fixed sized virtual blocks of memory, eliminating the possibility of fragmentation in their memory space. In contrast, the Large Object space does incur virtual address fragmentation. Since Large Space objects all reside in dedicated 2MB pages, compacting the virtual space is a simple matter of remapping the pages containing the objects to new virtual locations using the same relocation scheme described in section 2. As described, the tiered allocation spaces scheme limits the worst case headroom waste to 12.5%. The worst case Small Object Space waste is 12.5% (256KB out of 2MB). The worst case space waste for both the Medium and Large Object Space is 11.1% (2MB out of 18MB). However, arbitrarily small worst case sizes can be similarly engineered by modifying the object size thresholds and block sizes in the scheme, as well as by adding additional tiers.

6.2 Allocation pathway

Objects that fit in the Small Object Space are allocated using TLABs [10], on which we piggy-back the test for object size and fit into the Small Object space. Each TLAB tracks a TLAB end-of-region pointer, and a fast-allocation end-of-region pointer. The TLAB end-of-region indicates the end of the 2 MB TLAB. The fast-allocation end-of-region is checked by the fast path assembly allocation code. It would never point more than 256 KB past the top pointer, thus forcing middle size and large size object allocation into the slow path. The slow path bumps forward the fast-allocation end pointer as needed, until the actual TLAB end-of-region pointer is reached.

Allocation in the Medium Object Space shares allocation blocks across Java threads. A Java thread trying to allocate into a Medium Object Space block claims the required sized chunk by atomically updating the top pointer of the page.

Allocation in the Large Object Space is achieved by atomically updating a global top pointer for the space.

6.3 Relocating medium space objects

Middle space blocks are compacted using an algorithm similar to that of small space pages, combined with support for incrementally copying object contents in 4 KB chunks as they are concurrently accessed. This reduces the copy delays imposed when a mutator tries to access an unrelocated object of non trivial size. Compaction is done with a protected page shattering virtual memory remap operation, followed later by a copying page healing merge operation, defined below:

- Page Shattering Remap operation: Remaps virtual memory in multiples of 4 KB pages to a new virtual address, shattering contiguous 2MB mappings in the process. The new address is protected against both read and write access, forcing protection faults if the contents are accessed prior to page healing.
- Page Heal/Merge operation: A 2 MB aligned compacted region comprised of previously shattered 4KB virtual memory pages is "healed" by the collector to form a 2MB virtual mapping. The healing operation uses a contiguous 2 MB physical page as a copy-on-demand target, sequentially copying the individual 4KB contents to their proper position in the target physical page while at the same time supporting asynchronous on-demand fault driven copying of 4KB section as the mutators access them. Once the 4KB sections of a 2MB aligned region have been copied to the target physical page, their original physical pages become free and are recycled, facilitating hand-over-hand compaction of the Medium Space.

The shattering remap and healing merge operations are among the features in the new Linux virtual memory subsystem discussed in the section 5 . With these two new calls, the relocation algorithm for Medium Space objects becomes:

1. Remap each live object to a new 4KB aligned location in target to-blocks. The new virtual address is shattered and protected in the same operation.

2. Publish the new virtual address as the forwarding pointer for each object.

3. Heal/Merge each 2MB page in the to-blocks in a hand-over-hand manner, using the physical memory released from each 2MB Heal/Merge operation as a target resource for the next Heal/Merge operation.

4. As Mutators concurrently access Middle Space objects during the relocation, faults are used to heal only the 4KB section in which the fault occurred, minimizing the mutator blocking time.

The 4 KB remap granularity is the source of needing to allocate medium sized objects at a 4 KB alignment.

7. Experiments

Our experiments are intended to highlight the behavior of simultaneous generational concurrency by comparing the response time behavior of C4 to that of other collectors. We compared C4 with an intentionally crippled version of C4, with simultaneous generational concurrency disabled (dubbed C4-NoConcYoung), as well as with the OpenJDK HotSpot CMS and Parallel collectors.

C4 is intended to maintain consistent response times in transaction oriented programs running business logic and interactive server logic on modern servers, using multi-GB heaps and live sets, sustaining multi-GB/sec allocation rates, as well as common application and data patterns found in such enterprise applications. With low end commodity servers reaching 96GB or more in main memory capacity in 2011, it is surprisingly hard to find widely used server scale benchmarks that measure the response time envelope of applications that would attempt to use such capacities within managed runtimes. Large, mutating object caches that occupy significant portions of the heap, fat state-full sessions, rapid messaging with in-memory replication, and large phase shifts in program data (such as catalog updates or cache hydration) are all common scenarios in server applications, but benchmarks that require more than 1-2GB of live state per runtime instance (1% of a modern commodity server's capacity) are virtually non-existent. Furthermore, industry benchmarks that do include response time criteria typically use pass/fail criteria that would be completely unacceptable for business applications - with most including average and 90%'ile response times and standard deviation requirements, but no max time, 99.9%'ile, or even 99%'ile requirements.

Since response time behavior under sustainable load is the critical measure of a collector's operational envelope that we are interested in, we constructed a simple test bench that demonstrated the worst case response time behavior of various collector configurations. The test bench measured response times for an identical working set workload run on various collector and heap size configurations. A modified version of the commonly used SPECjbb2005 transactional throughput workload was used, changed to include a modest 2GB live set cache of variable sized objects that churns at a slight newly cached object rate of about 20MB/sec. The test bench also included a mechanism to measure the response time characteristics of transactions throughout the run. The modified SPECjbb2005 workload was run for prolonged constant-load runs with 4 warehouses, and we focused our measurements on worst case response times seen in sustained execution. The tests were all executed on the same hardware setup; a 2 socket, 12 core Intel x5680 server with 96GB of memory. On this platform, the test bench exhibits an allocation rate of about 1.2GB/sec, and live sets were consistently measured at about 2.5GB. All runs were executed at least long enough to proceed through multiple full heap collection cycles, and to allow the normal object churn and heap fragmentation to produce at least one major compaction event. The worst case response time for each run was collected and plotted. Figure 4 shows the results, depicting worst case response time of the various collectors at different heap sizes. For reference, Figure 5 provides the test bench throughput measured for each test[3].

As expected the worst case response times of collectors that do not perform concurrent compaction [i.e. CMS and ParallelGC] start off at multi-second levels, and get significantly worse as the heap

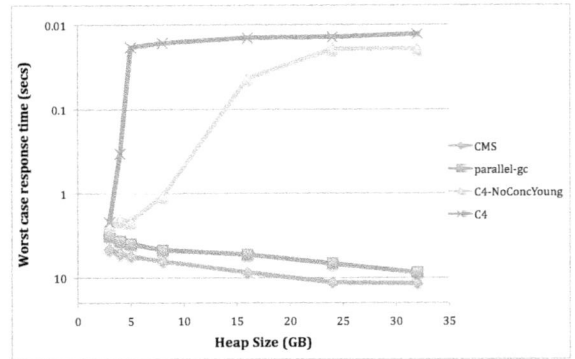

Figure 4. Worst case response times

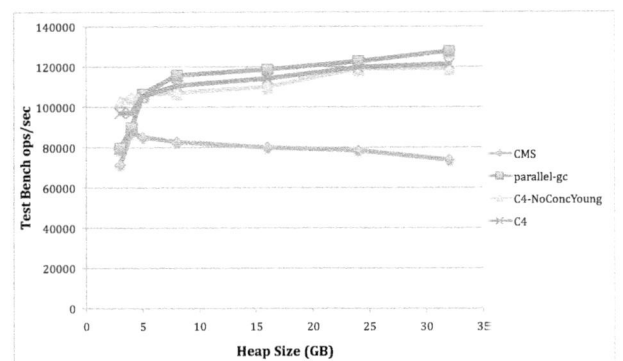

Figure 5. Test Bench Raw Throughput

size grows, even with the relatively modest 2.5GB live sets maintained across all tests. C4-NoConcYoung, due to its lack of simultaneous generational concurrency, exhibits problems maintaining pauseless operation and low response times when the heap size is not large enough to absorb the 1.2GB/sec allocation rate during full heap collections, and its results improve with heap size (reaching pauseless operation at 24GB). C4 exhibits a wide operating range with consistent response times, and is able to sustain pauseless operation at the test bench's allocation rate even with relatively low amounts of empty heap.

8. Related Work

The idea of using common page-protection hardware to support GC has been around for a while [1]. Appel et al [1] protect pages that may contain objects with non-forwarded pointers (initially all pages). Accessing a protected page causes an OS trap which the GC handles by forwarding all pointers on that page, then clearing the page protection. Compressor [13] uses techniques similar to our work and Pauseless GC [7], in that they protect the to-virtual-space. They update the roots to point to their referents' new locations at a safepoint and the mutator threads are then allowed to run. Their mutator threads encounter and use access violation traps to fixup the references they follow.

Incremental and low-pause-time collectors are also becoming popular again. Pizlo et al [15] discuss three such algorithms. The Chicken algorithm uses a Brooks-style read barrier and a wait-free "aborting" write barrier that in the fast path only requires a read operation and a branch followed by the original write operation. The Stopless algorithm [14] uses an expanded object model with tem-

---

[3] While measuring raw throughput is not the objective of these tests (non-SLA-sustaining throughput numbers are generally meaningless for production server environments), Figure 5 shows that C4 closely matches ParallelGC in throughput (to within 1-6% depending on heap size) on this test bench workload. Average latencies, which are also not the objective here, can be directly derived from throughput, knowing that exactly 4 concurrent threads were transacting at all times.

porary object while the Clover algorithm relies on a probabilistic model and writes a random value to a field and does field by field copy. It uses this technique in conjunction with a barrier to provide concurrency.

Attempts to deal with the stop-the-world atomic nature of young generation collection are relatively new. While we are not aware of concurrent young generation collectors, [11] presents a stop-the-world incremental young generation collector for real time systems. The algorithm uses a combination of a read-barrier and a write-barrier to capture remembered set changes during incremental collection.

9. Conclusions

C4 is a generational, continuously concurrent compacting collector algorithm, it expands on the Pauseless GC algorithm [7] by including a generational form of a self healing Loaded Value Barrier (LVB), supporting simultaneous concurrent generational collection, as well as an enhanced heap management scheme that reduces worst case space waste across the board.

C4 is currently included in commercially shipping JVMs delivered as a pure software platform on commodity X86 hardware, and demonstrates a two-orders-of-magnitude improvement in sustainable [worst case] response times compared to both stop-the-world-ParallelGC and mostly-concurrent CMS [8] collectors executing on identical hardware, across a wide range of heap sizes.

The C4 implementation currently supports heap sizes up to 670GB on X86-64 hardware, and while this represents some significant headroom compared to the commonly sold and used servers, commercially available commodity servers holding 1TB and 2TB can already be purchased at surprisingly low cost points as of this writing. As explained in the implementation notes (see Section 4), while the C4 algorithm is fully concurrent (with no required global stop-the-world pauses), the current C4 implementation does perform some very short stop-the-world phase synchronization operations for practical engineering complexity reasons. While these operations now measure in the sub-millisecond range on modern X86 servers, future work may include further improvement, potentially fully implementing the complete concurrent algorithm, and expanding the supported heap sizes to 2TB and beyond.

A. Appendix: Metadata encoding and LVB pseudocode

Section 2 describes C4's Loaded Value Barrier (LVB), its interactions with reference metadata, NMT state, and page protection. The specified LVB behavior and reference metadata encoding can be implemented in a wide variety of ways. This appendix discusses some of the encoding options and presents an example encoding and matching pseudocode for LVB logic.

For LVB to correctly impose the marked-through invariant on loaded references described in section 2.1, metadata describing the reference's NMT state and the reference's generation (the GC generation in which the object that the reference points to resides) must be associated with each reference. The most straightforward way to associate metadata with the reference is to store it within a 64 bit reference field, using bits that are not interpreted as addresses. Ignoring the metadata bits for addressing purposes can be achieved by stripping them off of the reference value ahead of the using the value for addressing purposes. Alternatively, on architectures where such stripping imposes a high overhead, virtual memory multi-mapping or aliasing can be used such that, otherwise identical addresses (for all metadata bit value combinations) are mapped to the same physical memory contents. Our enhanced Linux virtual memory subsystem includes support for efficiently aliasing 1GB aligned address regions to each other, such that any virtual memory

operation applied to an address in an aliased region would apply identically to all the addresses aliased to it as well.

The reference metadata bit-field itself can be encoded in various ways. The simplest examples would encode NMT state using a single bit, and encode the reference generation (young or old) using a single, separate bit. However, other considerations and potential uses for metadata encodings exist. For example, for various practical runtime implementation considerations, it is useful to have NULL values and non-heap pointers encoded such that their interpretation as a reference value would not appear to be in either the old or young generations, leading to a useful encoding of a multi-bit "SpaceID" where the young and old generations occupy two of the available non-zero spaceIDs. Additional SpaceIDs can be useful for purposes that are either orthogonal to or outside the scope of C4 (e.g., stack-local and frame local allocation space identifiers, such as those described in [17]). When encodings with a larger number of spaceIDs is desirable, a combined SpaceID+NMT encoding in a common bit field becomes useful for address space efficiency purposes, avoiding the "waste" of an entire bit on NMT state for SpaceIDs that do not require it.

In the interest of simplicity, we describe a simple encoding using 2 bits for SpaceID, and a single bit for recording NMT state. Figure 6 shows the layout of this metadata in a 64 bit object reference. Figure 7 describes the SpaceIDs field value interpretation, and gives pseudocode for an LVB implementation with the metadata encoding that matches the discussion in sections 2.1 through 2.4 .

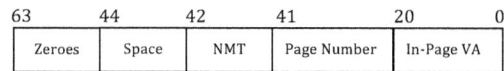

63	44	42	41	20	0
Zeroes	Space	NMT	Page Number	In-Page VA	

Figure 6. Object Reference Word Layout

References

[1] A. W. Appel, J. R. Ellis, and K. Li. Real-time concurrent collection on stock multiprocessors. In *Proceedings of the ACM SIGPLAN 1988 conference on Programming Language Design and Implementation*, PLDI '88, pages 11–20, New York, NY, USA, 1988. ACM. ISBN 0-89791-269-1. doi: http://doi.acm.org/10.1145/53990.53992. URL http://doi.acm.org/10.1145/53990.53992.

[2] Azul Systems Inc. Managed Runtime Initiative. http://www.managedruntime.org/, 2010.

[3] D. F. Bacon, P. Cheng, and V. T. Rajan. A real-time garbage collector with low overhead and consistent utilization. In *Proceedings of the 30th ACM SIGPLAN-SIGACT Symposium on Principles of Programming Languages*, POPL '03, pages 285–298, New York, NY, USA, 2003. ACM. ISBN 1-58113-628-5. doi: http://doi.acm.org/10.1145/604131.604155. URL http://doi.acm.org/10.1145/604131.604155.

[4] H. G. Baker, Jr. List processing in real time on a serial computer. *Commun. ACM*, 21:280–294, April 1978. ISSN 0001-0782. doi: http://doi.acm.org/10.1145/359460.359470. URL http://doi.acm.org/10.1145/359460.359470.

[5] S. M. Blackburn and K. S. McKinley. Immix: a mark-region garbage collector with space efficiency, fast collection, and mutator performance. In *Proceedings of the 2008 ACM SIGPLAN conference on Programming Language Design and Implementation*, PLDI '08, pages 22–32, New York, NY, USA, 2008. ACM. ISBN 978-1-59593-860-2. doi: http://doi.acm.org/10.1145/1375581.1375586. URL http://doi.acm.org/10.1145/1375581.1375586.

```
struct Reference
{
  unsigned inPageVA   : 21;   // bits 0-20
  unsigned PageNumber : 21;   // bits 21-41
  unsigned NMT        : 1;    // bit 42
  unsigned SpaceID    : 2;    // bits 43-44
  unsigned unused     : 19;   // bits 45-63
};

int Expected_NMT_Value[4] = {0, 0, 0, 0};

// Space ID values:
// 00   NULL and non-heap pointers
// 01   Old Generation references
// 10   New Generation references
// 11   Unused

LVB pseudocode:

doLVB(void *address, struct Reference &value)
{
  int trigger = 0;
  if (value.NMT != Expected_NMT_Value[value.SpaceID])
    trigger |= NMT_Trigger;
  if (value.pageNumber is protected)
    trigger |= Reloc_Trigger;
  if (trigger != 0)
    value = doLVBSlowPathHandling(address, value, trigger);
}

doLVBSlowPathHandling(void* address, struct Reference &value, int trigger)
{
  struct Reference oldValue = value;

  // Fix the trigger condition(s):
  if (trigger | NMT_Trigger) {
    value.NMT = !value.NMT;
    QueueReferenceToMarker(value);
  }
  if (trigger | Reloc_Trigger) {
    if (ObjectIsNotYetRelocated(value)) {
      relocateObjectAt(value);
    }
    value = LookupNewObjectLocation(value);
  }

  // Heal source address:
  AtomicCompareAndSwap(address, oldValue, value);

  return value;
}
```

Figure 7. LVB Pseudocode

[6] R. A. Brooks. Trading data space for reduced time and code space in real-time garbage collection on stock hardware. In *Proceedings of the 1984 ACM Symposium on LISP and functional programming*, LFP '84, pages 256–262, New York, NY, USA, 1984. ACM. ISBN 0-89791-142-3. doi: http://doi.acm.org/10.1145/800055.802042. URL http://doi.acm.org/10.1145/800055.802042.

[7] C. Click, G. Tene, and M. Wolf. The Pauseless GC algorithm. In *Proceedings of the 1st ACM/USENIX International Conference on Virtual Execution Environments*, VEE '05, pages 46–56, New York, NY, USA, 2005. ACM. ISBN 1-59593-047-7. doi: http://doi.acm.org/10.1145/1064979.1064988. URL http://doi.acm.org/10.1145/1064979.1064988.

[8] D. Detlefs and T. Printezis. A Generational Mostly-concurrent Garbage Collector. Technical report, Mountain View, CA, USA, 2000.

[9] D. Detlefs, C. Flood, S. Heller, and T. Printezis. Garbage-first garbage collection. In *Proceedings of the 4th International Symposium on Memory Management*, ISMM '04, pages 37–48, New York, NY, USA, 2004. ACM. ISBN 1-58113-945-4. doi: http://doi.acm.org/10.1145/1029873.1029879. URL http://doi.acm.org/10.1145/1029873.1029879.

[10] D. Dice, A. Garthwaite, and D. White. Supporting per-processor local-allocation buffers using multi-processor restartable critical sections. Technical report, Mountain View, CA, USA, 2004.

[11] D. Frampton, D. F. Bacon, P. Cheng, and D. Grove. Generational Real-Time Garbage Collection: A Three-Part Invention for Young Objects. ECOOP '07, pages 101–125.

[12] U. Hölzle. A Fast Write Barrier for Generational Garbage Collectors. In *OOPSLA/ECOOP '93 Workshop on Garbage Collection in Object-Oriented Systems*, 1993.

[13] H. Kermany and E. Petrank. The Compressor: concurrent, incremental, and parallel compaction. In *Proceedings of the 2006 ACM SIGPLAN conference on Programming Language Design and Implementation*, PLDI '06, pages 354–363, New York, NY, USA, 2006. ACM. ISBN 1-59593-320-4. doi: http://doi.acm.org/10.1145/1133981.1134023. URL http://doi.acm.org/10.1145/1133981.1134023.

[14] F. Pizlo, D. Frampton, E. Petrank, and B. Steensgaard. Stopless: a real-time garbage collector for multiprocessors. In *Proceedings of the 6th International Symposium on Memory Management*, ISMM '07, pages 159–172, New York, NY, USA, 2007. ACM. ISBN 978-1-59593-893-0. doi: http://doi.acm.org/10.1145/1296907.1296927. URL http://doi.acm.org/10.1145/1296907.1296927.

[15] F. Pizlo, E. Petrank, and B. Steensgaard. A study of concurrent real-time garbage collectors. In *Proceedings of the 2008 ACM SIGPLAN conference on Programming Language Design and Implementation*, PLDI '08, pages 33–44, New York, NY, USA, 2008. ACM. ISBN 978-1-59593-860-2. doi: http://doi.acm.org/10.1145/1375581.1375587. URL http://doi.acm.org/10.1145/1375581.1375587.

[16] F. Pizlo, L. Ziarek, P. Maj, A. L. Hosking, E. Blanton, and J. Vitek. Schism: fragmentation-tolerant real-time garbage collection. In *Proceedings of the 2010 ACM SIGPLAN conference on Programming Language Design and Implementation*, PLDI '10, pages 146–159, New York, NY, USA, 2010. ACM. ISBN 978-1-4503-0019-3. doi: http://doi.acm.org/10.1145/1806596.1806615. URL http://doi.acm.org/10.1145/1806596.1806615.

[17] G. Tene, C. Click, M. Wolf, and I. Posva. Memory Management, 2006. US Patent 7,117,318.

[18] D. Ungar. Generation Scavenging: A non-disruptive high performance storage reclamation algorithm. In *Proceedings of the first ACM SIGSOFT/SIGPLAN Software Engineering Symposium on Practical Software Development Environments*, SDE 1, pages 157–167, New York, NY, USA, 1984. ACM. ISBN 0-89791-131-8. doi: http://doi.acm.org/10.1145/800020.808261. URL http://doi.acm.org/10.1145/800020.808261

[19] M. T. Vechev, E. Yahav, and D. F. Bacon. Correctness-preserving derivation of concurrent garbage collection algorithms. In *Proceedings of the 2006 ACM SIGPLAN conference on Programming Language Design and Implementation*, PLDI '06, pages 341–353, New York, NY, USA, 2006. ACM. ISBN 1-59593-320-4. doi: http://doi.acm.org/10.1145/1133981.1134022. URL http://doi.acm.org/10.1145/1133981.1134022.

[20] P. R. Wilson. Uniprocessor Garbage Collection Techniques. In *Proceedings of the International Workshop on Memory Management*, IWMM '92, pages –42, London, UK, 1992. Springer-Verlag. ISBN 3-540-55940-X. URL http://portal.acm.org/citation.cfm?id=645648.664824.

Handles Revisited: Optimising Performance and Memory Costs in a Real-Time Collector

Tomas Kalibera   Richard Jones

University of Kent, Canterbury

{t.kalibera, r.e.jones}@kent.ac.uk

Abstract

Compacting garbage collectors must update all references to objects they move. Updating is a lengthy operation but the updates must be transparent to the mutator. The consequence is that no space can be reclaimed until *all* references have been updated which, in a real-time collector, must be done incrementally. One solution is to replace direct references to objects with handles. Handles offer several advantages to a real-time collector. They eliminate the updating problem. They allow immediate reuse of the space used by evacuated objects. They incur no copy reserve overhead. However, the execution time overhead of handles has led to them being abandoned by most modern systems.

We re-examine this decision in the context of real-time garbage collection, for which several systems with handles have appeared recently. We provide the first thorough study of the overheads of handles, based on an optimised implementation of different handle designs within Ovm's Minuteman real-time collector. We find that with a good set of optimisations handles are not very expensive. We obtained zero overhead over the widely used Brooks-style compacting collector (1.6% and 3.1% on two other platforms) and 9% increase in memory usage. Our optimisations are particularly applicable to mark-compact collectors, but may also be useful to other collectors.

Categories and Subject Descriptors D.3.4 [*Programming Languages*]: Processors — Memory management (garbage collection); C.3 [*Special-Purpose and Application Based Systems*]: Real-time and embedded systems

General Terms Measurement, Performance, Algorithms

1. Introduction

A real-time garbage collector must address fragmentation. Some collectors do this by splitting objects (Jamaica [37], Sun's RTS [9]), some move objects (Aonix's PERC [30]) and some combine both techniques (Metronome [3], Fiji [34], Ovm [2]). A real-time collector must also be incremental so as to cause only short and bounded pauses of the mutator. This complicates object moving significantly. After an object is moved, all direct references to it must be updated but all mutator threads must see a consistent view of the heap at all times.

If objects are referenced directly — the case for most virtual machines today — reference updating is a lengthy operation that involves scanning the stacks, global data and all live objects in the heap. The mutator must to be allowed to run during this period. The use of direct references typically requires that both the old and the new copy of an object (or at least some portions of both) co-exist during that time, since the mutator may have references to both and the new location of an object is stored in the old copy. This copy reserve leads to a memory usage overhead similar to that of a copying collector [16] rather than that of a mark-compact collector [20]. A mostly non-copying collector [3] may copy fewer objects, but the worst-yet-unlikely-case overhead is still close to all live objects plus floating garbage.

If two copies of an object may co-exist, the system has to ensure that the application still runs as if there was only one. This transparency can be achieved with indirections. With Brooks forwarding [8], every read and write includes a dereference of a forwarding pointer stored in the object header. Every access is then performed on the *newest* copy of the object. With replication [19, 21, 29], any copies of a single object are kept in sync: writes are executed on *all* copies, while reads can proceed without any indirection. However, access to a field that is `volatile` or through an atomic primitive is problematic. Some systems remove the need for a copy reserve by calculating new addresses on the fly and moving objects on demand, but this requires operating system or hardware support and cannot provide real-time guarantees [11, 22].

In this paper, we explore how objects can be managed with *handles* [31], unmovable entities that represent objects and include a direct pointer to their contents. The heap, global data, and stacks use only handles to refer to an object, and thus all accesses are indirect. If an object is moved, only its handle needs to be updated, which is trivial and can be done atomically. Consequently, the old location of a moved object can be re-used immediately, without need for the copy reserve required by direct pointer implementations. Depending on how much of an object header is moved into the handle, some dereferences can be elided.

Handles have further advantages over direct pointers (not all of which are applicable to real-time systems). In contrast to direct references, no special action is necessary for pointer comparison. Because references are never updated, memory compression is easier [10], conservative collectors may move objects [31], and objects can be moved *at any time* (not just during a particular GC phase) or even multiple times during a cycle. The handle as a unique proxy to an object allows a hash code to be implemented simply as the handle address with no further space overhead [1] and allows objects to be represented even if swapped out to external storage or resident on a remote machine [18].

Handles have been used in the past for non real-time VMs, most notably by Sun's Classic and earlier VMs. Today most memory managers use direct references which are believed to offer better performance, and certainly do so for collectors that do not move objects while mutators are running. Real-time systems managed by incremental collectors change the trade-offs. These systems already incur the overhead of actions to support incremental updating of references *by the collector*: it is no longer self-evident that handles have to be more expensive than these actions. Handles offer the advantage that old copies of objects need not be kept. This is important not only because it can save memory but also because it makes worst-case memory usage easier to analyse, which is particularly nice for mostly non-copying collectors. On the other hand, the price for handles includes increased allocation time due to handle allocation and the memory overhead of reserved but currently not used handles. Implementation of the collector is also more complex. While some real-time collectors use handles [14, 27, 35], to the best of our knowledge, no publicly available study compares different handle designs or implementations, or compares these to direct pointers. We provide such a study here. In summary, our contributions are:

- Designs and implementations of different variants of handles in a (mostly non-moving) mark-sweep/compact collector in Ovm [32], an open-source real-time Java Virtual Machine.
- Optimisations to handle free-list manipulation and sweeping that significantly improve mutator and collector performance, and are applicable to any handle based mark-sweep/compact collector.
- An experimental comparison of different variants of handles with each other, and with Brooks forwarding and replication.
- We find that handles can keep up with other mechanisms for incremental, mostly non-copying collection. Our best configuration — of uni-sized fat handles — has no execution time average overhead compared to Brooks (1.6% and 3.1% on other platforms), 1.8% (5.2%) over replication, but needs 9% more collection cycles to run within the same sized heap.

2. Design issues

Implemented naïvely, handles offer poor performance compared to other techniques for incremental compacting collection. However, there are many opportunities for optimisation. We consider the following.

- What information should handles hold? Should they include any header words as well as the pointer to the object?
- How should handles be allocated? The simplest solution would be to pre-allocate a fixed-size table but this makes the worst case utilisation of memory. Instead, we allocate and release *handle blocks* dynamically.
- Fragmentation is a significant issue for this handle space. Unlike objects, handles cannot be moved. Instead, we explore techniques that tend to avoid fragmentation. Can we encourage dense utilisation of handle blocks, thereby allowing other handle blocks to be recycled?
- There is substantial evidence [5, 15] that objects tend to live and die together. Can we take advantage of this both to reduce fragmentation in the handle blocks and to improve locality in the mutator?
- How can the collector trace and sweep both the handle and the data space in the most cache-friendly way?
- Some objects, including those in the boot image are known to be immobile. Can the compiler take advantage of this to short-circuit handle indirections?

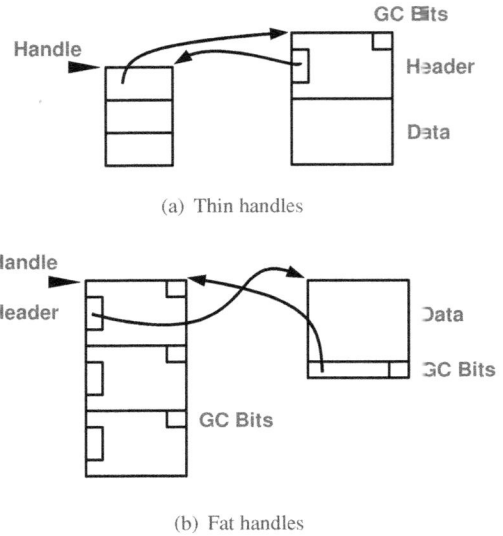

(a) Thin handles

(b) Fat handles

Figure 1. Object layout of movable objects.

3. Handles

In this section we describe our handle design and optimisations in a way largely independent of Ovm. The design should thus be applicable to any mark-sweep/compact collector. Ovm-specific details are provided in Section 4 and performance implications are evaluated in Section 7.

3.1 Object layout

We support three types of handles. *Thin* handles hold just a pointer to the object. Thus accesses to the object's header and fields require an indirection. By including the header in a *fat* handle (Figure 1), the indirection to access the header is removed but array and non-array handles now have different sizes, which makes it impossible to reuse handle slots between different object kinds. *Uni-sized fat* handles solve this by placing the array length with the payload rather than in the handle (header) — scalar and array handles have the same size but an indirection is needed for the array length field.

Compacting collectors sweep the object space (not the handle space) in order to discover objects to move. When an object is moved, its handle must be updated to refer to the new location. For this, we need to be able to find the handle from the object. Thus, objects hold a *back-pointer* to their handle.

Real-time systems cannot halt mutator threads to perform a collection, so objects are marked with a *colour* rather than a single bit [33]. All phases of collection require access to the GC colour. The colour is always part of the object header in Ovm, merged with the type information word. With thin handles, the header is already part of the object, so colours can be accessed during sweeping and compaction directly. Fat handles store the header (and hence the colour) in the handle. To avoid unnecessary cache traffic particularly while sweeping, we cache the colour in the back-pointer (Figure 1(b)). The back-pointer is used only by the collector, so the overhead of masking out the colour is not a problem. On the other hand, we do not cache colours in thin handles, because the speed-up we might gain in marking and so on would be outweighed by the slowdown of masking by the mutator.

The compiler can exploit knowledge that an object can never be moved. The object layout of unmovable objects is shown in Figure 2. This layout must be compatible with that of movable objects, because code may access both movable and immovable ob-

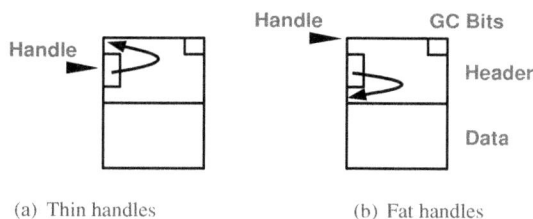

Figure 2. Object layout of unmovable objects.

jects. Unmovable objects thus still need handles. By keeping the handles with the objects, we exploit the likelihood that loading the handle into the cache will also load part of the header, thus reducing cache misses. The compiler can also replace a handle dereference by pointer arithmetic in code that is known to access only unmovable objects; this can eliminate completely some dereferences. Furthermore, unmovable objects do not need a back-pointer to their handle, as they are treated specially by the collector.

A consequence of having both movable and unmovable objects of the same type in the system is that, with fat handles, the header of an unmovable object has to be padded so that the payload starts at an 8-byte aligned address. This is because the payload of a movable object must start at an 8-byte aligned address and all fields of the object are laid based on this assumption. With uni-sized fat handles this is not a problem, because the header size is 16 bytes.

3.2 Handle allocation

We store handles in dedicated handle blocks, which are treated specially by the collector. Our handle space is not contiguous. Free handles are organised into a single-linked free-list, threaded through individual handles, which may be in different handle blocks. The allocator always takes the first handle from the head of the free-list. The handle space grows on demand — if no free handle is available, a new handle block is acquired, and new handles are initialised and linked to form a new handle free-list.

For fat handles, we maintain two independent handle spaces, one for scalar objects (smaller handles) and one for array objects (larger handles). To avoid the additional overhead of, and risk of fragmentation from, two handle spaces, we also implement uni-sized fat handles; we expect the overhead of the dereference to access the array length field to be relatively low, as this access will commonly be followed by ones to the array data, so there should be no extra cache load in most cases.

3.3 Handle release

When the garbage collector discovers a handle of a dead object, it has to return it to the free-list and zero the header part. We implemented different strategies on where to insert the handle, as we found that different choices have significant performance implications. The naïve yet simplest solution is always to add free handles to the head of the free-list (*naïve release*). Unfortunately, this solution has very poor performance, which we believe is caused by the resulting poor locality of this list. Consecutive handles in the list might well be in different handle blocks and the free handles of a particular handle block can be far apart in the list.

Consecutive free handles. A relatively simple but highly beneficial improvement is to keep all the free handles from a single handle block together in the free-list, not necessarily in address order. This rule can be enforced without any additional overhead on the allocator. For every handle block, the collector remembers the position of the last free handle in that block (the one that is last in the free-list). This information is not updated by the allocator, but only by the collector when it sweeps. When the collector needs to

insert a newly freed handle into the free-list, it first checks the last known free handle in the respective handle block. The block for a handle can be found easily using address arithmetic. If this handle is still free, the collector inserts the newly freed handle in the free-list after that one. Otherwise, the newly freed handle is the only free handle in the block, so it can be connected to the head of the free-list. Discovering whether a handle is free is also relatively cheap. We maintain a bitmap indicating whether a given block is a handle or object block: a handle is free if and only if it points into a handle block. Most importantly, this test is needed only for sweeping by the collector and not for allocation by the mutator.

Free-list rebuilding. We support further optimisations to increase the locality of handles. After sweeping, we rebuild the free-list so that the free handles in a block are sorted in address order. Because all free handles in a block are stored consecutively in the list, this sorting can be implemented incrementally. The rebuild is just a linear pass through the free-list. Each time a new handle block is detected in the free-list, its sequence of handles is temporarily disconnected to avoid interference with mutator allocation, then incrementally sorted and re-connected. Note that the reconnection must be robust against the situation that the allocator has already consumed the previous handle block.

Free handle block release. We support opportunistic release of free handle blocks. While this is not a worst-case optimisation, handle blocks can be often released in practice. Just as objects tend to live and die together in clumps [5, 15], so do their handles. This optimisation is vital to reduce handle space fragmentation caused by peak demands on handles: allocation of many small objects that die quickly, followed by a period with a lower rate of allocation. Note that handle space fragmentation is worse for a real-time collector than a non real-time one. A stop-the-world collector can ensure that the number of used handles never exceeds a threshold unless all the handles belong to live objects; otherwise it triggers a collection. There is no such option in a real-time collector. An alternative is to pre-allocate the maximum number of handles that could be needed before the system runs out of memory. This approach, however, leads to excessive wasting of memory.

Sorting handle blocks. Our collector can sort the handle free-list while it is being re-built so that blocks with fewer free handles are included first (and hence re-used sooner by allocator). The motivation for this optimisation is to make the handle space more compact and to increase opportunities for releasing blocks of free handles. Sorting is performed incrementally in the linear pass of the free-list already done for rebuilding. We use a variant of bucket sort to find the location in the free-list at which to insert a given block, maintaining an array of blocks that records the last block in the free-list of given occupancy. As this array may be sparse, we use a bitmap to speed-up access to it. We also support reverse sort order, where mostly-free handle blocks are held first. This order may improve the locality of handle allocation, by giving longer runs of handles allocated from the same block.

Pre-initialised caching. If handle blocks are released as soon as all the handles they contain are free, and the handle space is nicely compact, new blocks for handles are needed soon. The time spent initialising them (and previously clearing empty handle blocks) is then wasted. Thus it makes sense to retain some empty handle blocks, initialised with a free-list threaded through each one. It would be possible to vary this threshold dynamically, but we have not done so. Keeping these in the free-list would result in repeated re-building if they survive a collection cycle. To avoid this, we can cache a certain number of empty yet pre-initialised handle blocks. When the allocator exhausts the handle free-list, it first tries to use a handle block from the pre-initialised list and only if that list is empty does it acquire and initialise a fresh block from the system. Although this optimisation adds a branch, it is only to the allocator's (rare) slow path. Pre-initialised empty handle blocks are cached while rebuilding and perhaps sorting the free-list.

Colour caching. With both fat and uni-sized fat handles, we added a copy of the object colour into the payload, so that it can be accessed without dereferencing the back-pointer. This optimisation is important for sweeping, which is done in our collector by traversing the object space (not the handle space). Thus the sweeper does not need to access the header of live objects. We reduce cache traffic by updating the cached colour only when an object's fields are scanned (and hence must be loaded into the cache) rather than when the object (handle) is marked.

Independent handle release. Handles of dead objects need to be reclaimed. With thin handles, the sweeper does this (by following the back-pointer) as it discovers dead objects. This behaviour is not cache-friendly either. The handle free-list consolidation described above then runs *after* the object sweep has finished. With fat and uni-sized fat handles, the handle release can be done *while* sweeping objects, thereby improving locality and linearity of access of the sweeper. The sweeper passes through all used blocks of the heap in address order, sweeping both handle and object blocks. This handle sweep supports *consecutive free handles*. We also implement *free handle-block rebuilding* and *pre-initialised caching*. *Sorting* could be implemented as well, but instead we keep the blocks in address order, which could additionally improve locality. It also somewhat simplifies the handle sweep algorithm.

4. Minuteman RTGC and Ovm

Ovm [2, 32], developed at Purdue University, is an open-source implementation of the Real-time Specification for Java (RTSJ) [7] and a real-time garbage collector (RTGC). It compiles Java bytecode ahead-of-time into C, performing compiler optimisations including whole program analysis, devirtualisation, and inlining. The generated C code is then compiled by gcc to apply additional optimisations, including more inlining. The primary target platform is 32-bit Linux/x86, but Ovm has also been ported to the RTEMS/LEON embedded platform, used by the European Space Agency and NASA, and to other platforms.

Ovm is written mostly in Java, including the compiler, garbage collector, and runtime. At build time, Ovm runs in a hosted Java VM. It loads the bytecode for the whole VM and the application, compiles and optimises both, generates the C code, and then produces a final binary via gcc. It also generates a so-called boot image, which includes VM runtime classes, class information, and static data. We use a version of Ovm with green threading: all Java threads are run on top of a single native thread. Preemption points are inserted by the compiler only at back-branches. This has been shown to be sufficient to provide latencies below 6 μs [2] in response to external events including timer interrupts. Green threading greatly simplifies the collector: because the VM has control of scheduling it is straightforward to ensure that actions are atomic.

Minuteman is a highly configurable RTGC within Ovm. For this paper, we added handles as options for realising dynamic defragmentation. This implementation affected not only the GC, but other parts of the VM as well. We focus here on a GC configuration with arraylets, a fully incremental collector (all phases are incremental, but small objects are copied atomically), and GC barriers written for predictability (the barriers are on at all times, not just when needed by the GC). We use time-based periodic scheduling as in Metronome GC [3].

4.1 Memory layout and access in the boot image

As noted above, the memory layout and allocation is different for the heap and for the boot image. In the boot image, objects and ar-

rays are always allocated contiguously, at 8-byte aligned addresses. The contiguous representation for the boot image is designed to be accessible using the same code as the heap representation. Thus, the forwarding pointers for Brooks and replication are set to point to the object itself, handles are part of the object representation as shown in Figure 2, and arraylets are laid out one after another to correctly reflect contiguous representation of the array. The compiler sometimes knows statically that a particular piece of code only accesses objects in the boot image. Such accesses are then optimised (eliminating arraylet pointer dereferences, skipping forwarding with Brooks, omitting double-writes with replication and optimising out dereferences with handles). These optimisations are important for performance because the boot image also includes type information needed for non-devirtualised calls and type checks, as well as data structures used by the memory allocator

4.2 The heap

The heap is of fixed size, divided into 2 KB blocks. Each block can be free or dedicated to either small objects, arraylets, a large object, or handles. The kind of a block is stored in bitmaps and can be looked up at any time. Free blocks are always zeroed, organised in a single-linked free-list, and available to be allocated for any of the kinds. Small object blocks are allocated to size classes as in, for example, Metronome [3].

In fresh small-object blocks, new objects are allocated using a bump pointer. Once any objects in a block die, the block is no longer eligible for bump pointer allocation. Instead, free objects are organised into segregated free lists. There is a free-list per each small-object block, and a free-list of non-full small-object blocks of a given class. The small-object allocator preferentially allocates from a segregated free-list, and only if this list is empty does it acquire a new block and set it for bump pointer allocation. Small-object blocks that become free are zeroed by the collector and returned to the low-level block allocator. In general, zeroing is always done during the sweep in Ovm, to prevent pauses during allocation. Note that such pauses might affect the highest priority threads due to allocation activity of low priority threads. An adversarial allocation/lifecycle pattern may lead to very many almost-free blocks per size class; consequently, there may be no free blocks in the heap, and allocations may fail in another size class. This situation is prevented by dynamic defragmentation, which can move objects from one block to another within a size class. Arrays are formed by a spine which contains references to external arraylets (each the size of a heap block, marked as an arraylet block). The last arraylet can be allocated within the spine (as an internal arraylet) if it is smaller than 2 KB. Thus, arrays smaller than 2 KB have smaller access overheads. The spine is allocated either as a normal small object, if it small enough, or as a large object.

5. Modifications to support handles

In this section we outline the changes to the heap and to the write barriers to support handles.

5.1 Handle blocks

Each handle block holds only handles of one kind. Thin handles are 4 bytes long. Fat handles for scalars are 16 bytes and for arrays 20 bytes. Uni-size fat handles are 16 bytes. In addition to regular handle blocks that hold used and/or free handles, we keep pre-initialised handle blocks of free handles, sorted in address-order, which can be quickly re-used by the allocator. Free handles are allocated from a free-list, as explained in Section 3. Large objects do not use handle blocks but have their handles inlined in the same way as unmovable objects in the boot image.

In Ovm/Minuteman, the object header includes the type information word (with GC bits), a lock word, a pointer for RTSJ scopes, the forwarding pointer, and a hash word (except in handle configurations). Thus, without handles, scalars have 20-byte headers, and arrays 24-byte; the hash word is initialised when the object is allocated. With handles, the hash code is the handle address so the hash word is redundant and the headers are 4 bytes smaller. Thus, compared with Brooks and replication, *there is no per-object overhead for handles* although unused handles may incur memory overhead in the handle space.

5.2 Barriers and dereferences

The collector uses a Yuasa style [39] snapshot-at-the beginning (deletion) barrier, which marks the old target of the overwritten field. Stacks are scanned on-the-fly, one by one — scanning a single thread's stack is atomic (recall that Ovm uses green threads) but the mutator can run before the collector scans the next thread. This incrementality requires the collector to also use a Dijkstra style [13] incremental update (insertion) barrier, which marks the target of the newly written reference. The collector uses card marking to record pages in the boot image that it needs to scan for references into the heap. Whenever a reference is stored into an image object, the barrier marks the appropriate bit for the respective image page.

Brooks forwarding. Any read or write from/to the heap has to be preceded by a forwarding pointer dereference. However, immutable header fields, including the type information and the hash word, can be accessed directly. Array access does not need a dereference, because array length and the pointers to the external arraylets are immutable, and the pointer to the internal arraylet is updated by the GC to point to the up-to-date version in the new spine. Before any reference is written to memory, it is forwarded to prevent spreading of old references during collection. An indirection is also needed for reference comparison.

Replication. Reads from objects do not require a dereference. Writes store their value to both replicas of the object. Arrays are accessed in the same way as with Brooks forwarding. References are again updated before they are written to memory. Minuteman also supports incremental object copying with replication, during which time the mutator holds only references to the old replica – but we use only atomic copying in this work. A dereference is also needed for reference comparison.

Thin handles. Any access to an object needs a handle dereference, be it to data or header. The hash code is the address of the handle, and thus can be obtained without a dereference. No updating is necessary when writing a handle, as handles cannot become old. Array access works exactly as in Brooks forwarding and replication, except for the initial handle dereference. Reference comparison is cheaper: it is just comparison of the handles' addresses.

Fat handles require fewer dereferences than thin handles, as all header fields can be accessed without a handle dereference. Fast access to type information (type checks and virtual method calls) is particularly important. The array length field is in the handle, so requires no dereference to access it (e.g. for bounds checking).

Uni-size fat handles behave like fat handles but also require a dereference to access an array's length.

6. The collection cycle

The collector is implemented in a single thread, which wakes up when free memory (the number of free blocks) is running low, runs a GC cycle, and goes back to sleep. The thread is interruptible at almost any time: the longest atomic operation is a copy of a small object (up to 2 KB). The VM can be configured for other operations not to process more than a given number of bytes atomically. The GC cycle is as follows. In each phase, we distinguish the actions required for different configurations.

1. `waitUntilMemoryIsScarce` The GC thread sleeps. All references are black, and objects are allocated black.

2. `scanStacks` The meaning of black and white is inverted, making all objects white. The allocation colour is made black. Thread stacks are scanned and any directly reachable objects are marked grey (this also stores the reference into a list of reachable not-yet-scanned references).
   Brooks forwarding and replication. Marking always uses the up-to-date location (forwarding the reference if necessary; replication identifies the old copy with a special bit). Note that references on the stacks cannot be updated yet because the heap may still include old references.
   Thin handles. Marking dereferences a handle.
   Fat and uni-sized fat handles. Need no dereference as they include the colour.

3. `scanImage` The marked (dirty) pages of the boot image are scanned for objects, which are in turn scanned for references to heap objects which are marked grey.
   Brooks forwarding and replication. References are also fixed to point to up-to-date locations.

4. `markAndCleanHeap` For each reference in the list of grey (reachable not-yet-scanned) references, the target object is removed from the list and scanned for references, which implicitly marks it black.
   Brooks forwarding and replication. The defragmentation phase of the previous GC cycle (see below) duplicated live objects but did not forward references. This was deferred to the mark phase of this cycle. Consequently, there may be references in the heap and stacks to both the old and the new location of a single object. Marking updates stale references.
   Fat and uni-sized fat handles. Mark handles of live objects; this colour is cached in the object only when it is scanned for child pointers.

5. `cleanStacks`
   Brooks forwarding and replication. Stacks are scanned again, just to update references to point to the new locations of objects. Handles do not require this step.

6. `sweep` All white objects are unreachable, and will be reclaimed. After the sweep phase, all objects in the heap are black. All references point to up-to-date locations (there are no old copies).
   Brooks forwarding and replication. All references in reachable objects now point to up-to-date locations. The old locations of relocated objects are reclaimed as they are white (unreachable). The external arraylets of a garbage array are released only when the non-old copy is swept (as we must not release them twice). Replication must update the forwarding pointer of the new copy to point to itself when the old copy is reclaimed.
   Thin handles. Handles of small objects require additional work. Those added to free-lists are kept linked to the objects. Thus, when the allocator acquires a free slot in an object block, it obtains a handle and back-pointer 'for free'. This optimisation would not work with fat handles, because scalars and arrays use different size handles (although scalar and array objects may be interleaved in the same size class). On the other hand, when a small object block is completely unused, the block is recycled and the handles of any objects that it contained are added to the handle free-list.
   Fat handles. All handles of dead objects are zeroed and released for re-use. With *independent handle release*, the handles are released independently of their objects. To do this reliably, the small object sweeper has to be able to distinguish an array from a scalar (without accessing the header that may already have been zeroed or re-used). In the case that it is an array, the

sweeper needs to free the external arraylets of the array. With fat handles, we distinguish arrays from scalars by the type of the handle block to which the back-pointer points as there are no bits spare for this purpose in the back-pointer. Thus, *independent handle release* cannot return a free scalar- or array-handle block to the system in case it is reused for a different purpose before we have swept all garbage objects whose handle was stored in that block. Instead, all freed handle blocks are pre-initialised.

Uni-size fat handles. We solve this problem with uni-sized fat handles. As these are all 16-byte aligned, we can use a spare bit of the back-pointer as an array indicator. This bit is initialised at allocation time. We can thus reliably detect arrays at any time, and return free handle blocks to the system, once a threshold of pre-initialised handle blocks has been used.

7. `rebuildHandleFreelist(s)` The handle free-list is rebuilt as described in Section 3. With all optimisations enabled, this means that the list is sorted so that handle blocks with fewer free handles are first, and that the free handles of a single block are together and in address order. Some free handle blocks are cached as pre-initialised for further allocation, and others are zeroed and returned to the allocator. This step is only needed with handles, and only in certain configurations:

Thin handles. Whenever the handle free-list should be rebuilt or sorted or free blocks be returned or pre-initialised.

Fat and uni-sized handles. Under the same conditions, but not for independent release. With fat handles, this step uses two passes, one for scalar handles and one for array handles.

8. `defragment` If the amount of free memory is below a given threshold, defragmentation is started, relocating objects from less occupied to more occupied blocks.

Brooks forwarding and replication. The old locations of objects remain reserved until the next sweep. Only then can they be reused for allocation. Atomically with object relocation, forwarding references are updated so that the old location points to the new location and the new location to itself. Note that evacuation is not guaranteed to release a block, as free slots in the block may be reused by the mutator while the collector is attempting to evacuate it, that is until the next sweep.

Replication. The copies' forwarding addresses point to each other, and the old location is also marked by a bit shared with the type information in the header.

All handles. Relocating an object updates its handle to point to the new location. Fully evacuated blocks are zeroed and returned to the system.

Thin handles. If an object is relocated to a location that already has a cached handle (see point 6 above), this handle is relocated to the old location of the object. And in case of successful evacuation of a block, it is then freed.

7. Evaluation

The primary goal of our evaluation is to discover how much slower handles are compared to the faster non-handle configuration of replication and Brooks. The secondary goal is to compare execution time and memory requirements of different handle configurations.

For our experiments we use a subset of the DaCapo 2006-10-MR2 benchmarks [6] that run with Ovm. We use periodic scheduling of the garbage collector as in Metronome: the collector is scheduled periodically, always in fixed duration time slots (500 μs), targeting mutator utilisation of at least 70% with a time window of 10 ms [3]. The collector, however, does not start a new cycle unless the free heap blocks account for less than half the heap. We run eager compaction, so all size classes are fully compacted at every

	Linux	Intel platform	Clock	Cache
A	2.6.35	x86/64 Core2 Duo	2.4 GHz	4M 16-way L2
B	2.6.35	x86/32 Pentium 4	3.2 GHz	1M 8-way L2
C	2.6.32	x86/64 Nehalem/Xeon	2.27 GHz	8M 16-way L3

Table 1. Platforms used for experiments, including last level cache size.

GC cycle, since we find its cost negligible. Our statistical summary differs slightly with each experiment, but we always follow a common set of rules. We repeat every invocation of a benchmark (that is, start the VM binary multiple times) to average out noise due to memory placement. We iterate every benchmark within an invocation, as supported in DaCapo, to average out random perturbations of the system. We discard the first one third of measured iterations within each execution to limit the influence of start-up noise (note this is not possible with the experiments where the measurements are done by the VM, not the benchmark). We estimate the error bounds using non-parametric methods, and we round the results so as not to show digits invalidated by those error bars. When summarising relative overheads we use the geometric mean. When summarising execution times from different invocations and iterations of the same benchmark, we use the arithmetic mean, as the summary of execution time has a physical meaning [26].

We ran our experiments on three different platforms listed in Table 1. Note that while two platforms have multiple cores, Ovm only uses one. It has always been built as a 32-bit x86 executable.

Execution time overheads of handles. For this experiment, we choose the best configuration for thin handles, fat handles, and uni-sized fat handles, and we compare against replication (Table 2). The overhead of uni-sized fat handles (the best handle configuration) is about 1.8% over replication, 0.1% over Brooks, the error is within 2.3/2.4 percentage points respectively, and hence the slowdowns are not statistically significant (confidence intervals include 1, which is zero overhead). Fat handles seem slower than uni-sized fat handles, but the difference is not statistically significant (based on the confidence intervals in the table). However, we can conclude that thin handles are slower than other handles and direct pointers.

Memory usage with handles. Table 4 shows the total volume of objects moved during a benchmark execution (multiple iterations), measured in megabytes. The numbers are averaged over five executions (no error bars are shown as the numbers are extremely stable). The table shows that handles drastically reduce the number of objects moved. This is most likely because, with direct pointers, free slots in evacuated pages are often reused by the allocator, and hence after the next sweep the page is again only partially populated, and so once more is a candidate for evacuation. On average (not shown in the table), the amount of copied memory compared to replication is reduced to 4% (that is by 96%) with thin handles, to 5% with uni-sized fat handles and to 6% with fat handles. Fat handles move more data than other handles, probably because they use more GC cycles.

All the experiments for each benchmark were run with the same heap size. Handles are allocated in the heap. As the collector runs every time as soon as the heap is half-full, the number of GC cycles is a measure of memory requirements. Table 5 shows the number of cycles for the same experiment as in Tables 2 and 4. Numbers are again averaged over five executions, but left without error bars as they are extremely stable. Handles use more memory than direct pointers, but with thin handles the difference is tiny: they increase the number of GC cycles by only 1%. With uni-sized fat handles the number increases by 9% on average, which can be explained by the fact that they are larger, and thus the handle space fragmentation takes up a greater proportion of the heap. Fat handles increase the number of cycles by as much as one third — this is the fastest fat

94

	Antlr	Bloat	Fop	Hsqldb	Lusearch	Pmd	Xalan	**Geo-Mean**
Brooks	1.0328±0.0075	1.02 ±0.077	1.033±0.024	1.086±0.068	1.007±0.023	0.96 ±0.13	0.995±0.025	**1.018**±0.023
Uni-size Fat H.	1.0587±0.0072	0.973±0.084	1.021±0.019	0.999±0.056	1.046±0.061	1.0 ±0.1	1.06 ±0.03	**1.018**±0.023
Fat Handles	1.0815±0.0074	0.983±0.075	1.05 ±0.018	1.292±0.084	1.12 ±0.089	0.882±0.074	1.058±0.026	**1.061**±0.024
Thin Handles	1.0942±0.0071	1.25 ±0.15	1.053±0.026	1.152±0.074	1.214±0.087	1.11 ±0.13	1.081±0.032	**1.133**±0.032

Table 2. Execution time overheads of handles and Brooks forwarding. The baseline is replication [21]. Run on platform A.

	Antlr	Bloat	Fop	Hsqldb	Lusearch	Pmd	Xalan	**Geo-Mean**
Brooks	1.0393±0.0056	1.046±0.074	1.0217±0.0028	1.0014±0.0038	1.019 ±0.005	0.9955±0.0027	1.0212±0.0043	**1.021**±0.011
Uni-size Fat H.	1.0705±0.0054	1.05 ±0.08	1.0862±0.0025	1.013 ±0.002	1.0295±0.0054	1.0776±0.0027	1.0413±0.0073	**1.052**±0.012
Fat Handles	1.097 ±0.0053	1.026±0.083	1.076 ±0.002	1.173 ±0.013	1.0599±0.0056	1.1118±0.0051	1.0676±0.0049	**1.086**±0.013
Thin Handles	1.0974±0.0056	1.066±0.088	1.1051±0.0032	1.0768±0.0037	1.0982±0.0057	1.1612±0.0061	1.112 ±0.005	**1.102**±0.013

Table 3. Execution time overheads of handles and Brooks forwarding. The baseline is replication. Run on platform C.

handle implementation, which never returns free handle blocks to the system. Worse, fat handles need two handle spaces, thus adding to the handle space fragmentation.

It follows that the reduction in copy reserve for defragmentation does not outweigh the amount of memory wasted in unused handle slots. This is because although the amount of copying is reduced drastically, very few objects are copied anyway: in all configurations, there were at least 10,000× more objects allocated than moved. On the other hand, the amount of memory wasted in unused handles slots is very large (handle space utilisation is low).

The utilisation is the ratio of used handles to the current number of handles in the handle space. Unlike fragmentation in the object space which can be reduced by compaction, the handle space by its nature cannot be compacted. We aim to improve handle space utilisation by releasing free handle blocks. Out of the three selected configurations with best performance overhead (Table 2), thin and uni-fat handles release free handle blocks but fat handles do not (all blocks are pre-initialised). Further, fat handles use two handle spaces, which might worsen handle space fragmentation. Utilisation reported is the median of five runs, measured after every sweep; we report the geometric mean across benchmarks run on platform C. As expected, the utilisation with fat handles is worst (about 28% on average). Thin handles and uni-sized fat handles are better: 42% and 45% respectively. This is interesting: there are 4× as many handles per block with thin handles as with uni-sized, so one would expect far fewer opportunities to release a block with thin handles. But this is not the case: objects are probably allocated and are dying in long enough chunks [15]. Since the utilisation is nearly the same, the amount of memory wasted is almost 4× smaller with thin handles. This confirms Table 5 in that on average thin handles have much smaller memory overhead.

Execution time overheads on a platform with a larger cache.
Table 3 shows relative execution time overheads measured on platform C (compare with Table 2 which ran on platform A). Brooks is faster than uni-sized handles, which are followed by fat and thin handles. The overhead of thin over fat is however within error bars. Compared to platform A, the overhead of fat and uni-sized handles seems larger (and is significant) while the overhead of thin handles seems smaller (and is not significantly larger than that of fat). We believe that this is because platform C has a very large last level cache (8 MB): with thin handles, more of the hot handles can remain in the cache. The average execution time overhead of uni-sized fat handles over Brooks is 3.1±1.2% (not shown in the table). On platform B, the overhead of uni-sized fat handles over Brooks is 1.6%±1.2 (significant, but seems smaller than on C).

Collector- and mutator-only overheads. Some of the overheads of handles over replication or Brooks shown in Table 2 can be attributed to the mutator (more complex allocation, more frequent dereferences, poorer locality in dereferences) and some to the col-

lector (additional processing of the handle space, need for handles and/or back-pointer dereferences). The overheads exclusive to either the mutator or the collector are shown in Table 6. The results seem to suggest that the mutator overheads of handles may be higher than for Brooks, as expected, although the error bars overlap. However, the differences in collector overheads are large and significant, even given the errors. Best of the handles is the uni-sized handles configuration, which spends around 32% more time on GC than replication does (first column). This is partially because the GC runs more often, and partially because it is slower by about 24%: the second column normalises GC times by the number of cycles executed. The GC is faster with uni-sized fat handles than with thin handles, which is expected, because of *independent release* of handles and objects, which improves the locality of sweeping and also eliminates post-sweep handle space processing. It is a bit surprising that the GC with fat handles is also much slower than with uni-sized fat handles. This could be caused by poorer locality during collection due to the two handle spaces.

The average percentage of time spent in GC with the heap sizes we use is, however, small: 6% for Brooks and replication, 7% with thin handles and uni-sized fat handles, and 9% with fat handles. The GC time is dominated in all configurations by sweeping (50–60%, largely due to the cost of zeroing memory) and marking (30–40%). Stack scanning and updating each take less than 0.1% of GC time. Post-sweep handle processing (only thin handles in these experiments) takes about 5%. Compaction takes about only 0.4% (handles) to 1% (direct pointers) of GC time. Table 7 shows execution time overheads of marking, sweeping and compaction over replication. These numbers are normalised per cycle. The slowest sweep is with thin handles, which is not surprising because of their poor locality when releasing handles of dead objects. The sweep is about the same for fat and uni-sized fat handles. Handle marking is fastest with thin handles. This suggests that the overhead of the handle dereference to find the colour is smaller than the overhead of caching the colour when scanning objects of (uni-sized) fat handles plus the overhead of loading unneeded header fields of fat handles into the cache. Marking is much slower with fat handles than uni-sized fat handles. Compaction time per cycle is reduced to about 35% (that is by 65%) with thin handles, 46% with uni-sized fat handles and 56% with fat handles. Although (uni-sized) fat handles copy less memory per object because they do not copy headers, they copy more objects and hence more data (Table 4), and they take more time to compact.

Performance benefit of various handle optimisations. Execution time overheads of different configurations of uni-sized fat handles against the best one — *independent handle release with pre-initialised caching (Indep)* — are shown in Table 8. The fastest two configurations are *independent handle release* without *pre-initialised caching (IndepNopreinit)* as well as with caching all free handle blocks releasing none to the system (*IndepMaxpreinit*). The

	Antlr	Bloat	Fop	Hsqldb	Lusearch	Pmd	Xalan
Replicating	32.08	75.74	97.06	3.12	4.93	24.18	277.31
Brooks	33.65	74.96	99.87	3.15	4.93	24.4	270.81
Uni-size Fat Handles	2.69	0.84	0.66	0.06	2.17	0.97	18.27
Fat Handles	3.42	0.93	0.6	0.12	2.6	1.08	19.83
Thin Handles	2.04	0.81	0.57	0.04	2.16	0.78	15.86

Table 4. Total number of megabytes of data moved during defragmentation (platform A).

	Antlr	Bloat	Fop	Hsqldb	Lusearch	Pmd	Xalan	**Geo-Mean**
Brooks	1.0	0.97	1.01	1.0	1.0	1.0	1.0	**1.0**
Uni-size Fat Handles	1.19	0.94	1.06	1.07	1.04	1.29	1.09	**1.09**
Fat Handles	1.43	1.02	1.15	2.0	1.11	1.64	1.2	**1.33**
Thin Handles	1.02	0.93	0.97	1.0	1.01	1.1	1.02	**1.01**

Table 5. Number of GC cycles executed compared to replication (platform A).

	Collector	Col. per Cycle	Mutator
Brooks	1.045±0.015	1.05 ±0.015	1.021±0.029
Uni-size Fat H.	1.322±0.039	1.242±0.036	1.046±0.036
Fat Handles	1.78 ±0.03	1.393±0.026	1.049±0.031
Thin Handles	1.399±0.028	1.43 ±0.03	1.076±0.033

Table 6. Exclusive collector and mutator execution time overheads over replication. Relative mutator overheads are over the number of executed cycles. Run on platform A.

	Mark	Sweep	Compact
Brooks	1.14 ±0.016	0.999±0.015	1.065±0.037
Uni-size Fat H.	1.467±0.072	1.163±0.025	0.463±0.034
Fat Handles	1.8 ±0.034	1.18 ±0.02	0.555±0.023
Thin Handles	1.381±0.023	1.374±0.028	0.348±0.014

Table 7. Execution time overhead of GC phases, normalised per GC cycle. The baseline is replication. Run on platform A.

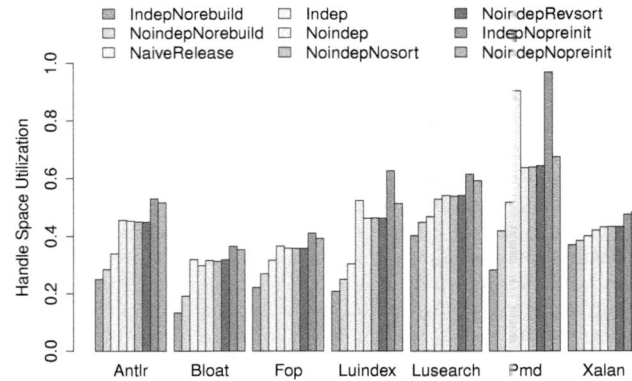

Figure 3. Handle space utilisation with different configurations of uni-size fat handles (platform B). Higher is better.

differences between *IndepNoPreinit*, *Indep*, and *IndepMaxpreinit* are negligible and within error bars, hence pre-initialisation does not make a difference on platform B. We have, however, observed a significant impact of the level of pre-initialisation on platform C and even more on platform A, where tuning the threshold (*Indep*) lead to the same overhead as with Brooks. *IndepNoRebuild* lacks *free-list rebuilding* and is slower than the previous configurations. The results show that *independent handle release* is also a good optimisation, as configurations lacking it are significantly slower (error bars do not overlap). Without *independent* handle release, *pre-initialised caching* does not improve the average overhead either (*NoindepNopreinit* is the same as *Noindep*, *NoindepMaxpreinit* seems even slower, but the difference is within error bars). By far and significantly the worst is *naïve releasing* free handles to the head of the free-list (*NaïveRelease*), which has overhead as much as 26% over the best version. This confirms that *consecutive free handles* are a crucial optimisation.

Sorting free handle blocks by occupancy has no performance effect: *Noindep* (free-list rebuilding, pre-initialised caching, sorting blocks by decreasing number of free handles), *NoindepNosort* (the same without sorting), and *NoindepRevsort* (the same, but sorting in reverse order) all have about the same average overhead over the best version and error bars overlap. *NoindepRevsort* has only slightly smaller average overhead than *NoindepNosort* and *Noindep*, the difference being well within the error bars. This suggests that sorting does not make a difference. *NoindepNorebuild* is a version with only *consecutive free handles*, but no *free-list rebuilding*. The average overhead seems higher than that of *Noindep* (sorting, pre-initialised caching), but it lies within the error bars.

Memory usage of various handles optimisations. We aim to increase handle space utilisation by releasing free handle blocks and by increasing the chance of free handle blocks (by sorting handle blocks). Median handle space utilisation with uni-sized fat handles is shown in Figure 3. The first three configurations (also first column of the legend) are those that do not release free handle blocks. The remaining six do: for every benchmark, releasing free handle blocks significantly improves the utilisation. Note that the actual values depend on allocation pattern of the application. The configuration giving highest utilisation is *IndepNopreinit*, which follows our expectations: it releases all free handle blocks. The configurations with maximum preinitialisation, *IndepMaxpreinit* and *NoindepMaxpreinit* (not shown in the graph) have very close utilisations to *NoindepNorebuild* and *IndepNorebuild*. It is not surprising that configurations that release free handle blocks also have better utilisation. With *preinitialised caching*, the utilisation is then very sensitive to the setting of the threshold of the maximum number of preinitialised blocks. For several benchmarks, configurations with *independent handle release* have better utilisation than without. This can be caused by the GC running faster, and thus fewer new handle blocks allocated during the GC. The graph also shows that *sorting handle blocks* does not make a difference: *Noindep*, *NoindepNosort*, and *NoindepRevsort* all have the same utilisation. Configurations with better utilisation run fewer GC cycles (not shown in the figure). This follows our expectation, as the GC is triggered when the amount of free memory falls below a given threshold. Increasing this threshold, and thus running the GC more often, should increase utilisation with all configurations.

	Antlr	Bloat	Fop	Luindex	Lusearch	Pmd	Xalan	Geo-Mean
IndepMaxpreinit	1.0135±0.0025	1.014±0.088	0.9851±0.0018	1.0098±0.0018	1.0093±0.0018	1.0352±0.0083	1.0025±0.0026	**1.009**±0.012
IndepNopreinit	1.003 ±0.002	1.031±0.086	0.9954±0.0026	1.0012±0.00095	1.0097±0.0025	1.0012±0.0052	0.9998±0.0033	**1.006**±0.012
IndepNorebuild	1.0179±0.0025	1.017±0.085	0.9901±0.0018	1.012 ±0.001	1.0133±0.0017	1.0478±0.0067	1.0012±0.0025	**1.014**±0.012
Noindep	1.0558±0.0023	1.05 ±0.091	1.0312±0.0025	1.0388±0.0013	1.0623±0.0054	1.165 ±0.011	1.0204±0.0029	**1.059**±0.013
NoindepMaxpre.	1.0636±0.0025	1.078±0.093	1.014 ±0.002	1.0444±0.0015	1.0602±0.0018	1.192 ±0.013	1.026 ±0.0026	**1.067**±0.013
NoindepNopre.	1.0549±0.0023	1.061±0.092	1.0138±0.0025	1.0415±0.0015	1.0536±0.0018	1.175 ±0.012	1.026 ±0.0039	**1.059**±0.013
NoindepNoreb.	1.0804±0.0026	1.048±0.098	1.036 ±0.002	1.056 ±0.002	1.077 ±0.0035	1.212 ±0.013	1.0263±0.0025	**1.075**±0.013
NoindepNosort	1.0534±0.0031	1.038±0.093	1.0303±0.0024	1.037 ±0.0015	1.054 ±0.002	1.16 ±0.01	1.0207±0.0029	**1.056**±0.013
NoindepRevsort	1.053 ±0.0026	1.016±0.093	1.0272±0.0025	1.0358±0.0012	1.0522±0.0016	1.161 ±0.012	1.0191±0.0026	**1.051**±0.013
NaïveRelease	1.1846±0.0032	1.25 ±0.11	1.1264±0.0021	1.23 ±0.002	1.2365±0.0073	1.848 ±0.068	1.0856±0.0031	**1.261**±0.016

Table 8. Execution time overhead of uni-size fat handles configurations against the best (Indep). Run on platform B.

8. Related Work

Recently, there has been renewed interest in handles for memory management, mainly for real-time and embedded systems [12, 14, 35, 38]. JOP [35] is a hardware implementation of a real-time Java VM for embedded systems with an incremental copying collector. The collector uses fat handles to support incrementality. Handles are allocated in a separate handle space of sufficient fixed size that it has enough handles for the worst-case demand of a particular application. Array and scalar handles have the same size — the array length field is used for the method table pointer in scalar handles. Each handle is either on a free-list or on a used-list. Allocation takes place from the free-list, and the allocator adds the new object to the used-list. Handle sweep operates on the used-list, adding unused handles to the head of the free-list. Handles allocated together will end up together on the list, if they also die together. It seems that no additional reorganisation of the handle free-list is performed. The handle dereference is implemented by hardware and can run in parallel with a corresponding null check and/or scope check. Fat handles with all metadata in the handles are argued to be good for memory mapped hardware structures, particularly arrays [36]. The payload does not include a back-pointer to the handle or any mark bits because collection is controlled from the handle space.

An alternative mark-compact real-time collector for JOP has been provided in [14]. It uses fat handles, allocated from a dedicated contiguous space that can grow but not shrink. The payload includes a back-pointer to the handle as well as to a mark-list. Free handles are organised in a free-list. Handles are allocated from its head, and added to the tail by the sliding compactor. Thus, although the handles freed in one collection cycle are appended in address order, overall the free-list is not address ordered.

Thin handles are used as a substitute for a mark stack in another mark-compact collector [38]. Outside a GC cycle, all pointers are direct. The GC replaces them by handles while scanning an object. An object is greyed by allocating a handle for it and linking it by a back-pointer. An object is blackened by removing that back-pointer. After sliding compaction, the handles are again replaced by direct pointers. The locality of the allocated handles should be good as it copies the live heap structure. The temporary nature of handles, on the other hand, leads to the need for not one but two rounds of pointer updating during a collection. Unlike most handle solutions, the addresses of handles cannot be used for hashing.

Compact-fit [12] is an allocator for explicit memory management which uses handles with size-class allocation and compaction. Compaction happens potentially after each object deallocation, with atomic update of the handle. Handles are allocated in a dedicated contiguous space and objects have back-pointers to handles. Free handles are stored in a free-list. Our optimisations for increasing handles locality should be applicable to compact-fit, together with the support for non-contiguous extensible handle space.

Handles are also apparently used in a garbage collector for BlackBerry devices [23]. The collector uses two memory spaces, RAM and flash. Handles were used in compressing mark-sweep

and sliding mark-compact collectors [10] for Sun's KVM in order to eliminate the need for updating direct pointers in objects, which would require costly decompression of these objects. The handles were 8 bytes wide (pointer plus type information) and objects had back-pointers to handles. Arrays used arraylets and had array length in the spine. In the mark-compact version, the handle space was contiguous, expandable, but not shrinkable. One configuration eliminated handles by refraining from compression of reference fields. It turned out that this pays off: more memory is saved by avoiding handles than by compressing reference fields.

A hardware-assisted real-time collector with handles has been proposed in [27], using reference counting. Handles are allocated in a dedicated handle table and contain a reference count, the direct pointer and object size. It is not clear whether the design has been implemented or only simulated.

Another collector with handles has been implemented for Scheme [25]. The mark-compact GC uses thin handles, allocated out of the heap in dedicated chunks. Whenever a new block for objects on the heap is allocated, the GC also allocates a new handle chunk large enough to contain handles for all (the minimum size) objects that might be allocated in a heap block. Free handles are linked into a free list, but it is not specified how the list is managed. Movable objects have back-pointers to their handles. Unmovable objects have handles attached to their headers, as in our collector.

A two-space copying collector [31] used thin handles, allocated in dedicated handle blocks of 32 handles, outside the semi-spaces. Handles are used to allow conservative scanning with dynamic defragmentation. Free handle blocks are linked into a free-list and used (non-free) handle blocks are linked into a used-list. The handle space is swept by scanning the used-list, avoiding the free handle blocks. This is similar to the *pre-initialised caching* that we support. The total number of handle blocks in the system is fixed. As with [35], objects do not need back-pointers.

Handles have also been used in earlier Smalltalk implementations [24] and in early versions of Sun's JVMs [17, 28] in stop-the-world non-incremental collectors. Finally, the space overhead bounds for a system with segregated free-lists and partial compaction is discussed in [4], and the worst-case bound for a fixed-size handle space in [35].

9. Conclusion

Recently, there has been a renewed interest in handles for memory management and particularly for real-time garbage collection. Anecdotally, handles are believed to be very slow compared to direct pointers. We provide the first empirical comparison of handles to direct pointers (such as Brooks forwarding pointers) and describe optimisations to reduce their overhead. Our findings are that handles can be surprisingly fast with proper optimisations. We even obtained the same average performance as with Brooks forwarding (then 1.6% and 3.1% overheads on other platforms).

Our implementation is within Ovm's Minuteman RTGC. The results are applicable to mark-sweep or mark-compact collectors with handles and some even to non real-time systems which use handles for distributed computation or persistence. A key optimisation to achieve such low overhead was a careful placement of free handles into a free-list: handles close to each other in memory should also be close in the free-list. This simple optimisation can be implemented without allocator overhead. In contrast, if free handles are added naïvely to the head of the free-list, the consequent overhead is very high — we measured 26%.

An important optimisation that reduced handle space fragmentation was releasing the memory occupied by unused handles. Still, the fragmentation can be around 40-60%. The amount of space consequently wasted depends on the handle size. When the handle was just a single pointer, we were able to run with almost the same number of collections as Brooks, but at a cost of 13% performance overhead (10% on another platform).

We show how to reduce the overhead of sweep by sweeping the handle space and data space independently in order to provide a more linear and local access pattern. The compaction phase of our collector (which is almost a reproduction of that in Metronome) is easier with handles than with Brooks: there is no copy reserve and many fewer objects need to be copied, resulting in much shorter compaction time. The lack of the copy reserve also means that it no longer needs to be part of the worst-case memory usage estimate, although the handle space size has to be included instead. Far shorter compaction time, however, does not make a difference overall in Ovm, because compaction is extremely rare in practice.

Finally, we thank the anonymous reviewers for their thoughtful comments and suggestions. We are grateful for the support of the EPSRC through grant EP/H026975/1.

References

[1] O. Agesen. Space and time-efficient hashing of garbage-collected objects. *Theor. Pract. Object Syst.*, 5:119–124, 1999.

[2] A. Armbruster, J. Baker, et al. A real-time Java virtual machine with applications in avionics. *Trans. Embedded Comput. Sys.*, 7(1), 2007.

[3] D. F. Bacon, P. Cheng, and V. Rajan. A real-time garbage collector with low overhead and consistent utilization. In *Principles of Programming Languages*, 2003.

[4] A. Bendersky and E. Petrank. Space overhead bounds for dynamic memory management with partial compaction. In *Principles of Programming Languages*, 2011.

[5] S. Blackburn and K. McKinley. Immix garbage collection: Mutator locality, fast collection, and space efficiency. In *Programming Language Design and Implementation*, 2008.

[6] S. Blackburn, R. Garner, et al. The DaCapo benchmarks: Java benchmarking development and analysis. In *Object-Oriented Programming, Systems, Languages, and Applications*, 2006.

[7] G. Bollella, T. Canham, et al. Programming with non-heap memory in the real-time specification for Java. In *Object-Oriented Programming, Systems, Languages, and Applications*, 2003.

[8] R. A. Brooks. Trading data space for reduced time and code space in real-time garbage collection on stock hardware. In *Lisp and Functional Programming*, 1984.

[9] E. J. Bruno and G. Bollella. *Real-Time Java Programming with Java RTS*. Prentice Hall, 2009.

[10] G. Chen, M. Kandemir, et al. Heap compression for memory-constrained Java environments. In *Object-Oriented Programming, Systems, Languages, and Applications*, 2003.

[11] C. Click, G. Tene, and M. Wolf. The Pauseless GC algorithm. In *Virtual Execution Environments*, 2005.

[12] S. S. Craciunas, C. M. Kirsch, et al. A compacting real-time memory management system. In *USENIX*, 2008.

[13] E. W. Dijkstra, L. Lamport, et al. On-the-fly garbage collection: An exercise in cooperation. *Communications of the ACM*, 21(11). 1978.

[14] F. Gruian and Z. Salcic. Designing a concurrent hardware garbage collector for small embedded systems. In *Asia-Pacific Computer Systems Architecture Conference*, 2005.

[15] B. Hayes. Using key object opportunism to collect old objects. In *Object-Oriented Programming, Systems, Languages, and Applications*, 1991.

[16] R. Henriksson. *Scheduling Garbage Collection in Embedded Systems*. PhD thesis, Lund University, 1998.

[17] C.-H. A. Hsieh, M. T. Conte, et al. Optimizing NET compilers for improved Java performance. *Computer*, 30, 1997.

[18] Y. C. Hu, W. Yu, et al. Run-time support for distributed sharing in safe languages. *Trans. Comput. Syst.*, 21, 2003.

[19] R. L. Hudson and J. E. B. Moss. Sapphire: copying garbage collection without stopping the world. *Concurrency and Computation: Practice and Experience*, 15(3-5), 2003.

[20] R. E. Jones and R. Lins. *Garbage Collection: Algorithms for Automatic Dynamic Memory Management*. Wiley, 1996.

[21] T. Kalibera. Replicating real-time garbage collector for Java. In *Java Technologies for Real-Time and Embedded Systems*, 2009.

[22] H. Kermany and E. Petrank. The Compressor: Concurrent, incremental and parallel compaction. In *Programming Language Design and Implementation*, 2006.

[23] M. Kirkup. Taking out the trash: Garbage collection, 2005. http://us.blackberry.com/devjournals/resources/journals/jan_2005/garbage_collection.jsp.

[24] G. Krasner, editor. *Smalltalk-80: Bits of History, Words of Advice*. Addison-Wesley, 1983.

[25] M. Larose and M. Feeley. A compacting incremental collector and its performance in a production quality compiler. In *International Symposium on Memory Management*, 1998

[26] D. J. Lilja. *Measuring Computer Performance: A Practitioner's Guide*. Cambridge University Press, 2000.

[27] C.-M. Lin and T.-F. Chen. Dynamic memory management for real-time embedded Java chips. *Real-Time Computing Systems and Applications*, 2000.

[28] S. Meloan. The Java HotSpot performance engine: An in-depth look. http://developer.java.sun.com/developer/technicalArticles/Networking/HotSpot/.

[29] S. Nettles and J. O'Toole. Real-time replication garbage collection. In *Programming Language Design and Implementation*, 1993.

[30] K. Nilsen. Differentiating features of the PERC virtual machine. http://www.aonix.com/pdf/PERCWhitePaper_e.pdf, 2009.

[31] S. C. North and J. H. Reppy. Concurrent garbage collection on stock hardware. In *Functional Programming and Computer Architecture*, 1987.

[32] Ovm. The Ovm virtual machine. http://www.ovmj.net.

[33] P. P. Pirinen. Barrier techniques for incremental tracing. In *International Symposium on Memory Management*, 1998

[34] F. Pizlo, L. Ziarek, et al. Schism: fragmentation-tolerant real-time garbage collection. In *Programming Language Design and Implementation*, 2010.

[35] M. Schoeberl. Scheduling of hard real-time garbage collection. *Real-Time Systems*, 45(3), 2010.

[36] M. Schoeberl, C. Thalinger, et al. Hardware objects for Java. In *International Symposium on Object-Oriented Real-Time Distributed Computing*, 2008.

[37] F. Siebert. Realtime garbage collection in the JamaicaVM 3.0. In *Java Technologies for Real-time and Embedded Systems*, 2007.

[38] S. Stanchina and M. Meyer. Mark-sweep or copying? a "best of both worlds" algorithm and a hardware-supported real-time implementation. In *International Symposium on Memory Management*, 2007.

[39] T. Yuasa. Real-time garbage collection on general-purpose machines. *J. Systems and Software*, 11(3), 1990.

Short-term Memory for Self-collecting Mutators *

Martin Aigner, Andreas Haas, Christoph M. Kirsch,
Michael Lippautz, Ana Sokolova, Stephanie Stroka, Andreas Unterweger
University of Salzburg
firstname.lastname@cs.uni-salzburg.at

Abstract

We propose a new memory model called short-term memory for managing objects on the heap. In contrast to the traditional persistent memory model for heap management, objects in short-term memory expire after a finite amount of time, which makes deallocation unnecessary. Instead, expiration of objects may be extended, if necessary, by refreshing. We have developed a concurrent, incremental, and non-moving implementation of short-term memory for explicit refreshing called self-collecting mutators that is based on programmer-controlled time and integrated into state-of-the-art runtimes of three programming languages: C, Java, and Go. All memory management operations run in constant time without acquiring any locks modulo the underlying allocators. Our implementation does not require any additional heap management threads, hence the name. Expired objects may be collected anywhere between one at a time for maximal incrementality and all at once for maximal throughput and minimal memory consumption. The integrated systems are heap management hybrids with persistent memory as default and short-term memory as option. Our approach is fully backwards compatible. Legacy code runs without any modifications with negligible runtime overhead and constant per-object space overhead. Legacy code can be modified to take advantage of short-term memory by having some but not all objects allocated in short-term memory and managed by explicit refreshing. We study single- and multi-threaded use cases in all three languages macro-benchmarking C and Java and micro-benchmarking Go. Our results show that using short-term memory (1) simplifies heap management in a state-of-the-art H.264 encoder written in C without additional time and minor space overhead, and (2) improves, at the expense of safety, memory management throughput, latency, and space consumption by reducing the number of garbage collection runs, often even to zero, for a number of Java and Go programs.

Categories and Subject Descriptors D3.4 [*Processors*]: Memory management (garbage collection)

General Terms Algorithms, Languages, Performance

Keywords Explicit Heap Management

---

* Supported by the EU ArtistDesign Network of Excellence on Embedded Systems Design, the National Research Network RiSE on Rigorous Systems Engineering (Austrian Science Fund S11404-N23), and an Elise Richter Fellowship (Austrian Science Fund V00125).

1. Introduction

At any time instant during mutator execution, an ideal dynamic heap management distinguishes the memory objects on the heap that are still needed by the mutator in the future (dynamically live) from the memory objects that are not needed anymore (dead). Heap management is correct if the memory allocated for the objects that are in what we call the needed set of objects is always guaranteed to be maintained. Heap management is bounded if the memory allocated for the objects in the (complementary) not-needed set of objects is always eventually reclaimed by deallocation or reuse.

Traditional heap management based on explicit deallocation or garbage collection implements different approximations of the needed and not-needed sets. Explicit deallocation, if used correctly, under-approximates the not-needed set. Tracing garbage collectors over-approximate the needed set by computing the set of reachable objects, which contains the needed set if used correctly, i.e., in the absence of reachable memory leaks. Reference-counting garbage collectors under-approximate the not-needed set by computing the set of unreachable objects, which is contained in the not-needed set. The needed and not-needed sets can also be approximated at the same time by tracing and reference-counting hybrids [5].

Despite the differences in approximation techniques, heap management based on explicit deallocation or garbage collection implements the same memory model for programming mutators. Allocated memory is guaranteed to be maintained until deallocation, either explicitly, or implicitly through unreachability. We refer to this model as persistent memory model throughout the paper. In the persistent memory model, memory is persistent until further notice. Thus objects in the needed set are safe without attention whereas objects in the not-needed set require action, either by explicit deallocation or garbage collection, hence the name. The advantages and disadvantages of explicit deallocation and garbage collection are direct consequences of the memory model. Explicit deallocation is fast but creates dangling pointers through premature deallocation and memory leaks through missing deallocation. Garbage collection removes the danger of dangling pointers but introduces cost and complexity for computing unreachability, directly or indirectly, and may therefore still allow for reachable memory leaks.

We propose short-term memory as an alternative model to the persistent memory model for studying an area of dynamic heap management that is in our opinion largely unexplored, at least by using a general model explicitly. In the short-term memory model, memory allocated for an object is only guaranteed to be maintained for a finite amount of time. Here, each object has, in addition to the memory that has been allocated for it, a so-called expiration date. When the object expires, its memory may be reclaimed by deallocation or reuse. If the object is needed beyond its expiration date, it may be refreshed before it expires, extending its expiration date but only by a finite amount of time. Refreshing may be repeated arbitrarily often but does not accumulate time.

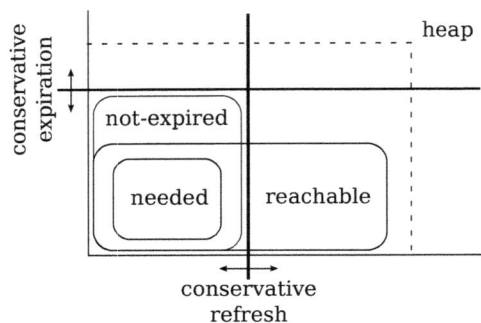

Figure 1. Approximation of the needed set by the not-expired set in the short-term memory model.

Thus, in the short-term memory model, memory is short-term until further notice. Now, objects in the not-needed set will be reclaimed without attention whereas objects in the needed set require action by refreshing.

Similar to the persistent memory model, short-term memory may be implemented by providing, in this case, refreshing information explicitly or implicitly. Note that explicitly refreshing needed objects can always be done since needed objects are always reachable, as opposed to explicitly deallocating not-needed objects, which may or may not be reachable. Moreover, unlike the persistent memory model, short-term memory induces the notion of two sets that provide structure that does not exist with persistent memory: the not-expired set of objects which have not yet expired, and the (complementary) expired set of objects. It is important to note that the two sets only exist if time is guaranteed to advance. Otherwise, all memory is permanent. As shown in Figure 1, the not-expired set is controlled by two concepts: conservative refresh of objects potentially preventing reachable but not-needed objects from expiring, and conservative expiration potentially delaying expiration of unreachable and thus not-needed objects.

Heap management in the short-term memory model is correct if the not-expired set always contains the needed set, and is bounded if the expired set always eventually contains the objects of the not-needed set, and time advances. Note that the mark phase of a mark-sweep garbage collector may readily be used to provide refreshing information that guarantees correctness by conservatively refreshing all reachable objects before time advances. However, this approach may again suffer from reachable memory leaks.

In this paper we focus on explicit refreshing. Unlike explicit deallocation, explicit refreshing only requires to know an upper bound on the lifetime of objects that may be arbitrarily large as long as it is finite. Explicit deallocation requires to know an upper bound that must be less than the time when the objects becomes unreachable. Like explicit deallocation, explicit refreshing may be done incorrectly. For example, incorrect use of explicit refreshing is missing refreshing information, resulting in memory being reclaimed too early creating dangling pointers. However, unreachable objects can never be explicitly deallocated in the persistent memory model (source of memory leaks) whereas refreshing needed and thus reachable objects is always possible. Other errors and their consequences are discussed at the beginning of Section 2.

We have developed a concurrent, incremental, and non-moving implementation of short-term memory for explicit refreshing called self-collecting mutators integrated into C as dynamic library using the ptmalloc2 allocator of glibc-2.10.1[1], the Jikes Research Virtual Machine [3] for Java, and the 6g runtime for Go[2]. The code is open source and available online [2]. In Jikes and 6g we use their mark-

[1] http://www.gnu.org/software/libc
[2] http://golang.org

sweep garbage collectors because they are non-moving (and there is anyway no other choice for 6g) and do not incur runtime overhead when not running (unlike, e.g. the Jikes reference-counting collector). Note that, for brevity, we generally use the term "thread" to refer to a thread (as in C and Java) and a goroutine (as in Go, developers forgive us) alike. We also use the term "object" to refer to a memory block (as in C) and an object (as in Java or Go) alike.

All memory management operations are lock-free, i.e., do not acquire any locks, and run in constant time modulo the underlying allocators. The progress of time for expiring objects is programmer-controlled by explicit "tick" calls. Each memory management operation may collect, in addition to performing its actual function, any number of expired objects. There are no additional heap management threads in the system for this purpose, hence the name self-collecting mutators. The default collection strategy is lazy for maximal incrementality where each operation collects at most one object. Currently, the only implemented alternative is eager collection for maximal throughput and minimal memory consumption where each operation collects all objects that have expired. In this case, however, operations may not run in constant time. Alternative, more dynamic designs remain future work.

The integrated systems are heap management hybrids with persistent memory as default and short-term memory as option. We show in a number of use cases and benchmarks that using persistent memory for permanent and long-living objects while using short-term memory for short-living objects simplifies explicit heap management at the expense of slightly increased memory consumption and improves temporal and spatial performance of implicit heap management at the expense of safety. Re-establishing safety, which may require the development of adequate program analysis tools, remains future work.

The paper makes the following contributions: (1) the short-term memory model, (2) the self-collecting mutators implementation in C, Java, and Go, and (3) an experimental analysis of several macro- and micro-benchmarks.

2. Model and Implementation

For programming with short-term memory we propose to use a fully backwards-compatible approach. The default is that objects are allocated as persistent and managed by the existing heap management systems (malloc/free, GC). Then, any time after its allocation (and before its deallocation),

- an object o may be flagged as short-term and, as a consequence, managed by our heap management system, by refreshing o with a so-called expiration extension of $e \geq 0$ through a constant-time, lock-free refresh(o, e)-call.

The effect is that the object receives an expiration date $(l + e)$ where l is the current value of a software clock, which is simply an integer counter that is local to the refreshing thread. From then on the object will not be managed by the existing heap management system anymore. Instead,

- the object is now guaranteed to exist until the thread that refreshed the object advances thread-local time to $(l + e + 1)$ by incrementing the value of its thread-local clock through $(e + 1)$ constant-time, lock-free tick-calls.

After that the object is said to have expired and will be collected by our system. Objects may be flagged as short-term any time after their allocation, e.g. when an exact or at least reasonable expiration date is known. If it later turns out that the object will expire too early, the object may be refreshed again with a later expiration date. However, an object once flagged as short-term may not be returned to persistent memory anymore although an appropriate memory management call would be easy to implement. It is rather a design choice we made because we did not find use cases.

There are a number of implications related to multiple refreshing of an object and the definition of time. We discuss them briefly right here before getting back to our use cases.

An object may be refreshed by multiple threads multiple times even in between time advance. As a result, an object may have multiple expiration dates (for one but also for different threads) since each refresh creates a new expiration date for the object. The expiration semantics is nevertheless simple. In general,

- an object in short-term memory expires when all its expiration dates have expired, and

- an expiration date has expired if its value is less than the thread-local time of the thread that created the expiration date through refreshing.

Thus multiple refreshing of an object by the same thread with the same expiration extension in between time advance has no effect other than wasting CPU time and memory (for creating and storing expiration dates). In contrast, multiple deallocations of an object with traditional explicit heap management systems (malloc/free) is an error. However, multiple refreshing across expiration, i.e., refreshing already expired objects, is also an error, which may lead to multiple deallocations of an object. The error may be detected at runtime to prevent multiple deallocations. An implementation remains future work.

Multiple refreshing of an object by different threads indicates that the object is not only shared but also short-term with respect to multiple thread-local clocks. The issue here is that refreshing and ticking requires coordination among the involved threads to prevent a shared object from expiring before all involved threads had a chance to refresh it. Coordination may either be done explicitly by the application (fast and space-efficient but difficult) or implicitly by our heap management system (easy and fast but less space-efficient), which effectively computes the notion of a global time for handling expiration dates of shared objects, see Section 2.6. For Go, there is a third option, namely for objects communicated through channels, to perform the necessary coordination implicitly and fast, and even without any space overhead.

Multiple refreshing may be avoided altogether by providing more than one clock per thread. The extreme case is that each object gets its own clock making short-term memory programming equivalent to persistent memory programming. Multiple clocks per thread are anyway interesting since, in terms of expressiveness, they are equivalent to non-zero expiration extensions if the clocks have a common base clock. Otherwise, multiple clocks are even more general, see Section 2.5.

Multiple refreshing does not make an object permanent but not advancing time does. Time advance may only be guaranteed by using real-time clocks rather than software clocks. This is an interesting topic for future work. However, even with software clocks, short-term memory may be used in real-time applications, see Section 2.4.

2.1 Single-Threaded Use Cases

We have manually ported a number of existing programs written in C, Java, and Go to short-term memory. We describe each port and argue informally about its correctness to provide intuition on the effort of using short-term memory explicitly in terms of lines of code and in terms of the difficulty of placing the needed code correctly. Table 1 shows the porting effort for each use case.

We first present single-threaded use cases: the mpg123[3] MP3 encoder and the x264 video encoder written in C, the Monte Carlo

	mpg123	x264	MC	Tree	WS
Original LoC	16043	61722	1450	104	29
Removed LoC	43	102	0	0	0
tick	1	1	1	3	1
refresh(0)	48	2	36	1	1
refresh((>0)	0	4	0	0	0
Aux LoC	0	63	0	11	0

Table 1. Original number of lines of code, number of removed lines of code, number of tick-calls, number of refresh(0)-calls, number of refresh(>0)-calls, and number of lines of auxiliary code, for each use case.

(MC) benchmark of the Grande Java Benchmark Suite [18] written in Java, and the Tree benchmark of the Computer Language Benchmarks Game[4] written in Go. In the next section we deal with multi-threaded use cases: a multi-threaded version of the x264 encoder and a simple web server (WS) written in Go.

The following improvements are achieved by short-term memory. The C use cases logically need fewer lines of code and establishing correctness is easy. In Java and Go, unlike with garbage collection, correctness with explicit short-term memory is not guaranteed. Nevertheless, in the presented use cases establishing correctness is easy. Moreover, by using short-term memory, the Java and Go use cases improve in terms of number of garbage collection runs, total execution time, and memory consumption. The performance improvements are shown in Section 4.

We apply an informal translation scheme that helps establishing correctness. We first place a tick-call at the code location that marks the end of the period of the most frequent periodic behavior of the benchmark where most of the memory expires, which was easy to find in all benchmarks. Code locations where less memory expires but more frequently are also an option, which we may consider in future work. In this case more refreshing work will be required but memory consumption may be reduced. Next, we flag all objects as short-term that can expire safely at the tick-calls by placing refresh-calls right after their allocation with expiration extensions that depend on the use case and range from zero, in most cases, to some positive value, in more complex cases such as the x264 benchmark. Multiple refreshing is only used for optimizations in the x264 benchmark.

mpg123 in C. The mpg123 benchmark decodes a set of mp3 files into a set of corresponding wav files. All memory is needed just for the conversion of a single file, which means that all memory is flagged as short-term with refresh(0)-calls, and one tick-call, conveniently placed in the code where processing a file finishes, suffices to let all memory expire. This removes the need for all 43 free-calls in the original code. Note that we placed a refresh(0)-call after each of the 48 allocation sites (of which some may never be executed). The result is obviously correct without introducing any memory leaks.

We are aware that this use case is somewhat trivial. Still, it shows the capabilities of our programming model and how easy it can be to use short-term memory.

x264 in C. As a second use case we have ported the open source video encoder x264 [20], which implements the H.264 standard [25]. We focus on the memory management of frames and frame buffers. All other memory is irrelevant for performance since it is only allocated once. Note that our port covers only the default configuration of x264, without additional features which may require additional memory.

Figure 2 shows the dataflow of frames in the x264 encoder. In the single-threaded use case, there is only a single (main) thread

---

[3] http://www.mpg123.de

[4] http://shootout.alioth.debian.org

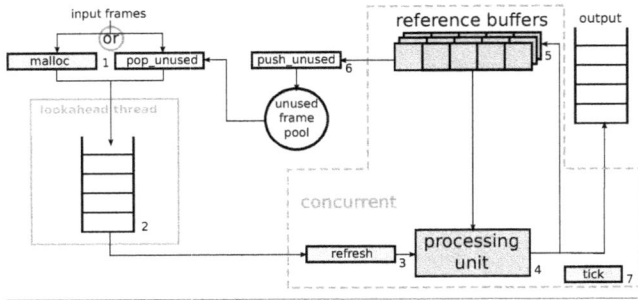

Figure 2. Dataflow of the x264 video encoder.

Algorithm 1 Pseudo code of the Monte Carlo benchmark

```
 1    monteCarlo(int repetitions)
 2    {
 3      ResultSet results = createResultSet(repetitions);
 4      for(int i = 0; i < repetitions; i++)
 5      {
 6        RandomWalk walk = createRandomWalk();
 7        refresh(walk, 0);
 8        results.add(doCalculation(walk));
 9        tick();
10      }
11      evaluateResults(results);
12    }
```

performing all work including frame lookahead and encoding. The numbers next to the boxes show the order in which the boxes are executed or activated. The malloc/refresh/tick boxes are introduced by the port to short-term memory. The original dataflow is as follows. Upon reading an input frame, memory is allocated for it. This frame is then encoded relative to previously encoded frames stored in so-called reference buffers. The result is output and written to the reference buffers for future reference.

One frame is an instance of a data structure consisting of multiple sub-objects, arrays, and management data. All frames require the same amount of memory. This allows for pool allocation and reuse of not-needed frames for new ones. Pool allocation may improve runtime performance and result in less memory fragmentation compared to general-purpose memory allocation. A frame can be reused (is returned to the pool) when it is removed from all frame buffers. Determining when this is the case is non-trivial since a frame may be stored in multiple reference buffers. The original implementation uses reference counting to determine when a frame can be reused. The reference counter of a frame increases when the frame is added to a frame buffer, and decreases when the frame is removed from a buffer. The frame is pushed into the unused frame pool when the reference counter becomes zero.

By porting to short-term memory we remove the need for reference counting. We have also removed pool allocation even though it can be used in combination with short-term memory. The relevant periodic behavior is given by encoding of a single frame. Therefore, we place a tick-call in the code where encoding a frame finishes. There are two approaches to refreshing: either refresh once with a long enough expiration extension, or else continuously refresh needed frames with an expiration extension of 1. Both approaches are implemented and tested, and described next.

The single-refresh approach leverages the fact that frames are removed from the reference buffers after a certain amount of time. The refresh-calls are placed such that a frame is refreshed when its encoding starts with an expiration extension that depends on the two x264 specific parameters bframes and ref which influence the size of the reference buffers. More details about the two parameters can be found in [20, 26]. We validated the calculated expiration extensions on several videos with different resolutions and length, and with different input parameters of the x264 encoder.

The expiration extensions in the single-refresh approach are conservative approximations of the lifetime of frames and thus introduce memory overhead when frames are actually needed for shorter amounts of time. In the continuous-refresh approach, we aim at removing that memory overhead by avoiding large extensions and instead refreshing all buffered frames right before the tick-call with an expiration extension of 1. The refresh(1)-calls guarantee that the frames will exist until the tick-call after the next frame encoding. Note that the runtime overhead of continuous refreshing is low due to the small number of frames in the frame buffers. Continuous refreshing is easy to do since it can be done right before a tick-call and is independent of the implementation of

the encoding unit, whereas the reference counting of the original implementation is done at every add- and remove-operation of the reference buffers.

Our experiments show that the effect of both refreshing approaches on throughput (total execution time) and memory management latency is negligible. Continuous refreshing is easier to use and consumes less memory than single refreshing in our benchmarks. In general, however, continuous refreshing may introduce more runtime overhead.

It is interesting to note that the memory usage pattern of the x264 encoder represents a bad case for many other memory management systems:

1. Explicit deallocation memory management is difficult to employ for x264 since it is unknown at compile time when a frame can be deallocated, which is the reason why the original implementation involves reference counting.

2. Generational garbage collectors are not suitable since at each collection of the nursery all live frames (which always exist and consist of multiple objects) need to be copied to the long-living part of the heap.

3. With region-based memory management for x264 it is difficult to form non-trivial regions (with more than one frame and not containing all frames).

Monte Carlo in Java. Algorithm 1 shows the Monte Carlo benchmark [18], which consists of a calculation loop to which we add a tick-call at the end. A result object is generated in every loop iteration. It is stored in a result set and exists until the end of the program. All other objects which are allocated in the calculation loop, e.g. the RandomWalk object and all objects allocated in the doCalculation method, only exist for one loop iteration and can be safely flagged as short-term.

With short-term memory all garbage collection runs are avoided by reusing the memory of expired objects. In Section 4 we show that with short-term memory every loop iteration takes nearly the same amount of time, in contrast to execution with a garbage collector where the loop iterations which are interrupted for garbage collection take significantly more time. Throughput and memory consumption also improve. Note that the same, although not with less effort, could be achieved with static preallocation, e.g. by reusing the same RandomWalk object for all loop iterations.

An interesting aspect of the Monte Carlo benchmark is that it contains a reachable memory leak. The result object contains a reference to the RandomWalk object which created it. Short-term memory fixes the memory leak by flagging the RandomWalk object as short-term, which lets the object expire at the end of the loop iteration. Clearly, the memory leak could also be fixed for garbage-collection use by deleting the reference from the result object to the RandomWalk object.

Tree Benchmark in Go. The Tree benchmark allocates one permanent tree and many short-living trees with different sizes. These trees are then dismissed after a validation step. For porting the benchmark to short-term memory we set a tick-call after every validation of a short-living tree. All but one short-living tree are allocated and validated in one loop, so two tick-calls are sufficient (one for the tree outside the loop, and one in the loop). Each loop iteration validates two trees. We therefore place a second tick-call in the loop for less memory consumption. The nodes of short-living trees are flagged as short-term right after their allocation by refresh(0)-calls. The permanent tree stays persistent and thus does not expire.

Using short-term memory in this benchmark results in higher throughput, lower near-constant latency, and less peak memory consumption, as shown in Section 4.

2.2 Multi-Threaded Use Cases

We ported two multi-threaded use cases to self-collecting mutators, a multi-threaded version of the x264 encoder written in C, and a simple web server written in Go. In the latter use case, objects are not shared among threads, which enables straightforward porting. The x264 use case includes shared objects, i.e., shared frames.

We explored two approaches of using short-term memory for shared objects. With the first, global-time approach, every thread refreshes the shared objects it needs according to the notion of a global time rather than its own thread-local time. Global time advances when the thread-local times of all threads in the system have advanced by at least one time unit. Refreshing an object according to global time thus conservatively approximates the effect achieved by refreshing an object according to the thread-local times of the threads that really need the object. The definition and calculation of global time is described in Section 2.6 in more detail. With the second, local-time approach, we use thread-local times even for shared objects. Some concurrent reasoning may then be necessary to ensure that a shared object does not expire before all threads that need it have refreshed it for the first time.

x264 in C. With the x264 encoder, there is little difference in terms of porting effort between the single-threaded and the multi-threaded use case.

The multi-threaded version of the x264 video encoder processes multiple frames in parallel. It consists of a main thread, a lookahead thread for prefetching frames, and a number of encoding threads. The lookahead thread deals with frames before they are flagged as short-term. As indicated by the area with dashed borderline in Figure 2, the encoding unit and the reference buffers exist in multiple instances, one instance per encoding thread. The encoder uses one mutex per frame for thread synchronization. We use a finalizer function to destroy such mutexes properly when collecting expired frames. Finalizers are described in Section 2.3.

The single-threaded ports of the x264 use case work for multiple threads without further modifications except for the registration of the finalizer that destroys the mutex of an expired frame. In this case, all short-term memory operations are invoked from within the main thread only. However, we also demonstrate multi-threaded short-term memory management by moving the refresh- and tick-calls into the encoding threads and then using either the global-time approach or else the local-time approach.

For the single-refresh approach, the formula calculating the lifetime of a frame can be refined using the number n of threads, i.e., the expiration extension e of a frame in the single-threaded case reduces to $e' = \lceil e/n \rceil$. It turns out that using the thread-local time approach for shared objects also works for both refreshing approaches, including the refined extensions for the single-refresh approach, since all threads are anyway synchronized by mutexes in a way that thread-local time and global time only differ by at most one time unit.

The usage and performance results of the multi-threaded use case are similar to the single-threaded use case, see Section 4.

Web Server in Go. We have ported the godoc web server to short-term memory but eventually decided to use our own simple implementation of a static yet multi-threaded web server in Go for benchmarking. The godoc web server indexes all library packages, which dominates the performance of the parts relevant to short-term memory. Our server creates a goroutine for each request, which simply serves a static web page. In the port to short-term memory, the objects storing web page content are flagged as short-term. We show with this use case that self-collecting mutators in Go maintain goroutine scalability as well as memory consumption while reducing memory management latency.

2.3 Implementation

The C, Java, and Go implementations of self-collecting mutators are based on the same algorithm and data structures, and differ only slightly in some low-level details that we point out whenever they are relevant. The implementations are available in source code [2].

Descriptors. An expiration date of a given object is represented by a descriptor, which is a pointer to the object. Descriptors representing a given (not-expired) expiration date are gathered in a descriptor list. In other words, the expiration date value represented by a descriptor is implicitly encoded by storing the descriptor in a descriptor list for this value. Note that an object may even have multiple expiration dates with the same value, which means that there may be multiple descriptors in a descriptor list pointing to the same object.

Object Header. Every object (also if persistent) is extended by a 64-bit object header that stores a descriptor counter, which is a 32-bit integer that counts, similar to a reference counter, the number of descriptors that point to the object, i.e., the number of expiration dates the object has. Incrementing and decrementing the descriptor counter of an object are the only operations that must be done atomically by atomic increment and atomic decrement-and-test instructions, respectively. All other operations involved in refreshing and expiring objects as well as advancing time are thread-local.

The remaining 32 bits of the object header are used differently in the C and Go implementations and unused in the Java implementation. For C, five of the 32 bits identify an optional user-implemented finalizer that gets invoked right before deallocation. The other 27 bits are unused. Finalizers receive a permanent and unique 5-bit identifier upon user-controlled, constant-time registration in a simple 32-entry identifier-to-finalizer table. A more dynamic service remains future work. For Go, 16 bits store the offset from the object address to its garbage collector status flag. Another 8 bits store an identifier of an internal Go size-class, needed to free an object of size smaller than 32KB. The remaining 8 bits are unused. Objects larger than 32KB actually require an additional 64-bit word in the object header for storing a pointer.

Descriptor Management. A descriptor list is a singly-linked list of descriptor pages represented by a fixed-size record containing a head and a tail pointer to the first and the last page, respectively. A descriptor page is a fixed-size record that consists of a pointer to the next page, an integer word that counts the actual number of descriptors stored in the page, and a fixed number of pointers for storing descriptors. A descriptor page is therefore properly initialized if just the first two entries are zeroed. The size m of descriptor pages is fixed at compile time. Descriptor pages are allocated cache- and page-aligned for better runtime performance. We distinguish different size configurations of m in our benchmarks. Note that using descriptor pages provides only a constant-factor, yet potentially significant, optimization over a singly-linked list of descriptors.

Given a compile-time bound n on the expiration extensions for refreshing, we use a thread-local descriptor buffer to store $n + 1$

descriptor lists in an array of size $n + 1$, which supports expiration extensions between zero and n. The buffer also stores thread-local time denoted by l. The descriptors in the buffer are interpreted against l as follows. The descriptor list containing descriptors representing an expiration date l is located at position $l \mod (n + 1)$ in the buffer. Given an expiration extension $0 \le e \le n$, a new descriptor representing an expiration date $l + e$ will therefore be appended to the descriptor list at position $(l + e) \mod (n + 1)$. Thus the descriptors in the descriptor list at position $l \mod (n+1)$ expire when thread-local time advances.

There are three descriptor management operations: create, move-expired, and collect, which all run in constant time.

Given an object and the index $i = (l + e) \mod (n + 1)$, the create-operation stores a new descriptor, i.e., a pointer to the object, in the last descriptor page of the descriptor list at position i in the buffer, if the page is not full. Otherwise, the descriptor is stored in a new page that is allocated, either from a thread-local descriptor-page pool or, if empty, from free memory, and appended to the list.

Given the index $i = l \mod (n + 1)$ upon thread-local time advance, the move-expired-operation removes the descriptor pages from the descriptor list at position i in the buffer, if it contains at least one descriptor, and appends the pages to a thread-local descriptor list called the expired-descriptor list. Unlike the descriptor lists in a descriptor buffer, the expired-descriptor list may contain descriptors that represent different expiration dates that have, however, all expired. Moreover, the expired-descriptor list stores, in addition to head and tail pointers, an integer counter that keeps track of how many descriptors in the first descriptor page of the list have already been collected.

The collect-operation only operates on the expired-descriptor list. If the list is empty, the operation immediately returns. Otherwise, the first descriptor in the list is removed from the list, i.e., from the first descriptor page in the list. If the page becomes empty, it is removed from the list. The empty page is then returned either to the descriptor-page pool, if the pool is not full, which is determined by a compile-time bound, or to free memory by calling the underlying free routine. Then, the descriptor counter of the object to which the removed descriptor points is decremented by an atomic decrement-and-test instruction. If the counter becomes zero, the object is deallocated, again by calling the underlying free routine. Note that, in the C implementation, we check if a finalizer has been set in the object header of the object. If yes, the finalizer is invoked right before deallocation.

In summary, each thread maintains a descriptor buffer containing $(n + 1)$ descriptor lists and an integer word for storing thread-local time, an expired-descriptor list, and a bounded descriptor-page pool.

Memory Management. We now describe the memory management calls, which do not require any locking and all run in constant time modulo the underlying malloc/new/free implementations.

A malloc-call or new-call simply calls the allocation routine of the underlying system to allocate a memory block that fits the requested size plus one 64-bit word for the object header with the descriptor counter initialized to zero.

In the C implementation, a free-call invokes the underlying free routine to deallocate the given memory block but only if its descriptor counter is zero. Otherwise, it returns without deallocation. The standard calloc and realloc routines have been wrapped in a similar way. If the realloc-call is invoked on a memory block that does not fit the requested adjustment in size, a new memory block that fits is allocated. The old memory block is then deallocated but again only if its descriptor counter is zero. This approach has an important consequence: our C library can readily be linked against any existing C code and used without introducing any new memory leaks and without any modifications to the code, unless the code

makes assumptions on the layout of memory management data in memory blocks. We tested this claim by successfully linking the library against Apache HTTP server-2.2.15 and executing it. Without using short-term memory, our implementations only introduce a per-object space overhead of one 64-bit word and negligible run-time overhead as shown in Section 4.

For Java and Go, we have modified the underlying garbage collectors such that all objects including all short-term memory objects are considered in computing reachability but short-term memory objects that ever had a descriptor counter greater than zero are not deallocated even when determined unreachable. Instead, the memory of expired objects is deallocated by our system to be reused later upon allocation, again into persistent memory first. Our modifications only involve a few lines of code in both cases and do not incur any runtime overhead. Similar to the C implementation, legacy Java and Go applications run without any modifications.

The refresh-call first atomically increments the descriptor counter of the given object. Then, a new descriptor pointing to the object is inserted into the descriptor buffer by the previously described create-operation.

The tick-call first increments the thread-local clock and then invokes the previously described move-expired-operation to move the just expired descriptors to the expired-descriptor list.

In principle, any memory management operation may collect expired descriptors and deallocate expired objects. Each operation may collect anywhere between one at a time (lazy) for maximal incrementality and all at once (eager) for maximal throughput and minimal memory consumption.

In our implementations, the default is lazy. Moreover, only the refresh-call and the tick-call collect by invoking the previously described collect-operation once after performing their actual function. Lazy collection at a refresh-call makes sure that the memory allocated for descriptors is bounded in the number of refresh-calls between tick-calls, similar to the memory allocated for objects.

The alternative of eager collection is only implemented in tick-calls. Interesting future work may be to study collection strategies for trading-off memory management throughput, latency, and space consumption dynamically. For example, we may choose to collect varying numbers of expired descriptors per call, and to collect expired descriptors also in other calls such as the malloc-call, new-call, and free-call, and even in code unrelated to memory management. Another option is running auxiliary threads that collect expired descriptors concurrently to the mutator.

Managing memory objects in persistent or short-term memory can now be done as follows. A malloc-call or new-call allocates persistent memory for a given object. As long as the object is not refreshed, it remains in persistent memory and thus requires, in the C implementation, explicit deallocation by a free-call. However, the first refresh-call on the object, even with an expiration extension of zero, logically transfers the object to short-term memory. Then, again in the C implementation, explicit deallocation is unnecessary and should be replaced by invoking tick-calls instead. Existing free-calls on short-term memory objects may nevertheless remain in the code as long as they are invoked before any tick-call makes the objects expire. Note that the malloc-call or new-call could also do both allocation and refresh in one step, which we nevertheless chose not to do for backwards compatibility and since reasonable expiration dates may not be known at allocation time.

Thread Management. All thread management operations for short-term memory run in constant time. A thread maintains thread-local metadata called descriptor root, which is a fixed-sized record that contains a descriptor buffer, an expired-descriptor list, a descriptor-page pool, and a descriptor-root pointer for constructing a global, lock-protected, and unbounded pool of unused descriptor roots. Memory for descriptor roots is allocated either from that pool, if not empty, or else from free memory. Descriptor roots obtained from free memory can be efficiently initialized just by allocating zeroed memory. Roots obtained from the pool do not require initialization. Descriptor roots and pages are the only two metadata types for short-term memory that require heap allocation.

Similar to the allocation of metadata storage for the underlying allocators, which is on demand upon the first invocation of a malloc-call or new-call, a descriptor root is allocated upon the first invocation of a refresh-call by a thread, effectively registering the thread with the short-term memory system. This approach minimizes the impact on scalability of threads that do not use short-term memory. Note that, by integrating the descriptor-root pool deeper into the underlying allocators, which already use a global lock to protect their metadata pools, it may be possible, as part of future work, to avoid introducing an extra global lock for protecting the descriptor-root pool. Without negative impact on scalability, all metadata storage may then be allocated upon the first invocation of a malloc-call or new-call.

When a thread terminates, its descriptor root is inserted into the descriptor-root pool for later reuse by another thread. In Java and Go, this is done transparently by the runtime system whereas, in C, a manual unregister-call is required. Interestingly, reused descriptor roots are not initialized since they may still contain uncollected, expired and even not-expired descriptors. Instead, the new thread may safely reuse a descriptor root expiring the not-expired and collecting the expired descriptors of the previous thread exactly from where they were left off. In particular, the new thread advances the root's thread-local time from where it was left off.

2.4 Real Time and Fragmentation

As shown by our Java and Go benchmarks, self-collecting mutators may, at the expense of safety, significantly decrease memory management latency by reducing the number of garbage collection runs, sometimes to zero, while even improving throughput. Real-time garbage collectors such as Metronome [4] reduce latency as well and are safe but only at a significant loss in throughput and increase in code complexity, which makes it difficult to certify them for hard real-time applications. Self-collecting mutators perform all operations in constant time and may therefore even be suitable for managing hard real-time applications if combined with a real-time allocator such as Compact-fit [11] or TLSF [17]. Lastly, real-time instead of software clocks may be used to guarantee time advance. However, using short-term memory correctly may become more difficult in this case and even require execution time analysis.

Our implementations of short-term memory are based on existing allocators unaware of short-term memory and, in particular, its effect on fragmentation. In our benchmarks fragmentation has not been an issue but it may become one in others. Addressing fragmentation in short-term memory is part of our future work.

2.5 Multiple Clocks

Self-collecting mutators use thread-local clocks and, optionally, the notion of a global clock, to expire objects. Each clock is stored in a descriptor buffer along with the descriptors that the clock expires. In principle, self-collecting mutators can readily be generalized to use a dynamic set of multiple clocks, i.e., descriptor buffers to be precise. Multiple, independent clocks are more expressive than a single clock in the sense that they may facilitate expiration of objects with different, independent lifetimes more accurately and thus decrease memory consumption. Note that advancing multiple clocks according to a common base clock is equivalent to using a single clock with non-zero expiration extensions for refreshing. An implementation of multiple clocks may require synchronization if threads share clocks, which may harm performance and scalability. Alternatively, a programming convention, as in Go for sharing

objects, could require each clock to be associated with a single thread at any time. Clock ownership along with object ownership could then be passed, as in Go through channels, from one thread to another. The issue of using short-term memory in library code may be addressed similarly, e.g. by maintaining dedicated library clocks. An implementation remains future work.

2.6 Global-Time Management

We describe a simple global-time management for brevity that suffices for the use cases considered here but does not support dynamically changing sets of threads. It also does not handle blocking and faulty threads properly since global time would not advance in their presence. However, we have developed a more general global-time management based on so-called thread-global time that does support dynamically changing sets of threads including blocking and faulty threads [1].

Shared objects in short-term memory may, in addition to regular refreshing, also be refreshed by a constant-time, lock-free global-refresh-call and expire according to a synchronized notion of global time, which is advanced by a constant-time, lock-free global-tick-call. The global calls operate on a new thread-local, global-time descriptor buffer, whereas the regular local calls still operate on the existing thread-local-time descriptor buffer. The clock in the global-time descriptor buffer is not used here but represents thread-global time in the more general global-time management [1].

Global time is represented by a global integer counter called the global clock. The expiration semantics remains simple. An expiration date created by a global-refresh-call has expired if its value is less than global time. The intention is that all threads sharing an object have a chance to refresh the object before it expires without coordinating refreshing and ticking explicitly.

In addition to the global clock, global-time management also requires a global ticked-threads counter and, for each thread, a thread-local integer counter representing the global phase of the thread. The global phase determines whether the thread performed a global-tick-call since global time has last advanced. Initially, the values of the global clock and phases are zero, and the ticked-threads counter is set to the (fixed) number of threads in the system. The global-tick-call increments the global phase of the invoking thread if the global phase of the thread is equal to global time, otherwise it immediately returns. In case the global phase was incremented, the ticked-threads counter is subsequently decremented by an atomic decrement-and-test instruction. If the counter becomes zero, global time is advanced and the ticked-threads counter is reset to the (fixed) number of threads in the system, marking the beginning of a new global period. Locking is not required since only one thread can decrement the counter to zero.

A global-refresh-call sets the expiration date of an object to the current global time plus the extension plus one time unit. The additional time unit is sufficient to guarantee that the object does not expire before one full global period has elapsed, i.e., all threads have invoked the global-tick-call at least once. Therefore, the global-time descriptor buffer needs to accommodate one more descriptor list. So far, we have implemented global-time management in C. Future work may focus on optimizing memory consumption, yet probably at the expense of runtime performance.

3. Related Work

We first discuss general memory management work related to the short-term memory model and then specific work related to the design and implementation of self-collecting mutators.

3.1 Short-term Memory

Implementing short-term memory essentially requires a representation of the not-expired and expired sets as well as an algorithm that determines expiration information and time advance. The algorithm may be an offline analysis tool or an online system, as with most related work, or a programmer who provides the information manually, as with self-collecting mutators. The representation may logically implement sets to support any algorithm, as in self-collecting mutators, or more specific data structures such as stacks and buffers that are more efficient but work only for specific algorithms, as in some related work.

Stack allocation can be seen as implementing a special case of short-term memory where the representation are per-thread stacks and the algorithm maintains per-frame expiration dates and per-stack time that advances upon returns from subroutines, which facilitates constant-time allocation and deallocation of multiple objects. General refreshing is not possible.

Short-term memory is originally inspired by cyclic allocation where the representation are cyclic fixed-size per-allocation-site buffers [21]. The algorithm maintains per-buffer expiration dates set to the size of the buffer and per-buffer time that advances upon each allocation in the buffer. For example, an allocation in a three-element buffer will always receive an expiration date equal to the current time plus three, i.e., memory allocated in the buffer will be reused after three subsequent allocations in the buffer, making deallocation unnecessary. Refreshing is again not possible. Note that cyclic allocation requires properly dimensioning the buffers, which is related to the more general problem of properly refreshing objects and advancing time with short-term memory.

Region-based memory management [13, 24] can also be seen as implementing a special case of short-term memory where the representation are regions, which allow deallocating multiple objects in constant time. The algorithm always uses expiration dates equal to the current time and maintains per-region time that advances upon events determined by either an offline analysis tool [24], or online reference counting [13], or explicit deallocate-region calls [13]. General refreshing is not possible but could be done by copying objects from one region to another. Similarly, choosing the appropriate region for an object must be done at its allocation and may only be avoided by copying the object. In short-term memory, each descriptor list forms a region and the associated clock is used to free (collect) the region. In contrast to the region-based approach, refreshing allows for choosing an appropriate region at any time after allocation and changing the region for an object without copying but at the expense of freeing a region in non-constant time. In addition, multiple clocks allow an object to be in multiple regions, i.e., to be associated with different clocks.

Objective-C [16] provides autorelease pools, which are a special case of short-term memory. The representation are stacked explicitly-allocated pools for delaying object deallocation. Objects can only be added to and removed from the top pool. The algorithm always uses expiration dates equal to the current time and maintains per-pool time that advances upon explicit deallocate-pool calls. An object may be in multiple pools and is deallocated when these pools have all been deallocated. General refreshing is again not possible.

Garbage collectors are implementations of the persistent memory model that compute unreachability, directly or indirectly, for reclaiming otherwise persistent memory. However, some portions of garbage collectors may be used to implement special cases of short-term memory. For example, as stated before, the mark phase of a mark-sweep garbage collector [19] may be used to implement an algorithm that prevents reachable objects from expiring. The transition from the mark to the sweep phase can then be seen as time advance for all objects. More recent work on object staleness, e.g. [7], and memory growth, e.g. [15], may be used to identify reachable memory leaks for expiring reachable but actually not-needed objects.

CPU	2x AMD Opteron DualCore, 2.0 GHz
RAM	4GB
OS	Linux 2.6.32-21-generic
C compiler	gcc version 4.4.3
C allocator	ptmalloc2-20011215 (glibc-2.10.1)
Java VM	Jikes RVM 3.1 0
Go compiler/runtime	6g, release 2010-11-02

Table 2. System configuration.

3.2 Self-Collecting Mutators

Reference-counting garbage collectors [9] determine reachability by counting references pointing to an object. In our implementations we determine expiration by counting descriptors pointing to an object. A drawback of reference counting are reference cycles which do not occur in descriptor counting. Moreover, the runtime overhead of descriptor counting is less than of reference counting since descriptor counters are only accessed at tick- and refresh-calls, which typically occur less frequently than reference changes.

Autorelease pools in Objective-C [16] approximate neededness by maintaining a so-called retain counter in each object that keeps track of the number of retain versus so-called release calls on the object. Thus the retain counters correspond to our descriptor counters. The pools contain references to objects and are thus similar to our descriptor lists.

The descriptor buffers in our implementations essentially implement priority queues [10] where expiration extensions correspond to priorities. Note that the time complexity of all our buffer operations is independent of the number of elements in the buffer, which may or may not be the case for general priority queues.

Global-time management in self-collecting mutators is related to epoch-based reclamation [12] and barrier synchronization [23]. A global period in global-time management corresponds to one epoch. A barrier forces a set of threads into a global state by blocking each thread when it has reached a particular point in its execution. Here, global time advance corresponds to the global state when all threads have ticked at least once in the current global period. However, threads that have ticked are not blocked until global time advance. We could also block threads, as in barrier synchronization, potentially reducing memory consumption at the expense of mutator execution speed. An implementation and adequate experiments are future work.

The idea of hybrid memory management systems is not new. One related example is the work presented in [8] and [14], which uses static analysis to insert free-calls in Java code, thus reducing the number of garbage collection runs. An interesting question is whether finding appropriate locations (and extensions) for refresh-calls as well as tick-calls is easier than for free-calls. In our Java implementation we collect expired objects in a way that is similar to the approach taken in [14].

4. Time and Space

We discuss performance results obtained with the benchmarks described in Section 2.1 and 2.2. The setup of the benchmarking environment is shown in Table 2. Memory consumption is reported as gross consumption including fragmentation. Net memory consumption is not shown since fragmentation turned out to be bounded by small constants in all benchmarks.

For the mpg123 benchmark in C we compare self-collecting mutators and ptmalloc2. For the x264 benchmark we run the original video encoder with and without pool allocation, and compare it with both porting approaches described in Section 2.1, the single-refresh and the continuous-refresh approach. We measure throughput (total execution time) and memory consumption of both benchmarks in all configurations. The effect on latency is negligible.

For the Java benchmarks we compare self-collecting mutators and two garbage collectors available with Jikes, the mark-sweep garbage collector that we already use with self-collecting mutators, and, as baseline, the standard garbage collector of Jikes, a two-generation copying collector where the mature space is handled by an Immix collector [6]. We measure the replay phase of replay compilation [22] provided by the production configuration of Jikes, which runs a JIT compiler in the recording phase. For the Go benchmarks we compare self-collecting mutators with the mark-sweep garbage collector of the Go runtime. We measure throughput (total execution time) and memory consumption of both the Java and Go benchmarks. Moreover, we measure latency (loop execution time for Java, time between two allocation operations in Go) and show that self-collecting mutators has lower latency than the garbage-collected systems.

Note that our use cases may also perform competitively when using other, more specialized memory management systems, e.g. a region-based allocator. However, a meaningful comparison requires a proper integration with self-collecting mutators that we have begun but not yet completed.

4.1 C

In both the mpg123 and the x264 benchmark runtime overhead through self-collecting mutators (SCM) is negligible. The mpg123 benchmark (and the x264 benchmark in some cases) runs even slightly faster than the unmodified baseline.

Figure 3 shows the memory consumption of the mpg123 benchmark. Self-collecting mutators with eager collection tracks the original memory consumption except for a final portion of memory before time advance. Maximum memory consumption is similar for lazy and eager collection. With lazy collection memory consumption lags the original memory consumption. The execution time of the tick-calls is around 20 times longer with eager collection (not shown) since there are around 20 objects to be collected per time advance, whereas the execution time of the refresh-calls is slightly lower with eager collection because no objects are collected during refreshing (not shown).

Figure 4(a) shows the memory consumption of the single-threaded x264 benchmark on the 300-frame foreman video sequence[5] (appended two times for 900 frames total) commonly used for video coding benchmarks. The first 150 frames and the last 300 frames are not shown for better resolution. The omitted data shows repetitive results or less memory consumption at the beginning and end. Single-refresh, while in principle faster, introduces some memory overhead by conservatively chosen expiration extensions. Memory consumption with continuous-refresh is always below memory consumption with pool allocation.

Figure 4(b) shows the memory consumption of the multi-threaded x264 benchmark on the same video running a main thread, a lookahead thread, and four encoding threads. We distinguish single-threaded short-term memory management where refreshing

[5] ftp://ftp.ldv.e-technik.tu-muenchen.de/dist/cif/

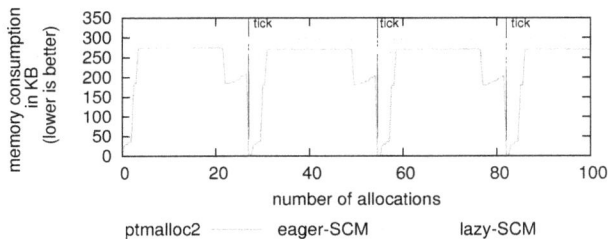

Figure 3. Memory consumption of the mpg123 benchmark.

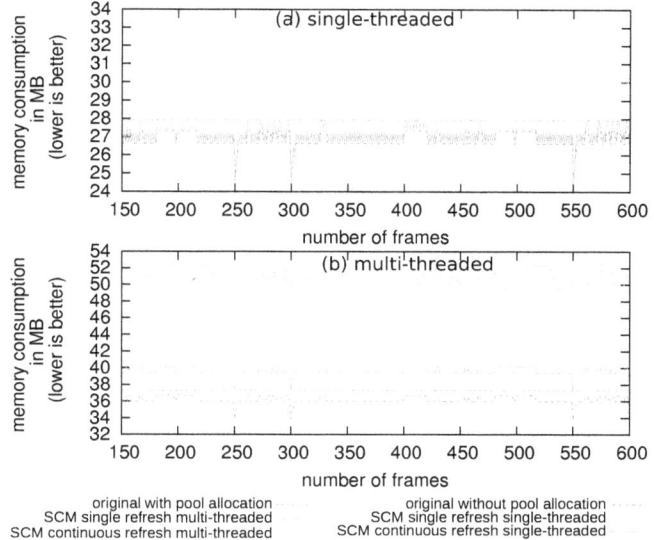

Figure 4. Memory consumption of the x264 benchmark (x-axis shortened for better resolution).

and ticking is done in the main thread from multi-threaded short-term memory management where refreshing and ticking is done in the encoding threads using either global time or else thread-local time. Both single-refresh and continuous-refresh perform well with single-threaded short-term memory management, introducing only low memory overhead over pool allocation (as expected the overhead of single refresh is slightly higher). With multi-threaded short-term memory management, memory consumption is higher except for continuous-refresh using thread-local time, which comes close to the maximum memory consumption of single-refresh in the main thread. Scalability is not affected, we obtain similar results on a 24-core machine.

4.2 Java

We execute the Monte Carlo benchmark 30 times and calculate the average of the total execution times.

The original Monte Carlo benchmark (MC leaky) produces a reachable memory leak which is not collected by a garbage collector. Self-collecting mutators (SCM) reuses the memory objects in the memory leak upon expiration. Therefore, the MC leaky benchmark can be executed in just 20MB with self-collecting mutators. The generational garbage collector (GEN) requires at least 95MB whereas the mark-sweep garbage collector (MS) requires 100MB. For this reason we benchmark MC leaky with heap sizes of 100MB as well as 1GB, which is enough memory to run the benchmark without garbage collection.

We then modified the Monte Carlo benchmark by removing the memory leak (MC fixed). The fixed benchmark runs successfully with a heap size of 20MB on all systems. For comparison we also benchmark MC fixed with a heap size of 50MB, which is the initial

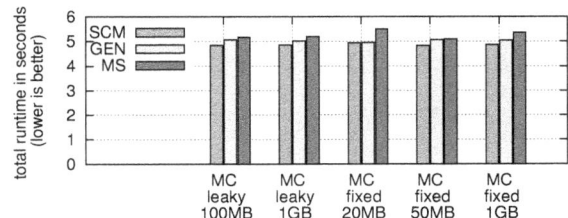

Figure 5. Total execution time of the Monte Carlo benchmarks.

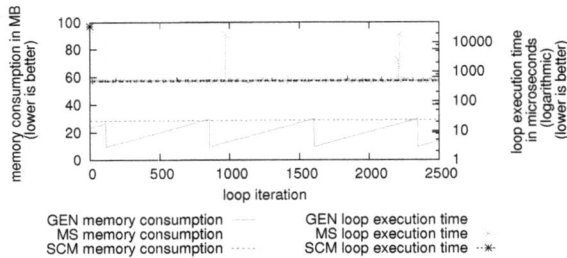

Figure 6. Memory consumption and loop execution time of the fixed Monte Carlo benchmark.

heap size of the production configuration of Jikes. The results are shown in Figure 5. SCM is slightly faster than the garbage-collected systems, even when more memory is available.

Figure 6 shows the memory consumption and loop execution time of the MC fixed benchmark recorded at the end of every loop iteration, with a heap size of 50MB. The results show that the memory consumption and latency of SCM are nearly constant, in particular there are no latency peaks (the loop execution time jitter is less than 100 microseconds) after startup. Both garbage-collected systems have similar loop execution times as SCM except for the iterations in which garbage collection is performed. The memory-consumption function of the garbage-collected systems has the typical saw-tooth shape with peaks right before each garbage collection run. The chart depicts the first 2500 loop iterations, further iterations show the same pattern. The measurements are done with all short-living objects flagged as short-term by 36 refresh(0)-calls. For avoiding all garbage collection runs it is sufficient to flag as short-term the objects of just 10 allocation sites (which allocate large objects).

Note that the first generational garbage collection run collects much more memory than the memory allocated by the application until then. The same is true for MS but to a lesser extent. This memory (not allocated by the application) is not collected when using SCM (it would be collected if garbage collection would trigger with SCM but it does not here). The overhead of SCM can be seen at time 0 as the difference between the GEN/MS versus the SCM memory consumption (=¡18%).

4.3 Go

The results of the Tree benchmark are similar to the results of the Monte Carlo benchmarks. Out of a total of 23 garbage collection runs all but one are avoided with self-collecting mutators improving latency and memory consumption, as shown in Figure 7, and total execution time by up to 28%. The remaining garbage collection run does not collect any objects.

The self-collecting mutators version of our implementation of a static multi-threaded web server in Go improves client-side server latency (from 1.87 to 1.54 milliseconds on average, from 1.7 to 1.05 milliseconds in standard deviation, and from 20.65

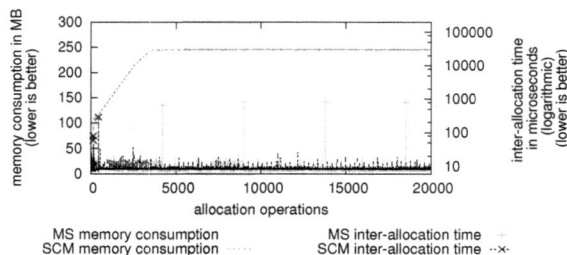

Figure 7. Memory consumption and inter-allocation time of the Tree benchmark.

to 10.85 milliseconds maximum) by decreasing the number of garbage collection runs while consuming about the same amount of memory as the unmodified server. The non-trivial aspect of this benchmark is that goroutine scalability is maintained since reuse of descriptor roots and pages across goroutines is effective.

5. Conclusion

We have proposed a memory model for heap management called short-term memory and developed an implementation of short-term memory for explicit refreshing called self-collecting mutators. Short-term memory may be particularly useful in applications with complex, data- rather than control-dependent object lifetime scenarios such as the x264 use case. Interesting, principled future work may be to develop an allocator aware of short-term memory using, e.g. regions, and to study alternative notions of time as well as program analysis for enabling safe use of short-term memory.

Acknowledgments

We are grateful to all reviewers of all previous versions of this paper, we have learned a lot from their comments and suggestions.

References

[1] AIGNER, M., HAAS, A., KIRSCH, C. M., AND SOKOLOVA, A. Short-term memory for self-collecting mutators - revised version. Tech. Rep. 2010-06, Department of Computer Sciences, University of Salzburg, October 2010.

[2] AIGNER, M., HAAS, A., AND LIPPAUTZ, M. Short-term memory implementation for C, Java, and Go, 2010. http://tiptoe.cs.uni-salzburg.at/short-term-memory/.

[3] ALPERN, B., ATTANASIO, C. R., BARTON, J. J., BURKE, M. G., CHENG, P., CHOI, J.-D., COCCHI, A., FINK, S. J., GROVE, D., HIND, M., HUMMEL, S. F., LIEBER, D., LITVINOV, V., MERGEN, M. F., NGO, T., RUSSELL, J. R., SARKAR, V., SERRANO, M. J., SHEPHERD, J. C., SMITH, S. E., SREEDHAR, V. C., SRINIVASAN, H., AND WHALEY, J. The Jalapeño virtual machine. *IBM Syst. J. 39*, 1 (2000), 211–238.

[4] BACON, D. F., CHENG, P., AND RAJAN, V. T. A real-time garbage collector with low overhead and consistent utilization. In *Proc. POPL* (2003), ACM.

[5] BACON, D. F., CHENG, P., AND RAJAN, V. T. A unified theory of garbage collection. In *Proc. OOPSLA* (2004), ACM.

[6] BLACKBURN, S. M., AND MCKINLEY, K. S. Immix: a mark-region garbage collector with space efficiency, fast collection, and mutator performance. In *Proc. PLDI* (2008), ACM.

[7] BOND, M. D., AND MCKINLEY, K. S. Leak pruning. In *Proc. ASPLOS* (2009), ACM.

[8] CHEREM, S., AND RUGINA, R. Compile-time deallocation of individual objects. In *Proc. ISMM* (2006), ACM.

[9] COLLINS, G. E. A method for overlapping and erasure of lists. *Commun. ACM 3*, 12 (1960), 655–657.

[10] CORMEN, T. H., LEISERSON, C. E., RIVEST, R. L., AND STEIN, C. *Introduction to Algorithms, Second Edition.* MIT Press and McGraw-Hill, 2001, ch. 6.5: Priority queues, pp. 138–142.

[11] CRACIUNAS, S., KIRSCH, C. M., PAYER, H., SOKOLOVA, A., STADLER, H., AND STAUDINGER, R. A compacting real-time memory management system. In *Proc. USENIX ATC* (2008).

[12] FRASER, K. *Practical Lock-Freedom.* PhD thesis, Computer Laboratory, University of Cambridge, 2003.

[13] GAY, D., AND AIKEN, A. Memory management with explicit regions. In *Proc. PLDI* (1998), ACM.

[14] GUYER, S. Z., MCKINLEY, K. S., AND FRAMPTON, D. Free-me: a static analysis for automatic individual object reclamation. In *Proc. PLDI* (2006), ACM.

[15] JUMP, M., AND MCKINLEY, K. S. Cork: dynamic memory leak detection for garbage-collected languages. In *Proc. POPL* (2007), ACM.

[16] KOCHAN, S. *Programming in Objective-C 2.0*, 2nd ed. Addison-Wesley Professional, 2009.

[17] MASMANO, M., RIPOLL, I., CRESPO, A., AND REAL, J. TLSF: A new dynamic memory allocator for real-time systems. In *Proc. ECRTS* (2004), IEEE Computer Society, pp. 79–86.

[18] MATHEW, J. A., CODDINGTON, P. D., AND HAWICK, K. A. Analysis and development of Java Grande benchmarks. In *Proc. JAVA* (1999), ACM.

[19] MCCARTHY, J. Recursive functions of symbolic expressions and their computation by machine, Part I. *Commun. ACM 3*, 4 (1960), 184–195.

[20] MERRITT, L., AND VANAM, R. X264: A high performance H.264/AVC encoder, 2006.

[21] NGUYEN, H. H., AND RINARD, M. Detecting and eliminating memory leaks using cyclic memory allocation. In *Proc. ISMM* (2007), ACM.

[22] OGATA, K., ONODERA, T., KAWACHIYA, K., KOMATSU, H., AND NAKATANI, T. Replay compilation: improving debuggability of a just-in-time compiler. In *Proc. OOPSLA* (2006), ACM.

[23] TANENBAUM, A. S. *Modern Operating Systems.* Prentice Hall, 2001.

[24] TOFTE, M., AND TALPIN, J.-P. Region-based memory management. *Inf. Comput. 132*, 2 (1997), 109–176.

[25] WIEGAND, T., SULLIVAN, G. J., BJØNTEGAARD, G., AND LUTHRA, A. Overview of the H.264/AVC video coding standard. *IEEE Transactions on Circuits and Systems for Video Technology 13*, 7 (2003).

[26] http://mewiki.project357.com/wiki/x264_settings.

Garbage Collection Auto-Tuning for Java MapReduce on Multi-Cores

Jeremy Singer

University of Glasgow
jeremy.singer@glasgow.ac.uk

George Kovoor *

kovoor.george@gmail.com

Gavin Brown   Mikel Luján

University of Manchester
firstname.lastname@manchester.ac.uk

Abstract

MapReduce has been widely accepted as a simple programming pattern that can form the basis for efficient, large-scale, distributed data processing. The success of the MapReduce pattern has led to a variety of implementations for different computational scenarios. In this paper we present *MRJ*, a MapReduce Java framework for multi-core architectures. We evaluate its scalability on a four-core, hyperthreaded Intel Core i7 processor, using a set of standard MapReduce benchmarks. We investigate the significant impact that Java runtime garbage collection has on the performance and scalability of MRJ. We propose the use of memory management auto-tuning techniques based on machine learning. With our auto-tuning approach, we are able to achieve MRJ performance within 10% of optimal on 75% of our benchmark tests.

Categories and Subject Descriptors D.3.4 [*Programming Languages*]: Processors—Memory management (garbage collection)

General Terms Experimentation, Performance

Keywords mapreduce, garbage collection, machine learning, Java

1. Introduction

The *MapReduce* programming pattern has its origins in functional programming [14]. However, MapReduce has been popularized by Google since they adopted this pattern as a highly effective means of attaining massive parallelism in compute clusters [13]. Given some input data, the `map` function operates on disjoint portions of the data, potentially in parallel, constructing a set of (key,value) pairs for each portion. The `reduce` function applies an associative, commutative operator to all values with the same key.

A MapReduce framework automatically handles issues like data-partitioning, load-balancing, and thread-scheduling. Thus the application programmer is not required to re-implement these basic threading mechanisms. Instead, the application logic is expressed simply in terms of `map` and `reduce` functions, at a suitably high-level of abstraction.

Over the past five years, MapReduce has attracted significant attention from industry, academia and the open-source community

---

* Work done while author was at Manchester

ISMM'11, June 4–5, 2011, San Jose, California, USA.
Copyright © 2011 ACM 978-1-4503-0263-0/11/06...$10.00

[3]. The pattern still has its detractors [15]. However, it has been demonstrated to give effective parallelism for important parts of the computer applications spectrum e.g. machine learning [10], databases [37], eScience [16].

Our objective is to investigate the MapReduce pattern in the context of multi-core architectures, rather than within compute clusters, as commonly used by Amazon, Facebook, Google and Yahoo, amongst others.

1.1 Motivation for Multi-Core MapReduce

The microprocessor product lines from all major vendors are now firmly entrenched in the multi-core era. Indeed, the industry trend is moving to *many-core*, with next-generation architectures like Intel's Single-chip Cloud Computer [22] which has 48 cores. However while the low-level architecture provides abundant parallel threads of execution, high-level programming models are not sufficiently mature or widespread to target this parallelism effectively. There has been a great deal of research effort in this area. For instance, new programming languages such as Fortress [4] and X10 [9] are under development. However these have not yet been widely adopted. At the same time, new parallelism frameworks have been introduced for existing languages, such as the Java fork/join framework [24], Pervasive DataRush [11], and the Task Parallel Library extensions to .NET [25]. These are complex libraries with significant APIs.

We have implemented our MapReduce for Java system on top of the Java fork/join framework [24]. In essence, we are treating fork/join like the assembly language of parallelism, and we are using MapReduce to provide a higher-level, simpler abstraction for application software developers.

Implementations of MapReduce that do not target clusters have started appearing recently. For example, He et al. [21] and Kruijf et al. [12] have developed MapReduce for GPGPUs and Cell processors, respectively. The Phoenix project [31, 38] is the only previous implementation that focuses on shared memory multi-core architectures. Our implementation targets the same system type as Phoenix, however we are working in Java, whereas Phoenix is based on C/C++. Java gives us certain inherent advantages, described in Section 1.2. However there can be a performance penalty caused by Java's automatic memory management, which Section 4 explores.

1.2 Motivation for MapReduce in Java

The MapReduce pattern is programming language agnostic. However in our opinion, there is plenty of synergy between the Java programming language and the MapReduce programming model. They both have a similar overall aim, in terms of reducing the burden of programming complexity. The Java language provides a runtime system that supports automatic memory management, hot code recompilation, and robust error handling, inter alia. MapReduce provides a runtime system that handles data distribution, thread scheduling, and error recovery. The philosophy underlying both frameworks can be summarized as: *Let the framework do the work*. Since the programmer is relieved from handling these complex and error-prone tasks manually, then he is free to focus on implementing the application logic of the program.

An explicit motivation for Java is its *platform independence*. MapReduce programs written in Java can be distributed as platform neutral JVM bytecode. In addition, a Java MapReduce framework is straightforward to port to new multi-core architectures, since its only requirement is a suitable virtual machine supporting lightweight parallel thread spawning on different cores.

The major open-source implementation of MapReduce, *Hadoop* [1] is also developed in Java. However Hadoop focuses on optimizing cluster-level parallelism. If a cluster node has n cores, the Hadoop runtime simply spawns n instances of a Java virtual machine on that node. This is a heavyweight approach to multi-core parallelism. We hope that our investigation of lighter-weight multi-core MapReduce using the Java fork/join framework (MRJ) can contribute directly to the evolution of the Hadoop project.

1.3 Motivation for GC Auto-Tuning

Because MRJ is implemented in Java, it depends on the automatic memory management provided by the underlying Java virtual machine. We find that Java runtime garbage collection interacts with MRJ application performance in non-obvious ways. The case studies in Section 4 demonstrate that this interaction is often benchmark-specific, or may only occur for certain heap sizes.

We argue that the MRJ end-user cannot be expected to perform expert analysis to determine (a) that GC activity is reducing the performance of MRJ, and (b) how to change the JVM configuration to improve the situation. Instead we propose the use of a GC auto-tuning system for MRJ applications. This system would have the following advantages:

1. It could adapt to benchmark-specific or heap-size-specific anomalies much more efficiently than a non-expert user.

2. It could be installed by the system administrator and automatically enabled for users that do not have sufficient permissions to change JVM parameters, e.g. on a utility computing platform [5] like Google AppEngine [18].

3. It would enable rapid deployment of MRJ on new multi-core architecture layouts. This is important due to the rapidly changing multi-many-core processor landscape.

1.4 Contributions

This paper makes several key contributions.

1. Section 3 demonstrates the scalability of our MRJ framework for standard benchmarks, on a commodity multi-core platform.

2. Section 4 highlights the major impact that Java runtime garbage collection (GC) has on MRJ, in a series of case studies.

3. Section 5 presents an auto-tuning approach to optimize GC for MRJ, giving speedups of up to 6x the default GC policy, with a 10% geometric mean speedup over all benchmarks with the largest input data sets.

2. MRJ Implementation

This section gives an overview of the design and implementation choices we made for MRJ, our MapReduce Java framework for multi-core architectures. A full technical description of MRJ is available in our earlier work [23].

```
1  public class WordCount implements
2      StringMapper , StringReducer {
3
4  public static void main(String[] args){
5    final WordCount wcinstance=new WordCount();
6    JobClient jobClient=JobClient.getInstance();
7    JobConf jobConf=jobClient.getConf();
8    jobConf.setInputtype(InputType.File);
9    jobClient.setMapper(wcinstance);
10   jobClient.setReducer(wcinstance);
11   jobClient.initialise(WordCount.class);
12   jobClient.submitApp(wcinstance);
13 }
14
15 public void map(String key, String value,
16             StringOutputCollector output) {
17   StringTokenizer tkn=new StringTokenizer(value);
18   while(tkn.hasMoreTokens()) {
19     String word=tkn.nextToken();
20     output.putKeyValue(word, ''1'');
21   }
22 }
23
24 public String reduce(String key, String value) {
25   StringTokenizer tkn = new StringTokenizer(value
       , ''|'');
26   StringBuilder strb=new StringBuilder  key);
27   int sum = 0;
28   while (tkn.hasMoreTokens())
29     sum += Integer.parseInt(tkn.nextToken());
30   return (strb.append('':'').append(sum).
       toString();
31 }
```

Figure 1. Actual implementation of WordCount in MRJ

2.1 Example MRJ Application

The design of MRJ shares many features with Hadoop at the application interface level (and also, e.g., for job submission, setting the configuration parameters, and initialising the framework) as both frameworks are implemented in Java.

The WordCount application is the canonical MapReduce programming example [13]. It counts the number of occurrences of each word in an input text file. The MRJ implementation requires the programmer to define only two methods: map and reduce since all other operations including task splitting and output sorting are provided directly by the MRJ runtime system.

Figure 1 shows the actual Java source code for the WordCount application, including a small amount of boilerplate initialization code. It is apparent from this listing that the MRJ API abstracts away all the details of the parallelization, runtime scheduling, etc, so the application programmer is enabled to focus on the application logic. The entire implementation of this simple application takes less than 30 lines of Java code. Other common string processing applications such as Grep, StringMatch and ReverseIndex may be implemented simply by altering the map and reduce methods in Figure 1.

2.2 MRJ Implementation Basis

The distinguishing feature of MRJ is that it exploits a recursive divide-and-conquer approach. The implementation takes advantage of this by relying on work stealing and the Java fork-join framework (part of pre-release version of java.util.concurrent package for JDK1.7) [2, 24].

The execution sequence of fork/join parallelism is analogous to the MapReduce pattern. In fork/join parallelism, a given computational task is divided into new subtasks and each subtask is executed in parallel on a separate core. The instantiation of subtasks in parallel is represented by the *fork* operation. The corresponding *join* operation ensures that the main execution context waits for the completion of all subtasks in a *barrier synchronization* before proceeding to the next stage. The significance of using fork/join parallelism is that it provides very efficient load balancing, if the subtasks are decomposed in such a way that they can be executed without dependencies.

Our MRJ framework builds upon the parallelism constructs provided by the Java fork/join framework to take advantage of the parallelism exposed by the functions `map` and `reduce`. Any MapReduce application has a high degree of parallelism, as the particular input to each `map` and `reduce` function is processed without any dependence on other portions of the overall application input.

We initialize a `ForkJoinPool` of worker threads, which will execute `map` and `reduce` methods as `ForkJoinTask` instances. In order to successfully complete any map or reduce phase, each worker thread needs to wait for other worker threads to finish execution before proceeding. The impact of such overhead is significantly reduced in MRJ framework by using a Cilk-style *work-stealing* technique [7]. This way of scheduling the subtasks minimises the load imbalance due to uneven distribution of the computation associated with each task. Each worker thread has a double-ended queue of map or reduce tasks awaiting execution. If any thread's queue is empty, it may steal a task from another thread's non-empty queue.

Dynamic load balancing is useful since some map/reduce tasks may finish quicker than others. For instance, the computation time may depend on values in the input data set, rather than just the size of the input data. Again, there may be architectural reasons for some tasks finishing quicker. Cache locality, or CPU turbo boosting on Intel Core i7 may make some cores execute faster. Indeed, heterogeneous multi-core architectures are an ideal target for a dynamic load-balancing system like MRJ.

2.3 MRJ Execution Details

Figure 2 presents an overview of the execution stages of the MapReduce pattern. Partitioning of the input data creates subtasks with equal size of partitioned data units. Worker threads in the `ForkJoinPool` execute the generated subtasks, at the map and reduce stages.

The number of worker threads is generally upper-bounded by the number of cores in the system. The particular task scheduling policy may be configured in the MRJ setup. With *static* scheduling, for each map or reduce phase, the number of subtasks created is equal to the number of worker threads in the fork-join pool. On the other hand, *dynamic* scheduling allows for more *fine-grained* parallelism. Many more subtasks are created than there are worker threads in the fork-join pool. The actual number of subtasks can be varied dynamically in the framework. This fine-grained parallelism improves load balance, cache locality and scalability (since it allows greater scope for the work-stealing mechanism to operate). However, generating more subtasks can increase the overhead due to task creation, garbage collection and scheduling. In all our experiments, we find that we can achieve good performance using around eight times as many subtasks as there are available threads. This is the recommended ratio for fork-join tasks to worker threads, in the fork-join library.

In order to improve performance for recursive calls to the MapReduce function, a job-chaining functionality, similar to Hadoop's, has been implemented in MRJ. Job chaining enables multiple calls to map and reduce phases during a single MapReduce execution. This feature is required, for example, to implement the kmeans benchmark in which the runtime iterates through the map and re-

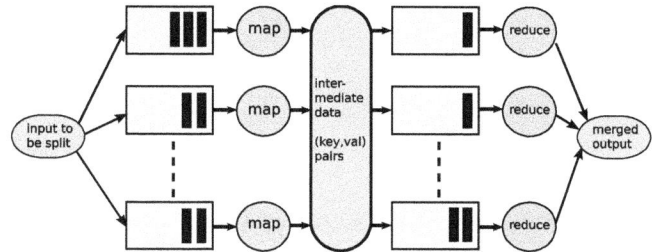

Figure 2. Schematic diagram for MapReduce execution

Vendor	Intel
Codename	Nehalem
Architecture	Core i7
Cores/Contexts	4/2
Per-core L1 i/d	32KB/32KB
Per-core L2	256KB
Shared L3	8MB
Core freq	2.67GHz
RAM size	6GB
OS	Linux 2.6.31
JVM (1.6)	14.0-b16
max fixed heap	4GB

Table 1. Multi-core architecture for evaluating MRJ scalability

duce stages to compute the final cluster for a given set of coordinates. The benefit of using the job-chaining feature is that all the worker threads and data structures created during the first Map and Reduce stages are *reused*, thus reducing memory management overhead.

3. Scalability Study

In this section, we evaluate the scalability of our MRJ framework on a commodity multi-core architecture described in Table 1. This is a shared-memory, uniform memory access multi-core processor.

All experiments take place using a fixed JVM heap size, that is large enough to minimize any GC activity. (We explore the impact of GC in more detail in Section 4.) Each experiment is run five times, and the arithmetic mean is reported as the result. We use a nanosecond resolution timer. Speedup is calculated as T_1/T_p, where T_1 is the execution time with a single MRJ thread, and T_p is the execution time using p MRJ threads.

Table 2 summarizes the seven MapReduce benchmarks we have ported to MRJ, and their input data sets. The porting process simply involves transliterating the application code from the open-source Phoenix implementation to our Java MRJ framework. (Phoenix is another multi-core MapReduce platform, developed in C [31].)

Figure 3 shows the scalability curves for all benchmarks, for increasing numbers of runtime threads allocated to the Java fork/join pool. The graphs only show the Large input data sets in this section.

The majority of benchmarks do not scale beyond 4 threads on the Core i7 platform, which has 4 cores, each with 2 hyperthread contexts. The intelligent JVM scheduler places the first four MRJ worker threads on separate cores. However hyperthreading does not give any significant performance gain for memory-bound applications. On a cache miss, a hardware thread is context-switched for a different hardware thread. However, if all threads incur frequent cache misses, then they are all stalled and no useful work can be done by the extra contexts. On the other hand, compute-bound applications such as matrix and pca show some further scaling beyond 4 threads on Core i7, gaining additional benefit from the hy-

benchmark	description	input data
grep	find string occurrences in input text file	S:10MB, M:50MB, L:100MB
kmeans	group 3d points into clusters based on their Euclidean distance	S:100k points, M:250K, L:500K
linearR	compute best-fit line for input data file	S:10MB, M:50MB, L:100MB
matrix	dense integer matrix multiplication	S:1000x1000 values, M:2000x2000, L:3000x3000
pca	principal components analysis on an integer matrix	S:1000x1000 values, M:2000x2000, L:3000x3000
sm	search input text file for a word	S:10MB, M:50MB, L:100MB
wc	count instances of each unique word in input text file	S:10MB, M:50MB, L:100MB

Table 2. MapReduce Benchmarks evaluated in the MRJ framework

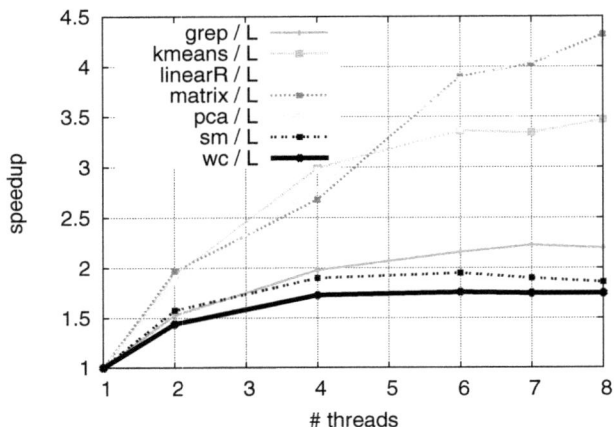

Figure 3. Scalability of MRJ benchmarks on Intel Core i7

benchmark	L3 miss rate	σ	DLTB miss rate	σ
grep	2283	90	556	41
kmeans	1547	30	38	2
linearR	2430	244	254	14
matrix	175	5	52	2
pca	231	5	48	1
sm	2377	161	251	14
wc	2271	89	6 7	26

Table 3. Oprofile samples for miss rates on Core i7, means and standard deviations for five runs of each benchmark

perthreading contexts. These benchmarks have more regular memory access patterns, which gives them relatively good cache locality.

Similar trends in behaviour for compute-bound and memory-bound benchmarks on simultaneous multi-threaded (SMT) multi-core architectures has been observed for the PARSEC benchmark suite [6].

In order to characterize which MRJ benchmarks are memory-bound and which are compute-bound, we run a set of simple profiling experiments. We use the Linux *oprofile* tool, to sample the LLC_MISSES and DTLB_MISSES hardware performance counters on the Intel Core i7 platform. We sample every 6000th retired memory load event that misses the L3 cache, and every 6000th memory access that incurs a DTLB miss, during MRJ benchmark execution. In order to make sure all cores are roughly equally loaded, we profile with 8 MRJ threads running. If we divide each sample count by the benchmark execution time, we should obtain values that correlate roughly with the L3 cache miss rate and DTLB miss rate for this benchmark. We say that MRJ benchmarks with high cache miss rates are memory-bound, conversely those with low cache miss rates are CPU-bound. Benchmarks with a low DTLB miss rate exhibit good locality of reference, whereas those with a high DTLB miss rate do not have good locality. Table 3 reports the mean of 5 measurements for each benchmark using 8 threads with large heap sizes to minimize GC.

We note that matrix has comparatively low miss rates, which account for its near-linear scalability. Since matrix multiplication is

implemented as simple linear array traversals, it exhibits excellent cache locality. The kmeans benchmark has *higher* miss rates, since it has little spatial locality. In the kmeans data, close points in the 3-d co-ordinate space are randomly distributed in the Java heap. The grep and wc benchmarks are operating on String based data, and have high miss rates.

4. Impact of Garbage Collection

Since MRJ is implemented in Java, it relies on the underlying JVM to provide garbage collection (GC) services. The impact of GC is more significant for execution with relatively small heap sizes: In the earlier experiments in Section 3, heap space is explicitly fixed at 4GB to minimize GC effects.

The Java 1.6 runtime provides three standard GC algorithms: serial, parallel, and concurrent. The *serial* collector is a stop-the-world GC (i.e. all application threads must be paused before GC takes place) which uses a single thread to perform all collection. Thus there is no inter-thread communication overhead for serial GC. The *parallel* collector is also a stop-the-world GC. However it uses multiple threads to perform the collection, thus it can out-perform the serial collector for applications with large data sets, running on architectures that provide multiple hardware threads. The *concurrent* collector [29] performs most of its work while the application threads are running. This minimizes GC pause time, which improves response time for interactive applications. However there is a runtime overhead to support concurrent GC, which means parallel GC generally gives better overall execution times.

When we run an MRJ application with n threads we allow the parallel and concurrent GCs to use n threads also. (The number of threads to use for GC can be specified as a JVM command-line parameter.)

For MRJ application execution, there are two major causes of heap memory usage. (i) The size of the input data set affects the heap space requirements. (ii) The specified number of map and reduce threads, and the granularity of the tasks, affects heap space requirements. This is because each individual task resolves to a

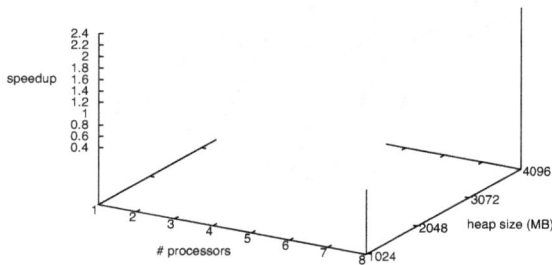

Figure 4. Scalability of grep degrades with increasing numbers of processors, for small heap sizes

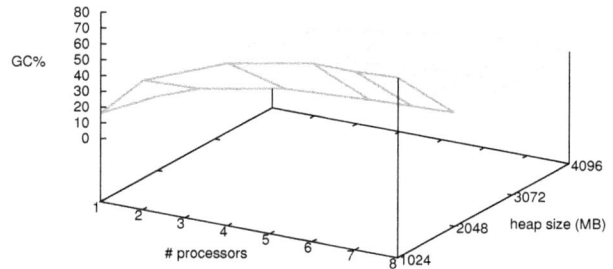

Figure 5. GC overhead increases with the number of processors, more significantly for small heap sizes

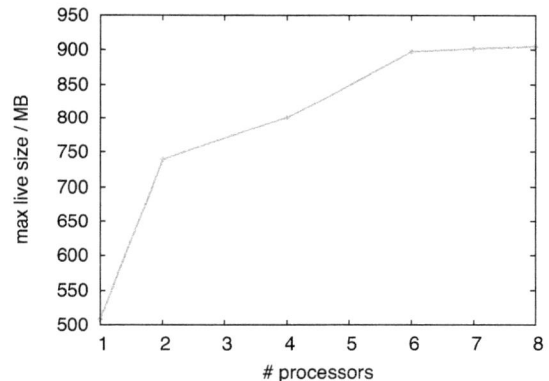

Figure 6. Max live size increases with the number of fork/join threads

ForkJoinTask instance, which requires its own book-keeping data structures in memory.

In the remainder of this section, we present some results that appear to be MRJ performance anomalies, but can be explained by considering the GC interaction with MRJ.

4.1 Inverse Scaling for Small Heaps

The first potentially surprising result is that the grep benchmark performance degrades with increasing numbers of threads, for small heap sizes. This is the case for all GC algorithms; Figure 4 illustrates the point for the serial GC, using the large input data set. When the heap size is 1024MB, the speedup drops below one when the number of processors is above two. However at all larger heap sizes, the speedup increases until the number of processors reaches four, then it hits a plateau (as shown earlier in Figure 3).

The reason for this slowdown at 1024MB, as the number of threads increases, is *heap space pressure* due to increasing memory consumption from the Java fork-join threads.

From an analysis using the Java *hprof* heap profiling tool, we see that the *total* amount of memory allocated in grep is generally invariant, no matter how many worker threads are allocated to the Java fork/join pool. However the amount of *live* data on the heap is proportional to the number of concurrently executing worker threads. This is because each thread has its own thread-local data structures, such as StringBuffer objects and backing char arrays. Thus with more concurrent worker threads, there is a higher proportion of live data on the heap, which increases heap space pressure. This causes a greater number of garbage collections, hence the slowdown in overall application execution time. Figure 5 shows how the proportion of application execution time spent in GC increases with the number of threads, for the 1024MB heap size with serial GC. With a single fork/join worker thread, the GC time is 16%. This rises to 74% with eight fork/join worker threads. At larger heap sizes, the proportion of time spent in GC is much less significant.

Figure 6 shows how the max live size statistic varies with the number of fork/join threads, for grep with the Large input in a fixed 1024MB heap. The max live size measure is an approximation of the minimum memory requirement for a program, based on the high-water-mark of live data over all GC events throughout the program execution. Note how this high-water-mark approaches the fixed heap capacity for larger numbers of fork/join threads. We

observe similar behaviour with the wc benchmark. At 1024MB it fails to execute the Large input data due to OutOfMemory errors for any more than two worker threads.

4.2 Relative GC Performance is Input Dependent

It is apparent that the behaviour of applications is often highly input dependent. Mao et al. [27, 33] establish the influence of Java program inputs on the minimum heap size required for successful execution, and the relative performance of various garbage collection algorithms.

We have three input data sets for each MRJ benchmark, classified as Small, Medium and Large. Using Small inputs, MRJ application performance is generally similar irrespective of the selected GC algorithm. This is because there is relatively little allocation, so the GC does not have much work to do. On the other hand, with larger inputs (or equivalently, smaller heap sizes [1]), there are significant differences in performance between the various GC algorithms. As a general rule, parallel GC outperforms serial GC on larger inputs, when the number of threads is above two. Since parallel GC uses multiple threads to perform collection, it reduces the GC pause time relative to serial GC.

Table 4 illustrates the point that the relative performance of each GC algorithm varies with application input. For the wc MRJ application, we evaluate each input data set with each GC algorithm, in a variety of heap sizes ranging from 1 to 4GB. So for each (inputsize, heapsize, numthreads) combination, we have three execution times, one per GC algorithm. We define a GC's performance as *good* if it gives an execution time within 10% of the optimal time from any GC algorithm for this (inputsize, heapsize, numthreads) case.

Table 4 enumerates all the cases: each table cell corresponds to a single case. For each case, the cell label indicates which GC algorithms are *good*. (Note that between one and three GC algorithms can be *good* for a particular case[2].)

For the Small input, the serial GC appears to be *good* for the majority of cases. On the other hand, for the Large input, the parallel and concurrent GC algorithms appear to outperform the serial GC for many cases.

Other benchmarks, such as matrix and kmeans, have negligible GC overhead at all the heap sizes we tested. These benchmarks do not exhibit significant GC performance variation with input.

4.3 Relative GC Performance is Application Dependent

It is a well-established fact that the relative performance of different GC algorithms is dependent on the characteristics of the application being executed [17, 28, 35] particularly at smaller heap sizes.

As one might expect, parallel GC (which is the default option on server class JVMs) generally outperforms serial and concurrent, especially for larger numbers of threads. However this is not always the case. For instance, the sm benchmark performs better with concurrent instead of parallel GC. For example in a 2GB heap, the sm benchmark with Large input executing on 8 threads takes an average of 2.26s with parallel GC, but only 0.61s with concurrent GC.

The unusual behaviour of sm can be understood by referring to its high object death rate. Figure 7 shows the death rates for all MRJ benchmarks. We compute the death rate as the total amount of collected garbage during the program execution divided by the total execution time of the program. The bar chart shows that sm has a significantly higher death rate than the other benchmarks.

Concurrent GC identifies and collects dead objects in the background, while the application is executing. This avoids long pauses for full-heap scans. We suggest that since the sm benchmark creates large numbers of short-lived objects, these are collected very shortly after their allocation, reducing overall heap consumption and increasing data locality. This has a significant impact on overall application performance.

As earlier, we use oprofile to quantify cache locality. We measure the L3 cache miss rates for sm with different GC algorithms, at a sampling rate of 6000, for 8 threads, Large inputs, 2GB heap. Table 5 shows this data, demonstrating that the cache locality is much better for concurrent GC.

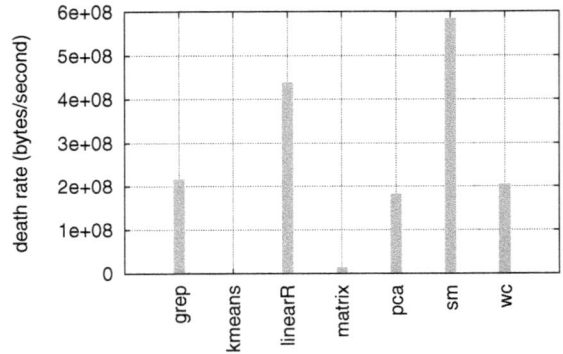

Figure 7. Object death rates for the MRJ benchmarks, running with 1 thread, serial GC, large inputs, 2048MB heap

GC	L3 cache miss rate	σ
serial	1973	57
parallel	3540	86
concurrent	1054	96

Table 5. Mean and standard deviation of L3 cache miss sample rates from oprofile over 10 runs of sm, for each GC algorithm

5. Auto-Tuning Garbage Collection for MRJ

In this section, we investigate the use of machine learning to select a suitable GC policy for each MRJ program. Previous sections have demonstrated that the GC performance is dependent on a number of factors, including benchmark characteristics, JVM heap size, and number of threads. In general, it is not straightforward to select the optimal GC policy without exhaustively testing all candidate policies. We show that it is *not* the case that a single GC policy is uniformly good for all programs.

Our objective is to implement a *GC auto-tuning framework* for MRJ. Given a new benchmark, input dataset, and system constraints on heap size and number of threads, the auto-tuning framework predicts a suitable GC policy. For this initial investigation, the GC policy consists of the GC algorithm (serial, parallel or concurrent) and the heap space layout (young:old generation ratio of 1:2 or 1:8). Thus there are six different GC policies, based on the various combinations of these configuration options. Other aspects of memory management could be incorporated into this auto-tuning framework, but these seem to be the most significant concerns relating to GC performance.

5.1 Motivation

Why should we have a specific GC tuning framework for MRJ? We feel there are several compelling reasons:

1. MRJ application developers will not be interested in the mechanics of GC. It is a low-level cross-cutting concern, to be addressed by the software platform architects, rather than application developers or users.

2. GC is crucial since it has effects on runtime behaviour, including thread scheduling, cache locality, response time, and overall execution time.

3. We can make use of MRJ-specific information as features to characterize applications, in order to predict appropriate GC

---

[1] Although this is a similar point to earlier, there is a distinction. Section 4.1 showed that small heaps magnify the impact of GC. Section 4.2 shows that in relatively small heaps, some GC variants are noticeably more effective than others.

[2] In a few cases the benchmark throws an OutOfMemory error for all GC algorithms, so no GC algorithm is good.

input heap/GB	Small			Medium			Large		
	1	2	4	1	2	4	1	2	4
#threads 8	P	S,P	S,P	C	P	P		C	P
7	P	S,P	S,P	C	P	P		C	P
6	P	S,P	S,P	C	P,C	P		C	P,C
4	P	S,P	S,P	S,P,C	P	P		S,P,C	P,C
2	P	S,P	S,P	P	P	P	C	P	P
1	S	S,P	S,P	S,P,C	S,P,C	S,P,C	C	S,P	S,P

Table 4. (S)erial, (P)arallel and (C)oncurrent benchmarks exhibit 'good' performance for different scenarios depending on input for the wc benchmark

policies. This might include allocated object types and sizes. For example, large `int` arrays tend to last for the lifetime of the application (consider the matrices in `matrix` multiplication or `pca`). On the other hand, smaller objects are more short-lived, such as `StringBuffer` objects in the wc or grep applications.

4. An accurate GC auto-tuning framework ought to give a time saving. When a new MapReduce application arrives, the framework will predict an appropriate GC policy for its execution given the system constraints. Without this auto-tuning, we would have to do exhaustive profiling, i.e. evaluate each individual GC policy. With auto-tuning, we can gather static features from the benchmark code and system parameters, and perhaps gather dynamic features from a small number of trial executions.

5.2 Data Set Generation

This section outlines the *features* that we use to characterize individual MRJ benchmark executions with specific constraints. These features will be used as inputs to the learning algorithm, which will predict a good GC policy.

The MRJ system constraints specified by the user are the JVM fixed heap size and the number of threads. In general, a larger heap and more threads should improve the overall performance of the application. However there may be other system-level restrictions that determine a particular MRJ application's resource usage.

Other features are dynamic characteristics of the individual application and its input data. We record the number of minor and major GCs that take place on a single run through the program, along with the time spent in GC as a proportion of the overall execution time. We measure the total amount of memory dynamically allocated by the application during its execution, and the proportion of this allocated memory occupied by `String` objects, and `int` arrays. These two are the most common datatypes manipulated by our MRJ benchmarks.

All of these dynamic features are collected on a single run of an MRJ program, using serial GC with 1 MRJ thread. In fact, we have two trial executions, one with a young:old heap ratio of 1:2, and the other 1:8. This gives us twice as many features for the GC-specific data. We make use of the extensive JVM profiling features, such as the `hprof` agent library and verbose GC logging. Table 6 presents a summary of all the features collected for each (benchmark,input) combination.

Next we collect the execution times on the Intel Core i7 machine. These execution times form the basis for the target class in our data set. For each (`bm`,`input`,`heapsize`,`numthreads`) combination, we run 5 experiments for each GC policy, and compute the arithmetic mean execution time.

From this information, we generate the data set for the machine learning algorithm as follows. For each experiment, there will be an *optimal* GC policy, i.e. the policy that gives the lowest execution time. We say that a GC policy is *good* for an application execution

feature	type	how collected
heap size (MB)	integer	system parameter
# MRJ worker threads	integer	system parameter
# minor GCs (x2)	integer	trial execution
# major GCs (x2)	integer	trial execution
% GC time (x2)	real	trial execution
bytes allocated	integer	trial execution
% String alloc'd	real	trial execution
% int array alloc'd	real	trial execution

Table 6. Summary of features collected for each (benchmark,input) combination

if the time is shorter than 95% of the time with the default policy, and if the time is no longer than 110% of the optimal time. (These thresholds require some experimentation, informed by the standard deviations of the execution time distributions for each application.)

So, for each application execution, we can say which GC policies are good, and which are not. We build a distinct classifier for each policy, to predict whether or not that policy is good for a particular experiment.

We create classifiers using leave-one-out cross-validation (LOOCV). We set up a training set to include experimental data for all benchmarks except one, and then *train* the classifiers using this data. Subsequently we *test* the generated classifiers on the missing benchmark to obtain fair predictions. (For *n* benchmarks, we have *n* rounds of LOOCV, each time eliminating one of the *n* benchmarks from the training set.)

The following section gives details of the classification technique we use.

5.3 Prediction Technique

We instantiate a separate classifier for each GC policy p, that predicts whether p enables good performance for an MRJ benchmark and its input, given their set of features. This is a variant of one-versus-all prediction [32], which is a commonly accepted way of decomposing a multi-class problem.

Each individual classifier is a *random forest*, which is an ensemble predictor consisting of many decision trees [8]. Decision trees automatically select the most relevant features for the classification problem, and discard less relevant features [30]. The ensemble technique introduces a small amount of randomness into the selected features to make the overall classifier more robust. We use the Weka [19] implementation of random forests, with all the parameters set to default except that we have 20 trees for each forest.

It may be the case that multiple individual classifiers predict that a program/input will be good with this GC policy. We apply the predictors in a simple *cascade* of classifiers [36]. This means that we impose an order on the policies, then apply the predictors in this order. If at any stage in the cascade, the predictor indicates good performance, then we go with this policy, otherwise we try

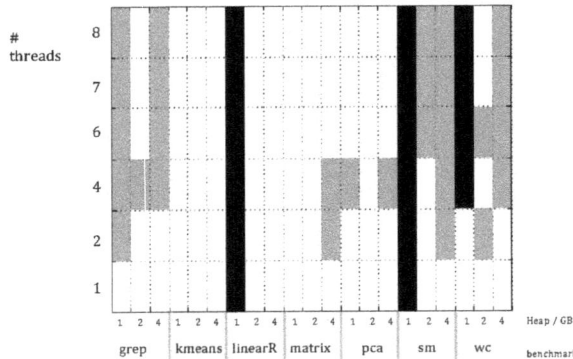

Figure 8. Heatmap showing GC auto-tuning performance relative to optimal policy, for each benchmark execution, at varying heap sizes (1,2,4 GB) and numbers of threads, with Large input data sets. White cells (around 75% of complete experiments) indicate that the predicted GC policy was close to the the optimal policy. Grey cells indicate that the selected GC policy gave clearly sub-optimal performance. Black cells indicate that the particular experiment did not complete with any GC policy due to OutOfMemory errors.

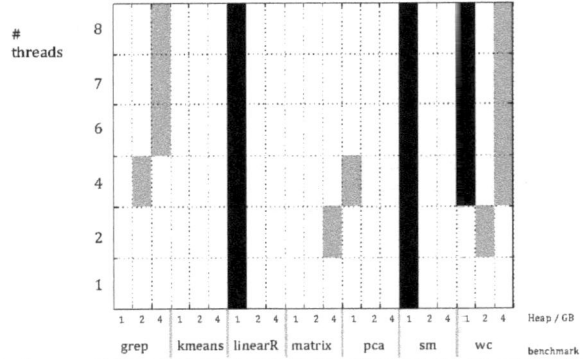

Figure 9. Heatmap showing GC auto-tuning performance relative to default GC policy, on benchmarks with Large inputs. White cells (around 90% of complete experiments) indicate that the predicted GC policy was at least as good as the default policy. Grey cells indicate that the selected GC policy gave worse than default performance. Black cells indicate that the particular experiment did not complete with any GC policy due to OutOfMemory errors.

the next predictor in the cascade. If no good policy is predicted, then we use the *default* HotSpot server GC policy, which is parallel GC with a 1:2 young:old heap layout.

The actual order of classifiers in our cascade, in terms of their predicted GC policies expressed as *algorithm-ratio* is: concurrent-1:8, concurrent-1:2, serial-1:8, serial-1:2, parallel-1:8, parallel-1:2. This ordering is another part of the learning that could be tuned directly. However to avoid complications we settled on this fixed order that gives good overall results.

5.4 Evaluation of Performance Tuning

We test the performance of this cascade of classifiers by using it to predict suitable GC policies for the (benchmark,input) combinations that we excluded from the LOOCV training data. We only give results for Large input data sets. For smaller inputs, there is less variation between the GC algorithms' performance.

Figure 8 presents the results of the GC auto-tuning, as a heatmap. For each benchmark, with a particular heapsize and number of threads, we compare the overall execution performance with the predicted GC policy against the best performance (optimal) of any of the six specified GC policies. In 82 cases out of 110 completed experiments, the predicted policy gives comparable performance with the optimal policy.

Even in cases that do not perform as well as the optimal time, we may still outperform the default policy, and thus get some improvement. For instance, this scenario occurs for the sm benchmark when using larger numbers of threads.

Figure 9 shows another map over the same experiments. Here, we report whether our predictive GC policy gives performance at least as good as the default GC policy. White cells indicate that the corresponding experiments are not more than 10% slower than the default execution time. In only 11 cases (out of 110) is the predicted performance significantly worse than default. These cases are indicated by grey cells in the heatmap.

The overall worst case is a 30% slowdown[3]. Across all 110 experiments, the maximum speedup of the predicted policy over

the default policy is 6.0 times[4], and the geometric mean speedup over all experiments is 1.1 times.

The predictor suggests using the default policy in only 5 out of 110 cases. However note that GC policy does not make much overall difference for benchmarks that do little dynamic memory management, such as matrix and pca.

6. Related Work

The original work on MapReduce [13, 14] applies to compute-clusters. Ranger et al. describe the first application of MapReduce to multi-core processors [31]. Yoo et al. later extend this to non-uniform memory access architectures [38]. They discuss the scalability of memory management in terms of malloc and mmap functions. Since their work is in C/C++, they do not have automatic memory management overhead.

Since the Hadoop MapReduce system [1] is implemented in Java, its performance can be affected by runtime garbage collection like our MRJ framework. The Hadoop developers give a limited amount of advice[5] on performance tuning for GC with Hadoop. However they do not appear to consider tuning for application-specific behaviour. Their chief concern is to minimise pause time by using a concurrent GC algorithm with a small nursery space.

The techniques for understanding interactions between an application and a runtime system are inspired by Hauswirth's work on vertical profiling [20]. He considers all levels from architecture through to application, to explore reasons for apparent anomalous behaviour. In the present paper, we have attempted to follow his holistic approach by considering and relating performance data from hardware counters, through JVM level statistics, to application performance.

A recent paper analysing the behaviour of multi-threaded Java workloads on multi-core systems shows that conventional memory management techniques do not scale to large multi-core envi-

---

[3] For execution of grep with 4GB, 8 threads, using the serial-1:8 GC policy.

[4] For execution of sm with 2GB, 2 threads, using the serial-1:8 GC policy. (Note that although both examples given use the serial-1:8 policy, all the other GC policies are predicted for various examples in the space of experiments.)

[5] http://wiki.apache.org/hadoop/PerformanceTuning

ronments, and require adaptation [40]. They identify an *allocation wall*, which refers to the maximum rate of allocation from concurrent JVM threads. In our limited experience with MRJ benchmarks, we have not hit the allocation wall. Most MRJ programs create major data structures up-front, then operate on these throughout the map or reduce phases, only allocating small objects (`String` instances, etc) during MapReduce computation. We have not hit a corresponding *de-allocation wall*, except as in Section 4.1 when the heap size is relatively small.

Singer et al. investigate the automatic selection of garbage collection algorithms for a set of standard Java benchmarks, using different feature sets and learning algorithms [34]. In the specific context of MapReduce for Java, we feel that the current set of features and learning strategies fit better.

We note that, in general, the application of machine learning to Java runtime performance auto-tuning is a growing trend [26, 39].

7. Conclusions

This paper presents MRJ: a Java-based framework for MapReduce parallelism that targets conventional multi-core architectures. We have demonstrated its scalability of performance, with increasing numbers of threads allocated to the underlying Java fork/join pool. We have highlighted the interactions between MapReduce benchmarks and the garbage collector, and shown how a machine-learning GC auto-tuning policy can improve runtime performance.

We intend to release MRJ shortly as an open-source project, since we hope it will be useful to a wider community.

Acknowledgements

Thanks to Angela Demke Brown for her careful and considerate shepherding of this paper. We are also grateful to EPSRC for supporting this research, under grant EP/G000662/1. Mikel Luján holds a Royal Society University Research Fellowship.

References

[1] Hadoop: Open source implementation of mapreduce. `http://lucene.apache.org/hadoop/`.

[2] Jsr-166, prelease of java.util.concurrent package. `http://gee.cs.oswego.edu/dl/concurrency-interest/index.html`.

[3] Organizations using hadoop. `http://wiki.apache.org/hadoop/PoweredBy`.

[4] E. Allen, D. Chase, C. Flood, V. Luchangco, J.-W. Maessen, S. Ryu, and G. L. Steele Jr. Project Fortress: A multicore language for multicore processors. *Linux Magazine*, Sep 2007.

[5] M. Armbrust, A. Fox, R. Griffith, A. D. Joseph, R. Katz, A. Konwinski, G. Lee, D. Patterson, A. Rabkin, I. Stoica, and M. Zaharia. A view of cloud computing. *Communications of the ACM*, 53:50–58, April 2010.

[6] M. Bhadauria, V. M. Weaver, and S. A. McKee. Understanding PARSEC performance on contemporary CMPs. In *Proceedings of the 2009 International Symposium on Workload Characterization*, October 2009.

[7] R. Blumofe, C. Joerg, B. Kuszmaul, C. Leiserson, K. Randall, and Y. Zhou. Cilk: An efficient multithreaded runtime system. In *Proceedings of the fifth ACM SIGPLAN symposium on Principles and practice of parallel programming*, pages 207–216, 1995.

[8] L. Breiman. Random forests. *Machine Learning*, 45(1):5–32, 2001.

[9] P. Charles, C. Donawa, K. Ebcioglu, C. Grothoff, A. Kielstra, C. von Praun, V. Saraswat, and V. Sarkar. X10: An object-oriented approach to non-uniform clustered computing. In *Proceedings of OOPSLA 2005*, 2005.

[10] C. Chu, S. Kim, Y. Lin, Y. Yu, G. Bradski, A. Ng, and K. Olukotun. Map-reduce for machine learning on multicore. In *Advances in Neural Information Processing Systems*, page 281, 2007.

[11] S. Daruru, N. M. Marin, M. Walker, and J. Ghosh. Pervasive parallelism in data mining: dataflow solution to co-clustering large and sparse netflix data. In *KDD '09: Proceedings of the 15th ACM SIGKDD international conference on Knowledge discovery and data mining*, pages 1115–1124, 2009.

[12] M. de Kruijf and K. Sankaralingam. MapReduce for the CELL B.E. architecture. *IBM Journal of Research and Development*, 53(5), 2009.

[13] J. Dean and S. Ghemawat. MapReduce: simplified data processing on large clusters. In *Proceedings of the 6th symposium on operating systems design and implementation*, pages 137–150, 2004.

[14] J. Dean and S. Ghemawat. MapReduce: simplified data processing on large clusters. *Communications of the ACM*, 51(1):107–113, 2008.

[15] D. DeWitt and M. Stonebraker. MapReduce: A major step backwards. *The Database Column*, 2008.

[16] J. Ekanayake, S. Pallickara, and G. Fox. MapReduce for data intensive scientific analyses. In *Fourth IEEE International Conference on eScience*, pages 277–284, 2008.

[17] R. Fitzgerald and D. Tarditi. The case for profile-directed selection of garbage collectors. In *Proceedings of the 2nd International Symposium on Memory Management*, pages 111–120, 2000.

[18] Google. Appengine. `http://code.google.com/appengine/`.

[19] M. Hall, E. Frank, G. Holmes, B. Pfahringer, P. Reutemann, and I. H. Witten. The WEKA data mining software: An update. *SIGKDD Explorations*, 11(1), 2009.

[20] M. Hauswirth, P. Sweeney, A. Diwan, and M. Hind. Vertical profiling: understanding the behavior of object-oriented applications. *ACM SIGPLAN Notices*, 39(10):251–269, 2004.

[21] B. He, W. Fang, Q. Luo, N. Govindaraju, and T. Wang. Mars: a MapReduce framework on graphics processors. In *Proceedings of the 17th international conference on parallel architectures and compilation techniques*, 2008.

[22] Intel. Single-chip cloud computer, 2009. `http://techresearch.intel.com/UserFiles/en-us/File/terascale/SCC-Overview.pdf`.

[23] G. Kovoor, J. Singer, and M. Lujan. Building a Java mapreduce framework for multi-core architectures. In *Proceedings of the Third Workshop on Programmability Issues for Multi-Core Computers*, pages 87–98, 2010.

[24] D. Lea. A java fork/join framework. In *Proceedings of the ACM conference on Java Grande*, 2000.

[25] D. Leijen, W. Schulte, and S. Burckhardt. The design of a task parallel library. In *Proceeding of the 24th ACM SIGPLAN conference on Object oriented programming systems languages and applications*, pages 227–242, 2009.

[26] F. Mao and X. Shen. Cross-input learning and discriminative prediction in evolvable virtual machines. In *Proceedings of the 7th annual IEEE/ACM International Symposium on Code Generation and Optimization*, pages 92–101, 2009.

[27] F. Mao, E. Z. Zhang, and X. Shen. Influence of program inputs on the selection of garbage collectors. In *Proceedings of the 2009 ACM SIGPLAN/SIGOPS international conference on Virtual execution environments*, pages 91–100, 2009.

[28] T. Printezis. Hot-swapping between a mark&sweep and a mark&compact garbage collector in a generational environment. In *Proceedings of the 1st Java Virtual Machine Research and Technology Symposium*, pages 171–184, 2001.

[29] T. Printezis and D. Detlefs. A generational mostly-concurrent garbage collector. In *Proceedings of the 2nd international symposium on Memory management*, pages 143–154, 2000.

[30] J. R. Quinlan. Induction of decision trees. *Machine Learning*, 1(1):81–106, 1986.

[31] C. Ranger, R. Raghuraman, A. Penmetsa, G. Bradski, and C. Kozyrakis. Evaluating mapreduce for multi-core and multiprocessor systems. In *Proceedings of the 13th International Symposium on High Performance Computer Architecture*, pages 13–24, 2007.

[32] R. Rifkin and A. Klautau. In defense of one-vs-all classification. *Journal of Machine Learning Research*, 5:101–142, 2004.

[33] X. Shen, F. Mao, K. Tian, and E. Z. Zhang. The study and handling of program inputs in the selection of garbage collectors. *ACM SIGOPS Operating Systems Review*, 43:48–61, July 2009.

[34] J. Singer, G. Brown, I. Watson, and J. Cavazos. Intelligent selection of application-specific garbage collectors. In *Proceedings of the 6th International Symposium on Memory Management*, pages 91–102, Oct 2007.

[35] S. Soman, C. Krintz, and D. F. Bacon. Dynamic selection of application-specific garbage collectors. In *Proceedings of the 4th International Symposium on Memory Management*, pages 49–60, 2004.

[36] P. Viola and M. Jones. Rapid object detection using a boosted cascade of simple features. In *Proc. IEEE Conf. on Computer Vision and Pattern Recognition*, pages 511–518, 2001.

[37] H.-C. Yang, A. Dasdan, R.-L. Hsiao, and D. S. Parker. Map-reduce-merge: simplified relational data processing on large clusters. In *Proceedings of the 2007 ACM SIGMOD international conference on Management of data*, pages 1029–1040, 2007.

[38] R. Yoo, A. Romano, and C. Kozyrakis. Phoenix rebirth: Scalable MapReduce on a NUMA system. In *Proceedings of the International Symposium on Workload Characterization*, 2009.

[39] C. Zhang and M. Hirzel. Online phase-adaptive data layout selection. In *ECOOP 2008 Object-Oriented Programming*, pages 309–334, 2008.

[40] Y. Zhao, J. Shi, K. Zheng, H. Wang, H. Lin, and L. Shao. Allocation wall: a limiting factor of Java applications on emerging multi-core platforms. *ACM SIGPLAN Notices*, 44(10):361–376, 2009.

Compartmental Memory Management
in a Modern Web Browser

Gregor Wagner[†§]   Andreas Gal[§]   Christian Wimmer[†]   Brendan Eich[§]   Michael Franz[†]

[†]University of California, Irvine   [§]Mozilla Corporation
{wagnerg, cwimmer, franz}@uci.edu   {gwagner, gal, brendan}@mozilla.com

Abstract

Since their inception, the usage pattern of web browsers has changed substantially. Rather than sequentially navigating static web sites, modern web browsers often manage a large number of simultaneous tabs displaying dynamic web content, each of which might be running a substantial amount of client-side JavaScript code. This environment introduced a new degree of parallelism that was not fully embraced by the underlying JavaScript virtual machine architecture. We propose a novel abstraction for multiple disjoint JavaScript heaps, which we call compartments. We use the notion of document origin to cluster objects into separate compartments. Objects within a compartment can reference each other directly. Objects across compartments can only reference each other through wrappers. Our approach reduces garbage collection pause times by permitting collection of sub-heaps (compartments), and we can use cross-compartment wrappers to enforce cross origin object access policy.

Categories and Subject Descriptors D.2.11 [*Software Engineering*]: Software Architectures - Domain-specific architectures; D.3.4 [*Programming Languages*]: Processors - Memory management (Garbage Collection)

General Terms Design, Performance, Experimentation

Keywords Web-Browser Architecture, Isolation, Memory Management, Garbage Collection

1. Introduction

Increasing bandwidth, faster computers, and a JavaScript performance boost over the last few years have enabled web developers to build highly complex web-applications. Browser-based office applications or games can now replace typical desktop applications. This rapid change in the usage pattern of a browser poses a big challenge for browser implementors. The functionality of a modern browser is moving towards the responsibilities usually provided by an operating system.

Memory management and garbage collection (GC) are now a severe bottleneck within the browser and the JavaScript virtual machine (VM) executing client-side web programs. While previously browsing speed was mostly degraded by rendering and network latency, GC pause times have now become an important factor of browser performance.

Architectural changes such as multiple browser tabs have changed the way users browse the web. The underlying JavaScript execution model has not kept up with this evolution. The implementation of the memory management subsystem of JavaScript VMs do not reflect the high-level configuration of the browser. For example, high level separations such as browser tabs are not reflected in the low-level design of JavaScript VMs. As a result, web pages loaded in separate tabs encounter interference with each other in ways that affect their memory management, security and performance.

Some web browsers such as Google Chrome or Microsoft Internet Explorer 8 address this separation problem by creating a new process for each new tab or origin. This is good for security since process boundaries act like "hardware fences" between browsing instances and memory management can be handled completely separately for every tab. Chrome also spawns separate instances of the JavaScript VM for every process. Since the created browsing instances are heavyweight, Chrome limits the number of processes to 20.

There are at least two problems with this approach: Certain web features such as iframe navigation require pages to maintain references to objects belonging to other pages. In order to support this pattern, Chrome loads such pages into the same rendering process, losing any benefits of process separation along the way. Furthermore, creating a new process for every origin is not an option for environments with limited resources such as mobile devices. One of the design constraints of our new system is that the new approach has to work on the desktop as well as on the mobile version of a browser.

In order to define the problem we look at the previous implementation of the JavaScript heap in Firefox. Figure 1 depicts the JavaScript heap with some tabs open in the browser. In this example we open some tabs and load popular web pages. The objects are not separated on the heap and it is likely that all the objects from different origins interleave within the heap. A Facebook object might reside next to a CNN object for example. We also load the V8 benchmark page in order to run the JavaScript benchmarks. Interleaving objects created by benchmark pages with other objects illustrates the drawbacks of the previous implementation:

- *Bad locality*: Objects that are often accessed at the same time are not grouped together.

- *No partial GC possible*: During a GC event, every single object must be accessed.

Our research proposes a new layer of abstraction for the JavaScript heap. We split the JavaScript heap into sub-heaps, which

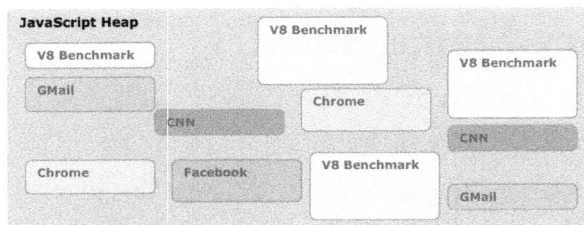

Figure 1. The previous implementation allows objects of different origins to be allocated in the same memory region.

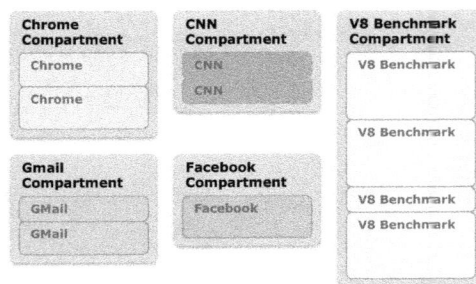

Figure 2. The new approach separates objects depending on their origin. New origins allocate a new compartment and only objects with the associated origin are placed in an arena.

we call compartments. JavaScript objects that are allocated from a certain origin are now placed into the compartment that is associated with the origin. This new abstraction level allows us to:

- Separate memory,
- Improve cache behavior, and
- Perform partial GC and therefore reduce GC pause time.

We implement our research in the open source web browser Firefox [16]. Firefox has about 400 million daily users with market share between 25% and 30% according to [24].

Having many open tabs is not unusual any more. User reports that are collected at Mozilla show that some users have 200+ open tabs. Running benchmarks in such an environment have shown drastic performance impacts. For example, the V8 benchmark score drops from 4511 to 3017 when 50 tabs are open in Firefox because the GC pause time increases dramatically. We reduce the GC pause time by 80% for such an environment. With our new approach, even users with 200+ open tabs now get the same performance as users with just one single open tab.

Our research has major improvements for performance and security. We explain some security aspects of our approach but the main focus of this paper is performance.

2. Compartments

In this section we introduce compartments representing sub-heaps in our JavaScript VM. The concept of separating data using heuristics has a long history in computer science. Applying this concept to a VM architecture for JavaScript that is embedded in a browser still raises some challenging research questions.

The JavaScript programming language is widely used for web programming. It allows web developers to extend web sites with client-side executable code. JavaScript copies many names and naming conventions from Java, but the two languages are otherwise not closely related and have different semantics. A lot of research was done in the area of memory management for Java but the results are often not applicable to JavaScript. First, there are fundamental differences between the two languages such as dynamic typing and the dynamic behavior of JavaScript programs. Second, JavaScript programs written in web pages tend to have a short execution time in comparison to Java applications. As with many dynamic languages, JavaScript objects are essentially associative arrays that lack static typing; object properties can be added and removed at runtime. JavaScript also provides a prototype-based inheritance mechanism to create complex object hierarchies.

For Firefox 4 we changed the way JavaScript objects are managed. Our JavaScript engine SpiderMonkey (sometimes also called TraceMonkey [3] and JägerMonkey, which are Spider-Monkey's trace-compilation and baseline just-in-time compilers) now supports multiple JavaScript heaps, which we also call compartments. All objects that belong to a certain origin (such as http://mail.google.com/ or http://www.bank.com/) are placed into

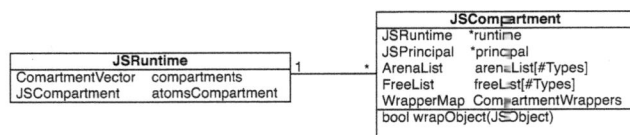

Figure 3. The runtime holds all compartments. The compartments themselves hold their corresponding principal, a list of arenas where all objects and strings are allocated, all wrappers and provide functions to wrap objects and strings

a separate compartment as shown in Figure 2. The same-origin policy [22] is the central security policy in today's browsers. The policy specifies that two documents from different origins cannot access each other's HTML documents using the DOM.

Our new compartment abstraction has a couple of implications:

1. All objects created by a page from the same origin reside within the same compartment and hence are located in the same memory region. This improves cache utilization by reducing false sharing of cache lines. False sharing occurs when we are trying to operate on an object and we have to read an entire cache line of data into the CPU cache. In the old model JavaScript objects could be co-located with arbitrary other JavaScript objects from other origins. Such cross origin objects are used together infrequently, which reduces the number of cache hits we get. In the new model most objects referenced by a website are tightly packed next to each other in memory, with no cross origin objects in between.

2. JavaScript objects (including JavaScript functions, which are objects as well) are only allowed to reference objects in the same compartment which means only same origin objects can reach each other. This invariant is useful for security purposes. The JavaScript engine enforces this requirement at a low level. It means that a google.com object can never accidentally leak into an untrusted website such as evil.com. Only a special object type can cross compartment boundaries. We call these objects wrappers. We track the creation of these cross compartment wrappers, and thus the JavaScript engine knows at all times what objects from a compartment are kept alive by outside references (through cross compartment wrappers). This allows us to garbage collect individual compartments, in addition to a global collection. We simply assume all objects referenced from outside the compartment to be live, and then walk the object graph inside the compartment. Objects that are found to be disconnected from the graph are discarded. With this new per-compartment GC we shortcut having to walk unrelated heap areas of a window (or tab) that triggered a GC.

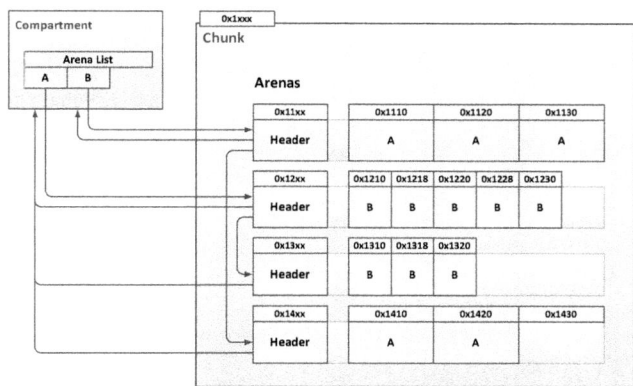

Figure 4. The basic data structures consists of 1MB chunks divided into 4KB arenas. Every arena has a header that stores basic information about the arena. The arena header also holds a reference to the corresponding compartment.

In Firefox this problem is even more pronounced than in other browsers, because our UI code (also called chrome code, not to be confused with Google Chrome) is implemented in JavaScript, and there are many chrome (UI) objects alive at any given moment. These UI objects tend to stick around and every time a web content window causes a GC, Firefox spends much time figuring out whether chrome objects are still alive instead of focusing on the active web content window.

Our design is based on an allocation model introduced by Hanson [5]. A simplified example of our memory layout is shown in Figure 4. We allocate 1MB chunks from the operating system and split them up into 4KB arenas.

Every arena has a header with basic information about the arena. With simple bit arithmetic (zeroing the last bits of each object address) we can obtain the address of the corresponding arena header. The arena header itself has a reference to the compartment it belongs to. This arrangement makes it easy and fast to lookup the corresponding compartment for each object.

Each arena holds a certain type such as strings or objects. This implies that all objects within an arena have the same size because all objects are allocated with an initial number of slots. If the objects grows beyond the initial size, additional memory has to be allocated for the object. Strings also have the same size and the actual payload is stored in dynamic memory. A free-list keeps track of all free objects within the arena and the reference to the first free object is stored in the arena header.

The compartment holds a reference to the first arena header for a certain size class and this arena header holds the reference to the next arena with the same size class for the same compartment. These links form a list of arenas which all belong to the same compartment and hold the same types. For fast allocation we have an array per compartment representing all size classes referencing the next available allocation slot in an arena or null if there are no slots available and a new arena must be allocated.

The compartments themselves live in our runtime. Compartments are created for new origins and are destroyed whenever all objects contained within become unreachable. The wrapperMap of the compartment holds all wrapper objects that intercept cross-compartment communications. The general Wrapper concept is explained in Section 3.

2.1 Allocation

Allocating an arena from a chunk now means that no other compartment can allocate objects in the same arena. In the previous

$$o1 \to o2 \Rightarrow \begin{pmatrix} c(o1) == c(o2) \\ c(o2) == AtomsCompartment \\ (o1, o2) \in WrapperMap \end{pmatrix}$$

Figure 5. An object can no longer point to an arbitrary object in the JS heap.

model, threads allocated multiple arenas from the arena list and kept them in the local thread storage. The allocation path had to be locked because other threads were also allocating arenas from the same list. After a GC, all arenas with available slots were placed on a global list and threads had to use a lock again for allocation. With the new model we can dispense with almost all the locking because arenas stay within the same compartment. After a GC we can simply traverse all arenas that already belong to a certain compartment without locking in order to allocate new objects. Once arenas are allocated they stay within the same compartment until they are empty and released.

Another popular optimization technique for JavaScript VMs is to create strings that are unique and immutable. We call them atoms but the technique is also called "interning" in Java VMs. The strings are shared between the different scripts and no other string can have the same content as the actual atomized string. The main advantage comes from string comparison where the actual content comparison can be avoided. This "sharing of strings" might become a problem since we want to have as little cross-origin references as possible. Our solution for this issue is a separate compartment for all the immutable strings. Atomized strings also do not depend on any other strings. This implies that there are no references from the atoms compartment to other compartments. Allocating atomized strings is the only place where we need fine grained locking because different threads can allocate atoms at the same time. The function that creates atomized strings locks the allocation path and ensures that only one thread is currently allocating from the atoms compartment at a time.

3. Wrappers

As mentioned before, we want to minimize the cross-compartment references. But if they become necessary, we do not allow direct communication between these two objects from separate compartments. We delegate the communication technique to a wrapper object that is explained in this section. In JavaScript we distinguish between strings and objects. Strings and objects are both heap allocated but strings cannot have cyclic dependencies.

References between objects must now follow several rules. As shown in Figure 5, an object o1 can only reference o2 if:

1. o1 and o2 reside in the same compartment and therefore have the same origin.

2. o2 is allocated from the atoms compartment meaning o2 is an immutable string.

3. o1 and o2 are in a different compartment and the VM explicitly allows this communication by adding a wrapper object representing o2 to the wrapper map in the compartment of o1.

Figure 6 shows all possible cross compartment communication mechanisms. The red dashed line represents the connection between two objects when they are in separate compartments. In the new model, each cross compartment reference is intercepted by a wrapper object that is stored in the wrapper map in each compartment. References to an atom and therefore into the atom's compartment do not need a wrapper object.

Wrappers are not a new concept in Firefox, or browsers in general. In the past they were used to regulate how windows (or

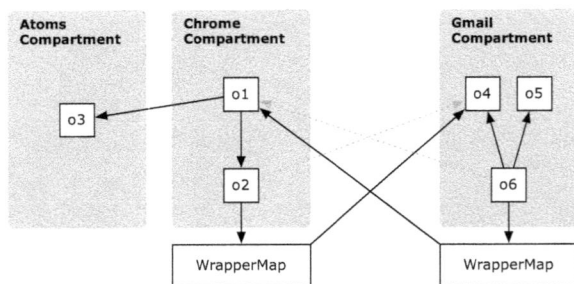

Figure 6. An overview of possible references between compartments.The red arrows represent the old way of communicating between two objects. In the new approach, we add a wrapper objects between 2 objects that reside in different compartments.

tabs) pass objects to each other. Cross-compartment Wrappers are much more than just a remembered set which is common in generational GC environments. Each wrapper is a real Proxy-Object with access-methods that are needed for security restrictions. No direct-communication between compartments is allowed. All communication between compartments must go through these wrapper objects.

When a window or iframe attempts to reference an object that belongs to a different window, we hand it a wrapper object instead. That wrapper object dynamically checks at access time whether the accessor window (also called the subject) is permitted to access the target object. For example, if one Google Mail window tries to access another Google Mail window, the access is permitted, because these two windows (or iframes) are same origin and hence it's safe to permit this access. If an untrusted website obtains a reference to a Google Mail DOM element, we hand it the same wrapper, and if it ever tries to access the Google Mail DOM Element the wrapper will, at access time, deny the property access because the untrusted website is cross origin with google.com.

A disadvantage of the Firefox 3.6 wrapper approach (which is similar to the way other browsers utilize wrappers) was the fact that these wrappers had to be injected manually at the right places in the C++ code of the browser implementation, and each wrapper had to do a dynamic security check at access time. With compartments we can do much better:

1. Since all objects belonging to the same origin are within the same compartment, and no object from a different origin is in that compartment, we can let all objects within a compartment reference other objects in the same compartment without a wrapper in between. Keep in mind that this does not just apply to windows but also to iframes. A single Google Mail session often uses dozens of iframes that all heavily exchange objects with each other. In the past we had to inject wrappers in between that continually performed security checks. This mediation is no longer necessary, and there is an observable speedup when using iframe heavy web applications such as Google Mail.

2. Since all cross origin objects are located in different compartments, any cross origin access that needs to perform a security check can only happen through a cross compartment wrapper. Such a cross compartment wrapper always lives in the source compartment, and accesses a single destination object. When we create a cross compartment wrapper, we consult with the wrapper factory to see what kind of security policy should be applied. For example, if evil.com obtains a reference to a google.com object, we create a wrapper referencing that object in the evil.com compartment. When the wrapper is created, the wrapper factory applies a stringent cross origin security policy,

which makes it impossible for evil.com to glean information from the google.com window. In contrast to our old wrappers, this security policy is static. Since only evil.com objects ever see this wrapper, and it only points to one single DOM element in the destination compartment, the policy does not have to be re-checked at access time. Instead, every time evil.com attempts to read information from the DOM element, the access is denied without even comparing the two origins.

3.1 Brain Transplants

A particularly interesting oddity of the JavaScript DOM representation is the existence of two objects for each DOM window (or tab or iframe), the inner window and the outer window. This split was implemented by web browsers a few years ago to securely handle windows navigated to a new URL. When such a navigation occurs, the inner window object inside the outer window is replaced with a new object, whereas the actual reference to window (which is the outer window) remains unchanged. If such a navigation takes the window to a new origin, we allocate the inner window in the appropriate new compartment. Of course, this action now creates a problem: The outer window might not point directly at the new window, because it is in a different compartment.

We solve this problem using brain transplants. Whenever an outer window navigates, we copy it into the new destination compartment. The object in the old compartment is transformed into a cross compartment wrapper that points to the newly created object in the destination compartment.

4. Partial GC

Having all JavaScript objects in the browser congregate in a single heap is suboptimal for a number of reasons. If a user has multiple windows (or tabs) open, and one of these windows (or tabs) created a large number of objects, it is likely that many of these objects are no longer reachable (garbage). When the browser detects such a state, it initiates a GC. Unfortunately, since objects from different windows (or tabs) are intermixed on the heap, the browser must walk the entire heap. If a number of idle windows are open, this can be quite wasteful, since those windows have not really created any garbage, so whenever a window with heavy activity triggers a GC, much of the GC time is spent walking unrelated parts of the global object graph.

The new approach allows us to perform partial-GC on single compartments. A single compartment GC or per-compartment GC is triggered whenever the allocation of a single compartment reaches some watermark that is set after a GC depending on the working set size. As a simple example, assume that a single compartment GC is triggered when 10MB of JavaScript objects are allocated. If we reach this level, we also check the overall allocation of all compartments. If the overall allocation exceeds 150% of the triggering compartment allocation (or 15ME in this example) we perform a global GC. There exist other GC triggers in the browser but they are not relevant to the per-compartment GC approach and beyond the scope of this paper. We also can not ignore of the global GC because the new approach introduces the possibility of cyclic data structures between compartments. Two objects in separate compartments that point to each other would never be collected with only per-compartment GCs since the wrapperMaps would keep them alive.

4.1 Marking

In order to find all reachable objects for a global GC we traverse the object graphs beginning with the following roots: First, we perform a conservative stack scan and mark all objects that are reachable from the native C stack. Then we mark all explicit roots that are stored in a roots hash table followed by marking all global objects.

Alias	URL
280s	280slides.com
AMAZ	amazon.com
BING	bing.com
DIGG	digg.com
EBAY	ebay.com
FBOK	facebook.com
FLKR	flickr.com
GDOC	docs.google.com
GMAP	maps.google.com
GMIL	gmail.com
GOGL	google.com
HULU	hulu.com
ISHK	imageshack.us
TECH	techcrunch.com
V8BE	V8.googlecode.com/svn/data/benchmarks/v6
YTUB	youtube.com

Table 1. Selected JavaScript-enabled web sites. All sites were visited on January 30th 2011. Some sites required an account in order to perform basic tasks.

Alias	Origin	Wrappers	IFrame	Wrappers
280s	1	26	2	85
AMAZ	4	280	16	563
BING	1	80	3	105
DIGG	3	114	3	115
EBAY	1	48	1	50
FBOK	1	249	6	445
FLKR	3	185	23	1094
GDOC	6	552	7	277
GMAP	1	88	2	82
GMIL	2	183	9	5654
GOGL	1	60	2	209
HULU	1	103	10	245
ISHK	6	776	41	1396
TECH	11	2324	154	3094
V8BE	1	35	1	35
YTUB	2	183	7	204

Table 2. Compartments and corresponding cross compartment pointers when creating new compartments per origin or per iframe.

Marking reachable objects for a single-compartment GC follows the same scheme as the marking for the global GC with one additional step. As mentioned before we assume all objects in other compartments to be alive. Since there are no direct pointers between compartments, marking all wrapper references from other compartments is sufficient to capture all reachable objects. The marking function checks every reference if the corresponding object is in the compartment currently performing the GC. Obtaining the compartment identity is done using simple pointer arithmetic and is very cheap as described in Figure 4.

4.2 Sweeping

JavaScript does not support a finalize() method as Java does. However the internal VM design calls a finalize function on every unreachable object during a GC where dynamically allocated memory for an object gets freed. The VM-API also allows overwriting this finalizer function. This is done by the browser and many embedders that use a standalone version of the JavaScript VM.

The sweeping phase for a global GC consists of traversing each arena and checking for unreachable (unmarked) objects. The advantage for a single compartment GC is that we do not have to traverse all arenas. It is sufficient to traverse only arenas that are allocated from the compartment involved in the single compartment GC since all other objects are considered alive as mentioned before. The sweeping process touches each object and checks the mark bit. If the mark bit is not set, a finalizer is called for the object and the location is added to the free list of the arena.

5. Granularity

Finding the right granularity for compartmentalizing web-content is the key for success. On the one hand we have the old approach with a single JavaScript heap and all objects regardless of their origin are intermixed in the heap. The other side of the spectrum is not that easy to define. "Web programs are easy to understand intuitively but difficult to define precisely" [20].

A web application such as GMail consists of many sub-structures. Typical components are parent-pages containing images, script-libraries, embedded frames, popup pages for chatting and messages. Placing each of these items into separate compartments would result in many compartments just for a single page like GMail. In order to argue that one compartment per origin is the right choice, we can compare it with an implementation where we separate objects based on iframes. The HTML `<iframe>` tag defines an inline frame that contains another document and is supported by all major browser vendors. The `src` attribute provides the location of the frame content which is typically an HTML document. There is no general way of telling how many iframes a web page has, but in order to compare our approach with a solution where each iframe gets its own compartment we compare typical web pages listed in Table 1. We compare our approach with an implementation that creates a new compartment for each iframe in Table 2. We can see that the finer granularity would be beneficial for some pages like Ebay and Digg, but for other pages the number of compartments increases dramatically. Techcrunch, for example, would have 154 compartments instead of 11. For GMail, the number of wrappers would increase from 183 to 5654.

6. Processes

Another question is how compartments compare to per-tab processes as they are used by Google Chrome and Internet Explorer.

Both processes and compartments shield JavaScript objects against each other. The most important distinction here is that processes offer a stronger separation enforced by the processor hardware, while compartments offer a pure software guarantee. However, compartments benefit by allowing much more efficient cross compartment communication that processes code.

With compartments, cross origin websites can still communicate with each other with a small overhead (governed by certain cross origin access policies), while with processes cross-process JavaScript object access is either impossible or extremely expensive. In the future, browsers will likely see both forms of separation being applied. Two web sites that never have to talk to each other can live in separate processes, while cross origin websites that do want to communicate can use compartments to enhance security and performance.

The space overhead can be shown by simply opening an empty tab and measuring the increased memory consumption. Opening another tab in Chrome creates a new process with about 30MB. Open another tab in Firefox is about 2.2MB and Safari about 10MB.

Another drawback that is introduced by the process level separation comes from the object communication mechanism. Two objects that want to communicate with each other have to go through an expensive inter process communication mechanism. A message sent from an object A to another object B does not have any guarantee to be received from B if there is no synchronization in place. The run-to-completion semantics defines that a state-machine has to complete processing one event before it can start processing the next.

Google Chrome supports 4 different process models: 1) monolithic process, 2) process per browsing instance, 3) process per site instance and 4) process per site. Models 1 and 2 do not provide memory protection across multiple origins. Model 3, (which is enabled by default) and model 4 still do not prevent origins that are embedded with the iframe tag from accessing objects from the parent page because they all execute in one process.

7. Evaluation

To evaluate our compartmental memory management approach, we implemented it in the open source JavaScript VM SpiderMonkey [18], which is used by Mozilla Firefox. As a result of this choice we are able to provide benchmark numbers for in-browser synthetic benchmarks as well as actual JavaScript web applications.

All experiments were performed on a Mac Pro with 2 x 2.66 GHz Dual-Core Intel Xeon processor and 4 GB RAM running MacOS 10.6 and beta version 10 of Firefox 4.0 that uses the compartments mechanisms we have introduced in this paper as its default configuration. It is easy to rerun the benchmarks by setting the `javascript.options.mem.gc_per_compartment` option in the `about:config` page of Firefox. This section uses baseline implementation, called *base*, where we only perform global GCs and per-compartment implementation or *comp*, where we also perform per-compartment GCs.

7.1 Cost in Space

The first question to answer is whether the new approach improves the memory footprint of the VM or introduces some space overhead. There are two scenarios that influence the space-overhead in a positive and negative way. Since we do not intermix objects of different origins within arenas any more, we must always allocate a new arena if all arenas are full for a certain compartment. This results in higher fragmentation because we end up allocating arenas even if there are some empty slots in arenas that belong to another compartments. On the other hand, if there are reachable objects within an arena, we cannot return the arena to the OS.

With the new approach it is more likely that objects with the same lifetime end up in the same compartment. Whenever we close a tab, the corresponding compartments including all its arenas are likely to become garbage. Once there are no reachable objects within the arenas, we can return them to the OS. In the old approach, objects from different domains might have kept arenas alive.

Figure 7 shows the difference between the old model and the new model. In this experiment, we open 50 tabs with popular web pages and close one after another with a forced GC in between. The y-axis represents the number of allocated 4KB arenas. As expected, the new approach has a higher peak demand because allocated arenas belong to a single origin. The difference for 50 tabs is, for this example, around 13% or 15MB. During the closing process, the new model shows its advantages. Since closing a tab releases all objects from a certain origin, the corresponding arenas become empty. The results of Figure 7 also show that our new approach is going towards a generational GC model. We can clearly see that objects separation based on their origin shows better results than when they are intermixed with other objects. This aspect is an interesting outcome that will lead to further investigation.

One of the key factors for our partial GC approach is the volume of missed space that does not get freed because we assume

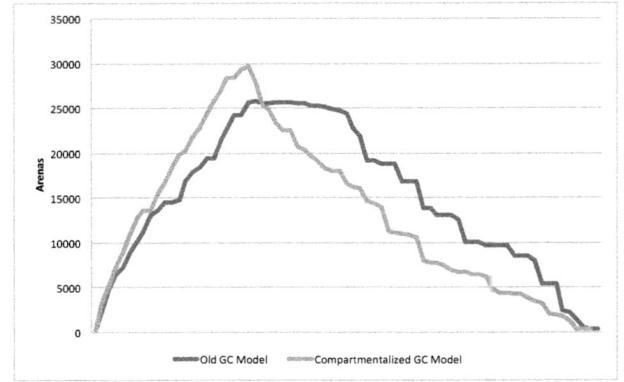

Figure 7. Opening 50 tabs and closing them again with the baseline and per-compartment approach. We can see a higher memory consumption peak for the opening process with the new approach but, once we close tabs, we also deallocate arenas faster.

all objects are reachable within this space. We changed the way our per-compartment GC works in order to get detailed information about unreclaimed objects because of our partial GC approach. Figure 8 and Figure 9 show detailed numbers for the GC workloads. We open 50 tabs in the browser with popular websites and, once all of them are fully loaded, we start the V8 benchmark suite. Whenever we would trigger a per-compartment GC, we perform a full GC but do not reclaim objects that are not part of the compartment that triggered the GC. *50 Tabs Reachable* represents all objects that are reachable in the JavaScript VM excluding the compartment where the V8 benchmark runs. *V8 Reachable* represents all objects that are reachable within the compartment that triggered the per-compartment GC (V8 compartment). This number also represents the marking workload for the partial GC.

Finalized represents all objects that are finalized during the GC event. *Missed* represents the number of unreachable objects that are not reclaimed because of the per-compartment GC.

Relative values are calculated as follows:

$$Reachable\ Rel. = \frac{V8\ Reachable}{50\ Tabs + V8\ Reachable} * 100\%$$

$$Missed\ Rel. = \frac{Missed}{Finalized} * 100\%$$

$$Rel.\ to\ Total = \frac{Missed}{Missed + Finalized + 50\ Tabs + V8\ Reachable} * 100\%$$

The first three GCs are global GCs and happen during loading of the 50 tabs. Once we start the V8 benchmark suite we see only compartment GCs until we shut down the browser. The shutdown process performs the last three global GCs.

Reachable Rel. is 0 for the first global GCs. After we start the V8 benchmark suite it is between 0.5% and 1%. For the Earley-Boyer benchmark we see a triangle allocation scheme and Reachable Rel. alternates between 1.5% and 7%. Only during the Splay benchmark, where a huge splay tree is created and modified, does the actual reachable objects within the V8 compartment represent around 60% of the whole browser heap.

More interesting is the ratio between finalized and missed objects. We can see that, during the benchmark, we create around 3% (Missed Rel.) garbage in other compartments that is not reclaimed. At GC event 37, we see a finalization spike during the Splay benchmark. This indicates that we perform a GC that does not free any memory and we have to increase the heap. The following GC events finalize around 4.5 million objects, but this is not shown due to readability of the graph.

124

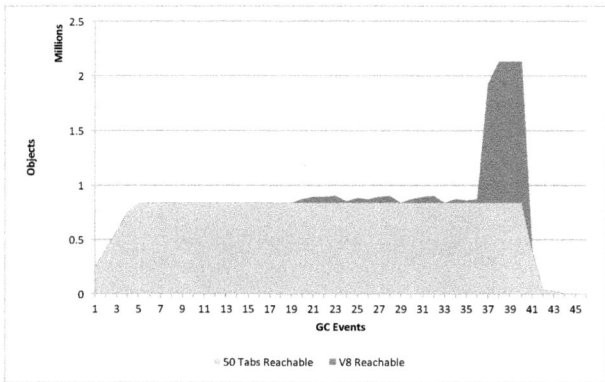

Figure 8. Reachable objects when opening 50 tabs and running the V8 benchmarks. *50 Tabs Reachable* includes all compartments except the compartment where the V8 benchmark runs. *Comp Reachable* means all reachable objects within the V8 compartment.

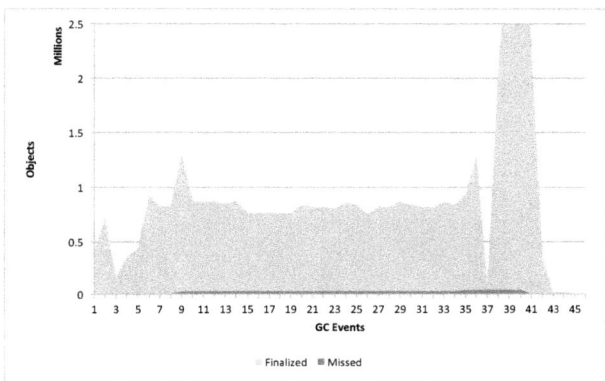

Figure 9. Finalized objects when opening 50 tabs and running the V8 Benchmarks. *Missed* represents the number of unreachable objects that fail to reclaim in other compartments because we only perform per-compartment GC.

Rel. to Total measures the ratio between total heap space and Missed to Finalized. We can see that we only miss to reclaim about 2% of the heap space because of the per-compartment GCs. Note that the number of GC events differs from the results in Table 3 because our instrumentation increased the GC pause time and therefore also influenced the benchmark scores.

7.2 V8 Benchmark

The V8 suite runs each benchmark for one second and computes a score per benchmark and an overall score based on each individual score. Since the benchmark runs for one second, the amount of memory that is used varies. An allocation-heavy benchmark allocates more objects and therefore more memory in the same amount of time if the allocation becomes faster and GC time is reduced. We also performed VM internal measurements in order to discuss the GC events happening during running the V8 benchmarks in more detail. We use the time stamp counter `rdtsc` [9] in order to measure the duration of each GC event.

Table 4 shows the results for running the V8 benchmarks for the baseline and our new approach. We can see that the reduced workload due to the partial GC increased the number of performed GCs from 63 to 75. The total time spent in marking increases because we perform more GCs but the average time spent in marking

	1 Base	1 Comp	50 Base	50 Comp
Richards	7929	7932	8211	8084
DeltaBlue	4198	5263	2142	4985
Crypto	8634	8598	8779	8596
RayTrace	3510	3527	1698	3464
EarleyBoyer	4357	4550	1514	3807
RegExp	1711	1692	1624	1651
Splay	5012	5134	3529	5041
Score	4505	4692	3017	4511

Table 3. Results of the V8 benchmark suite (higher is better). The numbers represent running the benchmark suite in a single tab for the baseline and per-compartment approach (Comp) and opening 50 typical web pages and running the benchmark suite for the baseline and per-compartment GC approach.

	Base	Average	Comp	Average	Relative
GC Events	63	-	75	-	+16%
Marking	2891	46	3075	41	-12%
Sweeping	2693	43	3319	44	+3.4%
Total	6117	97	6583	88	-11%

Table 4. Basic internal measurements for the V8 benchmark. The numbers represent 1E6 cycles measured with `rdtsc`.

reduces around 12%. The increase in finalization time results from the fact that more objects must be finalized. As explained in Section 4, we also check the mark bit of every single object during sweeping. Since we encounter fewer marked objects and more unreachable objects, the time spent in finalization increases. Marking fewer objects and finalizing more objects indicates a good separation technique.

Figure 10 through Figure 13 show the mark-to-sweep ratio for each GC event for the V8 benchmarks. Figure 10 shows the marking and sweeping ratio for starting the browser, running the V8 benchmarks and closing the browser again with our baseline approach. Figure 11 shows the marking and sweeping ratio with our new per-compartment GC model. We can see that even for a single tab we reduce the time spent in marking because we only perform the GC in the benchmark compartment and do not include the browser internal chrome compartment. Table 3 shows that the benchmark score increases from 4505 to 4692 for a single open tab. The big spike almost near the end is caused by the allocation intensive Splay benchmark. The finalization spike at the end is caused by the shutdown of the browser.

The real strength of the new approach shines with many open tabs. Figure 12 and Figure 13 show the mark-sweep ratio with 50 other open tabs. We start the browser, open 50 tabs, wait until they are fully loaded and start the V8 benchmark in a new tab. We can see that marking time dominates the GC pause time in Figure 12. If we compare this time to Figure 13 we can clearly see the improvements. We perform global GCs at the beginning because we open many web pages and the overall memory footprint increases. Once we start the V8 benchmark we see that the per-compartment GC is triggered because only the benchmark origin creates objects. There is one spike in the middle of the benchmark where the browser decides to perform a global GC. This is either caused by internal timers of the browser or an overall increase of the memory footprint. We can see that the time is identical to the baseline approach for this single spike. Table 3 shows that the benchmark score increases from 3017 to 4511.

125

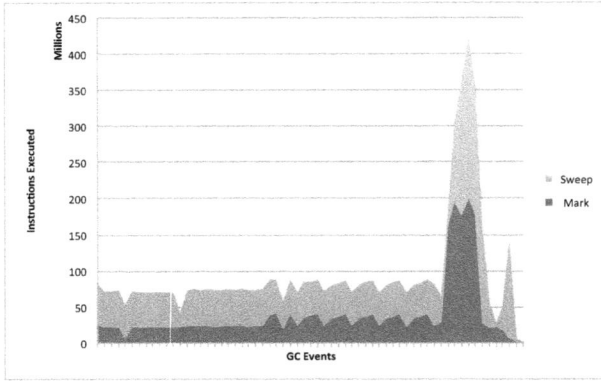

Figure 10. Running the V8 Benchmark Suite with a single tab using baseline approach. The y-axis shows a stacked representation of cycles measured with `rtdsc`.

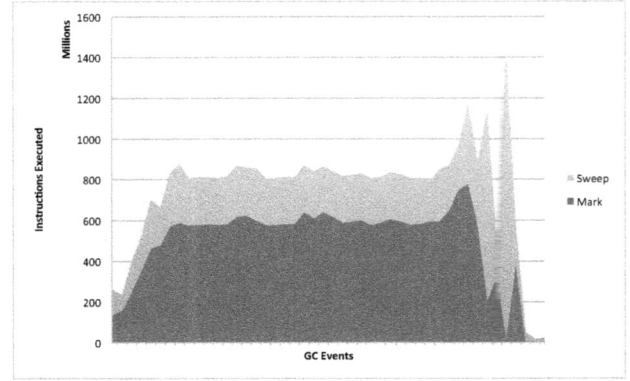

Figure 12. Opening 50 tabs with popular web pages and running the V8 Benchmark Suite using baseline approach. The y-axis shows a stacked representation of cycles measured with `rtdsc`.

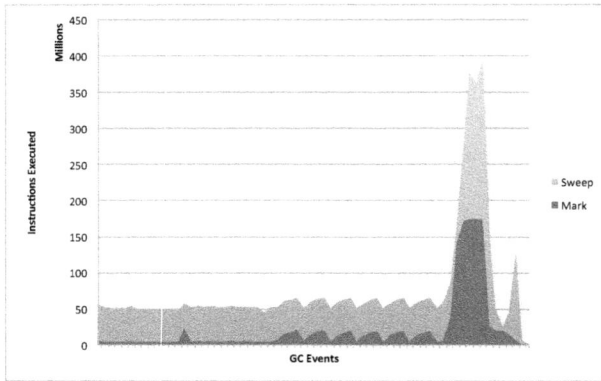

Figure 11. Running the V8 Benchmark Suite with a single tab using per-compartment GC.

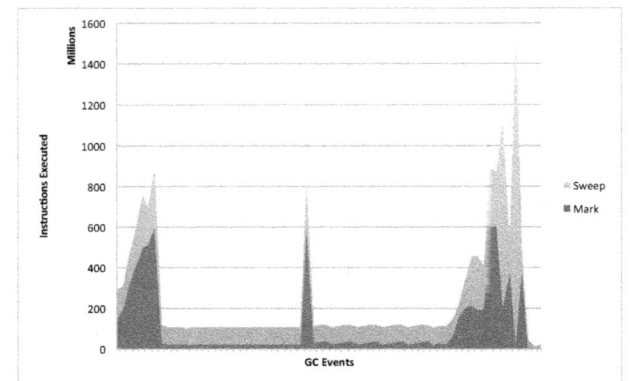

Figure 13. Opening 50 tabs with popular web pages and running the V8 Benchmark Suite using the new per-compartment GC.

Running the benchmark with an additional 50 open tabs now reaches the same performance as running the benchmark in a single tab without our new model. The average number of cycles for each GC event reduces from 885E6 to 294E6. If we only consider the interval where the benchmark is running and exclude the start and shutdown overhead, we reduce the average numbers of cycles 83%, from 998E6 to 170E6.

7.3 Kraken Benchmarks

Table 5 shows the Kraken benchmark [17] results. The benchmark was executed in a browser with websites loaded from Table 1 except the V8 benchmark suite. We can see an overall performance increase from 6.9% due to shorter GC pause times. The *Base* column represents the baseline and the *Comp* column represents the per-compartment GC approach. The new approach also introduces more stability for the individual benchmarks. As can be seen in Table 5, the random noise for the individual benchmarks is reduced.

7.4 SunSpider Benchmarks

We claim to improve locality of reference with our new approach. Since we do not allocate objects in already used arenas from another compartment and rather allocate a new arena, we place objects near other objects from the same origin. Running the SunSpider benchmark suite is an indicator for a better locality during the benchmark run because there is no GC event during the benchmark. Also the locking that is removed for arena allocation increases per-

formance. The benchmark suite executes all benchmarks 10 times with a forced GC in between that does not impact the benchmark scores. SunSpider is a time based benchmark suite where actual execution time is measured. Table 6 shows the results of the SunSpider benchmarks. We can see a 3% improvement with the new allocation scheme.

7.5 Non-Benchmarks

Reducing the GC pause time also has other advantages over increasing benchmark scores. An everyday Firefox user cares more about the performance for real workloads. Our new approach greatly improves the performance of all allocation heavy web apps such as JavaScript based animations and games. The GC pause time during an animation is no longer related to the number of open tabs and users do not have to close all other tabs in order to get the best performance for JavaScript based games.

8. Related Work

Jones and Lins [10] describe basic GC algorithms that are also used in our implementation. The current implementation of the memory management system in SpiderMonkey is based on the research from Hanson [5]. Mark and sweep GC implementations have a long history [13] and we do not claim to reinvent any of the basic ideas. We show how a new layer of abstraction can reduce the workload for such systems and make a real difference for every Firefox user.

Benchmark	Base [ms]	+/- [%]	Comp [ms]	+/- [%]
astar	1236.3	5.0	1182.7	5.8
beat-detection	457.0	12.9	418.5	3.4
dft	496.8	13.2	473.5	3.6
fft	343.2	13.5	348.6	3.7
oscillator	290.8	0.7	290.8	0.7
gaussian-blur	492.5	0.2	492.0	0.2
darkroom	221.7	0.5	221.0	0.2
desaturate	487.6	5.1	477.1	0.2
parse-financial	131.3	32.7	111.8	1.3
stringify-tb	96.2	51.2	71.8	2.3
aes	231.6	23.4	234.8	9.4
ccm	154.5	2.1	161.3	8.2
pbkdf2	313.4	23.8	237.6	7.4
sha256-it	198.2	39.0	95.9	2.7
TOTAL	5151.1	1.8	4817	1.7

Table 5. Kraken benchmarks

Our approach can also be described as a simplified version of distributed GC. The Emerald system [11, 12] supports moving objects between physically different nodes. Our solution differs in two ways: All the objects stay in the same process even if they are moved from one compartment to another, and a global GC still performs a GC on the whole heap rather than performing mark and sweep on each individual compartment.

Optimizing allocation patterns to improve the locality of reference in the virtual memory [19] and cache [14] has been studied over many years. Basic implementation like the "first-fit" approach [13] or improvements like the "better-fit" approach [25] still show bad reference locality characteristics. We use object separation based on their origin to obtain better reference locality. For example, internal objects created from chrome code no longer share pages with objects allocated from web sites.

Reis et al. [20] show the various process models supported by Google Chrome. They compare different process isolation models (monolithic process, process-per-browsing-instance, process-per-site and process-per-site-instance) that are all supported by Google Chrome. In contrast to our work, they attempt to create new processes for new domains. A more detailed discussion about the differences can be found in Section 6.

Microsoft [15] also uses OS processes to isolate tabs from one another in Internet Explorer 8. This protection mechanism is insufficient from a security standpoint since a user may browse multiple mutually distrusting sites in a single tab via iframes.

In more recent work from Microsoft Research, Wang et al. [26] present a secure web browser constructed as a multi-principal OS. The browser is called Gazelle and its kernel is an operating system that exclusively manages resource protection and sharing across web site principals. The main drawback is the performance. The page load time for a site like nytimes.com increases to around 6 seconds.

Hirzel et al. [7] do an interesting analysis on the connectivity of heap objects. They show the importance of understanding the connectivity of the heap objects and give hints on improving existing partition models. Their research is focused on Java but the overall connectivity idea is also relevant for JavaScript. Hirzel [6] also shows in his PhD thesis a connectivity based GC approach that relies on object connectivity analysis. Similar to our approach they try to place objects with the same lifetime and access frequency in the same memory area called "partition".

The Beltway [1] system also separates objects in "belts" with the main focus on comparing generational GC aspects.

Benchmark	Base [ms]	Comp [ms]	Speedup [%]
cube:	16.1	15.7	2.48
morph:	16.1	15.8	1.86
raytrace:	36.5	36.2	0.82
binary-trees:	19.9	19.1	4.02
fannkuch:	13	12.9	0.77
nbody:	4	4	0.00
nsieve:	5	5	0.00
3bit-bits-in-byte:	0.5	0.5	0.00
bits-in-byte:	6.7	6.7	0.00
bitwise-and:	1.3	1.2	7.69
nsieve-bits:	4.3	4.2	2.33
recursive:	21.3	20.9	1.88
aes:	10.5	10.3	1.90
md5:	5.3	5.2	1.89
sha1:	2.6	2.6	0.00
format-tofte:	20.1	19.4	3.48
format-xparb:	13.4	12.8	4.48
cordic:	8.3	4.6	44.58
partial-sums:	7.9	7.8	1.27
spectral-norm:	3.2	3.2	0.00
dna:	11.8	11.9	-0.85
base64:	3.3	3.1	6.06
fasta:	12.4	12.7	-2.42
tagcloud:	22.4	21.4	4.46
unpack-code:	29.6	28.9	2.36
validate-input:	5.3	4.9	7.55
TOTAL	300.7	291.1	3.19

Table 6. SunSpider benchmarks.

Seidl et al. [23] present a profile-driven object lifetime and access frequency predictor. They reduce the number of page faults by placing highly referenced objects next to each other on a small set of pages. Short lived objects on the other hand, are placed on a small set of different pages.

Cox et al. [2] use multiple VMs to completely isolate web applications. They present a solution to prevent cross origin communication with an overhead of up to 9 seconds to start a new browsing instance.

Grier et al. [4] present the OP web browser which is based on a browser- level information-flow tracking system. It enables them to analyze browser-based attacks after they have happened and show the possible root of the attack.

More recently, Inoue et al. [8] made a study of memory management for web-based applications on multicore processors. They compare a traditional and a region-based memory allocator for PHP applications and show speedups of up to 27%. They introduce a freeAll function that can be called from an application once all of the objects on the heap can be deallocated.

Richards et al. [21] present a study of currently used JavaScript benchmarks. They compare the behavior of V8 and SunsSpider benchmarks with popular web pages. One of the outcomes of this research is that the overall lifetime of benchmark objects is not comparable to actual web pages.

9. Conclusions

We demonstrated the advantages and an efficient implementation of per-compartment GC. We add another layer of abstraction to the JavaScript heap and separate JavaScript data based on their origin. Partial GC on a single compartment reduces the workload for the GC and therefor reduces the GC pause time. Our experiments show that the GC pause time for running the V8 benchmarks with 50 other open tabs is reduced by up to 83%.

The foundation we laid with the compartments work will also enable a number of future extensions. Since we now cleanly separate objects belonging to different tabs, future changes to our JavaScript engine will permit us to not only perform JavaScript GC for individual compartments, but we will also be able to do so in the background on a different thread for tabs with inactive content.

Our implementation is the default configuration for the current release version 4 of Firefox. It greatly improves the internet experience of several hundred million people every day.

Acknowledgments

We want to thank Jason Orendorff and Blake Kaplan from Mozilla that worked hard in order to make this research happening. Michael Bebenita and Mason Chang from UC Irvine gave valuable feedback. Other important help came from the Mozilla community. They tested our approach, reported bugs and helped us fixing them.

References

[1] S. M. Blackburn, R. Jones, K. S. McKinley, and J. E. B. Moss. Beltway: getting around garbage collection gridlock. In *Proceedings of the ACM SIGPLAN Conference on Programming Language Design and Implementation*, pages 153–164. ACM Press, 2002. doi: 10.1145/512529.512548.

[2] R. S. Cox, S. D. Gribble, H. M. Levy, and J. G. Hansen. A safety-oriented platform for web applications. In *Proceedings of the IEEE Symposium on Security and Privacy*, pages 350–364. IEEE Computer Society, 2006. doi: 10.1109/SP.2006.4.

[3] A. Gal, B. Eich, M. Shaver, D. Anderson, D. Mandelin, M. R. Haghighat, B. Kaplan, G. Hoare, B. Zbarsky, J. Orendorff, J. Ruderman, E. W. Smith, R. Reitmaier, M. Bebenita, M. Chang, and M. Franz. Trace-based just-in-time type specialization for dynamic languages. In *Proceedings of the ACM SIGPLAN Conference on Programming Language Design and Implementation*, pages 465–478. ACM Press, 2009. doi: 10.1145/1542476.1542528.

[4] C. Grier, S. Tang, and S. T. King. Secure web browsing with the OP web browser. In *Proceedings of the IEEE Symposium on Security and Privacy*, pages 402–416. IEEE Computer Society, 2008. doi: 10.1109/SP.2008.19.

[5] D. R. Hanson. Fast allocation and deallocation of memory based on object lifetimes. *Software - Practice and Experience*, 20(1):5–12, 1990. doi: 10.1002/spe.4380200104.

[6] M. Hirzel. *Connectivity-Based Garbage Collection*. PhD thesis, Department of Computer Science, University of Colorado at Boulder, 2004.

[7] M. Hirzel, J. Henkel, A. Diwan, and M. Hind. Understanding the connectivity of heap objects. In *Proceedings of the International Symposium on Memory Management*, pages 36–49. ACM Press, 2002. doi: 10.1145/512429.512435.

[8] H. Inoue, H. Komatsu, and T. Nakatani. A study of memory management for web-based applications on multicore processors. In *Proceedings of the ACM SIGPLAN Conference on Programming Language Design and Implementation*, pages 386–396. ACM Press, 2009. doi: 10.1145/1542476.1542520.

[9] Intel. Using the RDTSC instruction for performance monitoring, 1997.

[10] R. Jones and R. Lins. *Garbage Collection: Algorithms for Automatic Dynamic Memory Management*. John Wiley & Sons, Inc., 1996.

[11] E. Jul, H. Levy, N. Hutchinson, and A. Black. Fine-grained mobility in the Emerald system. *ACM Transactions on Computer Systems*, 6 (1):109–133, 1988. doi: 10.1145/35037.42182.

[12] N. C. Juul and E. Jul. Comprehensive and robust garbage collection in a distributed system. In *Proceedings of the International Workshop on Memory Management*, pages 103–115. LNCS Volume 637, Springer-Verlag, 1992. doi: 10.1007/BFb0017185.

[13] D. E. Knuth. *Fundamental Algorithms, The Art of Computer Programming, chapter 2*, volume 1. Addison Wesley, 2nd edition, 1973.

[14] S. McFarling. Program optimization for instruction caches. In *Proceedings of the International Conference on Architectural Support for Programming Languages and Operating Systems*, pages 183–191. ACM Press, 1989. doi: 10.1145/70082.68200.

[15] Microsoft. What's new in Internet Explorer 8, 2008. URL http://msdn.microsoft.com/en-us/library/cc288472.aspx.

[16] Mozilla. Firefox web browser and Thunderbird email client, 2011. URL http://www.mozilla.com.

[17] Mozilla. Kraken JavaScript benchmark, 2011. URL http://krakenbenchmark.mozilla.org/.

[18] Mozilla. SpiderMonkey (JavaScript-C) engine, 2011. URL http://www.mozilla.org/js/spidermonkey/.

[19] J. Peachey, R. Bunt, and C. Colbourn. Some empirical observations on program behavior with applications to program restructuring. *IEEE Transactions on Software Engineering*, 11(2):188–93, 1985. doi: 10.1109/TSE.1985.232193.

[20] C. Reis and S. D. Gribble. Isolating web programs in modern browser architectures. In *Proceedings of the European Conference on Computer Systems*, pages 219–232. ACM Press, 2009. doi: 10.1145/1519065.1519090.

[21] G. Richards, S. Lebresne, B. Burg, and J. Vitek. An analysis of the dynamic behavior of JavaScript programs. In *Proceedings of the ACM SIGPLAN Conference on Programming Language Design and Implementation*, pages 1–12. ACM Press, 2010. doi: 10.1145/1806596.1806598.

[22] J. Rudermann. The same origin policy, 2001. URL https://developer.mozilla.org/En/Same_origin_policy_for_JavaScript.

[23] M. L. Seidl and B. G. Zorn. Segregating heap objects by reference behavior and lifetime. In *Proceedings of the International Conference on Architectural Support for Programming Languages and Operating Systems*, pages 12–23. ACM Press, 1998. doi: 10.1145/291069.291012.

[24] StatCounter. Global Stats, 2011. URL http://gs.statcounter.com/.

[25] C. J. Stephenson. Fast fits: New methods for dynamic storage allocation. In *Proceedings of the ACM Symposium on Operating Systems Principles*, pages 30–32. ACM Press, 1983. doi: 10.1145/800217.806613.

[26] H. J. Wang, C. Grier, E. Moshchuk, S. T. King, E. Choudhury, and H. Venter. The multi-principal OS construction of the Gazelle web browser. In *Proceedings of the USENIX Security Symposium*, pages 417–432. USENIX, 2009.

Integrated Symbol Table, Engine and Heap
Memory Management in Multi-Engine Prolog

Paul Tarau

Department of Computer Science and Engineering
University of North Texas
tarau@cse.unt.edu

Abstract

We describe an integrated solution to symbol, heap and logic engine memory management in a context where exchanges of arbitrary Prolog terms occur between multiple dynamically created engines, implemented in a new Java-based experimental Prolog system.

As our symbols represent not just Prolog atoms, but also handles to Java objects (including arbitrary size integers and decimals), everything is centered around a symbol garbage collection algorithm ensuring that external objects are shared and exchanged between logic engines efficiently.

Taking advantage of a *tag-on-data* heap representation of Prolog terms, our algorithm performs in-place updates of live symbol references directly on heap cells.

With appropriate fine tuning of collection policies our algorithm provides an integrated memory management solution for Prolog systems, with amortized cost dominated by normally occurring heap garbage collection costs.

Categories and Subject Descriptors D.3.4 [*PROGRAMMING LANGUAGES*]: Processors—Memory management; D.3.2 [*PROGRAMMING LANGUAGES*]: Language Classifications—Constraint and logic languages

General Terms Languages, Performance, Algorithms, Design

Keywords atom garbage collection, Prolog memory management, multi-engine Prolog, Prolog runtime system architecture, integrated memory management

1. Introduction

Most Prolog implementations use variants of the Warren Abstract Machine (WAM) architecture [1] that provides efficient compilation of unification, backtracking and indexing operations. In the WAM, Prolog terms, built of function symbols (called *functors*), having as arguments constant symbols and variables, are represented on a heap using references (pointers in C and integer indices in Java) to their sub-terms. References to symbols are tagged integers pointing to entries in a symbol table that can acquire new symbols at run-time, leading to the need for symbol garbage collection mechanisms.

Symbol garbage collection is important in practical applications of programming languages that rely on internalized symbols as their main building blocks. In the case of Prolog, applications as diverse as natural language tools, XML processors, database interfaces and compilers rely on dynamic symbols (atoms in Prolog parlance) to represent everything from tokens and graph vertices to predicate and function names. A task as simple as scanning for a single Prolog clause in a large data file can break a Prolog system not enabled with symbol garbage collection.

The use in the implementation language of packages providing arbitrary length integers and decimals to support such data types in Prolog, brings in similar memory management challenges. While it is common practice in Prolog implementations to represent fixed size numerical data directly on the heap (given the benefits of quick memory reclamation on backtracking), conversion from arbitrary size integers or decimals to serialized heap representations tends to be costly and can add complexity to the implementation. While serialization can be avoided in C-based systems using pointers to "blobs" on the Prolog heap and type castings, this is not an option in strongly typed Java, where such data would need to be put on the Prolog heap (an `int` array) in a serialized form, incurring significant processing time and memory costs. For instance, under 64 bit Java 1.6.x, the BigInteger representation of 0 is serialized to as much as 202 bytes and its BigDecimal 0.0 to 290 bytes. Not counting conversion time, the memory impact is itself prohibitive.

Such problems can become particularly severe in multi-engine Prolog (defined here roughly as any Prolog system with multiple heap/stack/trail data areas) where design decisions on symbol memory management are unavoidably connected to decisions on symbol sharing mechanisms and engine life-cycle management. It is also important in this scenario to support sharing of data objects among engines and avoid copying between heaps as well as serialization/deserialization costs of potentially large objects.

Often, reference counting mechanisms have been used for symbol garbage collection. A major problem is that if the symbol table is used for non-atomic objects like handles to logic engines or complex Java objects that may also refer to other such handles, cycles formed by dead objects may go undetected. For instance, a Prolog clause can be contained in and can refer to an external HashMap while holding a handle to it. Another problem is that reference counting involves extensive changes to existing code - as every single use of a given variable in a built-in needs to be made aware of it.

These considerations suggest the need for an integrated solution to symbol and engine garbage collection as well as exchange of arbitrary Prolog terms between multiple engines.

This paper describes the implementation of such a solution in our ongoing *Lean Prolog* system that supports sharing of arbitrary size external data, as divers as collections, graphs, GUI components, arbitrary precision integers and decimals, between multiple logic engines.

Beyond Prolog implementation, our techniques are likely to be reusable for other scripting or domain specific languages implemented in languages like Java or C#.

We will discuss our design decisions and algorithms in the context of *Lean Prolog*'s lightweight BinWAM-based [13, 14, 22] runtime system, a minimalist Java kernel using logic engines as first class building blocks encapsulated as *interactors* [20, 23].

One might still legitimately ask: why do we need heap and symbol garbage collection in a Java-based Prolog implementation, when, by using Java objects to represent Prolog terms, Java itself provides automatic memory management?

The original reason for dropping this scenario, implemented as the compilation model used by jProlog, a BinWAM-based research prototype written by Bart Demoen in collaboration with the author back in 1996, [6], and some of its derivatives like Prolog Cafe [2] or P# [5], is that Java objects are too heavyweight for basic Prolog abstract machine functions. We have observed that a relatively plain, C-style integer based runtime system performs an order of magnitude faster than one using terms represented as Java objects, especially in the presence of "just-in-time" and "HotSpot" java compilers. The reader will find specific figures supporting our design decisions in section 5.

Unfortunately, giving up on Java objects for a low-level Bin-WAM engine [15, 24] meant also having to manage memory directly. On one hand, as an advantage, the Java-based *Lean Prolog* model can be moved seamlessly to faster languages like C or Google's new go language [1]. On the other hand, memory management becomes almost as complex as in C-based Prologs. In the case of our *Lean Prolog* implementation, this involves dynamic array management as well as heap and symbol garbage collection, the last task including also recovery of memory used by unreachable logic engines.

Fortunately, a number of simplifications of our runtime architecture, like separation of engines and threads (subsection 2.2) and a *tag-on-data* term representation (subsection 2.3) allow for *naive* shortcuts to potentially tricky memory management decisions within good performance margins. Some of these decisions also lead to additional benefits like efficient engine-to-engine communication and a uniform handling, *as symbols*, of arbitrary external objects including maps, arbitrary size numbers and logic engines (subsection 2.4).

As our approach to dynamic data areas and heap garbage collection (abbreviated from now on GC) is similar to typical Prolog systems, our focus will be on the symbol GC policy and algorithm and its integration with other memory management tasks.

The paper is organized as follows.

Section 2 overviews aspects of architecture of *Lean Prolog* that are relevant for the decisions involved in the design of our symbol GC algorithm and policy. Section 3 first outlines in subsection 3.1, and then describes the major components of the symbol GC algorithm (3.2 opportunity detection, 3.3 work delegated to engines, and 3.4 work in the class implementing the atom table). Subsection 3.5 focuses on the "fine tuning" of our symbol GC policy. Section 4 discusses interaction with multi-threading. Section 5 provides evidence supporting some of our design decisions and discusses an empirical evaluation of the costs and benefits of the integration of symbol GC with other memory management tasks. Finally, sections 6 and 7 discuss related work and conclude the paper.

---

[1] In fact, a C variant of *Lean Prolog* is now in the works, already covering pure Prolog + CUT + engines after just a few weeks of effort.

2. Architectural aspects of *Lean Prolog*

We briefly overview the architecture of our Prolog implementation as it is relevant to the description of the memory management aspects that the paper will explore in detail.

Lean Prolog is based on a compositional, agent oriented architecture, centered around a minimalistic Java-based kernel and autonomous computational entities called *Interactors*. They encapsulate in a single API stateful objects as diverse as first class logic engines, Prolog's dynamic database, the interactive Prolog console, as well as various stream processors ranging from tokenizers and parsers to process-to-process and thread-to-thread communication layers. The Java-based kernel is extended with a parser, a compiler and a set of built-ins written in Prolog that together add as little as 40-50K of compressed Prolog byte-code. This design fits easily within the memory constraints of the hundred millions of resource limited embedded Java processors found in today's mobile appliances as well as those using Google's new Java-centered Android operating system.

2.1 The Multi-Engine API

Our *Engines-as-Interactors API* has evolved progressively into a practical Prolog implementation framework starting with [17] and continued with [20] and [23]. We will summarize it here while focusing on the interoperation of Logic Engines.

A *Logic Engine* is simply a Prolog language processor reflected through an API that allows its computations to be controlled interactively from another *Engine* very much the same way a programmer controls Prolog's interactive top-level loop: launch a new goal, ask for a new answer, interpret it, react to it. Each *Logic Engine* runs a lightweight Prolog interpreter on a given clause database, together with a set of built-in operations. Engines are designed to interoperate with external resources in a modular way, to provide additional functionality ranging from GUI components and IO to multithreading and remote computations.

The API provides commands for creating a new Prolog engine encapsulated as an `Interactor`, which shares code with the currently running program and is initialized with a given goal as a starting point.

Upon request from their parent (a `get` operation), engines return *instances of an answer pattern* (usually a list of variables occurring in the goal), but *they may also return Prolog terms at arbitrary points in their execution*. In both cases, they suspend, waiting for new requests from their parent. After interpreting the terms received from an engine, the parent can, at will, resume or stop it. Such mechanisms are used, for instance, to implement exceptions at source level [17].

The operations described so far allow an engine to return answers from any point in its computation sequence, in particular when computed answers are found. An engine's parent can also *inject* new goals (executable data) to an arbitrary inner context of an engine with help of primitives used for sending a parent's data to an engine and for receiving a parent's data [21, 23].

Note that bindings are not propagated to the original goal i.e. fresh instances are *copied* between heaps. Therefore, backtracking in the parent interpreter does not interfere with the new Interactor's iteration over answers. Backtracking over the Interactor's creation point, as such, makes it unreachable and therefore subject to garbage collection.

2.2 Decoupling engines and threads

A typical "cooperative" multitasking use case of the engine API is as follows:

1. the *parent* creates and initializes a new *engine*

2. the parent triggers computations in the *engine* as follows:

(a) the *parent* passes a new goal to the *engine* then issues a `get` operation that yields control to the engine

(b) the *engine* starts a computation from its initial goal or the point where it has been suspended and possibly integrates (a copy of) a new goal or new data received from its *parent*

(c) the *engine* returns (a copy of) the answer, then suspends and returns control to its *parent*

3. the *parent* interprets the answer and proceeds with its next computation step

4. the process is fully reentrant and the *parent* may repeat it from an arbitrary point in its computation

As described in [17, 20, 23], the Interactor API encapsulates the essential building blocks that one needs beyond Horn Clause logic to build a practical Prolog system, mostly at source level. Prolog built-ins like `findall`, `setof`, `copy_term`, `catch/throw`, `assert/retract` etc. can be all covered at source level, and even if performance considerations require faster native implementations, one can use the source level variants as specifications for testing and debugging.

An important feature of our *Lean Prolog* implementation is the decoupling of *engines* and *threads* [21]. While it is possible to launch a logic engine as a separate thread, they are also heavily used in some built-ins like `findall`, that collects to a list all answers produced by a goal. Interestingly, our engine-based `findall` is about twice as fast as a direct findall implementation in which Prolog terms are saved as Java objects to an external ArrayList, as engine-to-engine communication uses significantly more compact heap representations.

The decoupling of engines and threads removes the need of thread synchronization in cases where engines are used in sequential or cooperative multitasking operations and allows for organizing multi-threading as a separate layer where synchronization and symbol garbage collection are aware of each other.

2.3 The *tag-on-data* term representation

When describing the data in a heap cell with a tag that indicates its type (variable, symbol, integer) we have basically 2 possibilities. One can put a tag in the same cell as the address of the data (pointer) or near the data itself.

The first possibility, probably most popular among WAM implementors, allows one to check the tag before deciding *if* and *how* a term has to be processed. Like in our previous Prolog implementations [16, 18, 19] we choose the second possibility, which also supports a form of term compression [24].

At the same time, it is convenient to precompute a functor in the code-space as a word of the form `<arity, symbol-number, tag>` and then simply compare it with objects on the heap or in registers[2]. Only 2 bits are used in *Lean Prolog* for tagging variables, small integers and functors/atoms. With this representation a functor or atom fits completely in one word:

arity	symbol-number	2-bit tag

As an interesting consequence, useful for symbol GC, the "tag-on-data" representation makes scanning the heap for symbols (and updating them in place) a trivial operation.

2.4 The case for internalizing all Java objects as symbols

Besides Prolog's atoms and functors, various Java objects can be *internalized* by mapping them to integers using hashing. Such integers are much "lighter" than Java's objects i.e. once one makes

sure that a unique integer is assigned to each external object at creation time, using them in Prolog operations like unification or indexing becomes quite efficient. For instance the term `f(X,Y)` would take 12 bytes in a WAM representation with 32-bit word size. The equivalent Java term would contain a functor object made of a string `"f"` and an array of length 2 containing arguments `X` and `Y` which in turn would be distinct variable objects containing an `int` field each. Assuming (conservatively, with a 32 bit JVM in mind) that the size of an object is 8 bytes + 4 bytes for each instance fields, we get `12 bytes` for `X` and `Y` each, `16 bytes` for `f/2` and 20 bytes for its argument array for a total of `12+12+16+20=60` bytes, not counting alignment constraints and possibly larger data sizes on a 64 bit JVM. The ratio between memory representations leads to comparable slowdowns of execution time. This justifies our design choice to use integer array representations for Prolog terms, and consequently a symbol table to interface between Java objects and their heap representations. Like in the case of Java's interning of a `String`, a single copy of the same Prolog symbol is shared and referenced as an `int` index in the symbol table, resulting in faster equality testing and memory savings.

Once the decision to have a symbol garbage collector is made, a number of consequences on the implementation follow, that break away from the design choices one would make in a typical C-based Prolog:

- serializing has minimal costs for an array of integers, but serializing an object graph containing complex objects, like HashMaps, TreeMaps or Java3D scene hierarchies is likely to be costly - that makes placing such objects on the heap less appealing

- while in a single-engine implementation heap reclamation on backtracking efficiently discards heap represented objects, the lifespan of objects created in an engine might extend over the lifespan of the engine

- placing an object in the symbol table is essentially a lazy operation, in contrast to eager serialization - what if the control flow never reaches the object - and the effort to serialize it is spent in vain?

One is then tempted by the following architectural choice: if symbol garbage collection is available and sharing is possible and needed between multiple independent computations, then all external objects (not just string atoms) can be treated as Prolog symbols.

Besides simplifying implementation of arbitrary size integers and decimals, internalizing everything provides cheap unification, as equality tests are reduced to integer comparisons and bindings to integer assignments. In particular, *internalizing logic engines* (Java objects at implementation level) allows treating them as any other symbols subject to garbage collection. This avoids likely memory leaks resulting from programmers forgetting to explicitly delete unused engines.

3. The multi-engine symbol garbage collection algorithm

We will first state a few facts that allow some flexibility with the policies on deciding *if* symbol GC should be performed and also on *when* that should happen.

PROPOSITION 1. *If a program creates new symbols in a multi-engine Prolog, they will eventually end up in the registers, choice points or the heap of at least one of the engines.*

PROPOSITION 2. *Checking for the opportunity to call the symbol GC algorithm, given that a flag has been raised by the addition of a new symbol, needs only to happen when either:*

---

[2] This technique is also used in various other Prologs e.g. SICStus, Ciao.

- *heap GC occurs in at least one engine*
- *at least one engine backtracks*

One might argue that a program like

```
loop :- loop.
```

does neither. Note however that such programs do not create new symbols, and therefore nothing is lost if they do not activate symbol GC.

PROPOSITION 3. *If a symbol does not occur on the heap, the active registers or in the registers saved in the choice points of any live engine, then the symbol can be safely reclaimed.*

PROPOSITION 4. *It is safe to use external (i.e. Java) Map, Set etc. references through a handle stored in the symbol table, provided that the interface ensures that new symbols contained in them are added to the symbol table on their first use.*

The multi-engine aspect of triggering the Symbol GC algorithm is covered by the following fact, easily enforced by an implementation:

PROPOSITION 5. *Given any chain of engine calls, happening all cooperatively within the same thread, executing the Symbol GC algorithm when one of the engines calls the heap GC, or when one of the engines backtracks, results in no live symbols being lost, if the heaps of all the engines are scanned at that point.*

Together, these assertions ensure that symbol GC can safely wait until "favorable" conditions occur, resulting in increased efficiency and overhead reduction.

As a side note, we have in *Lean Prolog* two implementations of the dynamic database that a user can chose from: one is a lightweight, engine based, all source level dynamic database [23]. The other one is a higher performance, multi-argument indexed external database that relies on Java's garbage collector and manages its symbols internally. Interestingly, both benefit from the work of the symbol GC, although for different reasons. In the first case, symbols in the database are handled by our collector as any other symbols on the heap of an engine. In the second case, symbols are lazily internalized, i.e. added to the symbol table only when occurring in the dynamic clauses that have passed all "the indexing tests"[3] - usually a small subset. In this case, from the symbol GC's perspective, database symbols are handled the same way as if read from a file or a socket.

3.1 Outline of the Symbol GC algorithm

As it is typical with GC algorithms, there are two phases:

1. heuristically recognizing that too many symbols or engines have been created since the previous collection (or being forced by a dramatic shortage of memory) - case in which a flag - let's call it `symgc_flag` is set to true

2. waiting within provably safe bounds until the actual garbage collection can be performed i.e. ensuring that as engines advance in their internal virtual machine loops, at least one of the opportunities will occur without the engines being able to create new symbols and crash as a result of running out of memory

As we want to make the symbol garbage collection available upon user request from a goal or the interactive prompt, we also need to ensure that the collector can be called safely right away in that case.

---

[3] Such indexing tests succeed when toplevel functors of the arguments in the heads of the clauses in the database match corresponding arguments in a goal atom.

The heap garbage collector used in *Lean Prolog* is a simple mark and sweep algorithm along the lines of [29]. As most GC implementations, it competes with heap expansion, as at a given time a decision is made if one or the other is retained as a solution to a heap overflow. On the other hand, we have avoided tight coupling of our GC algorithm with symbol table expansion, partly because we wanted to be free to use Java libraries like HashMap or possibly other Map implementations for our symbol tables. This has also simplified the decision logic and helped us to separate the detection of the need for symbol GC, from the activation of the collection process. This uncoupling had no negative impact on performance as the decision to call the symbol GC itself has been fine tuned as a self-contained process that is only activated when a significant amount of changes in the symbol table have occurred.

Note that while engines are internalized as symbols, a separate *engine table* is kept, providing the *roots* for the GC process.

The outline of our symbol GC algorithm is as follows:

- detect the need for symbol GC (automatically or on user demand) and raise the `symbol_gc` flag
- collect to the new table all live symbols from the heaps of all the live engines and relocate in the process all heap references using their symbol index in the new table
- remove all dead engines from engine tables
- replace the old symbol table with the new table

We will now expand this outline, filling in the details as needed.

3.2 Detecting the need for Symbol GC

The `symbol_gc` flag is raised when a new object is added to the symbol table (by the `addObject` method) or a new engine is added by the `addEngine` and some heuristic conditions are met. We will postpone the details of the *policy* describing how to fine tune such heuristics to subsection 3.5. We ensure that only one thread uses these methods at a given time either by sharing a symbol table only between coroutining engines or by synchronizing them in case of engines running on different threads. In this scenario it is ok if multiple threads raise `symbol_gc` flag independently as we will only act on it when opportunity to do it safely is detected. We start by describing the work done by individual engines as this is the simplest part of the algorithm.

3.3 Performing the symbol GC: work delegated to the engines

Individual engines are given the task to collect their live symbols. These symbols can be in one of the following *root* data areas.

- WAM registers
- temporary registers used for arguments of inlined built-ins
- in registers saved in choice points
- on the heap

Note that while the BinWAM [13, 22] does not use a local stack, an adaptation to conventional WAMs might require scanning for possible symbol cells there as well.

The scanning algorithm simply adds all the symbols found in these areas to the new symbol table. At the same time, some "heap surgery" is performed: the integer index of the symbol pointing to the old symbol table is replaced by the integer index that we just learned as being its location in the new symbol table. The same operation is applied to all roots. In our case, this is facilitated by the `tag-on-data` [24] representation in the BinWAM but it can be (with some care!) adapted also to Prologs using the conventional WAM's `tag-on-pointer` scheme.

3.4 Performing the GC: as seen from the class implementing the atom table

One can infer from Prop. 2 that we can avoid multiple flag testings in the inner loop of the emulators by only adding the test for the symbol_gc flag *after a heap garbage collection occurs* and when moving from a clause to the next, *on backtracking*.

We now focus on the tasks encapsulated in the class `AtomTable`, a Java `Map` object that *manages our symbols* and has access to the set of logic engines contained in a separate `Map`.

First, a new `AtomTable` instance, called `keepers`, is created. This will contain the *reachable* symbols, that we plan to keep alive in the future.

The `keepers` table is preinitialized with all the compile time symbols, including built-in predicates, I/O interactors, database handles etc[4].

Next we iterate over all the engines and *perform the steps described in subsection 3.3*.

If an engine (with a handle also represented as a symbol) has been stopped by exhausting all its computed answers, or deliberately by another engine, we skip it. A deliberate stopping happens, for instance, when the parent that has launched and engine is only interested in the first solution produced by the engine.

If an engine is `protected` i.e. it is the root of an independent thread running a set of related Prolog engines sharing the same symbol table and code (or managing the user's top-level), the engine is added to `keepers`.

If the engine has made it so far, the task to filter the current symbol table will be delegated to it. We will defer the details of this operation to the next section.

A check for self-referential engines is made at this point: if the engine did not make it into `keepers` before scanning its own roots and it made it there after, it means that it is the only reference to itself (like through a pending `current_engine(E)` goal, in the continuation still on the heap). In this case, the engine is removed from `keepers`.

The next steps involve removal (and dismantling) of dead engines.

An engine qualifies as dead if it is not a protected engine and it is stopped, as well as if it is unreachable from the new symbol table. At this point an engine's `dismantle()` method is called that discards all resources held by the engine[5].

Finally, the new symbol table replaces the old one and threads possibly waiting on the symbol GC are given a chance to resume.

3.5 Fine tuning the activation of the symbol collector

A simple scenario for symbol GC is to be always user activated. The `symgc` built-in of *Lean Prolog* does just that. A priori, this is not necessarily bad, users of a bare-bone Prolog system can learn very quickly that most new symbols are brought in by using operations like `atom_codes/2` and reading/writing from/to various data sources.

However, once the symbol GC algorithm is there and working flawlessly, few implementors can resist the temptation to design various extensions under this assumption.

In the case of *Lean Prolog*, components ranging from arbitrary length integer arithmetic to the indexed external database rely on symbol GC. Components like the GUI use symbols as handles to

buttons, text areas, panels etc. The same applies to file processing, sockets and thread control. Moreover, *Lean Prolog*'s reflection API, built along the lines of [25], makes available arbitrary Java objects in the form of Prolog symbols. And, on top of that, we have dynamic creation of new Prolog engines that can be stopped at will. As engines are first class citizens, they also have a place in the symbol table to allow references from other engines.

Clearly, predicting the dynamic evolution of this ecosystem of symbols with a wide diversity of life-spans and functionalities cannot be left entirely to the programmer anymore[6].

In this context, the fine-tuning of the mechanism that automatically initiates symbol GC i.e. a sound collection *policy* becomes very important. The process is constrained by the following goals:

- ensure that memory never overflows because of a missed symbol GC opportunity

- ensure that the relatively costly symbol GC algorithm is not called unnecessarily

- the GC initiation algorithm should be simple enough to be able to prove that invariants like the above, hold

We will now outline our symbol GC policy, guided by the aforementioned criteria.

First, we ensure that the symbol GC process should not be called from threads that try to add symbols when the symbol GC is already in progress. This is achieved by atomically testing/setting a flag.

We will also avoid going further if the size of the (dynamically growing) symbol table is still relatively small[7] or if the growth since last collection is not large enough[8].

On the other hand, upon calling the `addEngine()` method, one has to be more aggressive in triggering the symbol collector that also collects dead engines, given that recovering engines not only brings back significant memory chunks, but it also has the potential to free additional symbols. A heuristic value (currently an increase of the number of new engines by 256), is used. As engine number increases are usually correlated with generation of new symbols, this does not often bring in unnecessary collections[9].

Next, by iterating over all live (i.e. not stopped) engines, we compute the sum of their heap sizes. If the size of the symbol table exceeds a significant fraction of the total heap size[10], it is likely that we have enough garbage symbols to possibly warrant a collection, given that we can infer that live symbols should be somewhere on the heaps. Next we estimate the relative cost of performing the symbol GC and we decline the opportunity if the GC has been run too recently[11].

Otherwise we schedule a collection by raising the sym_gc flag.

3.6 An optimization: synergy with copying heap garbage collectors

An opportunity to run our symbol collector arises right after heap garbage collection. While we are using a mark-and-sweep collector in *Lean Prolog*, it is noteworthy to observe that in the case of a

---

[4] A total of about 1250 symbols in the case of our *Lean Prolog* runtime system. This includes 2 engines, the parent driving the top-level and the worker used to catch exceptions on running goals entered by the user.

[5] The main difference is that a stopped engine can still be queried, in which case it will indicate that no more answers are available. In contrast, trying to query a dismantled engine would be an indication of an error in the runtime system, generating an exception.

[6] This does not preclude allowing the programmer to manage directly the life-span of objects like files or sockets using open and close statements.

[7] This is decided by checking against a compile time constant SYMGC_MIN.

[8] This is decided by checking against a compile time constant SYMGC_DELTA.

[9] Nevertheless, future work is planned to dynamically fine tune this parameter.

[10] A compile time constant empirically set to 0.25, planned also to be dynamically fine tuned in the future.

[11] This is computed by the number of discarded attempts to initiate symbol GC since the time it has actually been performed, currently a heuristic constant set to 10.

copying collector, for instance [8], running in time proportional with live data, one might want to trigger a heap GC in each engine just to avoid scanning the complete heap. Even better, one can instrument the marking phase of the heap garbage collector to also collect and relocate symbols. Or, one can just run the marking phase if heap GC is not yet due for a given engine and collect and reindex only the reachable symbols. We leave these optimizations as possible future work.

4. Symbol GC and Multi-Threading

Clearly, in the presence of multithreading, special care is needed to coordinate symbol creation and even reference to symbols that might get relocated by the collector. Moreover, as our collector can also reclaim the engines that are used to support *Lean Prolog*'s multithreading API, consequences of unsafe interactions between the two subsystems can be quite dramatic.

Fortunately, Lean Prolog uncouples the multi-engine and multi-threading APIs and provides a number of high-level "design patterns" encapsulated as higher-order predicates for both cooperative and preemptive multi-tasking [21].

This allows source-level implementation of various scenarios ensuring the "peaceful coexistence" of multi-engine symbol GC and multi-threading.

The first approach, similar to the one used in systems like SWI-Prolog [28] is to ensure that all threads wait while the collector is working.

Alternatively, one can simply use a separate symbol table per thread and group together a large number of engines cooperating sequentially within each thread. In this scenario, when communication between threads occur, symbols are internalized on each side as needed. If one wraps up the communication mechanism itself, to work as a transactional client/server executing one data exchange between two threads at a time, safety of the multi-engine ecosystem within each thread is never jeopardized.

The other requirement for this scenario is the ability to have multiple independent symbol tables, a design feature present in *Lean Prolog* also to support an atom-based module system and agent-oriented extensions.

We have set as default behavior in the case of *Lean Prolog* the second scenario, mostly because we have started with a design supporting up front multiple independent symbol tables and strong uncoupling between the Engine API and the multithreading API.

However, for "system programming" tasks like adding *Lean Prolog's* networking, remote predicate call, Linda blackboard layer as well for supporting encapsulated design patterns like *ForkJoin* or *MapReduce* that are used as building blocks for distributed multi-agent applications, we have provided a simple synchronization device between threads, allowing full programmer control on the interactions with aspects involving sequential assumptions like the symbol garbage collector.

A synchronization device, called a Hub, coordinates N producers and M consumers nondeterministically, i.e. consumers are blocked until a producer places a term on the Hub and producers are blocked until a consumer takes the term on the Hub. Threads are always created with associated Hubs that are made visible to their parent and usable for coordinated interaction.

On the Prolog side Hub is introduced with a constructor hub/1 and works with following generic API:

```
hub(Hub)
ask_interactor(Hub, Term)
tell_interactor(Hub, Term)
stop_interactor(Hub)
```

A group of related threads are created around a Hub that provides synchronization and data exchange services. The built-in

Term	Java Object size	Int array heap size
f(a)	40 bytes	8 bytes
f((g(X),h(Y))	124 bytes	28 bytes
[1,2,3,4,5]	228 bytes	60 bytes

Figure 1. Java Object vs. int array heap representation

```
new_logic_thread(Hub, X, G, Clone, Source)
```

creates a new thread by either "cloning" the current Prolog code and symbol spaces or by loading new Prolog code in a separate name space from a Source (typically a precompiled file or a stream). The default constructor

```
new_logic_thread(Hub, X, G)
```

shares the code but it duplicates the symbol table to allow independent symbol creation and symbol garbage collection to occur safely in multiple threads without the need to synchronize or suspend thread execution.

We refer to [21] for ways to provide, using higher-order predicates, a convenient set of user-level built-ins that combine maximum flexibility in expressing concurrency while avoiding unnecessary implementation complexity or execution bottlenecks.

5. Empirical Evaluation

Comparing with C-based Prologs is quite tricky given the gap between the relative speeds of C and Java. Also the integrated management of conventional string symbols (atoms in Prolog parlance), arbitrary size numbers (these days present in most Prolog systems) and external Java objects is different from other Prologs' where symbol GC is restricted to managing string symbols. As a result, we will first justify with quantitative data the design decisions that entail some of our implementation choices and then focus on evaluating the performance benefits of our Symbol GC algorithm.

5.1 Evaluating the impact of our design decisions

Our first major design decision was to give up Java's free memory management in exchange for the speed-up provided by working with an int array-based BinWAM emulator. While we have not built a comparably refined implementation with Prolog terms represented as Java objects, one can estimate the performance gap based on the relative size of the Java objects representing Prolog terms and their direct representation on a heap implemented as a dynamic integer array, as shown in Figure 1. Note that Java object-size estimates are conservative, assuming atomic objects at 8-bytes, when in practice actual sizes can be much higher. For instance, a String object in Java 6 (HotSpot) starts with 38 bytes of overhead, to which one adds 2 times the number of 2 byte characters and one might lose a few more bytes due to 8-byte alignment requirements.

Figure 2 lists serialized byte-sizes of some of the Java objects that have been frequently used in our system when accessing Java libraries from Prolog, to give an idea on the space (and implicitly computation time) required for placing them on the heap in serialized form. As a further justification of our design decisions to use a shared symbol table for objects like BigIntegers and BigDecimals we have instrumented our runtime system to perform one serialization and one deserialization operation on the output value of arithmetic operations. As an estimate of how an alternative implementation using this technique would perform, Figure 3 shows the impact of these operations on two arithmetic-intensive benchmarks. As base line, we have provided also measurements for our actual emulator, with symbol GC turned off and on.

Class	Constructor argument	Bytes
java.util.ArrayList	()	58
java.util.HashMap	()	82
java.util.LinkedHashMap	()	135
java.lang.Integer	0	81
java.lang.Double	0.0	84
java.math.BigInteger	"0"	202
java.math.BigDecimal	"0.0"	290

Figure 2. Serialized sizes of minimal instances of some Java objects used in our implementation

Feature	Factorial	Factoradics
With serialization	10.30s	6.45s
With symbol GC off	1.82s	3.85s
With symbol GC on	1.53s	3.85s
Coded with BigIntegers in Java	0.41s	0.70s
With serialization overhead, in Java	11.66s	3.44s
SWI-Prolog with GMP integers	0.15s	0.26s

Figure 3. Impact of serialization on BigInteger performance

The *Factorial* benchmark is simply a tail-recursive computation of the factorial of 20000. Given the huge size of the integers computed, the performance gap is quite large in this case. Also the use of Symbol GC actually speeds up this benchmark as it reduces the overall memory footprint significantly. For comparison, we have also given the timings for the same, recursively coded factorial using BigIntegers, directly in Java. Interestingly, in the case when serialization/deserialization overhead is added, Java performs slightly slower than LeanProlog which switches between representations to plain `int` types when computing with small values and because recursive calls are faster in WAM-based LeanProlog than in the underlying Java VM.

The *Factoradics* benchmark computes 1234^{4578} then it converts this large integer to a *factoradic* representation and back. The impact is less significant in this case as the intermediate values are lists of mostly small integers, that LeanProlog detects and converts to tagged `int` objects on the heap. In this case, note that the same program written in Java is faster with or without serialization overhead, which, like in the case of LeanProlog, dominates costs. To help putting things in perspective, the last row in Figure 3 shows that a C-based Prolog, relying on the native code GMP (GNU Multiple Precision Arithmetic Library), outperforms both Java and LeanProlog, by a significant margin, on both benchmarks.

5.2 Performance benefits of our Symbol GC algorithm

We will divide our performance evaluation to cover two orthogonal aspects of the usefulness of our integrated multi-engine symbol garbage collector.

First, we evaluate, as usual, the relative costs of having the algorithm on or off on various benchmarks.

Second, we evaluate the benefits it brings to a system by comparing time and resource footprints with and without the collector enabled.

The table in Figure 4 summarizes our experimental evaluation on some artificial benchmarks. The table in Figure 5 summarizes our experimental evaluation on two fairly large applications.

As for the *Factorial* and *Factoradics* benchmarks, execution times have been measured for our 3 memory management operations on a lightly loaded, 8-CPU MacPro (with 2 2.26GHz Quad-Core Intel Xeon processors and 16GB of memory).

To make the experiments as realistic as possible, in each benchmark memory management operations are triggered automatically. This also tests the effectiveness of our collection policies. To measure the effectiveness of the symbol GC algorithm on reducing the total number of symbols and engines, we give as a baseline what happens when the symbol GC is switched off. These totals give indirectly an idea on the memory savings resulting from the use of symbol GC.

Given that *Lean Prolog*'s data areas are managed as dynamic arrays that expand/shrink as needed, expand/shrink operations, being often in the inner loops of the runtime interpreter actually dominate time spent on memory management.

As our symbol GC policy triggers symbol collection right after a heap GC in the engine that is most likely to have created most of the symbols, the cost of symbol GC is dominated by heap GC costs. Proceeding right after garbage collecting this "dominant heap" ensures that only live objects are scanned on the heap so relatively few unnecessary symbol creation operations happen when the old symbol table is replaced by the new one. *This also explains why symbol GC times are significantly lower than time spent on other memory management tasks.*

We have created a dedicated *"Devil's Own"* symbol GC stress test that uses 4 threads creating concurrently long lists of new symbols that are always alive on the heaps. This is the only benchmark where overall execution time is significantly slower with the symbol GC enabled. On the contrary, the memory bandwidth reduction that can be seen as an indirect consequence of the symbol GC, has in 3 other benchmarks beneficial effects on execution time.

The *Findall* benchmark computes a list of all permutations of length 8. As *Lean Prolog*'s `findall` is implemented using engines this benchmark focuses exclusively on the effect of the symbol GC collector on engines.

The *Pereira* benchmark tests a wide variety of operations. In particular, assert/retract operations and findall/bagof/setof operations benefit significantly from the presence of symbol GC, to the point that overall execution time improves. As this benchmark contains a fairly representative blend of Prolog predicates, we have also added in Figure 6 measurements of total Java memory usage and total symbol count with symbol gc off and on. We have manually called the collector after the end of the benchmark to show the additional amount of symbols that can be collected.

The *SelfCompile* application benchmark measures *Lean Prolog*'s time on recompiling its own compiler and libraries. As the symbols are all already there, no costs or benefits are incurred with or without symbol GC.

Finally, the Wordnet application benchmark reads in (and indexes) the complete Prolog version of the Wordnet 3.0 database (available from *http://wordnet.princeton.edu/wordnet/download*). A significant improvement in execution time is observed in this case, due to the overall reduction of memory bandwidth.

6. Related work

The current version of Lean Prolog and a few related papers are available at *http://logic.cse.unt.edu/tarau/research/LeanProlog* .

We have designed and implemented our symbol garbage collector by starting from scratch through an iterative process, that first worked with a single engine with serialized heap-represented external objects. Very soon, it has evolved to also manage arbitrary length arithmetic objects and Java handles. At the end, our overall architecture turned out to have some similarities with the Erlang atom garbage collector proposal described in [11].

Impact on Benchmark	Devil's Own	Findall	Pereira
Syms NO SYMGC	765692	1295	759001
Engines NO SYMGC	4	12	953
Total time NO SYMGC	18629	5280	19738
Syms SYMGC	530892	1295	69579
Engines after SYMGC	4	2	3
Time for useful work	8173	3647	18035
Time for SYMGC	666	1	43
Time for Heap GC	4352	1008	270
Time for expand/shrink	7724	721	406
Total with SYMGC	20915	5377	18754

Figure 4. Time (in ms.)/space efforts and benefits of our integrated symbol GC algorithm on three benchmarks

Impact on Benchmark	SelfCompile	Wordnet
Syms NO SYMGC	2017	613183
Engines NO SYMGC	2	2
Total time NO SYMGC	10482	412345
Syms SYMGC	2017	28590
Engines after SYMGC	2	2
Time for useful work	9358	367172
Time for SYMGC	0	14
Time for Heap GC	15	235
Time for expand/shrink	686	21428
Total with SYMGC	10429	388849

Figure 5. Time (in ms.)/space efforts and benefits of our integrated symbol GC algorithm on two applications

Memory Usage	Symbol GC off	Symbol GC on
Java Memory	158 MBytes	98 Mbytes
Symbols, after run	759793	69579
Symbols, after final GC	2670	2670

Figure 6. Statistics for the Pereira benchmark

The most important commonality is copying of live symbols into a new table, based on scanning, followed by symbol relocation in all roots (see also section 2.2 in [11]).

While our paper is based on a finished working collector, [11] describes a proposal for an implementation. While our description provides enough detail to be replicable in another system, [11] is fairly general and often ambiguous about how things actually get worked out. This makes a detailed comparison difficult, but we were able to point out a number of similarities and differences, as follows.

Among the similarities:

- comparable contexts: multiple Erlang processes on one side, multiple Prolog engines on the other - with the important difference that Erlang processes run in parallel and communicate using message passing while engines are uncoupled from threads in LeanProlog and use a different communication protocol

- separation in "epochs" with special handling of compile time symbols
- live atoms are migrated from an old table to a new one i.e. both approaches are "copying collectors"

Among the differences:

- engines, as first class citizens are themselves represented as symbols in our case
- a discussion of an incremental version of the collector is given in [11]
- constraints related to the use of the symbol table as an interface to arbitrary external objects in our case
- a detailed discussion on the policy used to trigger the collection is given in our case
- in contrast to Erlang, detection of symbol GC opportunity is complicated in our case by independent backtracking in multiple engines

In the world of Prolog systems symbol garbage collectors have been in use even in early pre-WAM implementations (Prolog1). Among them, SWI Prolog's symbol garbage collector, using a combination of reference counting and mark-and-collect has been shown valuable for processing large data streams and semantic web applications [27] and its interaction with multi-threading is discussed in [28]. Instead of copying however to a new, compact symbol table, SWI-Prolog leaves a symbol-table with holes. While managing them with a linked list can avoid a linear scan in the case of SWI's implementation, we have chosen to edit symbol cells in-place, partly because our tag-on-data representation made this operation simple to implement and partly because it added very little extra runtime cost to do so. Also, as Lean Prolog is finding some practical uses in applications working on terabytes of data, leaving holes in the symbol table would be an unpleasant limiting factor for the total size of the symbol space.

While not described in detail in a publication that we are aware of, the SICStus Prolog [3] description, in the user manual, of the built-in `garbage_collect_atoms/0`, mentions about scanning all data areas for live atoms.

The heap GC algorithm (a simple "mark and sweep") used by *Lean Prolog* is the one described in [29]. The heap scanning for symbols is, in our case, proportional to the total size of the heaps of all engines, (possibly after running the heap GC as well in some). With this in mind, a copying heap GC algorithm [7, 8, 26] is likely to provide also better symbol GC performance for programs with highly volatile heap data. The impact of such algorithms on integration with symbol GC remains to be studied.

Multiple Logic Engines have been present in a from or another in various parallel implementation of logic programming languages [9]. Among the earliest examples of parallel execution mechanisms for Prolog, AND-parallel [10] and OR-parallel [12] execution models are worth mentioning. While in these systems logic engines are not made available to the programmer through an API, independent virtual machine states are used internally, for instance, when implementing various scheduling policies.

In combination with multithreading our own engine-based API bears similarities with various other Prolog systems, notably [4, 28]. However, a distinctive feature of *Lean Prolog*, that allowed us to separate concerns related to thread synchronization, is that our engine API is completely orthogonal with respect to multithreading constructs [21].

7. Conclusion

While both reference counting and data area scanning symbol collection algorithms have been implemented in the past in various Prolog systems (and other related languages), we have not found in the literature a detailed, replicable description of all the aspects covering a complete implementation.

The main novelty of our integrated symbol GC is *support for allocation and exchange between multiple Prolog engines of arbitrary Java objects (including big integers and decimals) and seamless interoperation with various Java libraries*. Such benefits are likely to be replicated by using a similar architecture when implementing scripting or domain specific dynamic languages on top of Java or C#.

As a practical consequence, Prolog programmers can benefit from services provided by various Java collection and map classes whose complex object graphs are internalized as needed to garbage collectable Prolog symbols.

Our empirical evaluation indicates that the costs of symbol GC are amortized by consistent reduction of the memory footprint of Prolog's data areas resulting in reduced GC effort on the Java side as well. As a result, we have observed that on some large practical programs, activating our symbol GC can bring not only space savings but also execution time benefits.

We hope that our effort, that lifts symbol GC to a multi-engine context by integrating symbol and engine garbage collection, and generalizes it to manage handles to arbitrary external objects, will be useful to future implementors of logic languages as well as various scripting and domain specific languages built on top of Java or C#.

As virtually all Prolog and related logic programming systems in use today that support some form of concurrent execution can be seen as "multi-engine" Prologs, it is likely that they may benefit from an adaptation of our the integrated symbol and heap garbage collection algorithm independently of their virtual machine architecture and implementation language.

Acknowledgement

We are grateful to Kostis Sagonas and the anonymous reviewers of ISMM 2011 for their salient comments and constructive criticism. We thank NSF (research grant 1018172) for support.

References

[1] H. Aït-Kaci. *Warren's Abstract Machine: A Tutorial Reconstruction.* MIT Press, 1991.

[2] M. Banbara, N. Tamura, and K. Inoue. Prolog Cafe: a Prolog to Java translator system. *Lecture Notes in Computer Science*, 4369:1, 2006.

[3] M. Carlsson, J. Widen, J. Andersson, S. Andersson, K. Boortz, H. Nilsson, and T. Sjoland. SICStus Prolog user's manual.

[4] Manuel Carro and Manuel V. Hermenegildo. Concurrency in Prolog Using Threads and a Shared Database. In *ICLP*, pages 320–334, 1999.

[5] J.J. Cook. P#: A concurrent Prolog for the .NET Framework. *Software: Practice and Experience*, 34(9):815–845, 2004.

[6] B. Demoen and P. Tarau. jProlog home page (1996) http://www.cs.kuleuven.ac.be/~bmd.

[7] B. Demoen, P.L. Nguyen, and R. Vandeginste. Copying garbage collection for the WAM: To mark or not to mark? *Lecture notes in computer science*, pages 194–208, 2002.

[8] Bart Demoen, Gert Engels, and Paul Tarau. Segment Preserving Copying Garbage Collection for WAM based Prolog. In *Proceedings of the 1996 ACM Symposium on Applied Computing*, pages 380–386, Philadelphia, February 1996. ACM Press.

[9] Gopal Gupta, Enrico Pontelli, Khayri A.M. Ali, Mats Carlsson, and Manuel V. Hermenegildo. Parallel execution of prolog programs: a survey. *ACM Trans. Program. Lang. Syst.*, 23(4):472–602, 2001. ISSN 0164-0925. doi: http://doi.acm.org/10.1145/504083.504085.

[10] Manuel V Hermenegildo. An abstract machine for restricted and-parallel execution of logic programs. In *Proceedings on Third international conference on logic programming*, pages 25–39, New York, NY, USA, 1986. Springer-Verlag New York, Inc. ISBN 0-387-16492-8.

[11] T. Lindgren. Atom garbage collection. In *Proceedings of the 2005 ACM SIGPLAN workshop on Erlang*. ACM, 2005.

[12] Ewing Lusk, Shyam Mudambi, Ecrc Gmbh, and Ross Overbeek. Applications of the aurora parallel prolog system to computational molecular biology. In *In Proc. of the JICSLP'92 Post-Conference Joint Workshop on Distributed and Parallel Implementations of Logic Programming Systems, Washington DC*. MIT Press, 1993.

[13] Paul Tarau. A Simplified Abstract Machine for the Execution of Binary Metaprograms. In *Proceedings of the Logic Programming Conference'91*, pages 119–128. ICOT, Tokyo, 7 1991.

[14] Paul Tarau. Program Transformations and WAM-support for the Compilation of Definite Metaprograms. In Andrei Voronkov, editor, *Logic Programming, RCLP Proceedings*, number 592 in Lecture Notes in Artificial Intelligence, pages 462–473, Berlin, Heidelberg, 1992. Springer-Verlag.

[15] Paul Tarau. Low level Issues in Implementing a High-Performance Continuation Passing Binary Prolog Engine. In M.-M. Corsini, editor, *Proceedings of JFPL'94*, June 1994.

[16] Paul Tarau. Inference and Computation Mobility with Jinni. In K.R. Apt, V.W. Marek, and M. Truszczynski, editors, *The Logic Programming Paradigm: a 25 Year Perspective*, pages 33–48. Springer, 1999. ISBN 3-540-65463-1.

[17] Paul Tarau. Fluents: A Refactoring of Prolog for Uniform Reflection and Interoperation with External Objects. In John Lloyd, editor, *Computational Logic–CL 2000: First International Conference*, London, UK, July 2000. LNCS 1861, Springer-Verlag.

[18] Paul Tarau. Orthogonal Language Constructs for Agent Oriented Logic Programming. In Manuel Carro and Jose F. Morales, editors, *Proceedings of CICLOPS 2004, Fourth Colloquium on Implementation of Constraint and Logic Programming Systems*, Saint-Malo, France, September 2004. URL http://clip.dia.fi.upm.es/Conferences/CICLOPS-2004/.

[19] Paul Tarau. BinProlog 11.x Professional Edition: Advanced BinProlog Programming and Extensions Guide. Technical report, BinNet Corp., 2006. URL http://www.binnetcorp.com/BinProlog.

[20] Paul Tarau. Logic Engines as Interactors. In Maria Garcia de la Banda and Enrico Pontelli, editors, *Logic Programming, 24-th International Conference, ICLP*, pages 703–707, Udine, Italy, December 2008. Springer, LNCS.

[21] Paul Tarau. Concurrent programming constructs in multi-engine prolog. In *Proceedings of DAMP'11: ACM SIGPLAN Workshop on Declarative Aspects of Multicore Programming*, New York, NY, USA, 2011. ACM.

[22] Paul Tarau and Michel Boyer. Elementary Logic Programs. In P. Deransart and J. Maluszyński, editors, *Proceedings of Programming Language Implementation and Logic Programming*, number 456 in Lecture Notes in Computer Science, pages 159–173. Springer, August 1990.

[23] Paul Tarau and Arun Majumdar. Interoperating Logic Engines. In *Practical Aspects of Declarative Languages, 11th International Symposium, PADL 2009*, pages 137–151, Savannah, Georgia, January 2009. Springer, LNCS 5418.

[24] Paul Tarau and Ulrich Neumerkel. A Novel Term Compression Scheme and Data Representation in the BinWAM. In M. Hermenegildo and J. Penjam, editors, *Proceedings of Programming Language Implementation and Logic Programming*, number 844 in Lecture Notes in Computer Science, pages 73–87. Springer, September 1994.

[25] Satyam Tyagi and Paul Tarau. A Most Specific Method Finding Algorithm for Reflection Based Dynamic Prolog-to-Java Interfaces. In I.V.

Ramakrishan and Gopal Gupta, editors, *Proceedings of PADL'2001*, Las Vegas, March 2001. Springer-Verlag.

[26] R. Vandeginste, K. Sagonas, and B. Demoen. Segment order preserving and generational garbage collection for Prolog. *Lecture notes in computer science*, pages 299–317, 2002.

[27] J. Wielemaker, M. Hildebrand, and J. van Ossenbruggen. Using Prolog as the fundament for applications on the semantic web. *Proceedings of ALPSWS2007*, pages 84–98, 2007.

[28] Jan Wielemaker. Native Preemptive Threads in SWI-Prolog. In Catuscia Palamidessi, editor, *ICLP*, volume 2916 of *Lecture Notes in Computer Science*, pages 331–345. Springer, 2003 ISBN 3-540-20642-6.

[29] Qinan Zhou and Paul Tarau. Garbage Collection Algorithms for Java-Based Prolog Engines. In V. Dahl and P. Wadler, editors, *Practical Aspects of Declarative Languages, 5th International Symposium, PADL 2003*, pages 304–320, New Orleans, USA, January 2003. Springer, LNCS 2562.

Author Index

Afek, Yehuda 55
Aigner, Martin 99
Bai, Tongxin 65
Bard, JonathanE. 65
Blackburn, StephenM. 33
Brown, Gavin 109
Dice, Dave 55
Ding, Chen 43
Ding, Chen 65
Eich, Brendan 119
Frampton, Daniel 33
Franz, Michael 119
Gal, Andreas 119
Garner, Robin 33
Gross, ThomasR. 11
Gu, Xiaoming 43
Gu, Xiaoming 65
Haas, Andreas 99
Hertz, Matthew 65
Iyengar, Balaji 79
Jones, Richard 89
Kalibera, Tomas 89

Kane, Stephen 65
Keudel, Elizabeth 65
Kirsch, ChristophM. 99
Kovoor, George 109
Lippautz, Michael 99
Lujan, Mikel 109
Majo, Zoltan 11
Marlow, Simon 21
Morrison, Adam 55
Mutlu, Onur 77
Peyton Jones, Simon 21
Philippsen, Michael 1
Singer, Jeremy 109
Sokolova, Ana 99
Stroka, Stephanie 99
Tarau, Paul 129
Tene, Gil 79
Unterweger, Andreas 99
Veldema, Ronald 1
Wagner, Gregor 119
Wimmer, Christian 119
Wolf, Michael 79